The Moral Worlds of Contemporary Realism

The Moral Worlds of Contemporary Realism

Mary K. Holland

BLOOMSBURY ACADEMIC
NEW YORK • LONDON • OXFORD • NEW DELHI • SYDNEY

BLOOMSBURY ACADEMIC
Bloomsbury Publishing Inc
1385 Broadway, New York, NY 10018, USA
50 Bedford Square, London, WC1B 3DP, UK

BLOOMSBURY, BLOOMSBURY ACADEMIC and the Diana logo are trademarks of Bloomsbury Publishing Plc

First published in the United States of America 2020

Copyright © Mary K. Holland, 2020

For legal purposes the Acknowledgments on p. ix constitute an extension of this copyright page

Cover design by Eleanor Rose
Cover image © Vadim Sadovski / 123RF

All rights reserved. No part of this publication may be reproduced or transmitted in any form or by any means, electronic or mechanical, including photocopying, recording, or any information storage or retrieval system, without prior permission in writing from the publishers.

Bloomsbury Publishing Inc does not have any control over, or responsibility for, any third-party websites referred to or in this book. All internet addresses given in this book were correct at the time of going to press. The author and publisher regret any inconvenience caused if addresses have changed or sites have ceased to exist, but can accept no responsibility for any such changes.

Library of Congress Cataloging-in-Publication Data
Names: Holland, Mary, 1970- author.
Title: The moral worlds of contemporary realism / Mary K. Holland.
Description: New York, NY: Bloomsbury Academic / Bloomsbury Publishing Inc., 2020. | Includes bibliographical references and index. | Summary: "A literary history of our attempts to depict reality through Language"– Provided by publisher.
Identifiers: LCCN 2019057865 | ISBN 9781501362613 (hardback) | ISBN 9781501362644 (pdf) | ISBN 9781501362637 (epub)
Subjects: LCSH: American literature–20th century–History and criticism. | American literature–21st century–History and criticism. | Realism in literature. | Literature and society. | Modernism (Literature)–United States. | Postmodernism (Literature)–United States.
Classification: LCC PS228.R38 H65 2020 | DDC 810.9/112–dc23
LC record available at https://lccn.loc.gov/2019057865

ISBN: HB: 978-1-5013-6261-3
PB: 978-1-5013-6262-0
ePDF: 978-1-5013-6264-4
eBook: 978-1-5013-6263-7

Typeset by Deanta Global Publishing Services, Chennai, India

To find out more about our authors and books visit www.bloomsbury.com and sign up for our newsletters.

For Jeff

with me in all the many worlds

Contents

List of Figures	viii
Acknowledgments	ix
Preface: The Problem of "Realism"	xii
Introduction: A Brief History of Realisms	1
1 Metafictive Realism: David Foster Wallace and the Future of (Meta)Fiction	49
2 The Work of Art after the Mechanical Age: Materiality, Narrative, and the Real in the Fiction of Steve Tomasula	79
3 Material Realism and New Materialism: Literature from the 1990s to the Present	109
4 Quantum Realism: On Ted Chiang's "Story of Your Life" and Ruth Ozeki's *A Tale for the Time Being*	151
5 Quantum Realism Case Study: On Don DeLillo's *The Body Artist*	191
Conclusion: Realism and Periodizing after Postmodernism	251
Bibliography	261
Index	278

Figures

1. Ideas for depicting "overlapping realities" in *The Body Artist*. Don DeLillo Papers, Container 8.5, Harry Ransom Center, The University of Texas at Austin — 200
2. Ideas for constructing Mr. Tuttle outside linear time. Don DeLillo Papers, Container 6.5, Harry Ransom Center, The University of Texas at Austin — 201
3. Ideas for demonstrating that "time is in the body." Circa 1998–2000. Don DeLillo Papers, Container 7.1, Harry Ransom Center, The University of Texas at Austin — 219
4. Ideas for final scene of *The Body Artist*. Don DeLillo Papers, Container 6.5, Harry Ransom Center, The University of Texas at Austin — 226
5. Inside cover of notebook: "Otherwise it's only words." Don DeLillo Papers, Container 6.5, Harry Ransom Center, The University of Texas at Austin — 230
6. Outline of final pages of *The Body Artist*. Circa 1998–2000. Don DeLillo Papers, Container 7.1, Harry Ransom Center, The University of Texas at Austin — 232
7. Ideas for final chapter of *The Body Artist*. Circa 1998–2000. Don DeLillo Papers, Container 7.1, Harry Ransom Center, The University of Texas at Austin — 233
8. Handwritten draft of the end of *The Body Artist*. Circa 1998–2000. Don DeLillo Papers, Container 7.1, Harry Ransom Center, The University of Texas at Austin — 234

Acknowledgments

This project accompanied me through intense experiences over tumultuous years—in hospital rooms with both sons, waiting rooms of doctors and of family court, and during the last long, quiet nights at my grandmother's side. I cannot imagine its coming to fruition without the support of many people and the professional opportunities they offered me along the way.

The portion that became clear to me last grew out of the book's earliest research, an ecstatic week nosing around the DeLillo and Wallace archives at the Harry Ransom Center in 2012. I am enormously grateful to the HRC for the fellowship that enabled that research, and to Mr. DeLillo for allowing me to reproduce in Chapter 5 images of his drafts and notes for *The Body Artist*. My thanks to David Banash, whose invitation to write an essay for his *Steve Tomasula: The Art and Science of New Media Fiction* (Bloomsbury 2015), where about half of Chapter 2 first appeared, kicked off the writing of this project; and my thanks to Steve, whose generous response to that chapter told me I had gotten something right. In 2014, Charlie Harris invited me to give the keynote address for the First Annual David Foster Wallace Conference, which speech became the basis of Chapter 1. I will be forever grateful not only for his support of my work, but also for the mixture of friendship and mentorship he and his wife Victoria offered during my visit at ISU, and for the vision they provided of what a long, fecund, and collaborative career in literature can be.

I should therefore also thank Stephen J. Burn for becoming unable to give that keynote and trusting that I could do it justice in his stead. That is of course only the least intentional of the many thoughtful ways he has supported my work and career. He is largely responsible for my chapter on material realism, since he asked me to write on literary materiality for his *American Literature in Transition 1990-2000* (Cambridge UP 2017), where about half of Chapter 3 appeared previously. I hadn't known how central the topic was for my unfolding vision of contemporary realism until I wrote about it for him. Likewise, his suggestion that I write about "David Foster Wallace after Deconstruction" for the MLA volume we were coediting led me to clarify my argument about Wallace's impact on realism for Chapter 1. My writing on quantum realism was also much enriched by Stephen, as he passed along relevant titles of fiction and criticism that I hadn't yet stumbled across on my own. But I am most grateful for the sustaining friendship that has bubbled alongside our professional collaborations.

I owe a good deal of the book's Conclusion to my experience on an ACLA panel in May 2018, and for that I thank Ralph Clare and Matt Mullins, who invited me to speak on it. I doubt any of us expected that three days of discussing periodizing could be so lively, charged, and fruitful. I thank all of the participants on that panel—Matt, Alissa Karl, Jeffrey Severs, David Rudrum, Daniella Gati, Emily Johansen, Josh Toth, Jeffrey Gonzalez, and Laurin Williams—for the ideas in their papers and their contributions to the larger debate.

Once again, I feel so fortunate to acknowledge the many people at my home institution, SUNY New Paltz, whose support of all kinds enabled me to write this book. My early Americanist colleague Andrew Higgins steered me in the right direction when I asked him, in all my ignorance, where to start with late-nineteenth-century realism; I'm especially indebted to his directing me to James's "The Real Thing." Stella Deen and Nancy Johnson cheered me on as we struggled to protect research time while remaining committed teachers and (for two of us) mothers of teenagers, while Cy Mulready's enthusiasm for this topic lent me the encouragement of knowing I had an eager reader out there. I am most grateful to Laura Barrett, our dean, my friend, and a great DeLillo scholar, for reading my massive chapter on *The Body Artist* and helping me think about final revisions. Always my enormous gratitude goes to my students, especially those in my "Contemporary Realisms" seminar of Fall 2017 and my "Twenty-First Century Literature" class of Spring 2019, who helped me build and expand the arguments that became this book.

I am also indebted to the generous and astute comments of the external readers of this manuscript, whose suggestions improved the book in clear ways. And I am again grateful to have been privileged to work with Haaris Naqvi at Bloomsbury who, with Amy Martin and an excellent team, made the process of seeing this project into print a real pleasure.

A room of one's own is not enough: one needs emotional fortitude, focus, time, and some degree of self-confidence to be a writer. Few women, especially mothers, are encouraged to cultivate these things. So I am most grateful to the people who have enabled me to be the person and live the life that could produce this book. Every year I am filled with gratitude to return to Linwood, where I can feel my whole self regroup while my mind thrums and the word count rises. I thank the sisters who make and hold this peaceful space in the world. Discussing books, writing, and life with my friend and colleague Heather Hewett on our writing retreats there every year moves my work forward and sustains the rest of me throughout the year. My friend and fellow writer, Kirsten Wasson, likewise supports me in all the challenging facets of my life by being always available to discuss them in unnecessary detail and by being preternaturally gifted at sending the exactly right message through the mail exactly when I need it.

It is a pleasure beyond words and past my imagining to see my now-nearly-grown children, Evan and Camden, begin to know me as a person and a writer, rather than as just their invisibly ubiquitous mom. Their acknowledgment of intellectual work as integral to who I am—and as fitting seamlessly into my fierce momness—along with their obvious pride in that combination is one of the great windfalls of my life.

Finally, this book simply would not exist without Jeff Fisher. For the long runs and hikes during which we worked through the intricacies of literariness, Derrida, koans, and recursivity; for expanding my interest in Buddhism that runs through so much of my recent work and life; for reading early versions of some of these chapters and giving feedback that shaped them and the book as a whole; most of all, for holding me close while leaving me free to write, to be, to become, as I will: my deepest love and gratitude.

Preface

The Problem of "Realism"

Verisimilitude in a verbal expression or in a literary description obviously makes no sense whatsoever.

—Roman Jakobson, 1921[1]

Not so long ago, defining postmodernism—as distinct from modernism, and without wading into the morass of scholarly work still struggling to establish that it existed at all—was the toughest bit of literary historicizing I did with undergraduate students accustomed to the comfort of stark contrasts and bracketing dates. Meanwhile, I found my postmodern self unable to teach the realism of Howells and James without rampantly scare-quoting words such as "real," "true," and "objective," like Wallace's hideous man in "Brief Interview #48"—an impersonation that discomfited me and further confused those students not yet fluent in the nuances of irony. When I began exploring and then needing to organize for myself the diverse new modes of writing springing up from the fecund soil of the twenty-first century, all striving to do the work and many hijacking the terminology of the nineteenth-century realists, I wondered if the morass might be made into a neater throughline. And so the work on this book began.

How satisfying and provocative, then, to find (as experts in earlier periods already knew well) that "realism" as a literary-historical term has been, since its inception in America at least, nearly as resisted and contentious as "postmodernism." While those writers supposedly inaugurating it at times rejected the nomenclature of "realism" (as I will discuss in the Introduction), critics and theorists have pointed out the shortcomings, even uselessness, of the term since literary studies became a theorized field. In an early effort to coalesce a discipline out of the "slipshod" musings about art that preceded Russian formalism, Roman Jakobson targeted "realism" in his 1921 essay "On Realism in Art" as one of the most flagrant and consequential examples of impressionistic theorizing. He rightly labeled as absurd its central claim of verisimilitude, which he pointed out results not from a text's actual reproduction of reality—language can't do that—but from our ability to decode the text's conventions as having done so. Nor can "concrete content" distinguish realist writing, he pointed out, as "whoever senses faithfulness to life in Racine does not find it in Shakespeare." And since "classicists, sentimentalists, the romanticists [...], even the 'realists' of the nineteenth century, the modernists to a large degree, and finally the futurists, expressionists, and their like, have more than once steadfastly proclaimed faithfulness to reality [...]—in other words, realism—as the guiding motto of their artistic program,"[2] the only thing distinguishing nineteenth-century realists is their cheek in claiming for themselves a label that should rightly apply to most, perhaps all, writing.

Jakobson went on to suggest a formalist method of characterizing "realism" according to the author's intentions of verisimilitude, readers' perceptions of the same, and a handful of techniques employed to create it, as if categorizing existing formal attributes would clarify the field. But later critics, even while extending Jakobson's stylistic and technical examination into more recent writing, admit that such formalist analysis cannot distinguish "realist" writing in a meaningful way from the writing that surrounds it. His own impressive examination of style in American realism leads Harold Kolb, in *The Illusion of Life: American Realism as a Literary Form* (1969), to declare that all writing is mimetic, none is objective, and that "fiction is still a puppet show, still an illusion of life. The difference, largely introduced by the realists, is that a frame and covering have been built around the fictional stage. The puppeteer and the mechanism are now hidden, although the wires are still visible if one looks closely."[3] Kolb's colorful depiction of realism is perhaps the first of what will become many suggestions that "realist" writing is inherently metafictional, a notion that will occupy Chapter 1 in this book.

Thomas Clareson stretched the definition even further when in 1971 he called science fiction and fantasy "the other side of realism" and realism "one of the great delusions of the last century."[4] Of the first to consider "realism" not in relation to the reality it represents but according to its methods of representing reality, using Wittgenstein, J. P. Stern declared in 1973 that "realism" makes no sense as a periodizing term, "can't be identical with any one coherent ideology," and is "not a single style and has no specific vocabulary of its own." Rather, it is not a genre but "a disposition of mind and pen, like a humour, a mode of writing."[5] Even the critic who most clearly aimed at providing "a concrete description of the period concept of realism," René Wellek, conceded in 1963 that "all art in the past aimed at reality," and that defining a period of "realism" thus requires "a regulative concept, a system of norms dominating a specific time, whose rise and eventual decline it would be possible to trace and which we can set clearly apart from the norms of the periods that precede and follow it."[6] That is, Wellek argued that defining a period concept of "realism" requires making visible a conglomeration of habits that took shape in and then descended back into a long history of realist writing, like Debussy's "Sunken Cathedral" emerging out of its musical mist, only to melt back in again. More recently, Pam Morris's otherwise excellent *Realism* (2003), which traces concepts of realism from its international nineteenth-century inception, through the theoretical linguistic turn, to the present, similarly stalls out with this unhelpfully undifferentiating definition: realism for her is "any writing that is based upon an implicit or explicit assumption that it is possible to communicate about a reality beyond the writing."[7]

But *is* there any writing—any that we would call literature and attempt to read and talk about—that doesn't assume an outside world about which it can communicate? What would writing that doesn't make that assumption look like? Can you think of any? Of all the "anti-realist," "experimental," "conceptual" (all contentious labels) literature I read and teach and write about, none of which looks much like traditional realist literature, I can't think of any that does not intend to communicate about the world we live in, or the world its author lives in, or an imagined world that makes sense only in relation to the actual world we live in. I certainly can't think of any literature that believes it can't communicate with me. How would I know it can't? How would it communicate that, without communicating with me? How would it stop me from doing that obsessive human thing I do with all writing, with all image, with everything—interpret? And if all acts of representation, if all art and literature, are thus varieties of realism—attempts to represent the world through language—then how does "realism" have any meaning at all? How can we understand "realism" to mean something more precise than the history of literary forms used to represent reality, as posed first by Boris Eichenbaum during the early, New Critical establishment of literary study, and revised later by Fredric Jameson in his postmodern and deconstructive theory of history as the evolution of form?

One way of understanding "realism" as still, or ever, relevant is to recognize that claims of "realism" in literature always emerge in relation or reaction to a change in our ideas about what reality is or how language works. Most critics and writers view nineteenth-century realism as largely a reaction to romanticism and idealism, a need to reassert the reality of the material world over that of fantasy and idea. Though readings of realism in modernism differ from each other, they coalesce around a new notion of the multiplicity of reality as dialectical, struggling toward but resisting totalization; in this context, realism becomes one mode among many for representing a reality that is always also one mode among many.[8] But with the crisis of signification that attended the linguistic turn in theory and our entrance into a poststructural world, we see in literature new questions about both what reality is and language's capacity for representing it. Beyond nineteenth-century realism's turn from idea to material reality, literature under the influence of poststructural theory and postmodern image culture asks whether reality isn't after all merely an idea, or image, or whether language itself is the most real thing we can talk about. More recently, technological developments alter our sense of what is real and our abilities to represent it in altogether new ways, with ever-increasing computational power, the internet, virtual-reality technologies, and digitization simultaneously destabilizing and exploding our sense of what reality is while offering increasingly sophisticated ways of representing it. Rather than constituting a straight line, these changes in our concepts of reality and representation suggest that any attempt to talk about literary "realism," or representing reality through language, is a foray into a constellation whose points are themselves dialectics—of material/image, signified/signifier, real/representation, and, as this book will suggest, while extending and departing from Jameson's recent work on the dialectic of realism, of "realism"/"anti-realism."

Attempts to define literary realism date at least as far back as the nineteenth century, which saw the rise across Europe and into America of the first literature to be termed "realist" writing, and continue today, as critics reshape earlier fiction through new lenses while modifying the old lens of "realism" to read new literature. Thus definitions of "realism" and "realist" fiction vary widely, depending on the historical, theoretical, literary, and cultural contexts from which they arise. While some contemporary critics assert the folly of attempting to codify nineteenth-century "realism," others dare to posit distinctive versions of realism that are still emerging. Changes in literary practices and aesthetic values cause changes in critical and theoretical accounts of realism: what the nineteenth-century realists might have seen as the eclipsing of realism by modernist practices, some critics in the modernist and postmodern periods (notably Erich Auerbach) view as realism's culmination, while other critics after modernism look back at those same nineteenth-century realist practices with a skepticism born by the linguistic turn.

To add to the confusion, we begin to see, in the postmodern period and after, oppositions drawn between "realist" and "anti-realist," "experimental" or "conceptual" writing and techniques, even as many critics and writers point out the inaccuracy of such distinctions. Not only did Linda Hutcheon, along with other critics, undermine the divide between realism and anti-realism in her early work on metafiction, but primary practitioners of postmodern metafiction themselves refused to acknowledge a line between the "anti-realism" they were accused of practicing and the goals and aims of realism: John Barth saw himself as refusing to participate in the pretense of creating through language the truth of the world, and instead presenting the truth of the lie of those attempts. Such fiction, though conventionally audacious, remains committed to realism's desire to say something true about the world, in showing the reader the vast distance between that real world and the language that cannot possibly substitute for it. And both recent theorists of realism (such as Pam Morris and Steven Moore) and recent writers of what gets called "experimental" or "conceptual" fiction (notably Steve Tomasula and Ben Marcus) point out the many ways in which all writing has always been "experimental" in relation to what came before.[9] These concerted refusals to allow writing that deviated from realist norms in the post-modernist period to be ghettoized as reactive and negating ("anti-") or as tentative, transitory, or preliminary ("experimental," "conceptual") illustrate the work that remains to be done to connect today's generically and conventionally innovative fiction back to the realist writing it grew out of.

Yet so far we have seen few (and I will argue, insufficient) attempts to theorize exactly what has happened to realism in and after postmodernism,[10] and no sustained consideration of how the variety of new realisms that have sprung up in the last thirty years—over twenty at the time of my writing—relate to realism as it has been theorized thus far, or how they might force us to rethink how we define realism in particular and how we periodize or define literary modes in general. This book is one attempt to ask and answer these questions, informed by many others' past work on realism; rooted in readings of recent literature, criticism, and theory; and intended to contribute to an evolving conversation about the intersection of reality and language in literature—even as "language" and "literature" both transform in response to evolving philosophies, techniques, and technologies. Ultimately it aims to examine the variety of ways in which fiction today records the impact of changing ideas about how language works and what the real world is, while discovering and performing its power to shape the real world.

Notes

1 "On Realism in Art," in *Language in Literature*, ed. Kyrstyna Pomorska and Stephen Rudy (Boston: Harvard University Press, 1987), 21.
2 Ibid., 21, 23, 20.
3 Harold Kolb, Jr., *The Illusion of Life: American Realism as a Literary Form* (Charlottesville: University Press of Virginia, 1969), 35.
4 Thomas D. Clareson, ed., *SF: The Other Side of Realism: Essays on Modern Fantasy and Science Fiction* (Bowling Green: Bowling Green University Popular Press, 1971), 5.
5 J. P. Stern, *On Realism* (Abingdon: Routledge, 1973), 41, 52.

6 René Wellek, *Concepts of Criticism*, ed. Stephen B. Nichols, Jr. (New Haven: Yale University Press, 1963), 224–5.
7 Pam Morris, *Realism* (Abingdon: Routledge, 2003), 6.
8 For an extensive treatment of realism in modernism, see Gregory Castle's *A History of the Modernist Novel* (Cambridge: Cambridge University Press, 2015).
9 See for example Linda Hutcheon's *Narcissistic Narrative: The Metafictional Paradox* (Waterloo, CA: Wilfrid Laurier University Press, 1980), Steve Tomasula's "Where We Are Now: A Dozen or So Observations, Historical Notes and Soundings for a Map of Contemporary American Innovative Literature as Seen from the Interior," *Études Anglaises* 63, no. 2 (2010): 215–27, Ben Marcus's "Why Experimental Fiction Threatens to Destroy Publishing, Jonathan Franzen, and Life as We Know It," *Harper's*, October 2005, 39–52, Steve Moore's *The Novel: An Alternative History* (New York: Bloomsbury, 2010) and Morris's *Realism*.
10 The Introduction will consider two of these: Frederic Jameson's assertion that realism dissolved after modernism, and Pamela Morris's attempt to defang the postmodern critique of realism, both of which I see as negative models of post-modernist realism that do not help us understand what realism still is in postmodernism and "post-postmodernism."

Introduction

A Brief History of Realisms

One of the ways literature is actually quite a lot like reality is that it has its own unreal history, in the form of theory and criticism. What Stephen Greenblatt declared about reality and its deceptively deterministic history, we can say of that critical-theoretical history and of literature itself: "Everything can be different than it is; everything could have been different than it was."[1] Every so often, someone performs an act of literary theorizing or periodizing that reminds us of the tenuousness of all such historicizing acts. Linda Hutcheon did so when she identified metafiction with fiction; by pointing out that metafiction arose with what is often seen as the first Western novel, *Don Quixote*, she loosed metafiction from the postmodern period in which it later flourished and that has been erroneously seen as birthing and containing it. More recently, Steven Moore's "alternative history" of the novel traces its roots back far beyond Cervantes, and winds up proposing an alternative history for realism as well. Moore dates the novel back to "at least the 4th century BCE,"[2] and claims that the realist novel, more specifically, emerged first in Iceland 600 years before its nineteenth-century heyday in continental Europe:[3] realism for Moore, in the long history of the novel, is a mode that appears and disappears in various times and places over our long history of narrative.

Moore also echoes calls from "experimental" fiction writers Steve Tomasula and Ben Marcus to see fiction as a constantly evolving series of experiments, by considering nineteenth-century realism to be only one mode of many, rather than as the defining mode against which we should measure all subsequent fiction or novels, as has been the trend in twentieth-century periodizing. Pam Morris's *Realism* makes similar claims, from the opposite perspective.[4] Perhaps most interesting about Moore's claims for realism is that he insists not only that it is unremarkably one mode among others, but also that it is the least aesthetically compelling mode of writing to emerge so far:

> Instead of enjoying a brief fad and then losing favor, like the 18th-century epistolary novel, the realistic novel became thought of as the norm in fiction, instead of what it actually is: only one of many mutations in

the evolution of the novel, and one less concerned with exploring new techniques and forms than with pleasing audiences and enriching authors and publishers. Entertainment rather than art.[5]

That is, even critics who agree to expand our understanding of "realism" far beyond the nineteenth-century moment that named it, such as Moore and Morris, can't agree on how to read that eponymous period in relation to the fiction surrounding it. Is nineteenth-century realism unremarkable as a period because it is just as experimental as all fiction everywhere, or because it so panders to middlebrow tastes that it doesn't even qualify as art worth considering?

More aspects of the problem of defining "realism"—and of defining all literary periods—become clear when we consider what it means that Moore uses a nineteenth-century concept of realism as his basis for identifying pre-nineteenth-century appearances of the mode. Moore recognizes thirteenth-century Icelandic sagas as the origin of the nineteenth-century "social realist novel," describing the sagas as "narratives based on family histories but arranged as tales." These he contrasts with a "gloriously unrealistic Icelandic novella, *The Saga of the Volsungs*," which "doesn't distinguish between the natural realm and the supernatural, or between history and legend."[6] In so doing, Moore employs the distinction drawn by the nineteenth-century realists in the face of romanticism and idealism in order to categorize these earlier tales as "realist," in two different ways: by reading the Icelandic tales as "realistic" for favoring history—here assumed to be "true"—over myth, and, more specifically, for focusing on families. Indeed, in the many pages of "realist" sagas' plot summaries that follow,[7] Moore recounts family fortunes won and lost, with corresponding wielding and waning of social power, marriages of status forced and unions of love prevented by that power, social snubs and validations, and the chaos wrought by passion in all such social scheming. Moore's description of medieval Icelandic realism as "family histories" thus becomes a synecdoche for nineteenth-century realism's fascination with bourgeois reckonings with sex, wealth, power, and social status as organized by the institution of marriage.

While this similarity in fiction across cultures and centuries is fascinating, and surprising to those of us who have been too-long satisfied by grossly reductive definitions of "the novel" and "realism," the consequent backward defining of an earlier, perhaps originating mode of literature in terms of its much later descendant is troubling. Essentially, to say that the Icelanders invented the nineteenth-century continental European realist novel is to say that characteristics of writing popularized centuries later and elsewhere emerged first in Iceland, but in a time insufficiently obsessed with periodizing to name it. That privilege then got left to us, in our post-modernist, theory-driven (which is to say, academic publication-driven) fervor. We have done so by borrowing a term coined to describe literature of a particular cultural-historical moment—the *bourgeoisie* did not exist in thirteenth-century Iceland—and multiply interpreted over later decades of literary theorizing, and cast the term back to writing that actually paved the way for it to emerge. We fit the literature to the existing frame of literary history, a frame that was built centuries after the literature itself.

This method of writing literary history is not quite a palimpsest or simulacrum, since it acknowledges real origins or precursors. But the use of later examples to define and name their earlier examples or origins feels strikingly postmodern. To point this out is not to suggest that Moore has made an error—for what other frame of reference does he have?—but to recognize that in rectifying our foreshortened history of the realist novel, Moore is limited to terminology that drags its own historical moment with it. Essentially, Moore's extension of the history of the realist novel backward reveals that what critics have for decades criticized as a stuttering, zombie-like repetition of our most recent literary periods—postmodernism, and now "post-postmodernism," neither of which can quite escape the event horizon of modernism—is not unique to these periods. By grounding our categorizing of literature in the realism/modernism divide, all literature before and after the advent of such a schema becomes a descendant of those terms and of the contentiousness of their opposition. The coalescence of literary studies in the early twentieth century, followed by the explosion of theory in the 1960s and then of criticism, when academic employment became contingent on publication, produced a framework over one relatively brief period that must accommodate our entire history of known literature—and literature to come.

One largest aim of this book, then, is to use the proliferation of new "realisms" over the past thirty years or so as an opportunity to step out of this limited realism/modernism or realism/anti-realism context and examine not only these new modes of writing in and of themselves, but also to ask what their labeling as "realism" can tell us about the history of realism and our history of periodizing, and how we might rethink periodizing in more productive ways as we move forward. Considering such large diachronic questions requires first examining the specific synchronic ways in which writers and critics have attempted to define "realism" in their historical moments. In doing so, I depart somewhat from Moore, whose description of nineteenth-century realistic fiction as "entertainment rather than art" judges the formal and technical means used by that fiction as intellectually and aesthetically uninteresting. I wholeheartedly agree with Moore's impassioned defense of "difficult fiction," which seems to comprise for him all types of writing that does not obey the conventions of nineteenth-century realism, whether they pre- or postdate that era.[8] But I am less interested in comparing the aesthetic appeal of fictional approaches than I am in recognizing the problems that come from continuing to bind "realism" to a particular set of technical approaches in the first place. To that end, this chapter will examine concepts of realism written by the nineteenth-century realists, and then by theorists and critics throughout the twentieth century and into the twenty-first, with special attention to their accounts of the role played by technique, form, and genre. It will then consider the panoply of new realisms in this varied and contradictory context, asking how contemporary realisms intersect with nineteenth-century realism, how they radically diverge, and how both intersection and divergence force us to rethink long-standing habits of literary historicizing.

Realism as Theorized and Written by Nineteenth-Century Americans

Before formalism and Roman Jakobson's astute call for rigor in characterizing realist writing, authors and critics created and conceptualized realism in relation to existing literature and ideas about literature, in terms of the fiction's purpose and the stylistic devices and techniques it used to fulfill those intentions. The consistency of such descriptions in essays by key American realists William Dean Howells, Mark Twain, and Henry James is striking, with all three asserting the primary goal of fiction in terms of verisimilitude, or the representation through language of real life—terms that come to seem naïve after the linguistic turn. Howells describes fiction as "the expression of life," to be judged only by its "fidelity to it,"[9] and the novel as "the sincere and conscientious endeavor to picture life, just as it is";[10] Twain advocates (by way of a blistering critique of Fenimore Cooper's fictional crimes) that people and nature be depicted as they are in our lived experience of them; and James declares, in his seminal "The Art of Fiction," that "the only reason for the existence of the novel is that it does attempt to represent life," and that "the air of reality (solidity of specification) seems to me to be the supreme virtue of a novel."[11] All three of these writers assert fiction's responsibility to represent "truth," what is "real" and "natural" rather than "artificial" (as we see in Howells's famous grasshopper analogy[12]), and—establishing the second major purpose of realist fiction—to do so within a moral framework.

Twain and James go a step further in their commentary on realism, describing the methods that allow fiction to conjure the real world in convincing ways. Their recommendations for fiction overlap significantly, with both authors specifying the need for purposeful description, realistic dialogue, and well-drawn characters. Or, as Twain puts it, "personages in a tale shall be alive," "talk [...] as human beings would be likely to talk in the given circumstances," and "exhibit sufficient excuse for being there." While Twain goes on to make minute prescriptions concerning style ("eschew surplusage"), grammar (it should be "good"), fictional devices (they should be various), and even word choice ("use the right word, not its second cousin"),[13] James takes a more holistic approach in his recommendations. He reminds us of the interdependence of all aspects of fiction and of "idea and form"; of the need to allow all aspects of reality into fiction, not just the lovely ones; and, most interesting from today's perspective of proliferating "realisms," of the necessity of absolute "freedom of choice" in terms of form.[14]

Fiction by these authors offers abundant evidence of theory being put into practice. Howells's 1905 short story "Editha," for example, provides a textbook case of realism as Howells defined it in his essays. Editha is ultimately little more than an allegory for the dangers of fantasy and idealism. Her repetitive hyperbole in depicting all things, including war, as equally "mystical" and "glorious," combined with her constant theatricality, posturing, and fantasizing, and her susceptibility to the "current phrases," makes her a curiously unreal character, totally detached from objectivity and systems of judgment that might allow her to be a moral being. Howells opposes her ephemerality with the real bodily threat of death posed by the war—a death toward which she pushes George using seduction—so that her idealism becomes not simply a personal flaw but a dangerous weapon. The third-person narrator creates just enough space between the story's truth and "what she called her love, what she called her God"[15] to allow us to see and judge her hypocrisy, and then underscores her moral vacuity in the story's final tableau: Editha, sitting for her portrait, demonstrates her selfishness and lack of remorse for George's death even while being enshrined as a purely aesthetic object. Editha's decadence in this story is as straightforward as are Howell's ideas about how to represent it.

Twain's "The Man That Corrupted Hadleyburg" (1899) uses similar realist techniques, but complicates them through technique. Its external description reaches beyond physical setting, for example, to document the behavior of a variety of characters during the contentious speech of others, as if in a running set of stage directions. Pieces of dialogue overlap and obscure each other, in a realistic depiction of how much is lost during such a rancorous town meeting; multiple letters and messages and even a final image stand in for the "documents and records" that James identified in an essay as the storehouse of the "subject-matter of fiction," meaning truths of the world proven through documentation.[16] Meanwhile, Twain begins to give us access to characters' internal worlds as well, through liberal use of free indirect discourse. This view into the interiors of characters establishes the ironic moral point of the story: not that Hadleyburg becomes corrupted, but that its dominating middle class was corrupt all along.

The moral of James's "The Real Thing" (1892) is equally ironic: its main character, a painter, discovers that falsity is required to represent reality accurately. The story thus points to one of the significant ways in which some realist fiction presents much more complex visions of reality and of representation than does the criticism about that fiction. James's painter in "The Real Thing" confesses to feeling "an innate preference for the represented subject over the real one: the defect of the real one was so apt to be a lack of representation. I liked things that appeared; then one was sure." His attempts to create paintings of lords and ladies using a real former lord and lady as models are so bested by his paintings modeled after dressed-up servants that all involved are forced to acknowledge "the perverse and cruel law in virtue of which the real thing could be so much less precious than the unreal."[17] This story becomes a direct refutation of, or at least serious challenge to, his claim eight years earlier in "The Art of Fiction" that "as the picture is reality, so the novel is history":[18] the story asserts the need for the unreal, the fake, the un-lifelike, in creating a realistic version of either painting or fiction.

The realists create a similar contradiction between their essays' and their fiction's notions of reality. Whereas all three writers espouse in their essays rather naïve notions of the "reality" that fiction means to represent, the reality represented by much realist fiction is complex, contradictory, and not entirely knowable. Howells's critical notions of reality and realism are simultaneously most often used to represent the period and most unreflective. In his 1887 "The Editor's Study," he claims that we must judge the "fidelity" of any fictional "expression of life" according to its "relation to the human nature, known to us all." He further defines this universally known human nature in terms of "the glance of the common eye," as exemplified by Goethe's notion that "'boys and blackbirds' have in all ages been the real connoisseurs of berries," and his appeal to the wisdom of "the mass of common men."[19] In attempting to eliminate one exclusivity—that of the "stillborn, the academic"—Howells has asserted several more (of class, of gender), unwittingly illustrating the impossibility of this "common eye," this "human nature known to us all" against which we might judge any act of realism. His later attempt in "Novel-Writing and Novel-Reading" to define "truth" as "truth to human experience," as determined by the reader's own "knowledge of life," and exemplified by a list of "truthful novelists"—which does include women and writers of multiple nationalities, but does not range outside bourgeois settings and concerns—similarly limits "truthful experiences" to those like his own.[20] James seems to offer a less narrow and self-focused concept of reality than does Howells, reminding writers that "humanity is immense, and reality has a myriad forms." Still, he echoes Howells's call that the realist novel be above all "sincere" and, ultimately, "as complete as possible."[21] Yet fiction by Twain and James, as well as by their peer, Edith Wharton, depicts a reality whose sincerity is difficult to measure and can never be completely captured.

In "Hadleyburg," for example, even as the plot asks us to judge the townspeople for their greed, self-centeredness, and artificial honesty, it is structured around, even fueled by, a series of significant gaps—information that we, or the characters, sometimes both, never know. A stranger sends a note to the town announcing that whoever can identify himself as the person who helped him in a past encounter, by repeating part of their conversation, will receive a monetary reward. The stranger then anonymously delivers the answer to his question—the snippet of conversation—to every town leader, each of whom attempts to claim the reward, thus exposing his deceit. One, Edward Richards, is saved from public humiliation when the man in charge of reading the answers, Burgess, publicly withholds Richards's submission, in appreciation for what Burgess perceived as Richards's earlier kindness in warning Burgess that the town was after him to punish him for a crime he did not commit. But Richards later demonstrates his double hypocrisy by accidentally confessing to Burgess his guilt in telling neither Burgess nor the town that he could have proven Burgess's innocence. This already quite complex plot is considerably complicated by all that is left unknown for the reader and most of the characters: Who was the stranger? Who in Hadleyburg caused his "injury," and how? What was said between them? Why did he invent this scheme? What had made him so "revengeful"? What was Burgess accused of doing? Did Burgess know that Richards could save him? Ultimately the reality demonstrated by the story is not simply the ironic truth that "Hadleyburg was the most honest and upright town in all the region" because in the end it stamps its guilt into its official seal ("LEAD US INTO TEMPTATION"), but, more problematically, it is the fact that no amount of reading external signs—whether people's words and deeds or a town's motto—will divulge the true nature of reality, which is always at least partially hidden and unknown.[22]

Meanwhile, our free-indirect-discourse access to the thoughts of several characters—all "Nineteeners," or town leaders—exposes the greed, self-interest, and deceptiveness that characterize all members of the ruling class, and so, according to the story's moral center, seems to explain the leaders' powerful positions; we never gain access to the thoughts of a non-Nineteener. This extensive use of FID ultimately becomes proof of the truth that the main characters, Mary and Edward Richards, suspect from the beginning: that the town's celebrated honesty is purely "artificial," or as Mary says, "as rotten as mine is; as rotten as yours is." The FID also illustrates the extent to which reality for these townspeople is a product of our fantasies of the world, as we witness multiple characters struggling to manufacture through imagination a past in which they know the answer that will make the stranger's money their own.[23]

Similarly, Wharton's masterful "The Other Two" (1904), while proceeding according to the principles of realist fiction outlined by Howells, Twain, and James, also revolves around not the world we see so much as what we and the characters do not see. Alice's third husband, Waythorn, expresses ownership of everything in his reach, especially his house and the things in it, including his new wife and her daughter; once forced to meet Alice's two former husbands, he alleviates his anxiety about their challenge to his sense of possession by imagining the three of them as partners owning shares of Alice.[24] But as the story uses FID to follow Waythorn's colonizing perspective, it uncovers significant facts he has misunderstood (was Alice's first husband a "brute"? or steamrolled by his young wife?[25]) or totally missed (that Alice had spoken in person with her first husband against Waythorn's wishes[26]). By the end, when Alice takes total control of the awkward meeting of all three men in her drawing room—calmly using tea service to order them into her own submissive tableau—we realize that we have never gained access to her thoughts or feelings, because Waythorn has not. She remains unknowable, uncolonizable by him, as she has been by all three of her husbands.

Wharton's story is an excellent example of how realist writers used innovations in point of view and perspective not only to communicate the themes, moral and otherwise, of their work—as Twain and Wharton have done in these stories—but also to comment on the nature of the reality being represented. The focalization on Waythorn, which never floats to Alice, establishes Alice's freedom from her husband's attempts to possess her, as the exclusion of the non-Nineteeners from FID in "Hadleyburg" suggests their innocence in what ultimately reads as the greed of the striving middle class. Similarly, the sudden appearance of a first-person point of view in the penultimate paragraph of Twain's long short story adds another seriously distorting framework to the layers of performed "truth" and "honesty" in the story, throwing everything we have learned about the duplicitous, or multiplicitous, town leaders, seemingly from an authoritative third-person point of view, into another kind of questioning. David Foster Wallace would imitate and innovate on this sneakily shifting point of view in his own fiction a hundred years later, in his attempts to reshape tools for fiction capable of reflecting a reality so dangerously identified with fantasy (in the guise of image) and irony that these early realist writers might hardly recognize it (as I will discuss in Chapter 1). Even this one example of the link between changing fictional techniques and changing notions of reality belies Moore's dismissal of the "boring" techniques of realist fiction. More convincing still of the importance of realist technique are the many theoretical and critical accounts in the wake of nineteenth-century realism that use techniques—point of view primary among them—to characterize not just this particular mode of realism but also later evolution away from it.

Auerbach's Realism

Such evolution away from the easy objectivity and certainty theorized by Howells, as we see in the fiction of Wharton, Twain, and James, indicates that elements of nineteenth-century American realism were already moving toward the more representationally complex modernist realism that Erik Auerbach theorized in his *Mimesis: The Representation of Reality in Western Literature* (1946). And yet, even though the scope of Auerbach's work is so massive that after seven decades it has only been equaled by Fredric Jameson's recent *The Antinomies of Realism*, *Mimesis* scarcely mentions American realism. Instead, Auerbach grounds his wide-ranging characterization of realism in his discovery of two opposing types of representation in early Western literature, then charts the reappearance of and innovations on these types in European literature. The first type, classical-antique realism, represented by Homer's *Odyssey*, is characterized by

> fully externalized description, uniform illumination, uninterrupted connection, free expression, all events in the foreground, displaying unmistakable meanings, few elements of historical development and of psychological perspective.

The second type, represented by the Old Testament, comprises

> certain parts brought into high relief, others left obscure, abruptness, suggestive influence of the unexpressed, "background" quality, multiplicity of meanings and the need for interpretation, universal-historical claims, development of the concept of the historically becoming, and preoccupation with the problematic.[27]

Auerbach's study builds to an examination of realist techniques in Virginia Woolf's *To the Lighthouse*, whose modernist realism Auerbach argues is the culmination of the evolution of literary realism. Thus, the study provides a clear examination of changes in realism after the late nineteenth-century realists who theorized and produced the mode's namesake literature. Auerbach's meticulous, explication-based analysis of realism's types and definitive characteristics, the changing techniques used in its service, and the relationship of both realism and its techniques to changes in history, culture, and our understanding of reality, also serves as a useful model and stepping-off point for my contemporary exploration of what has happened in realism since modernism.

Auerbach treats Woolf's fiction as a profound development of the Old-Testament type of realism he has described—one that resists clear or singular meaning and leaves much important information and feeling unexpressed—through her innovations in point of view and uses of time. Pointing out that her changes to existing uses of point of view go beyond the recent and more general techniques of stream of consciousness and interior monologue, Auerbach argues that Woolf's point of view is unique not only because it is technically new—deployed in formally new ways—but also because the tone it crafts, or "the author's attitude toward the reality of the world he [sic] represents," is itself an innovation (535). In his exemplary scene, in which Mrs. Ramsey measures James's leg to repair a sock, Woolf frames events from multiple, abruptly shifting, and at times unidentifiable vantage points, none of which expresses total understanding of the moment, and behind which lurks no authoritative authorial vantage point to comprehend the scene. In fact, "The writer as narrator of objective facts has almost completely vanished . . . there actually seems to be no viewpoint at all outside the novel from which the people and events within it are observed, any more than there seems to be an objective reality apart from what is in the consciousness of the characters" (534). This lack of authorial viewpoint represents for Auerbach a distinct change even from Flaubert, who "never abdicated his position as the final and governing authority" of a scene (536). Auerbach considers this narrating device to be an outgrowth from and movement far beyond the "unipersonal subjectivism" of the totally anti-objective, but intensely personal, narrative of Huysmans's *A rebours*. Auerbach labels Woolf's device "multipersonal representation of consciousness," or "a close approach to objective reality by means of numerous subjective impressions received by various individuals (and at various times)" (536).

Auerbach then describes Woolf's constructions of time in the novel in ways that ultimately reflect back on her unique constructions not just of point of view, but of subjectivity. Noting that the sequence of "inner processes" that interrupt the external action—the measuring of the sock—"do not interrupt its progress [and yet] take up far more time in the narration than the whole scene can possibly have lasted" (529), Auerbach identifies in Woolf's fiction the ways in which, "in a surprising fashion unknown to earlier periods, a sharp contrast results between the brief span of time occupied by the exterior event and the dreamlike wealth of a process of consciousness which traverses a whole subjective universe" (538). This "elaboration of the contrast between 'exterior' and 'interior' time," along with the "naturalistic" depiction of characters' inner states and experiences of inner time, all provoked by random and discontinuous external events, makes significant claims about the author's attitude about reality and the author's beliefs about, and the characters' experiences of, subjectivity. Auerbach does not state such claims directly, but we can deduce them from what he does say about the aims for fiction that these technical developments reveal: to locate meaning not in "great exterior turning points" but in "any random fragment plucked from the course of a life" (547), and to communicate more faith in the "syntheses" of accounts of everyday life "than in a chronologically well-ordered total treatment which accompanies the subject from beginning to end" (547–8). Auerbach's description of these authors' aims indicates their belief in a very different universe and human experience than those created by orderly, totalizing, chronological realist fiction.

This modernist realist fiction is fragmented, discontinuous, nonchronological, and does not attempt to encompass a total vision that orders its many parts (as Auerbach reminds us, we never do know the meaning of Lily's "completed" vision at the end of *To the Lighthouse*). The reality it represents is likewise fragmented and discontinuous, as well as incapable of being fully seen, known, or grasped. Indeed, in perfect opposition to James's recommendation in "The Art of Fiction," Auerbach reveals how Woolf's text and fictions like it "are guided by the consideration that it is a hopeless venture to try to be really complete within the total exterior continuum and yet to make what is essential stand out" (548). Completeness is not just inadvisable and impossible as a representational strategy; it is also unrealistic, for "Life has always long since begun, and it is always still going on" (549). In the hands of Woolf and similar modernist writers, the singular subject's experience, though itself limited and incapable of grasping the whole, is vaster than any external account of events, and thus more real and true: the external, objective world exists, for the individual and for fiction, in order to provoke the mind's experiences of these truths, of this reality.

Such a characterization of modernist realism according to Auerbach sounds a lot like postmodernism, in terms of its concepts of truth, reality, and methods of representation—a similarity that identifies Auerbach's theory of modernist realism as a near ancestor of today's numerous realist offspring. Auerbach seems to gesture toward such a future evolution of modernist realism when he briefly considers the diverse writings that illustrate the wide influence of modernist realism on authors at the time of his writing, including "old masters" such as Thomas Mann and André Gide, and "writers of the sort whom discriminating readers are not in the habit of regarding as fully competent" (545). While Auerbach does not name any particular "incompetent" writers, he does specify writing practices that he sees as having descended from Woolf's masterful modernist realism but taken a "wrong direction" (545, 546). These writers he describes as offering "no strict continuum of events," or depicting "many fragments of events . . . loosely joined so that the reader has no definite thread of action which he can always follow," or forcing the "attempt to reconstruct a milieu from mere splinters of events, with constantly changing though occasionally reappearing characters" (546). All of these "reproachable" approaches share the lack of a unifying frame of reference, whether provided by a consistent timeline or by characters, which might organize and contain the nonchronological, discontinuous, incomplete fragments of time and narrated experience that he believes make up effective realistic fiction. Auerbach thus recognizes that realist techniques will evolve and are evolving beyond the forms that he identifies and valorizes, but he views the bulk of these innovations as not evolution but devolution, away from the apex of modernist representation of everyday experience.

Here, Auerbach's definition of the epitome of realism in modernism reveals the period specificity of his notions of realism. For he objects to those descendants of Woolf's modernist realism because he insists that fiction's ability to reflect the real world depends on its commitment to projecting the world as a definable totality of which any individual consciousness, writer, point of view, external event, or internal experience can only know or represent a tiny fraction. The unavoidable incompleteness is in the vision, not in the world itself. It is this difference, perhaps more than any other, which shapes literary postmodernism and post-modernist versions of realism as fundamentally different from modernism and its realism. Meanwhile, the resolute human-centeredness of this vision of the world differentiates Auerbach's realism from "post-postmodern" and posthuman realisms (as we will see in Chapters 4 and 5). Thus, Auerbach's historically specific theory of realism also suggests the need for a reassessment of our notions of realism in that future, now-present age, in light of its many new examples of realism.

Still, Auerbach's commitment to modernist realism as the epitome of the mode is instructive for any contemporary attempt to characterize today's realisms in the context of a long literary history that includes his contribution, in three ways. First, his theory of realism, despite its grounding in technique and meticulous textual explication, asserts a definitional breadth not unlike the one that troubles contemporary theorists. Auerbach illustrates this aspect of realism when he contrasts medieval realism, in the tradition of Homer's fully externalized representation, with modernist realism, an evolution of Old-Testament representation of incomplete knowledge and inner states. The former he calls "figural," in that its events correspond to other events and meanings, participating in a divine plan, whereas the latter suggests no such knowable larger framework and proceeds by way of random, unconnected occurrences. Yet he considers both modes of representation "realism," despite their profound differences in technique, tone, and concepts of reality. Such striking capacity in the umbrella of "realism" to contain these disparate approaches and worldviews indicates that for Auerbach, realism is characterized by the conventions that constitute acceptable literary modes for representing experience in *any* period, and remains much broader than any particular set of techniques, and so impossible to define by form alone.

This formal nonspecificity results from Auerbach's ultimate definition of realism simply as writing that renders and takes seriously quotidian human experience—or, as he puts it in his epilogue, writing that ignores the ancient doctrine of levels of styles. In thus grounding his definition of realism, Auerbach's approach reveals a second danger inherent in all acts of literary defining that rest upon the ever-shifting ground of literary historicizing. For Auerbach, every mode of writing that dared to represent "everyday practical reality" (meaning, the experiences of people excluded from the power dictated by class, lineage, title, etc.) outside the "frame of a low or intermediate kind of style, that is to say, as either grotesquely comic or pleasant, light, colorful, and elegant entertainment" marks a recurrence of realism. Thus, realism dates back at least as far as Homer and reasserts itself in a variety of ways after multiple attempts (for example, in the classical period) to mandate the separation of styles. Postmodernism's thorough blurring of high and low in terms of subject and style having killed off such a stylistic doctrine, Auerbach's definition of realism becomes not only overly broad, but no longer viable. Will all writing in and after postmodernism then become "realistic"?

That Auerbach ultimately makes such a specific and compelling argument for the superiority of one of those reassertions—the one most contemporary to his theorizing—demonstrates the third instructive aspect of his theorizing realism. From our perspective over half a century later, his argument for the ultimacy of modernist realism makes visible the criteria according to which we critics and readers judge the efficacy of our literary modes, and the transience of those judgments: we find most effective and appealing the techniques and tones that best reflect our current concepts of reality. But Auerbach's theorizing is also instructive in positive ways. Essentially, his account of realism notes that within this broad category of writing that treats seriously the everyday, multiple modes of realism develop, using changes in technique and tone to depict new concepts of reality, brought about by new historical and cultural contexts. He describes the emergence of modernist realism in just this way:

> At the time of the first World War and after—in a Europe unsure of itself, overflowing with unsettled ideologies and ways of life, and pregnant with disaster—certain writers distinguished by instinct and insight find a method which dissolves reality into multiple and multivalent reflections of consciousness. That this method should have been developed at this time is not hard to understand. (551)

It follows that as history continues to happen, culture continues to change, and new ideas of reality form, as they have continued to do since modernism, new kinds of realism will develop as well, beyond the type that epitomizes the mode for Auerbach in his time. Similarly, we should expect to see changes in realism resulting from changes in our concepts of representation, many significant of which occurred, in the theory of Lacan, Derrida, Foucault, Baudrillard, and others, after Auerbach's death in 1957. Meanwhile, the techniques that were already evolving in nineteenth-century realist writing, and whose innovations Auerbach credited with forming a new kind of realism in Woolf's writing, have evolved still further, as we see in the multiple and shifting point of view and perspective of authors such as David Foster Wallace (see Chapter 1) and unprecedented uses of time in the work of writers such as Ted Chiang and Ruth Ozeki (see Chapter 4). And technologies for creating and manufacturing fiction have evolved as well, with digital printing allowing writers to incorporate a vast array of new representational techniques and computers allowing texts to be digital-born, and thus to represent reality and subjectivity in entirely new ways (see Chapter 3).

As fiction responds to these new ideas and takes advantage of new technologies, it makes even more significant breaks from established habits of technique, form, and style, and from earlier notions of reality, than Auerbach observed in modernist literature. We must expect, then, to find that new kinds of realism have arisen. The following chapters of this book will examine a variety of post-modernist (or, by today's confusing terminology, "postmodern" and "post-postmodern") texts that strive to represent the complexity of everyday reality in a variety of ways, in order to identify recent trends in technique, tone, and notions of reality, and to begin to consider how we might understand these trends as types of realism, and in relation to the long history of realism described by Auerbach.

Mid-Century Critics on Realism

While Auerbach aimed to provide a definition of realism that could describe similarities among modes of writing originating in vastly different historical times and places, many other mid-twentieth century critics sought simply to offer a working definition of nineteenth-century American realism. Strangely, or perhaps tellingly, the tight focus of these critics resulted in more unhelpful contradiction than illumination. Some critics primarily repeat without question the obfuscating naïveté of Howells's own description of realism. Everett Carter, for example, in *Howells and the Age of Realism* (1950), describes the realism of Howells, Twain, and John William De Forest as distinctively unironic writing (Carter claims that Stephen Crane's irony ended the Age of Realism) that demonstrates "faith in the living" and "truthfully reports warped and maladjusted social relationships so that men may study and improve them."[28] Similarly, Warner Berthoff, in *The Ferment of Realism: American Literature 1884-1919* (1965), quotes Whitman to describe the style of realism as using the "voice of the natural man."[29] These critics incorporate Howells's "common eye" and "human nature, known to all," and the unquestioned universal "truth" proposed by Howells, Twain, and James in their definitions of realism.

René Wellek pursues (with questionable results) a more pointed understanding of realism in his chapter on realism in the 1963 *Concepts of Criticism*, placing American realism in a philosophical and literary history of realism dating to the eighteenth century, and covering continental Europe, in an effort to conceive of nineteenth-century American realism as demonstrably different from types of realism as they were stabilized in France, England, Germany, Italy, and Russia—and by Auerbach. Against these many definitions of realism, Wellek proposes his own, which he asserts as distinctly concerned with periodizing rather than recognizing style or technique, and thus required to apply to all major writers of the time. He follows Vernon Parrington's characterization of American realism from three decades earlier in saying it is more about conflict between faith in American individualism and the "pessimistic, deterministic creed of modern science." These idea-based criteria lead to a definition of realism that does not break with the American realists' own problematic definitions in any significant way, in that Wellek distinguishes realism according to its commitment to real-life events, rather than fantasy; inclusion of a variety of people and subject matters; didacticism; objectivity (here, in the form of the author's impersonality); and historicism.[30]

His emphasis on purpose, topic, and ideas over style and technique in defining realism as a mode of writing proves cautionary, however, when it leads him to end his chapter by recognizing a possible "pitfall of realism" as he has defined it. He worries that in this period-specific concept of realism, the distinction between art and mere information, communication, or manipulative rhetoric, such as propaganda and journalism, could disappear: "The theory of realism is ultimately bad aesthetics because all art is 'making' and is a world in itself of illusion and symbolic forms."[31] One might consider that Auerbach's formalist analysis of technique and style is exactly what allows his work to escape such a pitfall—to remain concerned only with the literary—and to propose a framework for realism that remains useful (to a point) in assessing a text's realism regardless of its historical period; and that perhaps the desire to restrict the concept to a particular period, but without sufficient regard to form, leaves too few criteria for inclusion and exclusion to designate a distinctive body of work.[32]

Other critics of the time also discuss realist literature as primarily defined according to the ideas it espouses, most notably George Lukács, whose *Realism in Our Time: Literature and the Class Struggle* (1962) differentiates types of realism based on their social and political philosophies. For Lukács, it is not enough to differentiate "critical realism," which identifies deleterious social and class relations, from "bourgeois realism," which quietly reproduces the cultural status quo; he advocates for a more specific "socialist realism," which offers a "concrete socialist perspective" and uses it to describe "the forces working towards socialism from the inside."[33] Warner Berthoff goes so far as to dedicate his book "to liberalism and democracy ... in whose service the work in this volume was mostly written," before asserting that "American literary realism was concerned less with problems of artistic definition and discovery than with clearing the way to a more profitable exercise of individual ambition." Uniting these works is "not form, certainly, not theme ... but fundamental motives to expression."[34] Both of these critics see realist writing as emerging not as a development of artistic practices in a long line of attempts to represent reality, but as a kind of rebellion against the tyranny of the status quo, whether economic or artistic.

One noteworthy critical study that continues the formalist analysis of realism established by Auerbach, while also beginning to place it in the context of an emerging new framework for literary studies—the linguistic turn—is Harold Kolb's *The Illusion of Life: American Realism as a Literary Form* (1969). Kolb recognizes the obfuscation inherent in the common, problematic terms used by the American realists to define realism (including "truth," "actuality," "accuracy," "reality," and "objectivity"), and notes how thoroughly scholarship had absorbed them: he observes that speakers on realism at the 1967 MLA convention invoked these terms, without critique, as characteristic of realism.[35] Since all writing is mimetic for Kolb and no writing is objective, or written without "cause, purpose, opinion,"[36] the only way to distinguish one type of writing from another is to examine *how* it accomplishes its goal of verisimilitude. Kolb thus characterizes late nineteenth-century realism according to its stylistic and technical innovations: rejection of omniscient point of view (here he points to James's exhortation in "The Art of Fiction" that authors not give themselves away by becoming present in the narrative[37]); crafting of multiple truths from multiple points of view;[38] pervasive ambiguity, missing information, and unresolved questions;[39] complicated, fully rendered characters that are "inextricably linked to" plot, and on which the complex point of view rests;[40] and "intrinsic, specific, and localized" imagery[41]—rather than evocative symbolism. Such a formalist characterization of realism indicates how we might draw a line between the literary innovations of American realism and those in high modernism that Auerbach described and championed. Their joint similarities to the innovations we will find in fiction after modernism, and the fundamentally metafictive framework in which Kolb describes the illusion that is the reality of all fiction, point forward to possible ways of productively characterizing realism after modernism—and remind us that any effective means of doing so must be to some extent *formal*.

Realism through the Lens of Linguistic Theory

Itself a massively complicated, varied, and definition-resistant thing, the "linguistic turn" as pertains to theory and criticism in the humanities might be shorthanded as the reformulation of all branches of academic inquiry, including philosophy, sociology, anthropology, psychology, and aesthetic theory, by the recognition that the deep structure of language profoundly shapes every aspect of the human experience and of subjectivity itself. Certainly Saussure's structuralist rethinking of linguistics as a distinctive branch of semiotics in the early twentieth century is one important origin of this turn, whose effects can be traced throughout the century in the philosophy and theory of Heidegger, Wittgenstein, and Derrida, the social and cultural studies of Foucault, Adorno, and Habermas, the psychoanalytic theory of Lacan, and into a new theory of narrative history by Hayden White. The late 1960s saw a surge of language-oriented theory with Derrida's 1966 landmark address at Johns Hopkins, "Structure, Sign, and Play in the Discourse of the Human Sciences," so that by the next decade, the fundamentals of poststructural thinking were influencing criticism and theory across Europe and America. It is easy to spot this influence on criticism about realist fiction, as we see the aims and methodologies of such criticism shift from largely political/idea-driven or formalistic—or, concerned with either the ideas about the world being represented or the techniques used to represent that world—to focused on the problem of the intersection of language and world.

In the contexts of poststructural theories, which question language's ability to say anything universally true about the world, and postmodern fiction, much of which demonstrates this difficulty or impossibility in overt and confusing ways, realist fiction (and early criticism about it) can feel quaint and simple, despite the technical and philosophical complexity that Auerbach's study uncovers, and which the fiction itself aptly demonstrates. J. P. Stern's *On Realism*, published in 1973, is an early example of the ways in which a post-modernist and language-oriented theoretical framework can fashion nineteenth-century realism into the strawperson whose naïveté illuminates poststructuralism's complexity in relief. Stern does acknowledge the long, varied history of the term "realism," and some of the ways in which earlier attempts to define the term in relation to one particular period or ideology have been unhelpfully vague or contradictory.[42] He proposes to narrow the term by framing it in the later linguistic theory of Wittgenstein, whose insights in *Philosophical Investigations* (1953) about how we define and use terms Stern calls "fundamental to any literary enquiry of this kind."[43] The two key concepts he borrows from Wittgenstein are that of "family resemblances," or the notion that we recognize meanings of words based on overlapping associations rather than direct connections between particular words and meanings, and the "double life of the word," or the recognition that different categories of language and meanings exist, for example literary and aesthetic versus everyday common language, and that words can occupy more than one set of vocabulary. Stern comments that recognizing these different types of vocabulary is important because critics tend to ignore the differences—a strange claim to make, given that such a recognition of literary versus everyday usage is fundamental to our earliest systematic literary theory, formalism.[44]

In any case, this philosophically sophisticated lens seems to lead to reductiveness and overstatement that erase the complexity of realist fiction already identified by other critics. In direct opposition to Kolb's assertion that "realistic fiction is devoted to the theme of unsimple truth,"[45] Stern calls realism "philosophically incurious and epistemologically naïve," essentially asserting that realist fiction questions neither the nature of reality nor what we know and how we know things about it—a claim that is easily disproved by "Hadleyburg"'s inquiry into honesty and postured sincerity, and "The Real Thing"'s discovery that the fake is a crucial component of represented reality. Likewise, Stern asserts that realism "implicitly denies . . . that in this world there is more than one reality, and that this denial is in need of proof,"[46] ignoring the "many truths, equally 'true' from some point of view"[47] uncovered by Kolb's stylistic and formalist analysis (and by Auerbach's central argument). And contrary to one of the key characteristics of the Old-Testament type of realism that Auerbach argues has most prominently endured into the twentieth century, Stern declares that "realism designates a creative attention to the visible rather than the invisible."[48] Ultimately, Stern argues that "the major end of realism (and of all literature) is to delight" rather than "distort," as idealism does,[49] which seems to equate reading pleasure with lack of intellectual and philosophical inquiry and complexity, quite at odds with Barthes's pleasures of the "text" and so with the linguistic-theoretical framework in which Stern locates his criticism. This method of "defining" realism seems, in the end, to do more to relegate realism to the literary junk heap in favor of newer and shinier, overtly poststructural kinds of fiction, than to offer a useful framework for understanding realism or reading any particular examples of it.

We can find ample evidence of the opposite tendency in postmodernist, poststructural and cultural-studies readings of realism as well. This approach does not dismiss realism as naïve in the face of poststructuralism and social constructivist theory, but rather rereads realism as already doing the work that would later be ascribed to such theory. One early example of such rereading is an anthology edited by Eric Sundquist and published in 1982, *American Realism: New Essays*. Several of its essays read canonical realist fiction as participating in the kind of linguistic uncertainty, and its resulting ontological uncertainty, that did not become thoroughly articulated in theory or criticism until poststructuralism had been well established; often these readings use specifically poststructural terms. Of Twain's *Pudd'nhead Wilson*, for example, Evan Carton writes that "truths are fictions as well as facts; lies, facts as well as fictions. The circuit of irony, unbroken and unbreakable, ensures a boundless freedom and imposes an inexorable enslavement."[50] Though grounding this reading in Kenneth Burke's 1962 definition of irony, Carton figures that irony in language reminiscent of Barthes's freeplay. More obviously, Fred See creates a bit of a mashup of Saussure, Lacan, and Derrida when he explores the "ontological . . . question of literary language"[51] as crafted by Henry James in terms of "a struggle taking place within language— the dramatic struggle of meaning with form: of signified and signifier, spirit and matter; language cannot exclude it; language is always haunted, always possessed."[52] Likewise, Alan Trachtenberg describes the city in Crane as "a swarming mass of signals, dense, obscure, undecipherable," "experienced as an absence," and characterized by the "'elsewhereness' of the street."[53]

The logic that holds together the collection's individual readings of realist texts—loosely—seems equally influenced by the postmodern period in which the book was born. Sundquist is careful in his preface to promise "no specific ideological or theoretical program on behalf of realism," for the same reason that Jameson will argue one year later, in "Postmodern and Consumer Society," that it is impossible to give a unified definition of postmodernism. Of realism, Sundquist claims in 1982 that

> the problem lies in part in the central difficulty of describing the program of a group of writers who virtually had no program but rather responded eclectically, and with increasing imaginative urgency, to the startling acceleration into being of a complex industrial society following the Civil War. Those responses became as varied and complex as the society itself.[54]

Of his introductory list of postmodernism examples, Jameson notes in 1983 that

> most of the postmodernisms mentioned above emerge as specific reactions against the established forms of high modernism, against this or that dominant high modernism which conquered the university, the museum, the art gallery network, and the foundations [...] This means that there will be as many different forms of postmodernism as there were high modernisms in place, since the former are at least initially specific and local reactions *against* these models.[55]

We might consider the significant difference between these two philosophies of literary period to be methodological: that is, while Sundquist's historicism locates the motivation for writing and reacting in historical events (the Civil War) and society, Jameson's Marxism focuses on ideological apparatuses, whether located in the institution (the university, the museum) or ideology itself (the "dominant high modernism which conquered the university"). But their similar approach to defining a mode through multiple, disparate, local examples is distinctly postmodern.

Indeed, Sundquist's anthology does more to blur the lines that had been dubiously drawn around realism by previous critics than it does to define the term. While the anthology's later essays illustrate realism's affinity for poststructural readings, its early essays demonstrate realism's resemblance to romance. Richard Brodhead argues that Hawthorne was an "exemplum" for, and anticipatory of, realist writing, especially Howells's;[56] Eric Cheyfitz reads the "self-realization" that is characteristic of realism as inherited from the romance;[57] and Sundquist himself concludes that "the psychological realism of James and Crane represents most evidently and most tellingly the continued presence of romance." Taken together, these essays deliver exactly what the preface promised, not a definition of period but "the complexity of response that defines the period itself."[58] The replacement of articulated period with disparate complexity—perhaps another example of what Lyotard termed "complexification,"[59] another characteristic of postmodernism—is so characteristic of postmodernism that critics were arguing that postmodernism was dead before it had barely begun, and continue to argue about its beginnings now that most agree it is dead.[60] Further aligning realism with the definition-averse, self-abnegating postmodern period in which he was writing, Sundquist describes realism as characterized by "intense experimentation" that "quite often betrays a supreme resistance to realism."[61] Certainly the diverse essays in this collection offer a far more nuanced examination of nineteenth-century American realism than had been produced by previous critics enthralled with the deceptively simplistic theories supplied by the realists themselves; as Sundquist's volume originated in an MLA panel on American realism at the 1979 convention,[62] the anthology is also evidence that thinking about realism in the academy had certainly progressed since the 1967 panel described by Kolb. But the essays also illustrate some of the ways in which new theories of literature cause radical rereadings that may say more about contemporary frameworks than about earlier periods or texts.

By the time its sixth edition came out in 1993, M. H. Abrams's *A Glossary of Literary Terms*, considered a standard in our field by students at all levels, reflected both the specific/nonspecific debate in decades of critical definitions of "realism," and contemporary, poststructural rereadings of the term. Abrams starts by describing "realism" as "applied by literary critics in two diverse ways":

(1) To identify a nineteenth-century movement in the writing of novels that included Honoré de Balzac in France, George Eliot in England, and William Dean Howells in America, . . . and (2) to designate a recurrent mode, in various eras and literary forms, of representing human life and experience in literature.

After characterizing realism in simple ways that are largely taken from the claims of the period—that it is "opposed to romantic fiction," represents "life as it really is," and concerns "the stuff of ordinary experience"—Abrams notes how structuralism forces us to look again at this seemingly straightforward representation, pointing to Barthes's and Culler's ideas about "naturalizing" texts through their "reality effects" as evidence that realism is an effect of conventions, not a property of one particular type of text. This step, naturally, leads Abrams to recognize the same trap that so many writers on realism, all the way back to Jakobson, have likewise discovered: "Since all literary representations are constituted by arbitrary conventions, there is no valid ground for holding any one kind of fiction to be more realistic than any other."[63] Meanwhile, in defining the "realistic novel" as one of the "two basic types of prose fiction,"[64] Abrams does a similar kind of dance, both grounding his definition in Howells, Eliot, Balzac, et al, and describing their work in far less direct ways than they did themselves: "the realistic novel is characterized as the fictional **attempt** to give the **effect** of *realism*."[65] Thus, an explicit definition of "realism," through the lens of structuralism, becomes another discovery of the impossibility of defining the term as a particular period, mode, or style of writing.

More telling still are the ways in which this sixth edition from 1993 revises Abrams's third edition, which he wrote in 1970. There, his second definition provided a broad description of realism, as in 1993, but kept it relative to the nineteenth century, whose writers "typified... this historical movement."[66] His explanation for the "illusion" inherent in realism likewise remained anchored in the past, as he attributed it to the fact that "the realist . . . is deliberately selective in his material and prefers the average, the commonplace, and the everyday over the rarer aspects of the contemporary scene"—a description of realism that owes much to Auerbach and has yet to register Culler, Barthes, Barthes, or even Saussure. Ultimately Abrams asserts that we must "reserve the term 'realist' for writers who render a subject seriously, and as though it were a direct reflection of the casual order of experience, without too patently shaping it"[67]—as if there is not more than one way of rendering subjects "seriously" or of "reflect[ing] . . . experience," as though what he has described as "realism" is not itself one method of "patently shaping" experience. This 1971 edition reflects a naïveté about realism as a historically distinct mode somehow free from the ideology of form and the pressures of language, all of which the 1993 edition communicates with its addition of structuralism. Perhaps it is not surprising, then, to find that Abrams's first edition of this long-lived glossary, which he wrote in 1957, does not even propose a historically delineated definition for "realism,"[68] or list the "realist novel" among the most common types of novel (though it does list "sociological novel" and "regional novel"[69]). These revisions suggest that, while the 70s' burst of criticism saw the increased concretization of "realism" as a historically delineated mode, the 90s reshaped the term again through the lenses of structuralism and poststructuralism. Taken together, these three editions of the highly influential *Glossary* illustrate once again how shaped by academic history and culture is any act of literary defining.

Morris's *Realism*

Like Abrams, and somewhat problematically, Pam Morris treats realism as both a specific (late-nineteenth century) literary period, with recognizable stylistic, thematic, and technical traits—which she spends a fair bit of time examining—and as a mode so broad that it offers little descriptive power. Realism is "a long, impressive tradition of artistic development during which writers struggled and experimented with the artistic means to convey a verbal sense of what it is like to live an embodied existence in the world"; it is "any writing that is based upon an implicit or explicit assumption that it is possible to communicate about a reality beyond the writing"; realism "as a form is witness to that juncture between the experimental and the representational."[70] One element of this broad definition might prove helpfully limiting one day. For, with digital literature thriving; social media forcing us all to live in a world of simulacra; literature, film, and television urgently pondering the implications of "advances" in computing, genetic coding, AI, and virtual-reality technologies; and science making real and present, in small but undeniable steps, those very technologies, we might imagine a time when a definition premised on "embodied existence" would demarcate some texts from others that have left the material world as a point of reference behind altogether. At that point, a moment ushered in more by technological advances and cultural absorption of their consequences than by aesthetic theory, Morris's definition of realism as a representational mode that "can and does rationally refer to a material domain beyond representation"[71] will distinguish everything written that presupposes the primacy of the material world from anything that does not (for more on this potential demarcation, see my Conclusion). But since even current theory of digital literature proceeds from the assumption that embodiment and the material are primary, that all electronic and virtual representation and projection are inevitably entangled with the material realm in which they are produced and which produces them, such a material-based definition of realism does little if anything in the early twenty-first century to designate a particular mode of writing.[72]

When Morris does treat realism as a restrictive term that points to a particular kind of writing, as exemplified by the late nineteenth-century realists, like Sundquist and (sixth edition) Abrams she reads it through expectations for fiction established by poststructuralism. Her basic premise incorporates the contexts of Barthes, Culler, and poststructuralist understandings of language in general: "realist novels *never* give us life or a slice of life nor do they reflect reality. In the first place, literary realism is a representational form and a representation can never be identical with that which it represents. In the second place, words function completely differently from mirrors."[73] Thus, she dismisses definitions of realism based on mimesis or verisimilitude, going so far as to note that

> the problem with definitions of realism and related terms that use phrases like "fidelity of representation" or "rendering of precise details" is that they tend to be associated with notions of truth as verifiability. There is a popular and somewhat paradoxical assumption that realist fiction is to be judged according to how faithfully it corresponds to things and events in the real-world.

Attempting to clarify her position in relation to such naïve notions of realism, Morris offers another analogy that she claims is popular and misleading: "Realist novels developed as a popular form during the nineteenth century alongside the other quickly popularized representational practice of photography. This coincidence may well have encouraged a pictorial or photographic model of truth as correspondence." Certainly, post-Saussure and post-Barthes, notions of realism as rendering the real in language through a one-to-one correspondence do seem ridiculous. But these notions came straight from the canonical writers who theorized and produced the literature she considers exemplary realism—Howells judging its success according to its "fidelity to [life]"; Twain excoriating Cooper's lack of such fidelity by pointing out the ways his fiction did not conform to the events and things in the world; James analogizing the story to the picture, which for him "is reality." So dismissing the picture analogy as irrelevant today seems at best historically amnesiac and at worst misleading and inaccurate. It is simply not true that "there is little evidence to suggest that the major realist writers of the nineteenth century ever saw their goal in terms of a one-to-one correspondence with a non-verbal reality."[74] It is much fairer to say that there is abundant evidence that the major realist writers of the nineteenth century in many ways did not see the paradox of believing that language could accurately and directly reflect reality.[75] Has literature changed, or just our way of reading it? Does Morris mean to define a type of literature, or a critical or theoretical understanding of it?

Morris is well aware of changes in critical perspectives of realism through the modernist and post-modernist periods. Like Auerbach, she reads modernism as an extension of realism,[76] and like Auerbach, her assessment of post-modernist evolutions of realism amounts to their dismissal in the interest of valorizing realism before and into modernism. Morris summarizes the critique of realism registered by Lyotard, Barthes, Derrida, and antihumanist thinking in general as "a rejection of the Enlightenment view of rational knowledge and human progress" that leads to a view of realist novels as "colluding with functional reason to produce philistine readerly narratives" that reaffirm rather than question the status quo and "naturalize" the sufferings it causes. She views poststructural rereadings of realist texts—perhaps of the sort anthologized by Sundquist—as condescending attempts to rescue realism from a blindness that has only been imagined and imposed upon it by poststructuralism itself.[77]

Ultimately, Morris rejects the entire critique of realism constructed by postmodernism and poststructuralism by reading poststructuralism's commitment to the freeplay of an open system of language, and the deconstructive acts it allows, as an elitist flight from common knowledge—or what those who erroneously equate postmodernism and nihilism would call "common sense": "As opposed to poststructuralism's grand liberation narrative into a discriminating realm of play, realism's contract with the reader is based upon the Enlightenment consensual belief in the possibility of a shared understanding."[78] Her opposition between the democracy of realism and the elitist individualism of postmodernism is an old one, but easily refuted. One of the primary motivations of postmodernism was, after all, a certain kind of democratizing, the recognition of difference, diversity, and particularity that had been so long obscured by totalizing gestures of realism and then modernism. But more importantly for my purposes, this opposition she draws between the nihilistic, individualistic elitism of postmodern and poststructural readings and texts—or perhaps simply of all post-nineteenth-century realist texts—and the realism that came before them has become inarguably false in the wake of critical studies that argue for exactly the continuities she denies between realist, Enlightenment-based texts and postmodern and post-postmodern texts.[79] One of the largest aims of this book, in fact, is to explore the ways in which contemporary fiction adapts and coopts realist aims and methods specifically in order to construct those continuities.

However hampered by a tendency to misread the postmodern, poststructural context that she argues misreads realism, Morris's argument does suggest interesting dilemmas of any attempt to define one literary mode or period in relation to a constellation of earlier or later theoretical and critical lenses. She acknowledges one of these dilemmas when she notes that Elaine Showalter's foundational feminist work on Woolf is unable to "adequately recognise Woolf's artistic achievement" because it proceeds from "within realist values," just as critics do not acknowledge the achievements of Pat Barker's realist work in a postmodern era.[80] Similarly, Morris's critique of poststructuralism's critique of realism stems from her analysis of the distortion involved in deconstructive readings of realist texts, such as Barthes's reading of Balzac:[81] for Morris, there are realist ways of reading and poststructural ways of reading, each proceeding from its own ideas of and values for language, literature, self, and culture, and applying one kind of reading to the other kind of text causes misreadings.

This conclusion seems to suggest that there must also be different kinds of *texts*, that is, realist texts and poststructural ones, as well. But her proposed solution to the problem of realist texts misread by ill-fitting lenses is *not* to separate eighteenth- and nineteenth-century European realism from later, "less systematic" uses of the mode in a diversity of cultures, but rather to unite them through the vague notion that "thematically and formally, realism is defined by an imperative to bear witness to all the consequences, comic and tragic, of our necessarily embodied existence."[82] It is this kind of extreme generalizing that seems to invite the very misreadings that Morris objects to. What does "realism" mean here, if it is not limited by culture, history, or technique, and if (as she also suggests) "realist" and "anti-realist" (and "experimental") techniques alike might be used to accomplish it?

Near the end of the book, she seems to erase even the binary of "realist" and "anti-realist" (which she has used throughout) when she attempts to widen the definition of "realism" to include even contemporary fiction whose ideas of reality stretch far beyond those contained in nineteenth-century realist texts: "From the perspective of the ideal of scientific knowledge as a continuing attempt to understand the world, Einstein's relativity theory 'is not in the least anti-realist, but on the contrary a great stride towards discovering the underlying structure of reality.'"[83] What do "realism" and "anti-realism" mean here? How is either of them related to the reality of the physical world, and/or how also to abstract literary conventions? What does the reality of the physical universe have to do with the efficacy of linguistic conventions for representing that materiality in language? And how can either of these terms be productive when usage of them obscures, rather than illuminating, this difference and the relationship between the material real and the linguistic referent? Whereas some contemporary writers and theorists contemplate exactly this generative difference, as I will examine in this book (see especially Chapters 3–5, on material realism and quantum realism), Morris's unexplained collapsing of that difference further undermines the usefulness of her attempts to define realism.

However ultimately unsatisfying, Morris's concerted efforts to define "realism" across the radically changing notions about language and reality of the twentieth century, and her characterization of that fiction in terms of meticulously examined "reality effects," helpfully elucidate four problems inherent to any such act of defining:

1. How do we distinguish realism as a period from realism as a set of techniques, or aims, or a value system (Enlightenment or otherwise), deployed in any time period? How can the term be useful without such a distinction?
2. Given the profound change in scientific descriptions of reality in the twentieth century, does any definition of realism have to consider what it means be "real"? How might it do so?
3. How might our uses of "realism" differentiate between realist ways of reading and realist texts?
4. Is metafiction, or self-reflexivity, as became a prominent feature in postmodern fiction, actually an inherent quality of all fiction, including realism, or is it a quality or technique that can be understood as opposed to realist fiction?

In its attention to technical and formal innovations that characterize contemporary realisms, this book aims to begin to address exactly such questions raised by Morris's and other earlier examinations of "realism."

Jameson's *Antinomies of Realism*

Quite in opposition to Morris—and to other post-modernist critics who look back on realism as always-already linguistically, epistemologically, and ontologically savvy, and engaged in the kind of ideological unmasking more often associated with poststructural texts—Fredric Jameson conceives of realism as a mode of writing that can neither deliver nor uncover truth, and is always invested in maintaining the status quo: "the realistic novel has a vested interest, an ontological stake, in the solidity of social reality, on the resistance of bourgeois society to history and to change"; "realism . . . is a hybrid concept, in which an epistemological claim (for knowledge or truth) masquerades as an aesthetic ideal, with fatal consequences for both of these incommensurable dimensions. If it is social truth or knowledge we want from realism, we will soon find that what we get is ideology."[84] Rather than a definable (or undefinable) single mode, realism for him is a process involving multiple aspects of fiction, an "aporia" or "dialectic" of two contradictory narrative impulses whose development in conjunction with and opposition to each other over time leads to its inevitable end. Realism is

> a historical and even evolutionary process in which the negative and positive are inextricably combined, and whose emergence and development at one and the same time constitute its own inevitable undoing, its own decay and dissolution. (6)

Jameson's Marxist-poststructural stance allows his theorizing of realism to bypass questions of universal truth that befuddle other formulations (even those of other Marxists, such as Lukacs), rendering it instead a matter of aesthetic modes for delivering ideological content. This shift away from the question of truth and verisimilitude enables his theory of realism to avoid some previous periodizing pitfalls, while proposing new terms in which to evaluate today's post-modernist realist innovations.

In defining realism as a process that unfolds over time, Jameson makes a literary-historical argument that we can only grasp realism as a kind of writing by looking at it in relation to the writing that predates it (romance, epic, melodrama, idealism) and that comes after its undoing. Such an argument is akin to others that posit realism as emerging out of other modes only to sink down again into the sea of writing, but with the significant addition of close attention to the mechanisms of that emergence and dissolution: his argument puts a powerful magnifying glass to the comparatively gross observations of Wellek, making visible the complex moving systems left invisible in more superficial accounts. This vision into the workings of realism as a process taking place on the level of form over time rescues "realism" from languishing uselessly as a large umbrella term that contains all other modes of writing (or, all those that believe a real world exists). Because this definition does not posit a particular mode or style of writing, with a set of stylistic, thematic, or formal devices, or particular historical or cultural dimensions, it also avoids becoming a strawperson term of questionable precision to be easily knocked aside by whatever slightly differing definition arises, as is sure to do over time and through changes in literature and ideas about literature. Perhaps we should see Jameson's dialectical definition of realism as the literary-historical counterpart to his dialectical concept of history as the evolution of form, as articulated in "The Political Unconscious," with nineteenth-century realism being one phase of literary history in the way that tribalism is one phase of an evolving history that is currently stalled out in (late) capitalism.

The dialectic of realism for Jameson comprises the old narrative impulse of the tale, or "récit," which preceded realism and is characterized by its pastness, unchangeability, and entanglement with fate, in conflict with a new "scenic" impulse toward representing an eternal-present moment of unprocessed affect. "Affect" here means not conscious emotions but "bodily feelings" (32, as theorized by Rei Terada) or feeling without meaning. In essence, realism for Jameson is writing that is attempting to throw off the bonds and structures of fiction that limit its expression of feeling and meaning by imposing particular form on it, especially the form and conventions of genre. Thus, Jameson characterizes realism in terms of the features of affect being expressed in a text; the new techniques and uses of language being used to express those features; and ways in which any given text demonstrates the tension between its narrative/descriptive/fated impulse and its desire to arrest time and escape limited knowledge or meaning.

Most diachronically, for Jameson, we can recognize the workings of realism in a text in the ways in which we can see it dissolving a particular element of the tale/récit in order to render affect—and in the ways it begins to destroy the very genres it created in doing so. Jameson demonstrates this argument by reading the work of Zola, Tolstoy, Pérez Galdós, and George Eliot as dismantling aspects of realism that it had inherited and solidified into its own conventions—not just character structure but even the "agent of conflict" that forms the backbone of realist plot structure (114). He further demonstrates this process of building then dismantling convention on the level of genre, arguing that any genre created in realism must be destroyed in realism:

> Realism as a formal strategy gradually begins to form new genres in its own right: hardening over, as it were, in a few tale-types, genres which the novel sometimes inherits but most often invents or reinvents, in a process in which they serve as a scaffolding which must in turn be dismantled. (144)

While breaking from the more descriptive and less useful attempts to codify realism as a particular set of themes or techniques, Jameson's account meaningfully develops other more holistic approaches. It extends, and in some ways rests on, Auerbach's concept of realism as a "flight from classification" that attempts to make space for the "everyday" or "existential," which Jameson has "named as affect—the everyday as the outside, or *Stimmung*; the existential as the lived or inside, namely affect as such" (143). And because this dialectic also describes realism's own emergence as a genre—"realism is opposed to romance only because it carries it within itself and must somehow dissolve it in order to become its antithesis" (139)—it also complicates the context in which we read the line-blurring between romance and realism accomplished by Sundquist's 1993 anthology.

Inherent in Jameson's definition of realism, as in Auerbach's, which reads modernism as the culmination of realism, is its own demise. So what is left after realism? For Jameson, as realism orchestrates its own death—as it kills off the genres it has built in its attempts to render affect through narrative—its primary techniques morph as well, so that both realism and its tools end up as mutated, zombiefied versions of themselves: still hanging around, but to no good end. In a masterful reading of generic evolution through form and technique, Jameson charts the changes undergone by the same techniques Auerbach examined in his discourse on realism—irony, free indirect discourse, and point of view—as they developed in realism and beyond, noting that what many of us today think of as the building blocks of postmodern or poststructural (or "anti-realist," as Jameson calls it) literature were first used to build the realist literature against which that later literature is often seen as reacting (164). To these techniques, Jameson adds the less-often noticed "cataphora," or a text's use of a pronoun without antecedent, which creates a kind of abysmal lack, often, in and since modernism, at the beginnings of texts. I will consider his studies of the distortions and subsequent defanging of these techniques more closely in Chapters 1 and 5, and posit ways in which some authors after modernism *have* devised new uses of these realist techniques that make them newly powerful in a post-modernist literary and theoretical context. Jameson's own conclusions about the productivity and potential, even the possibility, of realism after modernism, however, are bleak.

Ultimately he argues that realism's evolution in terms of dissolving its own generic and technical tools for rendering affect results in 1. "serious"/literary writers giving up on the broken tools of realism but holding on to their desire to represent "singularity in the everyday," and thus writing affect without realism; and 2. "popular" writers continuing to use these broken tools to write realism, but thus being unable to render affect. This latter dilemma Jameson explains by way of the decadence of contemporary realist techniques, which results in "inauthentic narrative temporality" and uses of point of view, FID, and stream of consciousness that can produce only performance, or a kind of inauthentic subjectivity (184, 185). His final reading, of David Mitchell's *Cloud Atlas* (2004), illustrates Jameson's commitment to this bleak conclusion about the ultimate inefficacy of realism. Rather than reading the novel as a masterful use of postmodern multiplicity of voices and poststructural rejection of authenticity in order to construct non-totalizing connections and non-universalizing truths, as I do in my teaching and others do in print,[85] Jameson reads the novel as illustrating the failure of art and of the historical novel to do anything but offer "shabby ideological messages" whose greater point is the primacy of pastiche and material media (303–13).

Meanwhile, over the past three decades—concentrated in the early 1990s, when postmodernism began transitioning into something else—over twenty different "realisms" have been posited, most as descriptors of new types of literature. Such an explosion of realisms after what Jameson has argued is the death of realism raises intriguing questions about how, or whether, these new realisms relate to the dialectical realism Jameson has defined. Are these new "realisms," with their innovations in technique, form, and genre, the end of realism as it coalesced in the nineteenth century and the emergence of something else? Is that something else truly a new form of realism, or something altogether different? Or are they doing something integral to realism as a historically evolving mode in the manner of Auerbach and Jameson, making them a holdover from a realism they are working to dissolve? If we accept Jameson's definition, as the dialectic between narrative/telling and scene/showing, of pastness/fate and eternal present/affect, how do we recognize these elements in "post-postmodern" narrative, and what is happening to them? Is "post-postmodern" narrative, are new realisms, reversing their relationship in the dialectic? Resolving it? Or is a new dialectic altogether, composed of different antinomies, arising?

Likewise, the appearance of such a glut of realisms amid the emergence of "post-postmodern" literature, and in the context of this long, complex, contradictory history of theories of realism, raises other questions less specifically relevant to Jameson's argument and more catalyzing for this book's larger investigation: What does this proliferation of realisms say about "realism" as a useful term for literary description and literary history? How are these numerous attempts to create, name, and theorize new kinds of realism characteristic of, or a feature of, literature after postmodernism?

Realisms in and after Postmodernism

As critics and theorists were beginning to codify postmodernism as a cultural and literary phenomenon[86]—often as an intensification of modernism's break with realism—realism was making a resurgence. Whether the reappearance of this term in the context of postmodern literature signaled a comeback or something altogether new depended on who was using it, why, and when. By my count, over twenty different literary realisms have been proposed so far:[87]

- Dirty realism (Bill Buford, 1983)
- Neorealism (Kristiaan Versluys, 1992)
- Postmodern realism

- (Albert Borgmann, 1992)
- (Deborah Bowen, 2010)
- (Holland, 2012)
- British postmodern realism (Amy Elias, 1994)
- Crackpot realism (Melvin Jules Bukiet, 1996, after Richard Powers in 1988)
- Traumatic realism (Hal Foster, 1996)
- Tragic realism (Jonathan Franzen, 1996)
- Figural realism (Hayden White, 1999)
- Hysterical realism (James Wood, 2000)
- Meta-realism (Philip Tew, 2003)
- Speculative realism (Ramón Saldivar, 2007)
- Agential realism (Karan Barad, 2007)
- Disquieting realism (Katarzyna Beilin, 2008)
- Capitalist realism (Mark Fisher, 2009)
- Post-postmodern realism (Madhu Dubey, 2011)
- Poststructural realism (Holland, 2013)
- Metonymic realism (Pam Morris, 2013)
- Ecocritical realism (Reinhard Hennig, 2013)
- Relational realism (Zuzanna Jakubowski, 2013)
- Metafictive realism (Holland, 2014)

This list raises thorny—if not exasperating—questions for critics of contemporary literature, about the terms' implications for our understandings of realism and of literature after postmodernism. As I am guiltier than anyone of muddying these waters, having already offered three "realisms" of my own in publication or presentation, this book is in part my effort to set things right and begin to clean up the literary mess to which I have repeatedly contributed. But more than penance, this book was motivated by the desire to do more thoroughly and diachronically what my earlier dabblings in contemporary realisms attempted to do in particular, synchronic ways: understand the relationship between realism in earlier fiction and theory and contemporary innovations in technique and form.

The coinages alone, each anchored in "realism" but inflected by a term stemming from some aspect of postmodernism or its close cousin, cultural studies, themselves suggest ways of beginning to recognize these connections: they indicate a continued preoccupation with realism in the postmodern period and after (White's "figural," after Auerbach); a rejection of or reaction against pre-modernist realism ("traumatic," "hysterical"); interest in how realism changes when produced or read in a postmodern and/or poststructuralist context ("crackpot," "capitalist," "postmodern," "poststructural," "post-postmodern"); belief in the productive role of new or newly prominent literary techniques, including metafiction ("meta-realism" and "metafictive realism"); attention to the effects of postmodern genres on realism ("speculative"); and even proposals of entirely new frameworks for conceiving of the world, representation, and the relationship between the two ("relational"[88] and "agential" realism).

The earliest new realisms, "dirty," "neo," and Borgmann's "postmodern" realism, are the most retro, describing what amounts to a return of conventionally pre-modernist realism during the postmodern period. These realisms, according to their positers, are affected by the postmodern period in which they arise more in subject matter than in form: the "realism" of all of these terms refers, at least in early coinages, to their aesthetic and conventional indebtedness to pre-modernist realism, in direct opposition to what was referred to at the time as "anti-realist."[89] Buford describes dirty realism as "not self-consciously experimental,"[90] a claim that is echoed by Robert Rebein's work on dirty realism, and Josh Toth sees neorealism arising in response to the "failure" of metafiction.[91] Borgmann borrows from realism its "common order centered on communal celebrations" to "resolve the ambiguities" of the "postmodern critique" in his "postmodern realism,"[92] and while William Thornton and Songok Han Thornton reject Borgmann's desire for resolution a year later, their concept of postmodern realism also rests on the conventions and ethical certainty associated with pre-modernist realism. After these early establishments of the term, others deployed it diversely, in subjects ranging from philosophy to photography and fiction and drama.[93] My own argument for "postmodern realism" in a 2012 article on A. M. Homes expands significantly on these earlier definitions, to incorporate a metafictive commentary on realism itself, an aspect of contemporary realisms I will discuss in Chapter 1, "Metafictive Realism."

Other uses of "realism" remain invested in old realism but are more interested in the workings of realism broadly as a mode of representing reality, in the manner of Auerbach, Morris, and Jameson. Hayden White's *Figural Realism: Studies in the Mimesis Effect* (1999) takes the main term of its title straight from Auerbach, who uses it to differentiate the mimetic system of the Old Testament, in which every event stands in for and/or derives its meaning from another, and "the various components all belong to one concept of universal history and its interpretation" (17), which the *Iliad* and *Odyssey* lack. White makes both a comprehensive argument about the nature of realist writing in general and a more specific argument about how realist writing must change to accommodate changes in reality. Broadly, he argues that all literary writing is realism, not only the more obviously realistic literal writing, but also figural writing: "figural language can be said to refer to reality quite as faithfully and much more effectively than any putatively literalist idiom or mode of discourse might do."[94] We might consider this argument the literary equivalent of the groundbreaking claim he made for history as early as 1972, in "The Structure of Historical Narrative," in which he began a considerable body of work arguing that history is inherently structured as narrative and operates according to the techniques we have come to associate with literature rather than history.

But if all realism is figural, it is not all the same: following Barthes, White argues that modernist writing breaks down the binaries of subject/object, active/passive, and literal/figural that (pre-modernist) realist writing maintained. He explains this transformation of mode by a causal transformation in the world: "the kind of anomalies, enigmas, and dead ends met with in discussions of the representations of the Holocaust are the result of a conception of discourse that owes too much to a realism that is inadequate to the representation of events, such as the Holocaust, which are themselves modernist in nature."[95] Essentially White defines realism as a mode of representing reality that is forced to change when reality itself changes: "our notion of what constitutes realistic representation must be revised to take account of experiences that are unique to our century and for which the older modes of representation have proven to be inadequate."[96]

Likewise, Pam Morris's "metonymic realism" posits yet another way of understanding how modernist (or "experimental") writing changed the workings of realism. Morris maps a "Counter-Enlightenment discourse"—following Hume rather than Descartes—that understands self as relational and as "materially embedded"[97] rather than solitary, resulting in a new realist epistemology that requires a new aesthetic mode. Using Woolf's *Mrs. Dalloway* as her example, Morris argues that realism devoted to representing the relational self and world proceeds by way of metonym, in which individual objects and events point to larger social structures that the texts can critique. Rather than wholly departing from such a concept of realism, the present book adopts a similar framework for understanding realism as adapting its structures and methods to changing notions of self and world, while offering a more detailed and extensive examination of the formal techniques being invented, and why and how they are used (most noticeably in Chapters 4 and 5, which focus on quantum realism).

In positing new realisms, some critics are really more interested in declaring and mourning what they see as the death of old realism. James Wood's infamous "review" of Zadie Smith's 2000 *White Teeth* is an excellent example of this tactic. Really an attack not just on Smith but also Salman Rushdie, Thomas Pynchon, Don DeLillo, and Wallace—a précis of postmodern writing that carefully crosses lines of gender, race, and nation—

Wood's article invents "hysterical realism" to describe a newly "hardened" genre in which novels construct rampant storytelling as "grammar," use the mode of realism while "seem[ing] evasive of reality," create "inhuman" stories and unpersuasive characters and offer too many of both. This "excess," he claims, strains realism to the breaking point, in a perhaps Freudian attempt to hide the emptiness at its center. Curiously, Wood seems to expect his reader fully to agree with him, despite the wealth of criticism on all of these authors (perhaps least so on Pynchon, but notably, existing even on DeLillo) that reads their fiction as accomplishing exactly what Wood claims it cannot. As if to underscore his insinuation that such fiction sounds the death knell for the Great Novel, Wood ends by imagining the reader of *White Teeth* "perhaps think[ing] wistfully of Mr. Micawber and David Copperfield . . . weeping together in an upstairs room."[98]

Sounding an entirely different death knell, Mark Fisher proposed "capitalist realism" in 2009 as the successor to Jameson's "late capitalism." Fisher sees capitalist realism, like White's "figural realism," as "not a particular type of realism; it is more like realism itself,"[99] or, a redefinition of "realism" in which it can no longer escape capitalism. Whereas Fisher sees late capitalism as a specifically postmodern phenomenon, capitalist realism describes the even more pervasive sense of exhaustion since the 1980s, and the total loss of faith—rather than waning faith—that any economic or cultural mode will ever defeat capitalism, and in art's revolutionary power in the face of that bleak fact. By this understanding, capitalism *is* reality, and all attempts to represent reality are then capitalistic. No longer describing a mode of representation we might read for signs of ideology, realism for Fisher in "capitalist realism" *is* ideology; it already contains inside itself all possible gestures of resistance, which are, in Foulcaultian fashion, all part of ideology and therefore meaningless. This new realism is not an offshoot or disagreement with conventional realism, but an explosion of it, a proposed notion of reality—notably, a poststructural, anti-humanist, social constructivist reality—in which pre-modernist ideas of realism struggle to make sense at all.

Most of the new realisms on this list, however, are more productive and useful for critics of contemporary literature than these backward-looking versions, in that they aim to characterize a particular type of fiction in or after the postmodern period, which shares something of traditional realism's fundamental goals but is distinguished by its innovations in technique, genre, or form.[100] Madhu Dubey's tentative coinage in her "Post-Postmodern Realism?" might function as the umbrella term for several more specific terms proposed by others; in her 2011 article, Dubey claims we are seeing in "post-postmodern" fiction a return to social realism as called for in 1989 by Thomas Wolfe and identified by Robert McLaughlin.[101] Dubey's argument extrapolates from Wendy Steiner's 1999 reconsideration of postmodern fiction, which sought to close the considerable gap long imagined between formally innovative postmodern fiction (associated with white male writers) and political and social writing (identified with women and people of color). Steiner argued that both these types of writing blended in the postmodern period into a "redefined realism" that creates formal innovation not as an end in itself but to refer to "the current state of reality."[102] "Post-postmodern" realism for Dubey, then, might designate a type of fiction that uses formal, "anti-realist" innovation in the service of the social critique characteristic of pre-modernist realism. It is exactly the opposite of those early uses of "postmodern realism," in its reliance on formal innovation rather than the return of realism's conventions: "Given that the material conditions that gave rise to postmodernism still pertain, . . . the problem that postmodernism posed for the social novel . . . cannot be solved on formal grounds, by reviving narrative realism."[103] As such it is, perhaps, our best hope for fiction's continued relevance to the world.

Some of the new realisms proposed in the "post-postmodern" period, though, are more relevant to postmodernism than to the literature that followed it. Hal Foster's "traumatic realism," a mode he proposed for reading visual art in his 1996 *The Return of the Real*, proceeds from a Lacanian framework in which the Real, particularly the traumatic Real (or the Real that is always traumatic), cannot be represented, and so art can only gesture toward its absence. Cathy Caruth's de Manian formulation of trauma and language's inability to communicate that trauma applies a similar logic to written narrative.[104] Amy Elias's notion of "British postmodern realism" seems to me akin to Foster's traumatic realism, in that what starts as a realist text becomes postmodern in the wake of trauma, as the text encounters language's inability to express the reality of traumatic experience. All of these concepts belong more clearly to the postmodern period than to "post-postmodernism"; in *Succeeding Postmodernism*, I argue that the traumatic Real, which can only be represented as a gap, a defense against real suffering, or through the diseased or damaged body, is characteristic of postmodern American literature but not of the literature that comes after it (167–8).[105] The same is true for Melvin Jules Bukiet's "crackpot realism," despite its efficacy as pre-emptive rejoinder to Wood's "hysterical realism." Taking the term from Richard Powers, who first used it in his 1988 *The Prisoner's Dilemma*, Bukiet defines "crackpot realism" as fiction characterized by plot gone wild, stylistic "mesh-mosh,"[106] and paranoid characters who find meaning and redemption in linguistic and experiential pattern (not surprisingly, he names its main practitioners as Powers, Pynchon, and Franzen). But "lunatic" characters finding private significance in general absurdity does nothing to escape the solipsistic threat that literature after postmodernism aims to overcome by reconceptualizing self, world, and language in newly connected ways.

Productive "Post-postmodern" Realisms: Metafiction and Materiality

If we set aside all these new "realisms" that smuggle old realism into postmodernist fiction, mourn the death of realism amid new fiction's inhumanity, or portray realism as stalled out in the linguistic maze of postmodernism, we are still left with quite a few proposals for ways in which realism gets productively reimagined in the "post-postmodern" period. At this chaotic moment in our field, a good deal of overlap exists among these new terms—which makes sense, because for the most part the different realisms that have been posited rely on similar narrative strategies and formal innovations, which have yet to be neatly cordoned off from each other by critical consensus. Two of the terms, "disquieting realism" and "speculative realism," describe strikingly similar narrative innovations. While Katarzyna Beilin's "disquieting realism" merges assumptions of magical realism with those of traditional realism, to acknowledge the presence in reality of the inexpressible and impossible, Ramón Saldivar's "speculative realism" blends multiple genres, including the historical novel, bildungsroman, science fiction, fantasy, and the comic book, to illustrate the "constitutive role of fantasy in the post-postmodern world"[107] and the need for writers to invent new ways of imagining and representing in order to convey that changed world (here his argument is in line with Auerbach's, White's, and Dubey's).

These productive "post-postmodern" realisms share two significant traits, in terms of method and theme: metafiction and materiality, with the former being a more-or-less ubiquitous technique for bending post-modernist narrative toward pre-modernist function. In speculative realism, metafiction allows illusion to reveal itself as such in the "parabasis" that collapses boundaries between author, narrator, and characters; in disquieting realism, and more overtly, metafiction is the tool that constructs the fiction's realist lens (this reading is akin to the larger argument I will make for "metafictive realism" in Chapter 1). My own proposed "postmodern realism," in 2012, shares aspects of both of these new realisms, in that it operates according to a shift between modes or genres and by way of metafiction. In a significant departure from Borgmann's and Thornton and Thornton's traditional realism-based concepts of postmodern realism, I argue that Homes's work is postmodern realism because it *seems* to proceed according to postmodern conventions and assumptions about the world, while ultimately recouping realist form and morality—a return to realism that can only be accomplished by the metafictive strategy of forcing the reader to become aware of the expectations provoked by the novel.[108]

Two eponymously metafiction-based realisms have also been posited, which I will outline here and then explore in depth in Chapter 1. Will Slocombe's 2010 "Is Metafiction an Other Form of Realism?" provides a broad starting framework. Expanding on Patricia Waugh's insight in her 2003 *Metafiction*, that metafiction is not disconnected from the real world but is rather a different, "anti-realist" way of representing that world, Slocombe points out the realism in metafiction and the metafiction in realism, positing the interrelationship of the two modes rather than a new mode altogether. My 2014 speech on Wallace's metafictive realism examined three metafictive techniques—innovations in point of view, perspective, and structural dialogism—constructed by Wallace and used toward realist ends. In my chapter on metafictive realism in this book, I will place these innovations in the context of recent critical debates about the role of metafiction in relation to realism, and consider the realism-metafiction dialectic suggested by Slocombe and deployed by Wallace in relation to Jameson's *Antinomies of Realism*, to consider how we might begin to conceive of "metafictive realism" as a useful term to describe the variety of metafiction-based realisms that have arisen in "post-postmodern" literature.[109]

Terminology grows even more confusing when we look closely at the many ways in which attention to the material and real, over the linguistic or theoretical, has surged in recent decades. My concept of "poststructural realism" in *Succeeding Postmodernism* recognized this renewed focus on the real and material in narrative from within poststructural concepts of language and world, but with a breadth that now strikes me as unhelpfully vague, and as encompassing what this current book will posit as several different types of new realism, namely metafictive realism, material realism, and quantum realism. This book further develops that broad concept of the return to the real through language in Chapter 2, "The Work of Art after the Mechanical Age," by investigating more thoroughly poststructural realism's main idea, that contemporary narrative crafts attention to the real and the material specifically in a context infused by poststructural notions of the language and of the world. In proposing that term I also touch on materiality as a mode of representing the real through poststructuralism, a strategy that receives its own developed examination in Chapter 3, "Material Realism."

This attention to the material over the linguistic, post-metaphysical, or representational shows up in twenty-first century philosophy as well.

But it does so not as an aspect of poststructuralism but as a rejection of it. Providing further evidence of the confusion of terminology today not just in literary studies but across fields is the philosophical concept of "speculative realism," which shares virtually nothing with Saldivar's literary coinage of the same term. Whereas Saldivar's literary term identifies literature that blurs genre to expose the ways in which fantasy dominates our notions of reality, the philosophical term describes a commitment to "robust ontological realism" and "seek[s] to restore the dignity of metaphysical investigation and invention after a century in which any sort of metaphysics was almost phobically rejected"[110]—in other words, the belief that we *can* say true things about reality that are not dependent on the human mind. Karan Barad carries this philosophical rejection of poststructuralist ideas about the world and what we can say about it even further, or perhaps deeper, when she proposes a materialist philosophy of ontology that stems from quantum-physics ideas about reality. In her 2007 *Meeting the Universe Halfway: Quantum Physics and the Entanglement of Matter and Meaning*, Barad opposes our long-standing belief in "representationalism" and referentiality, in which language is inevitably detached from the material world just as every object in the world remains separate from each other, with "posthuman performatism," in which both language and matter participate in the making of the world. She grounds this startling assertion in the quantum understanding of matter as inherently relational and agential, and of the observer as inextricably part of anything being observed. Though primarily physical and philosophical, Barad's argument carries profound implications for literary studies, especially in terms of literature's new attention to materiality: Barad asks us to rethink our ideas about language and its relationship to the world in light of a new understanding of what the world, or matter, is, and how we relate to it. Barad's quantum-based realism points to another important source or cause of new kinds of realisms—not changes in our ideas about language, representation, and fiction (epistemological and poststructural), but changes in our ideas about physical reality. A few critics have begun to examine the impact of quantum physics on literature, and to characterize a new kind of "quantum fiction." Chapters 4 and 5 will expand on this thinking to propose another type of new realism, "quantum realism," in which fiction attempts accurately to represent a quantum world, and to explore the ontological implications of such a world.

All of these new kinds of literary representation have in common the goal of making us aware of our and the book's presence in a real world, so that one aspect of "post-postmodern" realism that seems clear from the outset is its movement beyond the question of solipsism that so preoccupied postmodern literature (for example, David Markson's *Wittgenstein's Mistress*, 1988) and criticism (Wallace's 1990 essay on Markson's novel, and so many critical essays on Wallace). In this way, these new realisms seem to earn their awkward nomenclature, while also participating in (and perpetuating) the misnomer that so far has distorted all of literary history in its totalizing lens, in a kind of literary-critical version of the intellectual ethnocentrism that opens and motivates Derrida's explosive *Of Grammatology*.

That these new realisms primarily use metafiction, or metafiction overtly in relation with traditional realism, in order to conjure this real world suggests another clear achievement of "post-postmodern" realisms: they end once and for all any debate about the merits of the term "anti-realism," which, in the context of these contemporary realisms that aggressively depart from realist conventions while pursuing realist questions of ontology, epistemology, and morality, finally fully dissolves.[111] The bulk of this book will examine these technical, formal, structural, and stylistic innovations made by literature of the last thirty or so years in order to bridge language and reality in a poststructuralist, post-realist, post-Newtonian world, and in a post-postmodern literary landscape. In doing so, I identify three main innovations to nineteenth-century realism: metafictive realism, which uses self-reflective devices to allow language to invoke and connect the reader to the real world (rather than absorbing the reader into a linguistic construction that invisibly replaces the real world); material realism, which uses language and physical form to draw attention to the physical reality of the book and of language's impact on the physical world, while emphasizing the embodiment of all acts of reading and writing; and quantum realism—a subset of material realism—which uses literary representation to make us consider the quantum reality we live in and its effects on our experience and on literary form.

Of course, even this seemingly neat classification of productive postmodernist realisms into two major categories of metafictive and material breeds more paradox. On one hand, we see emphasis on the real, material, and physical over language and representation, while on the other we see an explosion of metafiction and innovations in textuality, style, technique, and form—what had previously been considered "anti-realism"—in accomplishing that real-world emphasis. But rather than frustrating any attempt to characterize post-modernist realism, this tendency to develop into unresolvable paradox will become a third primary characteristic of contemporary realisms. In fact, most of the new realisms examined in this book aim to escape the limits of realism as a literary mode, the limits of representationalism as an ontological model, or both. In this way, we might consider them to be literary forms of Derrida's philosophical exorbitant, building looping spaces of narrative multiplicity, structural excess, and logical paradox using the same literary tools that once erected lines with beginnings and ends.

Not surprisingly, fiction that rejects the neatness of nineteenth-century realism in some ways while extending its influence in others likewise sits uneasily in any literary history that builds neatly upon a stable foundation of nineteenth-century realism. Thus, any attempt to classify these new realisms according to the terminology of an old system in which "realism" was an anchoring singularity will necessarily raise more questions than answers—questions about "realism" as a period, about periodizing in general, and about possibilities for periodizing after postmodernism, that require the same kind of radical rethinking that has produced the exhilaratingly new landscape of contemporary realisms. I will leave these large conceptual questions for the Conclusion, and use the following chapters to explore in detail a more immediately fruitful set of questions: how exactly is the literature of these new realisms related to nineteenth-century realism? What is it doing that is new, and how, and why? What is the role of realism in shaping "post-postmodern" literature? What kinds of worlds, literary and real, does it in turn shape?

Notes

1 Stephen Greenblatt, "Resonance and Wonder," in *The Norton Anthology of Theory and Criticism*, 2nd ed., ed. Vincent B. Leitch (New York: Norton, 2010), 2155.
2 Moore, *The Novel*, 3.
3 Ibid., 147.
4 See Marcus's "Why Experimental Fiction Threatens to Destroy Publishing, Jonathan Franzen, and Life as We Know It" and Tomasula's "Where We Are Now." On Morris's *Realism*, see pages 23–7 of this chapter.
5 Moore, *The Novel*, 7.
6 Ibid., 147.
7 Ibid., 150–64.
8 Ibid., 21–30.
9 William Dean Howells, "The Editor's Study," in *Heath Anthology of American Literature*, 7th ed., vol. C, ed. Paul Lauter (New York: Boston: Cengage, 2014), 147.
10 William Dean Howells, "Novel-Writing and Novel-Reading: An Impersonal Explanation," in *The Norton Anthology of American Literature*, 7th ed., vol. C, ed. Nina Baym (New York: Norton, 2007), 917.
11 Henry James, "The Art of Fiction," in *Heath Anthology of American Literature*, 7th ed., vol. C, ed. Paul Lauter (New York: Boston: Cengage, 2014), 240, 246.

12 Howells, "The Editor's Study," 147.
13 Mark Twain, "Fenimore Cooper's Literary Offences," in *The Norton Anthology of American Literature*, 7th ed., vol. C, ed. Nina Baym (New York: Norton, 2007), 295, 296.
14 James, "The Art of Fiction," 246, 251, 353, 248.
15 William Dean Howells, "Editha," in *Heath Anthology of American Literature*, 7th ed., vol. C, ed. Paul Lauter (New York: Boston: Cengage, 2014), 162, 163, 170.
16 Mark Twain, "The Man That Corrupted Hadleyburg," in *Heath Anthology of American Literature*, 7th ed., vol. C, ed. Paul Lauter (New York: Boston: Cengage, 2014), 240.
17 Henry James, "The Real Thing," in *The Norton Anthology of American Literature*, 7th ed., vol. C, ed. Nina Baym (New York: Norton, 2007), 434, 446.
18 James, "The Art of Fiction," 240.
19 Howells, "The Editor's Study," 147.
20 Howells, "Novel-Writing," 916.
21 James, "The Art of Fiction," 244–5, 254, 255.
22 Twain, "Hadleyburg," 93, 92, 127.
23 Ibid., 100, 105.
24 Edith Wharton, "The Other Two," in *The Norton Anthology of American Literature*, 7th ed., vol. C, ed. Nina Baym (New York: Norton, 2007), 841.
25 Ibid., 837.
26 Ibid., 839.
27 Erich Auerbach, *Mimesis: The Representation of Reality in Western Literature*, trans. Willard Trask (Princeton: Princeton University Press, 1953), 23. I will note subsequent references parenthetically.
28 Everett Carter, *Howells and the Age of Realism* (Philadelphia: J B Lippincott Co., 1950), 24, 171.
29 Warner Berthoff, *The Ferment of Realism: American Literature 1884-1919* (New York: The Free Press, 1965), 7.
30 René Wellek, *Concepts of Criticism*, ed. Stephen B. Nichols (New Haven: Yale University Press, 1963), 25, 240–53.
31 Ibid., 255.
32 And perhaps it is telling that Wellek seems to misread Auerbach in any case, identifying Auerbach's two types of realism as "historical" and "existential" (rather than as external/illuminated and internal/obscured) and thus as contradictory, and claiming Auerbach excludes all moralistic fiction, while focusing on the bible and Dante.
33 George Lukács, *Essays on Realism* (Boston: MIT Press, 1980), 93.
34 Berthoff, *Ferment*, 2, 3.
35 Kolb, *Illusion*, 25–6.
36 Ibid., 60.
37 James, "The Art of Fiction," 66.
38 Kolb, *Illusion*, 92.
39 Ibid., 97.

40 Ibid., 105.
41 Ibid., 127.
42 Stern, *On Realism*, 41, 52.
43 Ibid., 28.
44 As we see in Boris Eichenbaum's "Theory of the 'Formal Method'" (1926), which itself relies on the work of Roman Jakobson and Victor Shklovsky, among others.
45 Kolb, *Illusion*, 93.
46 Stern, *On Realism*, 54.
47 Kolb, *Illusion*, 92.
48 Stern, *On Realism*, 171.
49 Ibid., 56.
50 Evan Carton, "*Pudd'nhead Wilson* and the Fiction of Law and Custom," in *American Realism: New Essays*, ed. Eric J. Sundquist (Baltimore: Johns Hopkins University Press, 1982), 92.
51 Fred See, "Henry James and the Art of Possession," in *American Realism: New Essays*, ed. Eric Sundquist (Baltimore: Johns Hopkins University Press, 1982), 120.
52 Ibid., 135.
53 Alan Trachtenberg, "Experiments in Another Country: Stephen Crane's City Sketches," in *American Realism: New Essays*, ed. Eric Sundquist (Baltimore: Johns Hopkins University Press, 1982), 138, 139, 154.
54 Eric Sundquist, "Preface," in *American Realism: New Essays*, ed. Eric Sundquist (Baltimore: Johns Hopkins University Press, 1982), viii.
55 Fredric Jameson, "Postmodernism and Consumer Society," in *The Norton Anthology of Theory and Criticism*, 2nd ed., ed. Vincent B. Leitch (New York: Norton, 2010), 1847, original italics.
56 Richard Brodhead, "Hawthorne among the Realists: The Case of Howells," in *American Realism: New Essays*, ed. Eric Sundquist (Baltimore: Johns Hopkins University Press, 1982), 26.
57 Eric Cheyfitz, "A Hazard of New Fortunes," in *American Realism: New Essays*, ed. Eric Sundquist (Baltimore: Johns Hopkins University Press, 1982), 45.
58 Sundquist, *American Realism*, 23, viii.
59 Jean-Francois Lyotard, "Defining the Postmodern," in *The Norton Anthology of Theory and Criticism*, 2nd ed, ed. Vincent B. Leitch (New York: Norton, 2010), 1467.
60 On postmodernism's questionable existence, see M. H. Abrams's "How To Do Things with Texts," in *Doing Things with Texts*, ed. Michael Fisher (New York: Norton, 1989) and Charles Altieri's *Act and Quality* (Amherst: University of Massachusetts Press, 1981), among others; on postmodernism's debatable beginnings, see Brian McHale's "When Did Postmodernism Begin?" *Modern Language Quarterly* 69, no. 3 (2008) and Andrew Hoberek's "After Postmodernism," *Twentieth-Century Literature* 53, no. 3 (2007) among others.

61 Sundquist, "Preface," vii.
62 Ibid., ix.
63 M. H. Abrams, *A Glossary of Literary Terms*, 6th edn (New York: Harcourt, 1993), 174.
64 Ibid., 131.
65 Ibid., 132; original italics, bold added for emphasis.
66 M. H. Abrams, *A Glossary of Literary Terms*, 3rd edn (New York: Hold, Rinehart, and Winston, 1971), 140.
67 Ibid., 141.
68 M. H. Abrams, *A Glossary of Literary Terms*, 1st edn (New York: Holt, Rinehart, and Winston, 1957), 73.
69 Ibid., 59.
70 Morris, *Realism*, 4, 6, 162.
71 Ibid., 141.
72 On the centrality of embodiment in posthumanism and its attending artistic forms, see especially N. Katherine Hayles's *How We Think* (Chicago: University of Chicago Press, 2012)—and many of the comparative media studies scholars she cites in that book.
73 Morris, *Realism*, 4, original italics.
74 Ibid., 5.
75 At least in James's case, we might say this belief was short-lived, as "The Real Thing" proves the lie of his picture analogy.
76 Morris, *Realism*, 17–23.
77 Ibid., 37.
78 Ibid., 42.
79 See for example my *Succeeding Postmodernism: Language and Humanism in Contemporary American Literature* (New York: Bloomsbury, 2013).
80 Morris, *Realism*, 43.
81 Ibid., 37.
81 Ibid., 44.
83 Ibid., 154, quoting Christopher Norris, *New Idols of the Cave: On the Limits of Anti-Realism* (Manchester: Manchester University Press, 1997), 228.
84 Fredric Jameson, *The Antinomies of Realism* (New York: Verso, 2013), 5–6. I will note subsequent references parenthetically.
85 See for example Heather Hicks's "'This Time Round': David Mitchell's *Cloud Atlas* and the Apocalyptic Problem of Historicism," *Postmodern Culture: An Electronic Journal of Interdisciplinary Criticism* 20, no. 3 (2010), John Shanahan's "Digital Transcendentalism in *Cloud Atlas*," *Criticism: A Quarterly for Literature and the Arts* 58, no. 1 (2016): 115–45, and Kevin Brown's "Finding Stories to Tell: Metafiction and Narrative in *Cloud Atlas*," *Journal of Language, Literature and Culture* 63, no. 1 (2016): 77–90.
86 E.g., Baudrillard's *Simulations* (1981); Lyotard's "Defining the Postmodern" (1986); Jameson's "Postmodernism and Consumer Society" (1988).
87 I have presented the author and date of each term's first appearance in publication to the best of my ability. With the exception of my own, the

2013 coinages come from the anthology *Realisms in Contemporary Culture: Theories, Politics, and Medial Configurations*, ed. Dorothee Birke and Stella Butter (Berlin: de Gruyter, 2013), which collects diverse considerations of realism as deployed over the last thirty years or so in texts across media platforms. Examining social, cultural, and political concerns that shape and are shaped by realism, this anthology nicely complements my own formalist, fiction-focused, literary-historical project.

88 Zuzanna Jakubowski's "relational" realism ("Exhibiting Lost Love: The Relational Realism of Things in Orhan Pamuk's *The Museum of Innocence* and Leanne Shapton's *Important Artifacts*," in *Realisms in Contemporary Culture: Theories, Politics, and Medial Configurations*, ed. Dorothee Birke and Stella Butter (Berlin: de Gruyter, 2013), 124–45) conflates aspects of new realism that I have developed in two different chapters and terms: one is realism's return to "the real," or a reorientation away from language and representation and back toward a real, physical world. (Interestingly, when I first published on this topic in *Succeeding Postmodernism*, I used several of the same methods and thinkers she used in her chapter from the same year—including Barthes's "reality effects," Latour's "thing theory," and Foster's "return of the real.") In Chapter 2 of this book, I expand that argument using Steve Tomasula's fiction to consider how recent fiction reorients us toward the real being represented and the real world in which every literary text participates; in Chapter 3, I develop an argument about material realism, using a wide variety of postmodern and "post-postmodern" texts, which Jakubowski's essay foresees with her analysis of Leanne Shapton's *Important Artifacts and Personal Property from the Collection of Lenore Doolan and Harold Morris, Including Books, Street Fashion and Jewelry* (New York: Sarah Crichton Books, 2009).

89 Similarly, Reinhard Hennig's "Ecocritical Realism," in *Realisms in Contemporary Culture: Theories, Politics, and Medial Configurations*, ed. Dorothee Birke and Stella Butter (Berlin: de Gruyter, 2013), 109–23—which is more concerned with examining practices in ecocriticism than in defining a new literary realism—considers why nature ecocritics often assume that nature writing must be "realistic" (rather than experimental) in order to express its investment in the real world rather than in theories or culture that shapes our experiences of that world.

90 Bill Buford, "Dirty Realism: New Writing in America," *Granta* 8 (1983): 4–5.

91 Josh Toth, *The Passing of Postmodernism* (Albany: State University of New York University Press, 2010), 20. For a fuller account of dirty realism and neorealism, see my *Succeeding Postmodernism*, 172–3.

92 Albert Borgmann, *Crossing the Postmodern Divide* (Chicago: University of Chicago Press, 1992), 115.

93 For a fuller account of postmodern realism, see my "A Lamb in Wolf's Clothing," 229–33. On postmodern realism in photography, see Bowen (1995); in philosophy, see Ronen (1995); in fiction, see Robertson (1992) and den Tandt (2003); in drama, see Sauer (2000, 2011).

94 Hayden White, *Figural Realism* (Baltimore: Johns Hopkins University Press, 1999), vii.
95 Ibid., 39. This concept of conventional realism as incapable of representing experiences that challenge the notions of orderly reality inherent in it is nowhere more evident than in Jonathan Safran Foer's representation of horrific events in the Holocaust in *Everything Is Illuminated* (2002). As Alex reports his grandfather's narration of the Nazi torture and extermination of the people of Kolki, the straightforward realism he has employed throughout his section of the novel gives way to experimentation, particularly the loss of spaces between words—as if realist writing simply cannot express the pain of the events, or of the grandfather's feelings of immediacy and urgency as he describes them.
96 Ibid., 41-2.
97 Pam Morris, "Making the Case for Metonymic Realism," in *Realisms in Contemporary Culture: Theories, Politics, and Medial Configurations*, ed. Dorothee Birke and Stella Butter (Berlin: de Gruyter, 2013), 16.
98 James Wood, "Human, All Too Inhuman," *The New Republic*, July 24, 2000: np.
99 Mark Fisher, *Capitalist Realism* (city: Zero Books, 2009), 4.
100 An exception to this characterization is Bowen's "postmodern realism" (*Stories of the Middle Space*, Montreal: McGill-Queen's University Press, 2010). While Bowen does define her "postmodern realism" as characterized by formal innovation (magical realism and metafiction) yet committed to traditional realism's goals (ethics and "the good"), by anchoring those goals in specifically Christian ethics, she makes the mode a misnomer.
101 In "Stalking the Billion-footed Best: A Literary Manifesto for the New Social Novel," *Harper's Magazine*, November 1989: 45–56, and "Post-Postmodern Discontent: Contemporary Fiction and the Social World," *symploke* 12, nos. 1–2 (2004): 53–68, respectively.
102 Wendy Steiner, "Postmodern Fictions, 1960-1990," in *The Cambridge History of American Literature*, ed. Sacvan Bercovitch, vol. 7 (Cambridge: Cambridge University Press, 1999), 499, 526-7.
103 Ibid., 369.
104 See *Trauma: Explorations in Memory* (Baltimore: Johns Hopkins University Press, 1995) and *Unclaimed Experience: Trauma, Narrative, and History* (Baltimore: Johns Hopkins University Press, 1996).
105 Meanwhile, in the same year in which Foster explored "traumatic realism," Jonathan Franzen floated another, seemingly related notion of "tragic realism" in his essay "Why Bother?" in *How To Be Alone* (Picador, 2002), 55–97. But, as Dubey points out (and unsurprisingly), Franzen's notion is "essentially a liberal humanist conception of the value of literature," rather than anything new ("Post-Postmodern Realism?" *Twentieth-Century Literature* 57, no. 3-4, (2011): 369).
106 Melvin Jules Bukiet, "Crackpot Realism: Fiction for the Forthcoming Millennium," *Review of Contemporary Fiction* 16, no. 1 (1996): 14.

107 Ramón Saldivar, "Historical Fantasy, Speculative Realism, and Postrace Aesthetics in Contemporary Fiction," *American Literary History* 23, no. 3 (2011): 585.
108 Interestingly, Mark Fisher makes a similar argument for his culture-based "capitalist realism," pointing to metafiction as a narrative strategy that seems to aim for truth in exposing the text's mechanisms of production but ultimately only validates our sense of our own sophistication by re-establishing our belief in the naïveté of the fiction that came before it.
109 Though Philip Tew's "meta-realism" appears—at least to one convinced of the ubiquity of metafiction—to offer another metafictive realism, his formulation in "A New Sense of Reality? A New Sense of Text: Exploring Meta-Realism and the Literary-Critical Field" (in *Beyond Postmodernism: Reassessments in Literature, Theory, and Culture*, ed. Klaus Stierstorfer (Berlin: de Gruyter, 2003), 29–49) is more concerned with ontological assertions than with formal ones. His core argument is that "one must insist that all literary texts...whatever their imaginative excursions and deviations presuppose a reality both as constituent of themselves and existentially independent of themselves" (46). While he quotes many philosophers and theorists in making this basic argument, his assertion remains primarily assumption, rather than argument, and remains unsupported by literary textual analysis or formal arguments about *how* language and structure represent that presupposed reality. Thus his essay asserts that texts remain connected to an unprovable reality, without examining any particular set of techniques, such as metafiction, which forge such a connection through language.
110 Steven Shaviro, *The Universe of Things: On Speculative Realism* (Minneapolis: University of Minnesota Press, 2014), 5.
111 Beginning in Chapter 1, I will use "Realism" to stand for traditional, nineteenth-century realism, following Wallace, leaving "realism" to mean, more generally, any mode of writing attempting to represent reality (following Morris, Jameson, and others). Then "anti-Realism" will continue to function specifically in relation to traditional realism, meaning a mode of writing whose form or techniques break conventions of nineteenth-century realism.

1

Metafictive Realism

David Foster Wallace and the Future of (Meta)Fiction

When we think of metafiction, we almost certainly think first of tonally sly, language-obsessed literature written by white men in the middle of the twentieth century: John Barth, Robert Coover, Donald Barthelme. Less prominent while more subversive is the metafiction wielded by writers seeking to overturn not just the constricting conventions of literature but also those of social and institutional norms, such as Doris Lessing's *The Golden Notebook*, Angela Carter's *Nights at the Circus*, and Ishmael Reed's *Mumbo Jumbo*. Thinking still further, we will concede a longer history for self-conscious literature, recalling the author addressing the reader in *Tristram Shandy* (1759) or *Don Quixote*'s second half referring to its first (1615). In fact, incidents of metafiction—or fiction that is aware of itself as fiction, or makes us aware of it as fiction—span more widely still, outside the bounds of the Enlightenment era and of its European cauldron, at least back to the eighth-century Persian and Indian origins of *The Arabian Nights*. And its reach now appears endless, as it describes a great deal of our most exciting recent literature, by authors as diverse and dispersed as Ali Smith, Roberto Bolaño, Flann O'Brien, Lily Hoang, David Mitchell, Salvador Plascencia, Rachel Cusk, W. G. Sebald, Ruth Ozeki, Mark Danielewski, Karen Yamashita, and Steve Tomasula. "Metafiction" also describes techniques used increasingly in fiction of the last two or three decades not simply to play language games, but to accomplish the most vital stuff of fiction: develop character, convey meaning, create empathy. Evocative and productive, metafiction is everywhere, is what arises from the storytelling urge itself. Before we can begin to understand this most primal human need, we must first consider the essential role of metafiction in every act of fiction. Likewise, in order to understand and characterize the diversity of fiction that comprises this "post-postmodern" moment, we need to ask what role metafiction plays in it, and how the metafiction of "post-postmodernism" might differ from that of early postmodernism.

Enormously complicating any investigation of metafiction, however, is a historical tendency to oppose it not only to fiction, but more specifically to other modes of fiction, especially realism—to equate metafiction with "anti-realism." Following the explosion of self-reflexive fiction in the 1960s, and William Gass's coinage of the term "metafiction" to describe it in 1970, came an accompanying eruption of terms used to set self-reflexive fiction generically apart from "normal" fiction, from realism: "anti-novel," "introverted novel," "surfiction," "irrealism," "fabulation," and the "self-begetting novel."[1] And yet at the same time, our earliest major studies of metafiction, by Linda Hutcheon and Patricia Waugh, take as their central assumptions not just that metafiction is as old as fiction itself but that it is an inherent aspect of realism, and thus of the novel as well. In fact Hutcheon takes this stance against Robert Alter's earlier argument that nineteenth-century realism, by suppressing self-reflexivity, acted as an "eclipse" of the self-consciousness inherent in the genre.[2] Instead, Hutcheon charts the steady progression of one kind of novelistic mimesis to another, all of them inherently metafictive, just as Aristotle saw all diegesis, or narrative, as part of mimesis: the narrative act is always part of the action of the story. Thus, for Hutcheon, nineteenth-century realism is a "reductive limitation of novelistic mimesis," of all of its self-reflexive possibility, rather than the pinnacle of mimetic achievement, as Auerbach, Watt, and others have claimed.[3] Similarly, Waugh asserted that metafiction is not a subgenre of the novel—let alone some kind of "anti-novel"—but a "tendency *within* the novel which operates through exaggeration of the tensions and oppositions inherent in all novels: of frame and frame-break, of technique and counter-technique, of construction and deconstruction of illusion."[4] Waugh points out that this tension is characteristic not just of metafiction but of all acts of representation when she connects her description of metafiction to Gass's description of "the dilemma of all art":

> In every art two contradictory impulses are in a state of Manichean war: the impulse to communicate and so to treat the medium of communication as a means and the impulse to make an artefact out of the materials and so to treat the medium as an end.[5]

From such a perspective, one might say that metafiction is not made of different stuff than is realism, but that in metafiction, unlike in realism, the second impulse wins.

Read with Waugh's and Gass's observations in mind, Jameson's recent theory of the "antinomies of realism" (see Introduction, pp. 27–31) likewise becomes evidence for the ubiquity of metafiction. For the overlapping of these three theories—all premised on contrary impulses and mechanisms for representation held in tension with each other—suggests that inherent in Jameson's dialectical theory of realism are the workings of metafiction. More particularly telling, however, are the ways in which Jameson's explanations of this dialectical realism are themselves inherently metafictive. For example, when Jameson uses Zola to illustrate his basic principle, that realism carries within itself the earlier narrative modes or genres that it must dissolve—in this case melodrama—the relationship he constructs between realism and melodrama in essence renders the latter metafictive. Jameson argues that the tension between the two modes causes us to "deplore" the fiction's (melodramatic) "narrative excesses"—those extreme events that move the plot along and eventually shut it down, and so which we also "admire." In this way, the text "seems to want to demonstrate, on its own, the gap between" depictions of "daily life," and "the gratuitous explosions, the fires, the bankruptcies, the monstrosities and . . . catastrophes, which are the price we have to pay for the novel's closure." This necessary/gratuitous excess, which he refers to as (Derridian) "supplements," "also announces the imminent breakdown of narrative as the form in which such 'reality' can be registered and conveyed" (154–5). Here, as in his later analysis of the reification and dissolution of melodrama in Eliot's *Middlemarch* (160), Jameson essentially argues that the nineteenth-century realist novel enlists an earlier generic device in order to draw attention to how this new, realist mode uses and dismisses that device. The new mode renders the older mode metafictive by rendering it visible and scrutable.

Taken as a whole, Jameson's analysis of dialectical realism suggests something even more interesting about metafiction: that its methods and aims change as realism changes in *its* mechanisms and aims, and in its relationship to the earlier modes it reifies and dissolves. Jameson's description of the struggle between récit and scene / tale and affect / old-past and eternal-present changes significantly when he examines realism's technical innovations in modernism. The metafictive nature of that struggle likewise changes. Jameson identifies in modernist narrative a new kind of third-person narrator, one that swallows the subjectivity of the first person into the formerly objective third, thus "incorporating everything we have attributed to the first-person narrator in order to reach some richer representation of subjectivity and thereby a more multidimensional representation of reality itself" (174–5). This "swollen third person" comes about because the modernist narrator emerges out of mystery, marking how little is known of the world, so that such novels

> bear witness to a modern necessity of constructing a narrative out of what were not initially narrative materials: in other words, they testify to the

weakening of the pole of the récit, of the past-present-future system itself, by the dominance of an eternal present which seeks then to disguise itself as récit and narrative to be told and story or destiny to be revealed. (176)

To say that a narrative uses a peculiar use of point of view to demonstrate its awareness that its dominant element is the fact and mechanism of its telling, rather than the established elements of its tale, is to say that it is metafictive. But this description also marks this fiction as realism quite differently than the realism of Zola or Eliot is marked: whereas nineteenth-century realism, for Jameson, is enabled and moved along by the tools of the earlier modes it simultaneously undermines, realism under the pressure of modernism creates new tools that undermine realism itself, by shifting our focus more overtly away from the story and toward its tools. Metafiction, always lurking, rises from realism's murky depths. We might say that by the postmodern 1960s it had fully surfaced, a shining cathedral shedding seawater. Where did it go, what does it do, what does it look like and how does it function in the "post-postmodern" twenty-first century? How does it continue to function in relation to realism—or does it? This chapter in part aims to address such questions that Jameson's theory of realism raises more than answering.

Looking backward in our history of literary periodizing, we find that just as early attempts to theorize metafiction link it to realism, early attempts to theorize realism link it to metafiction—again, without overtly identifying it as such. In a seminal Russian formalist essay, "The Theory of the Formal Method" (1926), Boris Eichenbaum reaches to metafiction to justify the formalist practice of analyzing realism. He enlists Shklovsky's analysis of *Tristram Shandy* and *Don Quixote* to demonstrate the difference between "motivated" techniques—those demanded by some thematic aspect of the text itself, such as episodic structure in a picaresque—and "exposed structure," whose aspects are not motivated by the content of the fiction and therefore dominate it. Eichenbaum concludes that

> neither a work fully "motivated" nor an art which deliberately does away with motivation and exposes the structure provides the most suitable material for the illumination of such theoretical problems [as the relationship between form and content]. But the very existence of a work such as *Don Quixote*, with a deliberately exposed structure, confirms the relevance of these problems ... and the fact that they are *significant* literary problems.[6]

Eichenbaum demonstrates the need for formalist analysis of literariness—those aspects of language peculiar to literature—by placing metafiction, which makes its literariness visible, at one end of a spectrum that contains all prose, all of which is "realist" narrative, with varying degrees of motivated and exposed structures.

Given this early and persistent integration in the theorizing of realism and metafiction, it is surprising to find such a lack of attention to metafiction in recent critical attempts to characterize the changing fiction of "post-postmodernism." Least helpful in this endeavor are critical treatments that persist in opposing nineteenth-century realism and metafiction in terms of their strategies, goals, and capacities. In 2011, Madhu Dubey's "Post-Postmodern Realism?," for example, investigated the possibilities presented by the traditional "social novel" in a "post-postmodern" era, concluding that "the problem that postmodernism posed for the social novel . . . cannot be solved on formal grounds, by reviving narrative realism"[7]—as if twentieth-century postmodernism and nineteenth-century realism as we have long known them are the only options; as if realism is as exhausted as metafiction; as if the two are somehow totally separate modes of fiction. In the same 2011 issue, David James, on the other hand, asserted the possibility of fictional recuperation in "post-postmodernism," but retained the same uninterrogated binary of traditional realism vs. postmodernism. His "Integrity After Metafiction" argued for the possibility of renewed literary integrity—defined, using Henry James, as "the integration of 'story and the novel, the idea and the form'"—through a revision of traditional realism that does not incorporate the lessons of postmodern metafiction so much as "reprise" Jamesian realism in the face of the "era of hermeneutic suspicion" that makes traditional realism no longer possible.[8] But what does it mean to say that we are or must be "after metafiction" in order to achieve literary integrity? Or to imply that only nineteenth-century realism, such as that practiced by James, integrates "idea and form"? If the Russian formalists taught us anything—and I continue to hope they taught us a lot—it should be that to be literary means to integrate idea and form, and that metafiction in fact, with its "exposed structure," might demonstrate this unavoidable integration best of all.

More recently and perhaps promisingly, Margaret Gram asserted the inappropriateness today of the form of the traditional realist novel, demonstrating its inability to accommodate the "narrative of anti-growth" required in an era that has become as suspicious of population growth and the sustainability of our cultural practices and natural resources as it is of epistemological clarity.[9] Rather than imagining a return to or reprisal of old forms, she posits the need for new representational models born of the very cultural and hermeneutic challenges they are meant to elucidate. Such a recognition that cultural and intellectual changes demand new forms makes perfect and explanatory sense at a time when literary output is characterized by new forms. However, the examples Gram imagines as possible solutions to the problem of stilted realism—open-ended stories, like Franzen's first; corporations as characters, as Richard Powers ventured in *Gain*; a turn from progressive to circular narrative—do not, in my opinion, offer nearly as much in terms of restructuring and newly empowering the forms of fiction, and revising our understanding of fictional form, as do solutions posed by other recent authors, whose formal innovations do not just add to but also expose and experiment with the workings of realism.

One way of elucidating the effectiveness of such inherently self-reflexive methods, then, might be to explore their understanding of realism and metafiction—not as stagnant forms defined in opposition to each other and by period but as approaches to writing that are definable only in relation to each other, and to their various uses and accomplishments over time. This is the dialectical model of realism and metafiction that Will Slocombe effectively brought to his reading of Paul Auster in 2010, using both "realist" and "metafictional" texts to demonstrate how strategies of realism and metafiction employ each other, each to its own ends ("Is Metafiction an Other Realism?"), a strategy on which I will expand here in my reading of David Foster Wallace. Certainly Wallace is only one among many writers in the late twentieth and early twenty-first centuries to harness self-reflexive narrative techniques toward overtly realist ends; several of the new realisms noted in the Introduction are either explicitly metafictive (meta-realism, metafictive realism) or operate by way of metafictive means (postmodern realism, speculative realism, disquieting realism, poststructural realism). The formal and technical innovations by which the fiction examined in the remaining chapters of this book creates its material or quantum realist effects are all in some way metafictive. So this focused exploration of metafiction and the detailed ways in which it functions in relation to realism in Wallace's work provides a foundation for understanding the formal innovations that undergird most if not all of the contemporary realisms this book investigates.

Meanwhile other questions remain, which expand and escape the formalist scope I have taken so far, in focusing on metafiction's relationship to realism as methods of representation. Waugh argued that metafiction exploded in the 1960s because the worldview that had supported realism—materialism, positivism, empiricism—had profoundly changed.[10] She emphasized that metafiction, like realism, is about the real world, and grounded in it, but that unlike realism, it "re-examine[s] the conventions of realism in order to discover—through its own self-reflection—a fictional form that is culturally relevant and comprehensible to contemporary readers."[11] More than half a century after that initial explosion of metafiction, our worldview has changed (at least) once again. How has metafiction changed to become newly culturally relevant? And what new tricks have evolved to allow it to work and mean differently? If we accept Gass's pithy description of the dilemma of art, that the impulse to communicate struggles against the impulse to make an artifact out of the medium's materials, how might we see metafiction, in a new world full of new technologies and media, making communicative artifacts in new ways? Chapters 3–5, on material realism (the conversion of the physical book into artifact) and quantum realism (the attempt to capture the quantum world in language), examine more materially extreme ways of answering this question. This chapter will consider specific ways in which metafiction as adapted by Wallace uses innovations in technique and genre to create an inherently metafictive realism capable of making present in language multiple dimensions of the "post-postmodern" world.

Metafiction versus Metafictive Realism

Revealing the realist impulses of metafiction, and using metafictive devices to invoke in fiction the presence of the real, David Foster Wallace's fiction demonstrates and capitalizes on this interdependency of fictional modes. In fact, one of the many interesting insights into Wallace's sense of his own work that we gain from his interviews is that Wallace was much more interested in realism, and the realism of his own writing, than he was in metafiction. Though he considered metafiction extensively in his much-cited interview with Larry McCaffery, he hardly referred to it at all outside that interview, and then only to reiterate points he had already established in the interview and the TV essay, "E Unibus Pluram," which was published alongside it. Similarly, while he referred to himself as a "realist" writer several times over his publishing years, he never allowed himself to be identified with metafiction. Instead, he reiterated and refined in interviews spanning thirteen years his ideas about what it meant to write realist fiction from within a culture and literary landscape so thoroughly changed from those that bore nineteenth-century realism. He theorized contemporary realist fiction in two ways: first, as fiction that "reproduces the texture of the world I live in," or "convey[s] the way stuff tastes and feels to you"—in other words, fiction that produces for the reader the internal chaos, self-division, and doubt caused by living in an age of pervasive mediation, information, and disconnection from the self and the other. Second, he considered writing "realistic" when it exposed the truth behind narrative itself, especially traditionally "big-R" "Realistic" narrative, as he called it: the truth that it is a construction, just as "familiarity is mediated and delusive." That is, realistic fiction for Wallace exposed "realism [as] an illusion of realism."[12]

Such concepts of fiction explain why this self-identified realist writer was also a master of metafiction: both of these definitions of realism rely on self-reflexivity. Whereas the first understands the foregrounded artifice of metafiction as expressing the reality or truth of the contemporary, postmodern world (a definition of metafiction also espoused by Patricia Waugh and Linda Hutcheon[13]), the second views metafiction as revealing the truth of the artifice inherent in fiction (as Barth earlier defined metafiction, in interviews with Enck and Reilly[14]). Wallace's realism, then, is really an act of anti-big-R-Realism, of self-aware narrative, of metafiction. Wallace in fact is one of many contemporary writers who recognize that, in a society that has absorbed into itself the cultural gestures of postmodernism and the signifying tricks of poststructuralism—originally intended to work against mainstream ideas of representation—producing "reality effects" (as Jonathon Culler describes traditional fiction) *requires* anti-Realism. Thus realism in the twenty-first century, born of poststructural notions of language, and into a culture steeped in irony and winking metamoments, harnesses traditionally anti-Realist tools such as nonlinear, nonchronological, and multiple narration, hypertext, self-reflexivity, and metafiction, in order to represent a highly signification-oriented textual world that feels as real to us as did the visually mimetic fiction of a more empirically minded nineteenth century: poststructuralism turned toward the ends of realism. But significantly, Wallace and his contemporaries use such poststructural realist strategies not simply to ape ironic cultural narcissism, but to provoke readers to interrogate our ways of inhabiting that culture, and our methods of knowing that build such culture.

Elsewhere, I have read Wallace's work as doing the work of realism and expanding his definition of that work—invoking a real world, even invoking a real author, and building an empathetic bridge between reader and author—using poststructural narrative devices. This "poststructural realism" is a literary equivalent to Bill Brown's and Bruno Latour's "thing theory," which illustrates how every thing in literature and critique is a thing read and represented, and how considered things cannot exist outside of systems of signification.[15] Any realism that recognizes the thing's enmirement in the sign must be made of, and, more importantly, *know* it is made of, systems of representation. Thus, one way to preserve the Thing in a text made of language, and in a poststructural world made of text—one potent form of poststructural realism—is through a self-conscious realism, a metafictive realism. This is exactly the kind of realism that becomes increasingly common in contemporary literature, and of which Wallace was one of our most skilled practitioners—though by no means the first.[16]

Such methods rely on a strategy that is very much akin to what Latour recommended for reattaching meaning and the real to critique: *multiplying* and making visible, rather than streamlining and hiding, the mechanisms of fiction at work in creating that sense of reality. These strategies for fiction shatter traditional realism's implied binary axis of thing versus sign and real world versus representation, freeing the representation from the mimetic economy that relegates it to the shadow of the real. Instead, metafictive realism creates a world of multiple planes and perspectives, in which it is impossible to locate an origin or original in relation to which the representation can be deemed unreal, or a center against which it can be measured as outlying. So this explosive decentering of the structures of mimetic fiction does not destroy or obfuscate the real, to make the sign primary over it or even its substitute (as Baudrillard argued), but rather it makes a space in which the real might be or seem present within representation—in order to make the representation itself invoke, and make present, the real.

Acknowledging the clearly metafictive strategies Wallace used to create the new realism that would, he hoped, revitalize fiction begs further consideration of his seemingly contradictory stance on metafiction. By now Wallace's early, two-pronged criticism of metafiction is well-known: in the early 1990s he characterized it as having been defanged by the absorption of irony and self-reflexivity into popular culture, and reduced to an onanistic gesture by "crank-turners." And yet it is clear that, even after declaring "metafiction's real end" to be "Armageddon," not all metafiction was the same for Wallace. Not only did he praise, in that same 1993 interview, early postmodern metafictionists including Nabokov, Barth, Barthelme, and Coover for their productive metafictive groundclearings, but he also described contemporary (1980s and 1990s) metafiction as having become "*conscious* of itself in a way it never had been," much as Skynet apocalyptically did in James Cameron's *Terminator*—also a product of the 1980s.[17] Further, in repeatedly describing his own earliest metafictive efforts, particularly *Broom of the System* and "Westward the Course of Empire Takes Its Way," as failures, while continuing to produce throughout the course of his career fiction that is no less metafictive than they, Wallace confirmed his faith in metafiction not only as his most effective tool for creating meaningful art, but as his most powerful way of writing what he called realist fiction. And however much we might disagree, as some critics do,[18] with Wallace's assessment of the ways in which his works variously fail and succeed, his intentions for redeeming a tired postmodern fiction by forcing readers to wrestle with the visible conventions and structures of texts are clearly expressed and fulfilled.

The problem of making sense of Wallace's relationship to metafiction, then, is semantic more than conceptual, part of the ongoing collective critical failure to adequately define metafiction in relation to genre, period, or technique. However, we might clarify Wallace's own ideas about what metafiction is, what it can and should do, and how it might do those things, by examining his essay "The Empty Plenum," in which he praises David Markson's *Wittgenstein's Mistress* as an exemplary piece of productive metafiction. Written in 1990, this essay provides a crucial example, specifically using metafiction, of the theoretical ideas for redeeming fiction that Wallace would articulate to McCaffery one year later.[19] As in that interview, Wallace's main concern in the essay is that self-reflexivity be "for the *sake* of something" other than self-reflexivity itself: "I personally have grown weary of most texts that are narrated self-consciously as *written*, as '*textes*.' But *WM* is different from the Barthian/post-Derridean self-referential hosts."[20] Here he differentiates types of metafiction as he will do later in the interview, designating some metafiction, like Markson's, as worthwhile because in the service to some larger (and, in Wallace's terms, Realist) goal of empathy and communication, and some, which he identifies here with Barth and deconstruction, as motivated by only linguistic tricks or empty poststructural gymnastics.

However, this division is not as neat as it first appears: only a few sentences later in the essay, he admires the "need" rather than "art" that motivates the main character's writing by describing it as "a kind of long message in a big bottle"—a clear allusion to the last pages of Barth's *Lost in the Funhouse*, in which the narrator depicts the massively self-reflexive writing that pervades the collection as earnest attempts at connection cast between lonely humans on our isolating islands. Thus, in the Markson essay as in the McCaffery interview, Wallace simultaneously rejects and invokes a Barthian model of metafiction—or presents Barth's metafiction as simultaneously estranging and to be eclipsed, and communicative and to be emulated. The well-documented ambivalence with which Wallace viewed his relationship to Barth as his most prominent metafictional ancestor[21] suggests that what seems like a self-contradicting stance on metafiction is more likely another expression of that ambivalence of influence. For the argument Wallace makes about the purpose of metafiction using Markson's novel remains clear: the thing other than itself that the text must be about in order for self-reflexivity to be meaningful for him is the *emotional implication* of philosophical ideas about language and the world—the human suffering brought by both. Attention to the functioning of language, then, is meaningful when it captures "the textual *urge*, the emotional urgency of text as both sign and *thing*," as he claims Kate's writing in *Wittgenstein's Mistress* does by expressing the ontological insecurity that forms the impulse behind every act of writing: language as attempt to deny the self-estrangement of the *Cogito*, as "a necessary affirmation of an Outside."[22]

Wallace reads *Wittgenstein's Mistress* as using metafictive attention to language and textuality in the service of exploring relationships among writer, text, and world in two broad ways. First, he examines Wittgenstein's picture-theory of language in the *Tractatus* and Markson's interrogation of it through Kate. But he does not do so simply to demonstrate either Kate's inability to escape solipsism using language, or our inability to know whether that impossibility comes from Kate's philosophical construction of the world or from the state of the world itself. To stop there would be to turn the crank. Instead, Wallace illuminates the many ways in which the novel is *not* about this "double bind" but is rather about Kate's *suffering* of it, as empathetic evidence of our own suffering of the same. Second, Wallace demonstrates how Kate's framework for understanding the world and her place in it—and for understanding the nature and possibilities of language and acts of writing—itself creates the walls of the cage that binds her. *Wittgenstein's Mistress*, according to Wallace, does what Wittgenstein never did, by illustrating the problem that atomic logic (and the positivism it led to) "denied the coherent possibility of things like ethics, values, spirituality, and responsibility" and "questions about what it is to be human."[23] Instead, he sees Markson as allowing Kate to recognize her spiritual emptiness as a result of an intellectual problem—that she has made the world empty by conceiving it as such. Thus Wallace reads Markson's novel as a text that considers its own textuality, and theories about language, to critique those theories and expose for our empathetic understanding the ways in which we suffer in the grip of them. This is exactly what Wallace's fiction, especially after *Broom of the System* and *Girl with Curious Hair*, aims to do, at times providing a glimpse of an "Outside," more often simply empathizing with our frustrated attempts to escape our own thinking.

As ironizing irony to produce earnestness has become a favorite critical trick for reading the "post-postmodern" turn, especially where Wallace is concerned, it would be neat to suggest that Wallace metas metafiction to return it to meaning. Such a reading, however, would be not just facile, but wrong. Rather than creating a *mise en abyme* of infinite textual self-reflection, the text only able to return diminishing images of itself, Wallace uses textual self-reflexivity to provoke the *reader* into acts of reflection, less on the status of the text than on how our *ways of reading* the text translate to ways of reading and relating to the world. Crucial to this operation is the text's ability to mimic the world in feel and construction, one of the key ways Wallace saw himself as a realist writer for a new age, creating texts that invoke the confusion and fragmentation of a heavily mediated and over-informed era. His realist writing, then, aims not for *trompe l'oeil* but a kind of *trompe l'esprit*, mimicking the *mind's* perception of the real world, rather than the eye's. The meta-ness of his fiction thus functions not just as mirror to the meta-ness of contemporary life, but to create possibilities and models for acts of meaning-making and communication within our ironic, self-referring world—or often, as *Wittgenstein's Mistress* does, simply to help us understand the difficulties or impossibilities of doing so, to keep misery company.

This shift in the focus of metafiction's acts of reflection—from internal, directed toward the text and self; to external, directed toward the reader's own desire to escape the text and self—is a central change Wallace made to the metafictive strategies he inherited from a previous generation of writers whose work carried the seeds of the shift that he would grow. It seems safe to suggest that, living and writing in the shadow of those seminal postmodern metafictionists, Wallace aimed to create space for his new methods of metafiction by rejecting the main term that described those of his ancestors' methods. And then, as now, no more nuanced term existed to mark the difference between the two. Yet, the decade since Wallace's last, posthumous publication have shown that this shift from *trompe l'oeil* to *trompe l'esprit* underlies other writers' work and other aspects of the recent period as well, so that we might ask whether it is a central feature of literature after postmodernism. When Steve Tomasula's artist in *The Book of Portraiture* (2006) illustrates that "the most important organ of sight is not the eyes, but the mind,"[24] he argues for this shift (see Chapter 2); and when Karan Barad proposes that the philosophy of new materialism engenders a movement away from the "play of images between two facing mirrors" to "questions of ontology, materiality, and agency,"[25] she suggests a similar shift as well (see Chapter 4). However imprecise and likely doomed to the quiet boneyard of old criticism, "metafictive realism" will serve for my current purpose of acknowledging the fundamental metafictive strategies that accomplish Realist goals, while marking Wallace's brand of realism, and its goals, as meaningfully different from the metafiction he inherited. More useful than a placeholding term, though, will be my endeavor to better understand Wallace's contribution to fiction by examining the *technical changes* he made to bend metafiction into the service of emotion, connection, and human "need" rather than cleverness or "art." To this end I will group these techniques into three major strategies: dialogism of perspective, the endless binary, and contrapuntal metafictive realism.

Dialogism of Perspective

The inherent dialogism of Wallace's writing has been well noted, especially in *Infinite Jest*.[26] But his commitment to dialogism goes beyond using multiple voices to escape monologism, to creating a persistent multiplication of perspective, in two ways: through shifting, multiple, and at times hidden *point of view*; and through intertextual splitting and layering of *perspective* (this differentiation enlists Wallace's own careful distinctions between the technical point of view that structures a narrative—first, second, or third; and perspective or focalizing, or the subjective position from which we get information, regardless of point of view). An obvious and beloved example of manipulated point of view occurs in "Good Old Neon," which *seems* to unfold from the first-person point of view of dead Neal in conversation with his live self on the cusp of suicide. Read in this way, dead Neal's beautiful key-hole revelation—that "it does have a knob, the door [between self and other] can open"—is only a solipsistic act of transient self-comfort in the face of his own death. But, as the narrator tells us, "what it really is, it turns out, is a matter of perspective": at the end of the story, we are asked to reimagine this act of self-understanding as the character "David Wallace"'s remarkable attempt to empathize with a man he had paid little attention to in life. This empathy with the suffering of the other allows him to attend to his own similar suffering of the mind's internal monologue of anxiety—ultimately to silence it, with the story's final words, "Not another word." Thus "Good Old Neon" uses its insistently textual voices and perspectives—one from beyond life and another impossibly empathizing with it—explicitly to induce healing self-reflection.[27]

Wallace also multiplies and shifts point of view in "Mister Squishy," this time not to imagine a way out of solipsism but rather, much as does *Wittgenstein's Mistress*, to demonstrate the variety of ways we suffer our inability to create or affect things outside ourselves. "Squishy" adds contemporary corporate America, its dominance over individuals via their submission to consumer culture, as a thematic explanation for the individual's loss of identity and power and her resulting inability to connect to others.[28] The story incapacitates the individual by manipulating point of view. At the heart of a story so steeped in corporate-speak that it is difficult to bear, much less finish, is Terry Schmidt, a group facilitator for an advertising firm, whose irrelevance and impotence in his job and life are even greater than he understands. We know his impotence, as we know how thoroughly his kindness, naïveté, and gentleness have been warped into murderous rage by that impotence, because the story seems to proceed, for 66 exhausting pages, through third-person free indirect discourse. We believe we are granted access to Schmidt's internal thoughts, which bleed through the external narration. When we discover—if we notice it—the invasion of first-person point of view briefly in a block of text on page 14, and again in a footnote at the bottom of page 57, several crucial things happen to our understanding of the story. First, this first-person point of view invalidates everything we thought we understood about Schmidt through free indirect discourse, essentially erasing his earnest struggle to define a self against the corporate forces that would efface him, as well as obliterating the palpable pathos of an otherwise alienating story. In fact, *all* of the free-indirect-discourse windows into characters' "real" internal selves become by definition products of the encompassing first-person point of view. So when Laleman's internal vision of himself in warpaint echoes Schmidt's much earlier sense of Laleman as predatory, "something that hunted on autopilot at extreme depths,"[29] what seems to be a confirmation of one character's sensitive perception of another through authentic revelation becomes, as does every seeming revelation, either impossible or imposed from the outside. Wallace detaches all such information from the characters even further by refusing to divulge the identity of the first-person character who delivers it. The monstrous control of all knowledge and characters in the story by this inscrutable first-person point of view mimics the absorption of individuals into consumer groups and corporate control.

No part of the story escapes it. The archive at the Harry Ransom Center shows how intent Wallace was that the story end by clarifying and restoring rightful power relations. On the draft of the story read by Dave Eggers, dated "6/00," Wallace notes Eggers's "dissatisfaction" with and query about the story's original, confusing ending: "Could whole climbing-w/ a gun thing be to rattle Schmid [sic]?" Wallace's responding note to himself resolves all early ambiguity:

> A: No. Britton knows Laleman's betrayin him for Cloe Jaswat. He's lettin Laleman run this absurd test [in the margin, pointing to "test," Wallace clarifies "w/ gun, crowds, etc."] so Laleman himself will get in trouble. Need 1 line indicating Britton knows of Laleman's betrayal.

Eggers's critique presumably resulted in the published story's single footnote on its final page, which establishes the ultimate omniscience and authority of Alan Britton, who sits at the top of the company's food chain ("Britton knew all about Laleman trying to jew him out to A. C. Romney-Jaswat; who did the smug puppy think he was dealing with").[30] But in true, convoluted Wallace fashion, even that bald final statement of omniscient authority does not stand unchallenged. Though its cocky, racist language seems ostentatiously to identify it as communicating the free-indirect-discourse voice of Britton, the barely present, never clarified, and perhaps already-forgotten first-person point of view absorbs and undoes even that titanic authority.

Rather than shifting point of view within one text, "My Soul Is Not a Smithy" multiplies perspective by multiplying texts and textual registers. The story gives an adult's recounting of the day a teacher experienced a mental break in a fourth-grade civics class, interrupted by all-caps reports on the trauma that add information gleaned from other sources, over time, and from the narrator's own adult understanding. The two differently typeset texts, though proceeding from entirely different perspectives (at different times in the narrator's life), share the same first-person point of view. Meanwhile, the recounting story, which begins in a traditional retrospective style, quickly fractures into four sub-narratives: the narrator's description of what was happening in the classroom that day; his observations of happenings in the world outside the classroom, as viewed, fittingly, through the multiply divided frame of a window; stories he created and told himself while looking out the window; and memories of his childhood relationships to his family and his resulting fears about adulthood. Only through the interplay between the different texts (report and narrative) and between the sub-narratives, and among the different subject positions they imply, can we, and the narrator, discover that the real trauma of the story is not the socially sensationalized mental break of the teacher but the narrator's own quietly growing, quotidian fear of becoming his self-alienated father. The story does not synthesize its pieces but rather holds them apart from each other to allow spaces in which empathy can arise: the boy's unconscious perception of his parents' suffering produces his imagined stories of overt suffering (of the accosted dog, the weeping Ruth Simmons, and her dismembered father); these emerge amid his partial awareness of the trauma unfolding around him in the classroom. This hypercomplex structure bearing the simple joy of revelation is classic Wallace and the way of the best metafiction, *bildungsroman* effected by dizzyingly anti-Realist narrative.

These three stories, "Neon," "Squishy," and "Smithy," demonstrate (as do many others) how Wallace's fiction creates a kind of dialogism of perspective or subject positions and suggests that anything we might take for meaning or identity depends on our negotiating this multiplicity of selves, and of self and other. As we can say that all of Beckett is an attempt to escape monologue,[31] we might say that all or most of Wallace is an attempt to escape solipsism by escaping the structural singularities of Realism. In this fundamental movement from the one to the many, Wallace's fiction acknowledges, as Borges did before him (though perhaps in reverse), the endless binary we construct with every attempt to understand the self, the other, or the world.

The Endless Binary

Positing a structural "endless binary" in Wallace's fiction essentially moves observations of the multiple planes of fictionality and reality of poststructural realism, and of multiple, competing perspective and point of view, to the realm of truth and sincerity. His "Brief Interviews" provide an easy initial example. These interviews, implying an audience/interlocutor, specifying their settings in time and place, and contained within an overall narrative generated by their shared interviewer,[32] are essentially dramatic monologues—they foreground scene and their own performativity. (They also point to Robert Browning as another ancestor of metafictive realism.) In so doing they illustrate how truth and sincerity depend on acts of storytelling and so on acts of intention and interpretation. We can read "Interview #20" in just this way (as I have done in "Mediated Immediacy"), demonstrating the layers of truth that fold back on themselves as the reader considers the story from multiple perspectives and with various information in mind: first we have the seeming sincerity and character growth of the male speaker, which reverses when we notice his continued objectification of the woman he supposedly loves *and* the one to whom he is speaking, inside which we must acknowledge the indisputably real moments of empathy described by the man, even as he is writing his self-promoting narrative of empathetic growth, and probably as an attempt to score with the woman who is interviewing him, whom he ultimately verbally abuses.[33] "The Devil Is a Busy Man" (the second of two) uses a similar strategy, the speaker seeming to reveal his selfishness while intending to represent his magnanimity (in the style of Browning's "My Last Duchess"), but also revealing his own self-loathing that drives the selfishness, which—since the story is about his "anonymous" giving of money—is also in a real way an act of charity. This kind of structural relativity, in which big things like truth, meaning, empathy, and morality can only exist as an uncomfortable sum of multiple incommensurate representations of each, produces a very different kind of *mise en abyme*: not the infinite textual self-reflection that reduces all the world to *text*, but the infinite gesture of reflection itself—one thing, person, perspective, or context reflecting upon another—that is our only way of knowing the world.

In this way, Borges is a crucial ancestor of Wallace, his philosophical metafictive strategies shaping Wallace's work at least as definitively as did the linguistic strategies of Barth and company. Wallace's (scathing) 2004 review of Edwin Williamson's biography, *Borges: A Life*, reveals Wallace's great admiration for Borges's work as a whole; the quotation from Borges's *Discusión* that serves as epigraph for "Good Old Neon" in the story's "2nd to last Draft"[34] indicates a more particular Borgesian inspiration in Wallace's fiction of the same time period. The epigraph, "Hay un concepto que es el corruptor y el desatinador [sic] de los otros," roughly translates to "There is a concept that is the corrupter and the fool of the other." Considered in conjunction with "Neon," it connects dead Neal's insights into the ways in which our concepts of time, language, and the separate ego/self limit human understanding—and the story's structural attempts to escape those limits through shifting and multiplied point of view and perspective—to the many thematic and structural ways in which Borges's own fiction explodes the concepts and constructs that limit our understandings of life and fiction.

Yet, with the exception of Lucas Thompson's recent and much-needed *Global Wallace* (2017), very little critical attention has been paid to Borges's influence on Wallace. Borges's fiction chases the impossible aleph—the point from which all other points can be seen—resulting in the labyrinthine structures and images of much of his fiction, its mirrors and mirroring, its creation of worlds through fictions that themselves recreate the world. Fueling them all is the attempt to do what Kate, of *Wittgenstein's Mistress*, cannot—to get "Outside," only to remember that every outside requires and constructs another inside—as in the library containing a book that contains the whole library ("The Library of Babel"), the man who dreams a man who is dreaming him ("The Circular Ruins"), the book that is the labyrinth of time and possibility through which we must move ("The Garden of Forking Paths"), and the encyclopedia whose imagined world rewrites the world of those who wrote it ("Tlön, Uqbar, Orbis Tertius"). While writers such as Mark Danielewski and Italo Calvino have, like Borges, used the text to recreate the world *as* textual labyrinth (or is it the other way around?), Wallace's fiction makes us confront the labyrinth in which we find ourselves in our own minds when we try to get outside ourselves and our ways of knowing. All of the strategies examined in this book are attempts to write fiction that, if it does not solve the problem of the binary that is at the heart of metafiction, and of fiction, and of philosophy, and of human thought and experience, at least constructs its components as interdependent, unable to dominate each other, unresolvable into unity, origin, or singularity, and generative—of mechanisms for attempted connection and understanding.

The Ultimate Endless Binary: Contrapuntal Metafictive Realism in *The Pale King*

According to the definitions of realism examined so far in this chapter, all of which incorporate metafiction, and some of which explicitly require the contrapuntal tension of Realist and metafictive strategies (namely, Jameson's and Slocombe's), the most realistic work Wallace attempted was his final novel, *The Pale King*. Like his short story collection *Brief Interviews with Hideous Men* (1999),[35] *The Pale King* mixes overtly metafictive pieces with

Realist ones such that each mode comments on the other, illustrating the integral interdependence of the two approaches in delivering the novel's story. But rather than the metafiction eclipsing the realism, or vice versa, as Jameson's dialectical model of realism would predict, the two modes work together, actually relying on each other to create the book's complex sense of verisimilitude—a blend of *trompe l'oeil* and *trompe l'esprit* in which each is only possible because of the other's presence. Wallace described the incredibly frustrating and ultimately unfinished experience of writing *The Pale King* as struggling with "a tornado that won't hold still long enough for me to see what's useful and what isn't, which tends to lead to the idea that I'll have to write a 5,000 page manuscript and then winnow it by 90%" (Max 289). When he died, he left behind—on disks and legal pads, in boxes and drawers—more of a 5,000-page tornado than a novel, and the bit we can hold in our hands and discuss is the result of the diligent winnowing of Michael Pietsch. But even allowing for the monumental excerpting and rearranging, and despite the fact that at the time of my visit to the Harry Ransom Center the full tornado was not yet on display, I believe the published novel justifies my argument that Wallace endeavored in his final novel to create a kind of total literary realism, one that might swallow and explode the binary of reality/fiction by doing the same to the dialectic of realism and metafiction.

Despite the loud and long "Octet"-style authorial intrusions that announce the novel's metafictiveness, headed "Author here," an "embryonic outline" of the novel (provided by Pietsch at the back of the book[36]) notes its "Central Deal: Realism." Indeed, anyone coming to *The Pale King* having read its numerous separately published excerpts would find these metafictive outbursts surprising, since all of the previously published excerpts are formally Realist. Likewise, with the exception of the ninety-eight-page Chris Fogle section, all of the novel's significant Realist episodes were separately published, and all but one were published before the posthumous novel: the novel made its literary entrance in the wake of a fanfare of Realism.[37] Perhaps unsurprisingly then, whereas critical attention to *Brief Interviews* tends to focus on its thematically and physically central metafictive story "Octet," academic and nonacademic attention to *The Pale King* so far tends to favor its structurally central Chris Fogle "novella," whose classic *bildungsroman* narrative provides the thematic focus of an otherwise scattered novel.

But the novel as a whole generates its sense of realism—of invoking a real world and a real author—much more from its metafictive sections, and from the relationship between the metafictive and Realist sections, than it does from those thematically grounding Realist sections alone. Wallace accomplishes this sense of realism via metafiction using some traditional (we might say first-wave) metafictive techniques: in the way of Barth, Calvino, Vonnegut, and others, the author-narrator distinguishes himself, the "real" author, from the author-persona that exists as a "pro forma statutory construct" elsewhere in the novel (66), and exposes conventions of fiction and of nonfiction, while insisting that he is writing the latter (73). This persona—the "real" author—then steps back to show us his concerted efforts to perform this task of nonfiction documentation, as when he blames the falsified perspective of his description of the Exam Center on narrative convention ("Part of this is artful compression"), on the physical circumstances of his writing ("part is that it's next to impossible to take coherent notes in a moving van"), and on his mediating material tools ("much of this is from the actual notebook in which these impressions were recorded," 276 FN 25). Similarly, he attributes defects of other aspects of his "real" account to the limitations of embodied human memory (289).

But the metafictive realism of *The Pale King* goes beyond such familiar devices, by employing new metafictive approaches that add another layer of reflection on the compositional process that leads back to the real. Wallace does so by putting his metafictional and Realist sections overtly in conversation with each other, allowing the relationship between them to do more work than does, for example, the loose contrapuntal Realist/metafictional structure of Barth's *Lost in the Funhouse*, or even than does the similar structure of Wallace's earlier *Brief Interviews*. In *The Pale King*, Realism becomes inflected through the prism of metafiction, whose shattering of Realism into its constitutive elements feels like the revelation of a reality not normally seen by the human eye. For example, the poignancy of "Good People" as a stand-alone short story, which seems so Realistic in the ironically explicit way of Hemingway—little is revealed, but that little bit is real, direct, and significant—feels a bit contrived when read as a carefully polished gem constructed by our untrustworthy narrator, David Wallace. This criticism of the Realist sections of the novel by the metafictive ones becomes a central truth being documented by our narrator. For example, five pages after we emerge, transported and perhaps transformed, from Chris Fogle's moving story of being "called to account," our narrator admits, in parentheses inside a footnote that is also a "N.B.," that Fogle's account, which had been presented to us as a transcript of his interview for a documentary film, is "heavily edited and excerpted" (257 FN 3). Of course, this novel was also heavily edited and excerpted, and the metafictive deflation of the Realist epiphany comes right on the latter's heels only because Pietsch put it there. But the basic point remains: Wallace bestows realism on his metafiction by invalidating his Realism.[38] He repeats this tactic of creating realism through metafiction that insists on its failure to narrate realistically—one he explored extensively in "Octet"—in many other moments of the novel, as when the narrator confides that "it's probably best to keep the explanations as terse and compressed as possible, for realism's sake," then continues to deliver densely detailed description for several pages, while admitting that "none of these truths yet existed, realistically speaking" (296, 297).

Similarly, Claude Sylvanshine's "fact psychicness" takes on a new meta meaning in the context of the narrator's critique of Realism as a mode of representing reality. Section 15 uses a Realist omniscient third-person point of view to describe Sylvanshine's gift and burden of being flooded by facts associated with people or objects that move through his life. Thematically, the character sketch provides an extreme example of the struggle faced by every human being, and epitomized by the novel's IRS "wigglers," to filter out unnecessary information and noise and remain aware of the present moment. But as seen through the larger, contrapuntally self-critiquing structure of the novel, this depiction of Sylvanshine becomes a metafictional critique of Realism on two levels. First, Sylvanshine's total knowledge metaphorically represents the position of a traditional omniscient realist narrator, and thus points out how *un*real, how contrived and impossible this convention of Realism is. Much of what Sylvanshine knows is unknowable: "Norbert Weiner's name for the little leather ball that was his only friend as a sickly child. The number of blades of grass in the front lawn of one's mailman's home" (119). No database containing such information exists: any depiction of such knowledge suggests a godlike perspective that is impossible, inhuman, and decidedly not lifelike. Second, as a portion of the larger novel, this section does even more damage to our notions about the possibility of verisimilitude in fiction by undermining the larger Realist/metafictional structure whose self-critique has seemed to offer truth. For if "Sylvanshine knew the name of his homeroom teacher's husband's first love's childhood cat ... verified only when he wrote a little illustrated booklet and the husband saw the name" (120), who verified this act of verification? And how might the section's narrator, David Wallace, know Sylvanshine's internal experience, or the unknowable facts or acts of validation that might verify them? Read through this larger self-reflexive lens, the implications of this section for the novel's inquiry into the possibility of truth in fiction become, as Sylvanshine feels at the end of this section, "Overwhelming" (121).

On the other hand—and there is always an other hand, in a novel that strives to envelop the entire endless binary—in some ways the novel also enacts the anti-Realist realism that it posits and critiques as impossible. The "Realism" that is the "Central Deal" in Wallace's "embryonic outline" is described as "monotony"; Wallace plans to "Plot a series of set-ups for stuff happening, but nothing actually happens" (546). He plants this concept of realism in the novel itself when an interviewee for the documentary film imagines a "totally real, true-to-life play" that "would be unperformable." In it, a wiggler would sit on stage doing nothing but occasionally turning a page, until audience members started leaving, after which "the real action of the play can start" (106). This concept of a "realistic" piece is not entirely new, even for Wallace, who already sketched it out in several of Incandenza's films in *Infinite Jest*; we might also see it as an echo of Lauren's *Body Time* in DeLillo's *The Body Artist* (see Chapter 5).[39]

What is new in *The Pale King* is that Wallace attempted not just to conceive of such realism but to enact it. Despite the neat circularity that Pietsch imposes by opening and closing with second-person pieces, the first inviting us to "read these" and the last offering a final lesson by provoking us to be aware of the body, breath, and presence (4, 538), the published novel as a whole mostly delivers the blank, peripatetic monotony that Wallace proposed as his "Central Deal." Several sections do as well, most prominently §25, which consists almost entirely of sentences describing wigglers turning pages. This section is thus Wallace's attempt to render through language the anti-Realist realist play proposed by the interviewee, invoking the boredom that might provoke us to turn our attention away from any narrative or even conventions of narrative and thus remain open to the real—perhaps to the Lacanian Real—that lies outside of narrative. Wallace rewards our attention to the monotony of this section by burying an enigmatic statement, itself defamiliarized by a line break, deep in the eventless litany: "Every love / story is a ghost story" (312). Certainly, this sentence is the only content readers take out of the section; the rest becomes the wash of unimportant moments to which we had to pay attention in order to experience that moment of meaning. In this way, the novel's anti-Realist sections create on the page, using language, the mental and physical conditions in which awareness might arise; Wallace creates through language an embodied experience of being that is unstructured by events and unorganized by recognizable conventions.

Thus they provide the novel's most powerful avenue to the real as defined by Chris Fogle's insight, that the "realest, most profound parts of me involved not drives or appetites but simple attention, awareness" (187). And it is Wallace's technical and structural innovations in metafiction—dialogism of perspective, the endless binary, and contrapuntal metafictive realism—that allow the novel to produce the simultaneously embodied and intellectual experience that illustrates that to be aware always means to be aware of multiple contradictory things. *The Pale King* thus uses two seemingly opposing representational modes—Realism and metafiction—to create a dialectic capable of expanding the powers of not only fiction, or of the novel, but of linguistic representation itself. Placed in conversation with each other, Realism and metafiction create a literary mode whose multiple planes seem to extend off the page to encompass the reader in the novel's complex reality. For the novel is not merely aware of itself but is also aware of awareness itself, and structured such that reading or naturalizing it requires the reader to become aware of both of these awarenesses. The first type of awareness is simply metafictive, but the second is more traditionally realist, as the novel strives to reflect and provoke the quality of awareness, much as Flaubert drew for us the ennui of Emma Bovary. *The Pale King* demonstrates how Wallace used technical innovations (in point of view, perspective, and self-reflexivity) to create larger generic innovations (interdependent Realism and metafiction) that allow language on the page to create real, embodied experience of the kind of awareness that he believed is necessary for staying present in real life. In this way, Wallace's final, posthumous novel stands as an unfinished experiment in ways of using language to connect readers not only to other readers, texts, and writers, but to their own embodied experience of the world around them.

The Future of (Meta)fiction: "Divid[ing] by Zero"

This reading of Wallace's last novel as an example of realism as a dialectic—between realism and metafiction, or Realism and anti-Realism—returns us to the question of how *The Pale King* relates to realism as defined by Jameson. I have argued that we see *The Pale King*, whose explicit aim is realistic literary representation, performing realism as a dynamic process of establishing traditional generic methods of such representation which it then resists or undermines. In this way, we might see *The Pale King* as enacting within itself the process that Jameson outlined for evolving literary representation as a whole, the "flight from classification" that Auerbach identified as the primary characteristic of realism.[40] But whereas Jameson suggests that realism is a pattern of establishing and resisting genres as part of realism, my reading of *The Pale King* suggests we might see realism, with its inherent resistances, as begetting a pattern of anti-realism, or of metafiction. Jameson names five genres established and then dissolved by realism: melodrama, *bildungsroman*, the historical novel, the novel of adultery, and naturalism (145). While one might quibble with individual generic categories—why does adultery merit its own category, and exactly whose adultery do we need that category to assess?—the overall list is a reasonable one for describing realist sub-genres, and for describing the sub-genres established and undermined by Wallace's metafiction. In this chapter, I have made plain Wallace's building and exploding of the *bildungsroman*-heart of *The Pale King*, a reading that also applies to a lesser extent to his *Brief Interviews*. Elsewhere I and others have read his other work as doing the same with this and other sub-genres—for example, we might read *Infinite Jest* as invoking and exploding, or at least parodying, all five of them.[41]

But more provocatively—and, I believe, more promisingly—my reading of Wallace's innovations in realism through innovations in metafiction fundamentally disagrees with Jameson's largest argument—that the realist novel has thoroughly dissolved itself through this dialectical process, leaving us with contemporary fiction that is incapable of accomplishing any of the things we look for in fiction:

> The breakdown of the realist tension between narrative and affect released uncontrolled linguistic production calculated to blacken endless pages of pseudo-realistic narratives classifiable by way of a return of the old genres and sub-genres that realism itself had attempted to dislodge (and had succeeded, but at the cost of its own destruction). (187)

Ironically, or fittingly, Jameson's conclusion about the destruction of realism repeats in new terms Wallace's now-famous lament about the "toothlessness" of irony and the "Armageddon" of postmodern metafiction from his 1991 interview. That proclamation itself revised Barth's assessment of the "Literature of Exhaustion" in 1967. In his essay, Barth argued that realism as a representational mode had become so ineffective that it needed to be revived from within, in the self-reflexive moves of 1960s metafiction. Declaring such metafiction itself exhausted thirty years later, Wallace called for, and began to construct, a revitalization of realism through reimagining metafiction, which I have demonstrated here and elsewhere. When Jameson declares the death of realism a little more than twenty years after Wallace began resuscitating it through metafiction, it seems reasonable to ask what metafiction's role might have been in this putative death, and whether attempts by Wallace (and by those who influenced him, and whom he influenced) to use metafiction to revive, rather than kill, realism, were a total failure. I argue that they were not.

Jameson concludes his study of "The Antinomies of Realism" with the depressing claim that the dissolution of realism has left in its wake a flood of what he calls "existential novels," which lack authentic temporality and subjectivity, allow no moral judgment, obscure the painful gap between subject and object through linguistic tricks, and feed our late-capitalist desire for easily consumed, affect-driven content that reassures our senses of self and of "endless possibility." Such is, he claims, the state of popular fiction. Literary fiction, or "the postmodern and its narrative production" as he terms it, is no more admirable and arguably no more lifelike. Using Alexander Kluge's tales as his example of "what happens to both narrativity and affect after the end of their brief union" (188), Jameson characterizes post-realism literary fiction as having no author, expressing no affect, and making no distinction between the fictive and the non-fictive, so that it "also testifies to the disappearance of 'fiction' as such, as a meaningful (narrative) category" (189). Since I (and others) read Wallace's quite challenging literary fiction as doing exactly the opposite—invoking an author, provoking and representing affect, and drawing a distinction between fiction and nonfiction precisely in order to preserve our sense of a real world,[42] and since I arrive at such a reading through attention to innovations in the same technical and structural devices that Jameson uses to arrive at his pessimistic conclusion (namely, point of view and perspective, irony, and the realism/anti-realism dialectic), the question arises, why do Jameson and I come to such different conclusions, using such similar means?

One way of answering this question is to consider our different approaches to analyzing the context and causality of changing literary technique. Like Auerbach, Jameson sees changes in narrative techniques as driving the evolution of structures and forms, which leads to changes in the status and function of realism, or literary representation of reality. For Jameson, the seeds of realism's death were sown by Faulkner's invention of a new, subjective third-person point of view (174). That technical innovation had, according to Jameson, itself been motivated by the problem of the inherent impersonality and atemporality of realist narrative, which causes any first-person point of view to be "a form of acting, of posing, feigning, taking up positions, before that spectator who is the reader" (169); Jameson offers Mark Twain's "wild succession of first-person dramatizations" as a prime example of such first-person inauthenticity (170). Jameson reads Faulkner's "swollen third person" as an attempt to avoid the first-person mask by absorbing that mask into the previously objective third person, which becomes an "incorporation of everything we have attributed to the first-person narrator in order to reach some richer representation of subjectivity and thereby a more multidimensional representation of reality itself" (174–5). This new, subjective third person then creates its own narrative problems that cause today's postmodern narratives, by Jameson's account, to destroy themselves in attempting to solve them. The Faulknerian swollen or "blank" third person, incorporating subjectivity into an undefined "objective" perspective, saturates its narrative in mystery and unknowability, which in turn suggests the impotence of the récit and the dominance of the "eternal present" disguising itself as tale (176). Although free indirect discourse and unstable irony (as pioneered by Henry James) proliferate in their own attempts to solve this latest problem of pervasive uncertainty, Jameson declares the former's attempts "facile" (177) and the latter's doomed, in that unstable irony combines with the new swollen third person to leave no objective point of view from which moral judgments can be made (181-4). In the wake of these new techniques, "what alone authentically survives" is affect, as the narrative impulse that once opposed and balanced it has been eviscerated of all temporal and subjective authenticity (184).

This brief overview, however admittedly unable to fully represent Jameson's dense argument, illustrates an important broader aspect of that argument clearly: Jameson's history of realism might as well be a history of technical problems of linguistically representing reality and technical solutions to those problems, as it is a history of dialectical generic formation and change. Essentially the former propels and undergirds the latter. It is curious, given his theoretical leanings, that his version of this story, however dialectical, seems to be more Realist than poststructural: it appears to have an end. Or, it has a strikingly postmodern end, one that shuffles along like the glimpse of "*closure*" that Derrida imagines as our undead passage out of metaphysics.[43] Jameson describes narrative after modernism and its invention of the swollen third person as "the omnipresent production of realism after realism" (185), but one that is "no longer the realism I have been describing here" (184), in that it no longer has the capacity to do what realism throughout its long evolution has aimed to do: represent time, place, subjectivity, and the judgments about reality that these allow.

What are we to make, then, of these over twenty new "realisms" that are emerging out of what Jameson calls the death throes of realism? On the largest level, I see these new realisms as evidence that fiction of the last thirty years has changed enough technically and generically to require a systematic investigation of the form and function of literary representation of reality after postmodernism. And I see the overwhelming viability and vitality of much of this technically innovative literature—its ability to pursue the aims of Realism using devices and frameworks constructed long after the initial phases of Realism—as inarguable evidence that Jameson's foreclosure on literary possibility and varieties of future literary evolution is premature. Even a cursory glance at Wallace's work and its criticism provides grounds for protest in exactly the terms used by Jameson to describe the failure of contemporary realism. A good portion of Wallace studies focuses on Wallace's surprising and refreshing ability to use masks, and often first-person masks, to convey a sense of authentic subjectivity; "Good Old Neon" is one of several examples of how Wallace's work reflects on the peculiar relationship of language and time in order to depict a different sort of temporal authenticity. Despite appearances to the contrary, Wallace's work often elicits our judgment, as I have argued in more than one reading of "Octet," while forcing us to reflect on those acts as well. Of course Wallace is not alone in crafting innovative techniques for renewing Realism. Carol

Maso's *AVA* (1993) and George Saunders's *Lincoln in the Bardo* (2017), for example, however otherwise formally experimental, both rely on the unity of time and place no less than does any Greek play; Saunders is widely regarded as our most accomplished inheritor of and innovator on Wallace's intimate first- and third-person voices. As for the accusation that fiction after Realism can no longer "presentify," or make the past-present-future temporality of the récit present for contemporary readers, the assortment of technical, formal, and material innovations of the texts examined in Chapter 3, on "material realism," largely evolve specifically in order to be able to preserve and/or present the past, and the experience of presence, for the reader.

Perhaps instead of diagnosing the death of realism, and the descent of literature into a state of inauthenticity and unreality, we should recognize another major shift in the continuing dialectic of realism. This one is caused by changes outside the realms of technique and genre, by pressures and influences beyond those considered so far by our major theorists, namely Auerbach and Jameson. We might see Wallace's work as creating empathy and authentic subjectivity by changing his technical construction of irony and point of view, but we must also consider how his fiction constructs self and judgment as equally necessary and impossible in the context of its Buddhist influences (see my "David Foster Wallace's 'Octet' and the 'Atthakavagga'"). Similarly, we might investigate how Saunders constructs selves with rich interiors capable of feeling and expressing empathy using innovations in voice and perspective that move past Wallace's, and even through formal experimentations in blending prose and drama structures. But certainly the Buddhist core of *Bardo* shapes these innovations as well, just as it shapes Ozeki's persistently innovative *A Tale for the Time Being* (see Chapter 4). Ozeki's formal innovations also result from the novel's investment in quantum theory, a recently influential alternative way of conceiving of physical reality, which likewise motivates technical experiments in representations of temporality. Meanwhile, all of the physically and materially experimental texts of Chapter 3 innovate new ways to tell tales, convey affect, and "presentify," using methods made possible only through recent advances in composition and print technologies. That is to say, however much technical problems beget technical solutions that beget new problems to keep the engine of formal and generic evolution moving, major changes happen outside the realm of literary representation too, out in the real world: changes in technology, material production, and concepts of physical and metaphysical reality all leave their marks on the techniques, forms, and genres of literature, and of realism.

Still, all of these new realisms are powered by metafiction, more specifically by a new kind of metafiction, metafictive realism: realism that knows any attempt to represent reality must also consider and represent the forms, conventions, and materials used to construct that representation.

Given the near ubiquity of metafictive strategies—not only in literature, but in film, television, visual art, even in advertising—it has become difficult to imagine fiction that is in no way also metafiction: even fiction that conforms to the conventions of Realism will likely be read through the self-reflexive lens of contemporary consciousness. The metafictive strategies of realism that I have explored in this chapter (using metafiction to represent the workings of the human mind, and the experience of presence and awareness), and the ones I will examine in this book's remaining chapters (using metafiction to draw our attention to the physicality of the book and to the implications of our quantum world), all aim to represent through language something real about the human experience that is particular to the late twentieth and early twenty-first centuries. The methods used and the realities represented differ dramatically from those of the mid-century metafictionists against whom Wallace positioned himself, and thus represent marked evolution of the techniques of metafiction and the workings of realism of which metafiction is an intregral part.

One of the ways Wallace described productive metafictionists as opposed to "crank-turners" in that first important McCaffery interview was as "bona fide artists who come along and really divide by zero and weather some serious shit-storms of shock and ridicule in order to promulgate some really important ideas."[44] Since he wrote a book on infinity, we can assume that Wallace knew that the result of dividing by zero only seems to be infinity, but is really "undefined." So, perhaps "divid[ing] by zero" is an apt way to characterize Wallace's distinctive strategies of writing, which resulted in fiction that reveals the seeming infinity of information and perspectives needed to reach an understanding and empathy that will always be undefined. Given the enormous influence his work has already had on many of the most fascinating writers today, and the growing variety of self-reflexive, anti-Realist practices that increasingly define these contemporary realisms, perhaps Wallace's analogy also illustrates not just how metafiction can be productive, but how dividing metafiction from fiction makes no sense at all.

Notes

1   Patricia Waugh, *Metafiction: The Theory and Practice of Self-Conscious Fiction* (Abingdon: Routledge, 1984), 13–14.
2   Robert Alter, *Partial Magic: The Novel as Self-Conscious Genre* (Berkeley: University of California Press, 1975).
3   Hutcheon, *Narcissistic Narrative*, 4–5.

4   Waugh, *Metafiction*, 14 (original italics).
5   Ibid., 14–15; quoting William H. Gass, "Philosophy and the Form of Fiction," in *Fiction and the Figures of Life* (Boston: Nonpareil Books, 1979), 3–26.
6   Boris Eichenbaum, "The Theory of the 'Formal Method,'" in *Norton Anthology of Theory and Criticism*, 2nd ed., ed. Vincent B Leitch (New York: W. W. Norton, 2010), 938 (original italics).
7   Madhu Dubey, "Post-Postmodern Realism?" *Twentieth-Century Literature* 57, no. 3–4 (2011): 369.
8   David James, "Integrity After Metafiction," *Twentieth-Century Literature* 57, nos. 3–4 (2011): 492–515.
9   Margaret Gram, "*Freedom*'s Limits: Franzen, the Realist Novel, and the Problem of Growth," *American Literary History* 26, no. 2 (2014): 295–316.
10 Waugh, *Metafiction*, 7.
11 Ibid., 18.
12 Stephen J. Burn, ed., *Conversations with David Foster Wallace* (Jackson: University Press of Mississippi, 2012), 60, 129, 151, 38, 129.
13 Waugh, *Metafiction*, 6; Hutcheon, *Narcissistic Narrative*, xii.
14 John J. Enck, "An Interview," *Wisconsin Studies in Comparative Literature* 6, no. 1 (1965): 6; Charlie Reilly, "An Interview with John Barth," *Contemporary Literature* 22, no. 1 (1981): 18.
15 See *Succeeding Postmodernism*, 138–47.
16 John Barth is a crucial predecessor for Wallace's metafictive realism, as Charles Harris argues in "'The Anxiety of Influence: The John Barth/David Foster Wallace Connection," *Critique: Studies in Contemporary Fiction* 55, no. 2 (2014): 103–26, and as I argue in "'Your Head Gets in the Way': Reflecting (on) Realism from John Barth to David Foster Wallace," in *John Barth: A Body of Words*, ed. Gabrielle Dean and Charles Harris (Champaign: Dalkey Archive Press, 2016): 201–31.
17 Burn, ed., *Conversations*, 30 (original italics).
18 See Bradley J. Fest's "'Then Out of the Rubble: David Foster Wallace's Early Fiction," in *David Foster Wallace and "The Long Thing": New Essays on the Novels*, ed. Marshall Boswell (New York: Bloomsbury, 2014), 85–105.
19 While the interview was not published until the 1993 *Review of Contemporary Fiction*, Wallace gave that interview in 1991.
20 David Foster Wallace, "The Empty Plenum," Afterword for David Markson's *Wittgenstein's Mistress* (Champaign: Dalkey Archive Press, 1990), 249 (original italics).
21 See especially Charles Harris's "The Anxiety of Influence: The John Barth/David Foster Wallace Connection."
22 Wallace, "The Empty Plenum," 250–1 (original italics).
23 Ibid., 259, 260.
24 Steve Tomasula, *The Book of Portraiture* (Tuscaloosa: FC2, 2006), 39.
25 Karan Barad, *Meeting the Universe Halfway: Quantum Physics and the Entanglement of Matter and Meaning* (Durham: Duke University Press, 2007), 135.

26 See Catherine Nichols's "Dialogizing Postmodern Carnival: David Foster Wallace's *Infinite Jest*," *Critique: Studies in Contemporary Fiction* 43, no. 1 (2001): 3–16 as one early example.
27 David Foster Wallace, "Good Old Neon," in *Oblivion* (Boston: Little, Brown and Company, 2004), 178, 180, 1.
28 In this way the story narrativizes Christopher Lasch's *The Culture of Narcissism: American Life in an Age of Diminishing Expectations* (New York: Norton, 1979).
29 Wallace, "Good Old Neon," 64, 12.
30 Ibid., 66 (FN).
31 James Goodwin in conversation, many years ago.
32 See Burn, *Conversations*, 90.
33 I have seen a troubling tendency in recent years, in print and in graduate student work, for readers of this story to be seduced by the narcissistic and objectifying techniques of this story's narrator, rather than to read the story as exposing and critiquing those techniques. Wallace has written the story such that it is absolutely not possible to read it as valorizing the male narrator and his experience of "growth." His violent verbal attack on his female interviewer at the end of the story is only the most obvious evidence that prevents such a sympathetic reading. And what would it even mean to say that a story, an author, chooses to use a woman's brutal rape as the occasion for male personal epiphany? Wallace's own attempts at feminism are fraught, as I have argued in "'By Hirsute Author': Gender and Communication in the Work and Study of David Foster Wallace," *Critique: Studies in Contemporary Fiction* 58, no. 1 (2016): 65–78, but his work does not suggest that he was so misogynistic or un-self-aware as to construct a story with misogyny as its main goal. Thus I would suggest that reading "Brief Interview #20" as sympathetic to its male narrator requires one to be oblivious to the misogyny that the story intends to critique, and so is not merely inaccurate but offensive. For an egregious example of this erroneous reading in print, see Christoforos Diakoulakis's "'Quote Unquote Love . . . a Type of Scotopia': David Foster Wallace's *Brief Interviews with Hideous Men*," in *Consider David Foster Wallace*, ed. David Hering (Los Angeles: Sideshow Media, 2010), 147–55. For a thoughtful refutation of such a reading, see Rachel Himmelheber's "'I Believed She Could Save Me': Rape Culture in David Foster Wallace's 'Brief Interviews with Hideous Men #20,'" *Critique: Studies in Contemporary Fiction* 55, no. 5 (2014): 522–35.
34 Typescript draft of "Good Old Neon," June 2000, Container 24.3. David Foster Wallace Papers, Harry Ransom Center, University of Texas at Austin.
35 For this reading, see my "Mediated Immediacy," in *A Companion to David Foster Wallace Studies*, ed. Marshall Boswell and Stephen J. Burn (New York: Palgrave Macmillan, 2013).
36 David Foster Wallace, *The Pale King* (Boston: Little, Brown and Company, 2011), 546. I will note subsequent references parenthetically.

37 §1 was published as "Peoria (4)," in *TriQuarterly*, Fall 2002; §6 was published as "Good People," in *The New Yorker*, February 2007; §8 was published as "Peoria (9) 'whispering pines,'" in *TriQuarterly*, September 2002; §16 was published as "A New Examiner," in *The Lifted Brow*, January 2010, and in *Harper's*, September 2010; §33 was published as "Wiggle Room," in *The New Yorker*, March 2009; §35 was published as "The Compliance Branch," in *Harper's*, February 2008; and §36 was published as "Backbone," in *The New Yorker*, May 2011. My thanks to the howlingfantods.com, for providing a helpful record of these publications and directing me to one I had not yet found myself.

38 Chapter 5 will argue that DeLillo uses different metafictive techniques to accomplish a similar kind of realism—as an attempt to represent the quantum truth of the universe—by invalidating his novel's Realism, in *The Body Artist* (New York: Scribner, 2001).

39 Perhaps not coincidentally, Wallace and DeLillo corresponded about *The Body Artist* in great detail in December of 2000 (HRC Container 101.10 of DeLillo archive).

40 Jameson, *Antinomies*, 143.

41 As one example, on *IJ* as a historical novel, see my *"Infinite Jest,"* in *The Cambridge Companion to David Foster Wallace*, ed. Ralph Clare (Cambridge: Cambridge University Press, 2018), 127–41.

42 See, for example, Marshall Boswell's reading of "Little Expressionless Animals," in *Understanding David Foster Wallace* (Columbia: University of South Carolina Press, 2003), 74.

43 Jacques Derrida, *Of Grammatology*, trans. Gayatri Chakravorty Spivak (Baltimore: Johns Hopkins University Press, 1974), 4 (original italics).

44 Burn, *Conversations*, 30–1.

2

The Work of Art after the Mechanical Age

Materiality, Narrative, and the Real in the Fiction of Steve Tomasula

The world according to Steve Tomasula—and according to the poststructural language, Darwinist nature, and systems-theory digital technology that inform his work—can only be experienced by the transient, particular human as fragmented, incomplete, relative, and irresolvably multiple. And yet art traditionally gathers and organizes these pieces into the wholeness and meaning that the world lacks, with the apparent passivity of a mirror. For Steve Tomasula, however, the work of art is most integrally about *work*. It exists materially and physically impacts the world; it is defined by its function and use, not by a cloaking aestheticizing of them; and it results from work done by humans: it is human-made, not a product of nature. At bottom, Tomasula's fiction aims to cram a wedge into the nearly non-gap between the Real and the endless ways we represent it to ourselves, while accusing itself of being no wedge at all. The essentially Lacanian—which is to say, Freudian, or perhaps Cartesian—notion that the self necessarily experiences everything as mediated by the self, and therefore has no direct access to reality, presents the basic problem of Tomasula's work. Whether and how art might offer a solution to that problem, or simply a way of comprehending the problem, while also identifying itself as part of that problem, motivates its unfolding. Ultimately for Tomasula, art is one of the many lies—like science, like history, like culture—that we can't live without, if we are to live at all. But unlike the other scaffoldings we cling to, the other masks of the untouchable Real, art for Tomasula offers the possibility of making the Real present, pointing to the Real (as in Hal Foster's "traumatic realism"; see Introduction), by exposing itself as nothing more than mask.

But Tomasula's work does not confine itself to critiquing systems of signification and their relation to an abstract Real. Rather, his novels connect that theoretical inequity between representation and reality to a materialist critique of the inevitable inadequacy of any individual vision of the physical world, and a social critique of the inequities of power producing those visions. Thus, in all of his novels, the frameworks we use to stand in for reality—whether conceived as abstract idea or material whole—change as the dominant ideology changes: in *VAS: An Opera in Flatland* (2002), music evolves from earthsounds to mouthsounds to melody to genetic duet, while *The Book of Portraiture* (2006) depicts the evolution of modes of perception using mechanisms of representation, from the invention of alphabetic language to the reinvention of human life via genetic alphabet. *TOC: A New Media Novel* (2009) goes one step further, imagining a looping creation myth in which frameworks of perception evolve in and out of complexity as humanity repeatedly builds and destroys the master framework of time. These texts suggest that our ways of understanding reality *are* culture, insidiously self-perpetuating in that it both results from the gathering of individuals' understandings, reactions, and desires, and invisibly shapes them.

VAS demonstrates how the most horrifying societal practices become accepted, even forgotten, not just through its story, but through its real-world examples of horrors we've assimilated, forgotten, or not even noticed. Years after learning in school of the Nazis' sterilization programs, Square (narrator of *VAS*) learns of those programs instituted decades before in America, "The Land of Free Choice" (54): he marvels that one can acculturate to his own commodification, as had Ota Benga, who killed himself after his removal from the Bronx Zoo where he had lived in the Monkey House with an orangutan (297); he fills pages with pictures of ads selling gene manipulation and the eggs of beautiful women, meticulous documentation of Miss America's decreasing dimensions, and reports of the eighteen surgeries required to transform a woman into a living Barbie—all of which we will find exist in the real world, if we check. The fact that we will have to check (how could I never have heard of Ota Benga?) indicates how little we know about the world we live in, how inaccurate any concept of reality is. The ultimate simulacrum, culture replaces the real so thoroughly that we forget, or never know, that reality is anything more than the set of assumptions, fragments, and misperceptions that we live in.

Such a wholesale substitution of representation for reality can't be helped: there is no Adam's Peak, which Tomasula imagines in both *VAS* and *IN&OZ* (2003) as a point on earth from which one can view all of creation, unframed. The danger, then, comes in confusing our methods of framing (narrative, schools of knowledge, facts) with the thing itself, and thus allowing particular lenses to dominate our vision in ways that distort or destroy our understanding of what it is to be human—that is, how we relate to the larger world, to each other, to the self. Tomasula's novels investigate our methods of representing and knowing reality (science, technology, history, language, image, story), the risks and benefits of each, and art's value as such a method, asking what kind of art best allows us to know the Real by confronting the necessarily incomplete, fragmented, irresolvable ways that we know reality. It considers the work art can do in an age defined by information systems, reproducibility, and technological manipulation of the material world and body.

Today's most respected mask/ideology being science and its technologies, Tomasula's writing focuses on the concerns of science and language as interrelated arms of the culture industry that shape our world and our bodies. His fiction considers what art is in that industry, and what it needs to be in order to resist it, to be revolutionary. Just as his art explores thematically how a science grown ever more atomic in scale, and a technology evolved from mechanical to digital, make increasingly profound alterations to the physical world and the human body, so does his fiction formally explore how literature in a digital age must grow increasingly and insistently material. The implications of his theory and execution of art revise the status of literature, the genre of the novel, and material theories of art. Thus, they also point toward a new theory of realism.

The Danger of Art

One aim of Tomasula's fiction is exposing the dangerous lie of narrative. As a mimetic method, narrative pleases by offering the appearance of knowledge, wholeness, and immediacy, but through the mechanisms of forgetting, partiality, and construction. *VAS* and *Book* enlist the constellation as metaphor for such constructive/destructive acts of understanding, in which "trying to see the constellations . . . was more a matter of not seeing than seeing, of ignoring patterns that the makers of charts didn't know were there in order to believe that their Scorpions and Dragons were outside and not just within."[1] The narrator of the "Chronos" section of *TOC* also explains the pull of art as its ability to meaningfully connect the random pieces of our lives: "She longed for a way to approximate the sense of a whole that was easier to fake in art than in life." *IN&OZ*, more allegorical art manifesto than novel, demonstrates the danger of traditional realism and its invisible methods by contrasting two kinds of cars as two kinds of art with two very different societal functions and meanings. Mechanic, who becomes the novel's artistic guru, transforms himself from worker to artist when he starts "fixing" cars in ways that make them inoperable as cars, but revelatory as art objects: "Having grasped the essence of Car, he could no longer participate in the lie that was Not-Car, the lie that blinded people from the beauty of the Truth that resided beneath the false beauty they mindlessly used to tool about their work-a-day lives."[2] Instead, he tools about the neighborhood pushing his car, whose wheels he has mounted to the roof and replaced with its doors like skis (35), allowing the car in its functional brokenness to showcase its essential carness, just as his broken hammer allows him to "see its hammerness for what it was" (26).[3] Having been Heideggerianly thrown into the mechanic's life simply because he grew up with a father who became a mechanic because cars often broken down under the bridge where they lived (101), Mechanic knows how material conditions shape our lives, how form determines function and fate—how form is the essence of meaning—as it is for his watchdogs with their "powerful bodies," and for the Designer's dog whose delicacy fits into her owner's petite lap. Only removing this function allows us to see things for what they are, for the function they lost.

Pointing to meaning/function by removing it is for Mechanic a true reproduction of the absent truth that all art is after; it testifies to his understanding that such a truth can only be made present in its absence, that art neither conjures nor substitutes for the Real but rather exists entirely separate from it, and more often obscures than illuminates it. Designer, on the other hand, creates designs that "mask the grotesque viscera of cars," as a dress or eyeglasses are "more of a language than an article of clothing or a medical aide." Her cars derive their power not from their ability to reveal their material function, but from their ability to "giv[e] desire form—and shap[e] the world by doing so" (17). In transforming the cars' essences into the language of desire, Designer creates "invisible cars" whose "wordless language" enables people to "change their selves by changing what they drove" (91, 16, 18), thus masking both the mechanism of the Car and the mechanism by which cars can be made to act ideologically on the world.

Like Mechanic's inoperable cars, Photographer's mental photographs and Composer's silent music present an argument for anti-Realist art. When Photographer finds that Mechanic has "fixed" his car by replacing the windshield with the radiator, he recognizes their kindredness: "All my life I have driven this car without once considering the beauty, the functionality of its radiator . . . but now I shall never drive again without first appreciating its handiwork, and yours, and all of those whose labor has helped make my locomotion and comfort possible." This attention to the object's material function and the labor that produced it Photographer calls the "true beauty of art," which he contrasts with the "lies and illusions we are expected to live by" (27). Photographer's own art expresses the same distrust of the "lies and illusions" perpetuated by mainstream art. Having abandoned filmmaking after being "sickened" by "the artificiality of time in films," Photographer turned to stills and then photos with increasingly tiny frames, in an attempt to minimize the opportunity for misreading: "the photos themselves, the mere flotsam of looking were what most people wanted in a photograph while the photos were the very thing that arrested looking" (30). His quest to escape the tyranny of the frame, of frameworks of representation that manipulate viewers who believe they are seeing unmediated reality, leads Photographer to "take pictures without any film in the camera," and then to abandon framing devices altogether by building a house as a "walk-in camera obscura," in which he stands, "eyes shut, letting the image that came in through the window that was a lens project itself onto his closed eyelids" (30).

Composer presents a similar argument for anti-Realist art that results in a similarly solipsistic alternative to mainstream art. His concert begins with a manifesto for anti-Realist art, which accuses mainstream art of distorting reality by "FRAMING the world in such a way so as to CROP from view the WHOLE OF MUSIC and make of it a standardized assemblage of sounds to play while in the car or vacuuming the house" (49). Later Composer will argue, as if he has been reading David Foster Wallace, that "by preventing audiences from slipping into the passive, dreamlike trance of listening, by forcing them to instead work for every note with their eyes, they apprehend the constructed nature of music. That is, . . . they see how there is nothing natural about it" (74). Further, he points out the structuralism of music, that it, like a language, operates and means only relationally, and that our investment of meaning in its distinct parts is also a construction: "We see how illusory is the concept of 'a' note. There can be no 'note' without an absence of sound between other sounds . . . . And so it is with all genres of music and the invisible assumptions that make them possible: No military music without a military. No church music without a history of churches" (75). In this description, traditional art, and our traditional understanding of art, hides not just the truth of function but also the historical, political, and cultural forces that brought the art into being. But Composer's methods of turning away from the lies of mainstream art, like Photographer's, produce art that cannot communicate at all. For the entrancement of aural music, he substitutes the intellectual exercise of reading sheet music, ironically for more hours than the most devoted musician could bear. And the sound of the music is replaced by the roar of the diesel engine used to power the machine that projects the sheet music, so unbearable that the audience must stop its ears. In his attempt to produce "real Music, true Music" that cannot be misconstrued as mindless pleasure, Composer makes "music" that cannot communicate, or even be endured, at all. It will be left for Mechanic to invent an art that can preserve function and communicable truth.

TOC, on the other hand, enacts anti-Realist practices while depicting in a variety of ways the seduction of Realism. The illusion of Realism and our helpless desire for it are the engine for the novel, which tells through many tales the story of our human quest to understand, explain, contain, and so control experience. At the heart of the multiplicitous narrative told by a host of voices spanning vast time and distance is the quest for a machine that can be more influential than time, that will allow us to register time without suffering it, that is, that will allow us to perceive our constructions of meaning as realer than the death-inducing reality of time. In "The Heart of the Machine," the character that variously appears as young woman and crone, and as hermit, inventor and persecuted, realizes that

> the most influential machine they could ever make would actually be a difference engine ... that could display these differences and yet on its face make the vast difference between spring and springs—and indeed all puns—as seemingly real as any good illusion—paintings of sunsets, or magic tricks, or words, but especially the divisions of time: realistic tricks, illusions that seemed real because they were fueled by desire, desire that they be real.

This definition of human-made meaning is strikingly linguistic and specifically structuralist. Indeed, all examples of human understanding in this book[4] operate through relative difference, as matters of perspective, dialectically dependent on others' understandings, therefore meaningless in themselves (as we see from the interdependent mythologies of the People of Tic and the People of Toc). The illusion of shared meaning is best generated and depicted by the Difference Machine itself, which, fueled by human desire—this woman's beating heart—codifies the seemingly meaningful differences of words and images into a perception of understanding and mastery, even of time itself. In *TOC*, this machine, the clock, is the ultimate Realist technique, the *trompe l'oeil* inside which we live, representing for us the reality we can never actually grasp. The clock is the art that contains all other attempts to represent the world.

In *Book*, Tomasula also uses *trompe l'oeil* to contrast Realist and anti-Realist art and its purposes. Chapter 2 develops another manifesto of art, this time from the point of view of Diego de Velázquez, a historical painter in the court of King Felipe IV of Spain during the reign of Louis XIII. Velázquez-the-character explains his arrival at anti-Realist technique as a reaction to his peers' enslavement to mimesis and his own perception of the dangers inherent in mimetic practice. In a competition of mimetic "traps," his colleagues content themselves to trick the eye with perfectly reproduced coins and water drops, while Velázquez tricks the mind by painting "an ambiguous golden disk" mistaken for a host by men of the cloth and a coin by men of the world (38). Thus he demonstrates his insight that "the most important organ of sight is not the eyes, but the mind" (39), which he then translates into increasingly sophisticated revelations of how representation works on the minds of its viewers: to "illustrate that which is already known," or "to make what man imagines into what is" (47). Here we see Tomasula theorizing a metafictional revision to mimesis that is broadly akin to Wallace's shift from *tromp l'oeil* to *trompe l'esprit*, or from reproducing the eye's experience of the world to reproducing the mind's (see Chapter 1, pp. 59–60). But Tomasula's work conceives of the mind's reflections on reality differently than does Wallace's, whose *trompe l'esprit* reproduces the infinite self-reflection of the individual mind. Tomasula's fiction, on the other hand, aims to reproduce the ways in which art shapes the mind's reflections of the world, and the ways in which the mind reflects upon and so shapes the world around it.

For Tomasula, *trompe l'oeil*, or visual mimesis, fails in the proper project of art as defined by Velázquez in two ways: by reflecting only what the viewer already knows and thus expects to see, and by fooling the viewer into believing the identity between her expectation of the real and its fulfillment in art—by creating an illusory connection between representation and thing, art and life, that seems to heal the pain of the gap that lies between us and experience/reality. Instead, Velázquez realizes that

> it is only by making visible the artist's artifice that the art of painting can express its own essence: the directions by which the viewer is to note the breach between the marks he sees and the things he believes them to represent. That is, it is only when paint represents itself as paint that its craft can become an art—a form of knowledge that signifies a way of being as well as represents. (53)

The opposite of mimesis (or, attempting to trick the viewer into believing the representation *is* the Real), the essence of art for Velázquez and for Tomasula is its ability to call attention to the gap between the two. Thus art becomes not a salve for or distraction from the painful gap, but a "form of knowledge"—which *VAS* pairs with pain in its opening line—and a "way of being" that is an alternative to the pleasant ignorance of mimetic magic.

The Work of Art

The church fathers in *Book* are right to panic at the implications of such a theory of art. By using as his mouthpiece for anti-mimetic art an artist who worked for the church when it asserted its power through the Inquisition,

Tomasula moves beyond the personal seduction of aesthetic Realism to examine the cultural dangers of aesthetic ideology. Rather than reinscribing the authority and power already concentrated in state and religious rulers, as portraiture had long done, art as evolved by Velázquez unmasks mimetic representation as itself a system of power that sanctifies certain "truths" while repressing others. Such anti-mimetic art has the potential to expose the repressive mechanisms of all inscribing systems, so that "a confusion of origins would replace the Origin . . . the Tower of Babel falling—forever," as a church father bemoans (72, 73). Velázquez unmasks mimetic art as a prime instrument of ideology via its inevitable reliance on perspective—its requirement that a viewer must occupy its point of view in order for the work to make sense:

> This is why a crucifix paint'd from the perspective of one on his knees then hung at the right height before a pad'd kneeler will act as an invisible hand, bringing its viewer down into alignment. It is only by aligning himself with the assumptions embody'd in the work that it will appear normal. (79)

And so with the huge hands of Michelangelo's David: we were meant to stand farther beneath him than today's ground-level installment allows; he was made for a roofline display. The work of art similarly imposes a physical relationship between itself and its viewer that moves the viewer into "proper" alignment with the contextual assumptions inherent in it. Velázquez's connection between art's ability to manipulate the body to take its perspective and its deployment of a belief system echoes Louis Althusser's explanation of "the material existence of an ideological apparatus," which, through ritual, governs the actions that dictate and contain people's beliefs.[5]

In order to avoid such tacit manipulation, Velázquez paints his masterful *Las Meninas*, which absorbs its viewer into it, moving her into place as witness to the scene. She shares this position with the implied mirror that reflects both the scene as the artist paints it and the marginalized subjects of the scene—king and queen, who end up trapped in an infinity of reflection. The painting makes plain the influence of every work of art over the viewer whose body it moves to accommodate its perspective, of the viewer who is conscripted into its making, and of the desires and beliefs of the artist that enable both. "Every portrait can only be a self-portrait; a portrait of its viewer, its author, a portrait of the I (*nosotros*)," Velázquez concludes, displacing the work's subject onto creator and viewer and dispersing self into the other that is its co-creator (84). From one origin, many: and so Velázquez transforms art from an instrument of placating, totalizing ideology into one of the painful knowledge of multiplication and separation, of the self from the self, and of the self from the Real.[6] Thus *Las Meninas* operates primarily as disruption: of the viewer's thoughtless absorption into art, and of the power structures that create the hierarchies and assumptions that invisibly shape art. It is a disruption of the self-perpetuating cycles of power—authority shaping cultural artifacts that reinscribe that authority—of which Realist art is a reliable handmaiden. All of Tomasula's books unmask these structures of power, and all of them aim to disrupt them, to be linguistic *Las Meninas*.

Whereas Velázquez exposes the church as an ideological state apparatus, to use Althusser's term, Mechanic exposes the ISA of the consumerist forces that transform everything and self into a commodity that is absorbed into the capitalist machine. Not only does Designer draft invisible cars used by people to remake themselves in the cars' own images, but she also demonstrates how a perspective of commodification creates the simulacra of OZ's music (which fills the elevators that have replaced the interior of the OZ building, means entirely replacing ends, 24), and the "Technicolor rainbow over amber waves of grain" (31) that accompanies her morning jogs. OZ^7 comprises and composes her world, a virtual patchwork of pieces—sounds, images, even branded verbal expressions—all of which quote something else unreal. Thus Designer's only way of appreciating the "unique" work of art she purchases (from a commodifying gallery of "authentic" art) is to bring it into the language of commerce that defines her expectations and assumptions: she makes the painting "less of a dominating sneer" by buying more products, more magazine images, that will align the work of art with their comfortable, commodified perspective, until "she found it harder and harder to say which was product and which art" (107).

Meanwhile, Composer and Photographer understand only in theory what Mechanic comes to understand through embodied experience: that all art participates in ideology that materially shapes the world. Composer teaches Mechanic this link between art and the material world as they, along with Photographer and Designer, sit and talk in an IN bar called DRINK BOOZE (its name, like all place names in IN, inviting function rather than creating desire, and so pointing to how different strategies of signification in IN and OZ create differences in inner states and behavior). Composer pontificates that "aesthetic decisions have real-world consequences," an assertion that is meant to support his argument for art that prevents viewer passivity but also, ironically, explains why his unbearable version of nontraditional art can never actually shape the world. But it does succeed in resisting commodification, by being as unreproducible as it is unsellable; for "any music that can be bought and sold . . . is a force in the maintenance of the status quo" (79). Ultimately, though, the novel exposes the limits of Composer's materialist theory of art, not just by showing the limits of his consuming audience, but by indicating the limited conviction of his purely intellectual understanding in the face of the forces of ideology and its capitalist cooption.

The bar scene foregrounds—for us and for Mechanic, if not for the less savvy other artists—this divide between embodied and intellectual knowledge as a framework for examining the impact of class on the human body and experience, in the tradition of Marx and Engels, and so on theories of art. Mechanic realizes he should have known that Composer and Photographer "had both been born in OZ and educated in OZ and still had the money to live in OZ, their families made up of wealthy OZ professors and business people, even doctors and judges...the first time they shook hands, their hands being as soft as the foam rubber of luxury-car seats" (72). He sees "the lifetime of premium, not standard, health benefits written in the luster of Designer's blonde hair, . . . the straightness and whiteness of Composer's teeth" (74). Designer, unapologetically of OZ, makes herself comfortable in this world of bodily labor in the same way that she made her piece of art fit comfortably in her commodified world—by appropriating the world of labor into her commodifying designs. She is "dressed down in a faux work shirt," wearing "matching stoker's cap," and "shoes designed to resemble work boots only not so much that it wouldn't be obvious that she didn't actually 'work.' . . . her faux work boots were too petite to contain the steel reinforcing that real boots needed to protect toes from being crushed by a dropped beam" (73). Designer converts real function into functionless fashion. On the other hand, Composer illustrates how one's alienation from the world of bodily labor can *inadvertently* convert function into fashion: though he and Mechanic buy their shirts at the same "resale and vintage boutiques of gas-station attendant uniforms and high-voltage-proof hip-waders, the work shirts that Mechanic wore looked like work shirts, while Composer's work shirts somehow came off as fashion" (73). The same signs signify differently depending on the experiences and uses of the body employing them. Thus, it is Composer's own limited experience of physical labor in the world that limits his understanding and therefore also the works of art he produces, in their ability to shape the material world and represent material relations.

Mechanic learns from this bar talk "the idea that art could shape its viewer" (80). But he knows from growing up in IN what the other, OZ-bred artists never will: how art necessarily arises from hands that have been shaped by the world. His embodied way of understanding the other artists' cerebral concepts of art is evident throughout the bar scene, not through anything he says but from what he notices as the others talk. He observes in the surrounding scene, which is mere window-dressing for the others, evidence of the hard lives lived by residents of IN. While Composer pontificates about aesthetics impacting the world, Mechanic notes the massive forearms of the sheet-metal worker and the protective paunch of the jackhammer operator, and he understands that the men's ferocious fist fight erupts not because of an adolescent prank but rather "because their bodies had been in the bargain, the big guy going nuts over the graffiti of chalk, his body being something so not-to-fuck-with because during the rest of the week all of their bodies were little more than tools that the factories they worked in would slowly consume" (79). While the others theorize art's ability to affect the world, while producing objects that either refuse to perform that impact (Composer's silent, alienating music; Photographer's mental pictures) or fail to be true art (Designer's commodified, invisible cars), Mechanic learns to make art that does not "shape its viewer" in the dominating way of labor and modes of production, but that instead allows its viewer to become aware of the various ways in which she is forever shaped by the world and by art. Mechanic's unusable cars point to our assumptions about the systems that constitute a car and make us see how each piece does its work, just as the "visual sonnet" he composes for Designer—a bouquet of car parts salvaged from the automobiles she designed—means to make her invisible cars and the labor they do and that produced them visible again. The art disgusts her, of course; what he creates as an ode to her as creator of Carness, she reads as "butchered parts of her children" (117), in a fundamental disagreement about what exactly it is that art creates or destroys.

If, in the language of Gramsci,[8] Mechanic is an organic intellectual and Designer an unabashedly traditional intellectual, Composer, in his unconvincingly worn work clothes, presents a more dangerous, insidious version of the latter. His collaboration with Designer by novel's end indicates that he replaces his romantic rejection of birthright and assertion of artistic independence with grateful acceptance of his place on the world's consuming stage. More damning still is the story about humanity's relationship to art-making with which he leaves us at the end of the novel. In a book that is already a parable about the dilemma of making art in a commodifying world, the three parables about ways of seeing and representing the world stand out as conspicuous devices for exploring that dilemma. Composer's later parable comes as a pessimistic rebuttal to the more productive theory of art espoused by Photographer, and by the novel. Expanding on the "Adam's Peak" image alluded to in *VAS*, Photographer explains that he moved his house to the "highest point around, even higher than OZ" in order to approximate that point "protruding from The Garden of Eden" from which "Adam could hold the entire world in one, unframed view" (129)—the artist's holy grail. When the sprawl of OZ and his own oncoming blindness conspire to teach him the impossibility of such a total view, he realizes that "the Sur myth for an artist is not the story of Adam's Peak . . . but The Tower of Babel" (131), which he reads as teaching these lessons: "resolve yourself to an earnestness of such intensity that you will succeed gloriously—or fail so tragically that your failure will become legendary as success," and "live where you work . . . work where you live" (132). In advising Mechanic to do earnestly what he loves and to live where he works, he advises Mechanic to resist commodifying culture by maintaining an identity between self and work that will protect his sense of self and make his work meaningful. Photographer's subsequent repetition of this advice in "some six thousand living languages," a surprising assortment of them painstakingly represented in the text in alphabetic and logographic characters, lends his parable the same power and earnestness that he urges Mechanic to adopt.

This advice resonates backward to a moment when Mechanic, whose home is his garage as Photographer's is his camera, hears Designer complain of her twenty-mile commute to work and innocently asks, "why don't you live closer to your work?" (54). Thus the novel aligns this Marxist work-art-self identity with a philosophy about art that Photographer lives, Mechanic learns, and Composer and Designer will never understand. Instead, Composer counters Photographer's evolution from Adam's Peak to the Tower of Babel with his story of the "Tunnel of Babble," dug to "undermine the foundations of not only their own tower but of all buildings," to bring down institutions, "the deconstruction of Babel" leading to "the lesson we live with to this day: Which is to say, I just can't say what is right any more" (138). It is impossible to read a Tomasula novel and conclude that this ultimate skepticism of meaning and value, beyond multiplication and decentralization and into destruction, is what his fiction intends. As much as his work insists on the relativity and multiplicity of meaning, the futility of fully articulating reality or of fully getting outside the biased frameworks necessary to express it, his fiction also insists that, at the least, this exposure of frameworks of meaning is one kind of truth art can aim for, and is the crucial job of art.

Whereas Tomasula ends Composer's intervention in Mechanic's education about art with this fantasy of total deconstruction, we leave Mechanic in yet another *physical* discovery of how the world stamps itself on us in ways we can't help but perpetuate, and how our art must be born of and participate in this material shaping. He aids in the births of two puppies, which "looked exactly like the other ones, exactly like the mother, and the father," and marvels at the materializing destiny of biology: "Not one bird. Not one cat" (141). This hand that birthed the dogs he then recognizes as "the most essential part of his art," just before crushing it in his counterweight. When he then catches Poet/Sculptor in the act of creating a poem from the dirt of his yard, recognizes the "beauty" and "simple logic" of her broken bike, and gestures to fix it with his broken hand, Poet's immediate attention to both hand and injury signals a collaboration of selves and ideas of art that directly opposes the commodifying affair of Designer and Composer. In the end, Mechanic sees art as exposing the essence of being as constituted by labor, function, the body, and home, and of the self crucially in relation with the other.

The Science of Art

While *IN&OZ* explores the more obvious threat to self and art posed by our commodifying age and its denial of the impact of class difference and the erasure of difference between art and commodity, Tomasula's first novel, *VAS*, examines the dangers of a more insidious form of ideology: science. The novel does for science what DeLillo's *White Noise* did for technology nearly twenty years earlier, demonstrating the ubiquity of scientific systems and products in our material quotidian experience, and exposing how our constant exposure to scientific methodology has allowed it to dominate our ways of representing the world to ourselves. In the world of *VAS*, the simulacrum of science has taken the place of the elusive Real. The novel opens and closes with an empirical example of the natural body readily absorbing and being visibly altered by scientific technique: Square's daughter's originally white carnation, transformed by "TV-red" water, carried by Square in his pocket in the book's last pages as he submits his own body to alteration via medical technique (10, 366). Later definitions of the Greek roots of "chromosome"—color (*chroma*) and body (*soma*)—reinforce the analogy. As our genetic elements color our bodies, so do our scientific stories about those elements color our understanding of the world we live in, and what is true. *VAS* insists that science is an evolving collection of stories, a narrative whose facts change as surely as do its forms, according to the assumptions of other frameworks of understanding that inform it: "How odd it was to go into a library and find the crumbling volumes of *The Eugenics Review* and other learned sciences now so completely dismissed that coming upon their artifacts was as startling and enigmatic as coming upon pyramids and great stone heads" (18). Science is reduced to the status of culture and religion, composed of irrational conviction and mass opinion, a "history of failed theories" that progresses by eliminating the problems it cannot solve or explain using its own limited, flawed framework of understanding (87). As Square realizes when contemplating the constellations, science can only present what seems like a complete picture of the Real when we ignore its gaps and outliers, as we do when we locate pictures of ourselves in the night sky. And it is so often pictures of ourselves we are looking for, and perhaps always it is our own visions of ourselves that we see. Like *The Book of Portraiture*, *VAS* points to the many ways that science is simply another human-made framework for understanding the world that can only return the human expectations and assumptions that make up the framework—that science is a portrait, and that "every portrait is and can only be a self-portrait" (*Book* 84). By novel's end, Square understands that this human imposition of its own face and expectations is one constant in the ever-changing story of truth told by science: "Like the thick glass lens Leeuwenhoek squinted through to see his own face on spermatozoa, the biochips would only give up what reflections the mind would let him, it being impossible for anyone to be from a time other than the time they were from" (365).[9]

As in all of his work so far, Tomasula goes beyond identifying the domination of truth by ideological narrative to exposing how language shapes ideologies. In *VAS*, science is made of language, is a matter of language. In an attempt to "step out of [his] diorama and look back at what [he] assume[s] to be normal," to get to some kind of nature that is "beyond the pictures" of his *Grant's Anatomy* (158, 168), Square kills and dissects a female Australopithecus. But instead of something true, he finds the many ways in which what we see and understand is governed by what we say about it, that "to name was to impose an order" and "to catalog was to see differently" (171). The true, unrepresented Real remains inaccessible even through the opened body: "the Origin" that he seeks in the woman's womb is no more real than is the representation of the boy who represented "The Origin" of humanity in "The Hall of Man" he visited as a child (29). It is only "a pink tissue bag," a "silky purse," empty of the narratives that give it power (169). Meanwhile, these languages that bestow power and meaning themselves gain or lose power to name according to struggles for power in the physical world. The novel observes that "within 90 years, another 3,000 languages are expected to be found nowhere but in museum display cases" and that "two thirds of all scientists worldwide [are] now writing in English" (77, 80). It thus links the historical culling of languages to the increasingly rapid homogenizing of versions of truth available for debate, with English of course leading the way in this verbal colonization of the world.

Contemporary science makes this process easy and invisible, having become a kind of language itself. The novel draws many equations between the letters it comprises and the ones that spell the body through the genetic alphabet, most directly when it gives 25 of its pages over to the linguistic representation of one gene (into which it inserts, barely visibly, "THE FACTS," 225). In the language of genes, mutations are simply "typos" (67), materializing in disease the aberrations of the telephone game, so that the human body and the human story are equally shaped by the change inherent in repetition, equally apocryphal. From this linguistic point of view, the body is "the species of free verse Darwin had helped midwife," and "all life spoke the same language, written in the same genetic letters and could be parsed like tenses" (179). After decades of fiction that frets over language's domination over the world of the human,[10] *VAS* describes the human body itself as vulnerable to the problems of inscription and translation of the language that constitutes it.

If, as the novel suggests, genes are "the material of people," and people the "material of families," and families the "material of society" (251), then the language of genes determines the reality of society, and whoever controls one controls the other. "Eugenics" then becomes a word in need of redefinition, as it describes not an outdated set of morally reprehensible practices used by less enlightened people in less enlightened times and places, but rather everything done by a society that views the language of genetics as a tool for affecting the means or outcome of human reproduction. Whether equating Hitler's attempted genocide with Churchill's and Washington's support for selective breeding (97, 96, 108), or comparing today's technological methods of gene manipulation and reproductive assistance with the Middle Ages' exiling of "undesirables" on a "ship of fools" (232) (and to our contemporary exiling of the old and infirm to nursing homes, 294), *VAS* asserts that those in power have always attempted to exert that power to shape the individual and society at the level of the body, and that today's technologies of genetic manipulation make that power increasingly effective and invisible by working in the language of the gene. Genetic manipulation is today's method of translating concepts of what makes a "desirable" human (dictated by those with the means to impose them, whether wealthy couples choosing the characteristics of their offspring or governments dictating reproductive rights, 122) into bodies, of making ideology material.[11] Like Mechanic's discovery about the relationship between labor and art and Velázquez's discovery about perspective and portraiture, Square's narrative is a process of making these invisible workings of science visible in the art he creates.

But *VAS* is also full of more macro, visible ways in which scientific technology alters bodies and thus dictates what it is to be human according to the culture's current definitions of human and animal. Square's impending vasectomy,[12] which he mentally resists throughout the novel and yet physically succumbs to on its last page, is one example that propels the entire narrative as Square contemplates the many ways we use technology to alter human reproduction in both means and outcome. Thus the novel becomes a kind of twenty-first-century narrativizing of Walter Benjamin's modernist redefinition of art and its potential for carrying ideology in the age of technological reproduction. In the age of the technological reproduction of the human being, whose reproduction threatens to become inseparable from technology and so an extension of the ideology that creates and disperses the technology, the role of art in carrying and/or exposing ideology becomes even more complicated and significant than it was for Benjamin. Square's response to the dilemma of the "vas" is to create art—the book we are reading—as a method of examining what it means to alter his body in such a way; the codex[13] of quotations, photographs, forms, graphs, and other historical and cultural documents about sexual and technological reproduction, genetic manipulation, cultural norms of beauty and ideas about truth, and historical and scientific and medical practices, which he gathers and inserts into his own narrative, argues with evidence the premise that his own narrative strives to understand: that all of our bodies are subject to remaking according to the concepts of humanness wielded by science, and thus wielded by those in power.

But Square ultimately understands the dilemma at play in writing a narrative in order to make visible the ways in which other narratives, like science and history, bend us and our bodies into their points of view, as the painted cross forces the Christian to kneel. After all, as he points out, "The first natural history museum in America began as an art gallery no one would have heard of it its owner didn't see the light" (284): art and history have always been two faces of the same mediation of the Real. How, then, to use art, specifically narrative, to expose the mediation of science?

Ultimately Tomasula asserts that art must both separate itself from the dominant ideological narrative and expose its own inherently ideological narrative work. Sitting in the clinic, awaiting his vasectomy, Square sees a collection of antique microscopes and considers how much of the "truth" they revealed to their users in their time has become eclipsed—falsified—by the technologies of today, whose own "truths" will one day become equally quaint, will become "history or art . . . not technology" (365). He realizes that only in their *un*usefulness, in their inability to perform acts of meaning-making consistent with the epistemological system that produced them (to "naturalize" them, as Jonathon Culler explained Realism[14]) can they expose the limits and framework of that system in which they no longer seamlessly belong, and so, like Mechanic's undriveable car and Poet/Sculptor's unrideable bike, say something true. "If his story, or any art, was to compete with surgery, it was in this way, he realized" (365): in order to convey truth that is as compelling as the "truths" of a society's dominant narrative, story and art must refuse to operate in the system of that dominant narrative, and must represent things and bodies in ways that are outside of their usefulness by that system and culture. Art must do for the body and thing what its techniques, according to Shklovsky, must do to its ideas and concepts: it must *defamiliarize* them, make the familiar strange and therefore visible.[15] Tomasula's book does this by failing to perform any of the mimetic devices of Realist fiction that offer the text as substitute for reality, as immediate, unmediated, unbiased, and true.

Square's own book within *VAS*, however, is less successful, in that his equated story and life end in equal failure. Not only does the book leave him aware of being trapped in his book, but he also winds up trapped in his wife's narrative, which leads inexorably to the vasectomy she insists on and he submits to, and which submits his reproductive power to technological destruction. In this way, the process of producing the book has been a process of castration, the final physical loss of manly power a materialization of the symbolic castration that has been unfolding for Square all along, as he repeatedly submits to his wife Circle's will, gives up his job for hers and then finds he has nothing productive to do at home, and then fills the emptiness with the writing that he will ultimately find equally disempowering: "his sail was a blank whiteness and his oar a pen and he began to write, *First pain, then knowledge*. . . . Of course castration imagery came to mind" (286). He can write no story for himself that will give him the power fully to make himself; always his life is made by other frameworks of narration. In allowing Square to discover through writing his inability to represent and control the thing he is after—whether truth about the world or his own sense of self—Tomasula makes narrative function productively in demonstrating the unproductivity of narrative.

That Square's narrative attempts to point to an unnarrativized Real lead to a physical loss of male reproductive power that is also a metaphorical castration invokes a telling comparison, between Square's understanding of his loss of the Real, and a Lacanian notion of the phallus as lost connection to the Real. *VAS* argues throughout not that narrative—whether scientific or literary—fails adequately to capture an ideal and available reality, but that the only reality we have access to as beings who know the self and world through language is the reality of the linguistic structure of knowledge that bars us from unmediated experience. In this way, the Real that escapes the various narrative and ideological attempts to package it is the *objet petit a* that both resists signification and is constituted as loss through the process of signification. To this missing thing that is not a thing but is a consequence of the structure of language and of the subject's dependence on language for knowledge, Lacan assigns the signifier of the phallus, whose loss we sense in our inability to come to total knowledge of the self, or to experience the self or the body immediately, rather than through language and in relation to the other. Lacan's "The Signification of the Phallus"[16] commits obvious offenses as a statement on gender difference and on human beings' roles in the process of coming to knowledge through signification. Still, it is admirably efficient in connecting to each other the consequences to subjectivity of dialectical and linguistic knowledge, the unfulfillable desire for completeness of self, and the variety of ways we displace that desire through acts of signification. In *VAS*, Square's narrative is both proof of Realist narrative's deceit in hiding that endless deferral of desire, and itself a failure to escape that desire for narrative satisfaction: both the book and his narrative end in the loss of the phallus.[17] Thus *VAS* expresses critique by critiquing its ability to critique, and points to the Real by demonstrating its absence, or the ways in which all narrative attempts to preserve it end in its loss. Its art must compete with the surgery not only of science but also of technologically advanced art, which, as Benjamin pointed out even before the postmodern age, pretends to stitch together a new and improved reality no less than does the surgeon's knife.[18] Tomasula's manipulation of the book's formal and physical dimensions to mount that critique of ideology and of art's complicity with it acknowledges his deliberate intervention in an evolving intimacy among art, ideological power, and the material conditions of the world.

The Work of Art after the Mechanical Age: The History of Form

The titles of three texts spanning modernism, postmodernism, and "post-postmodernism" announce their reflection on how changing modes of production evolve the role of art in society and shape the work it can do. First, Walter Benjamin's "The Work of Art in the Age of Mechanical[19] Reproduction" (1936) famously reevaluated for modernism the role, abilities, and risks of art that could be mass-produced by machine rather than painstakingly by human hand. Writing in a new cultural and literary period, Donald Barthelme's short story "At the End of the Mechanical Age" (1976) asks to be read in the context of Benjamin's essay, as a demonstration of the greatly diminished capacity of art to be meaningful as we move beyond even the age of mechanical reproduction and into the age of "metaphor." The narrative of his story is only a skeleton—assembling the bare bones of two people meeting, marrying, divorcing, and having a child, in that discombobulated order, and his characters are similarly skeletal, lacking interiority, acting as frames that carry the plots we have come to substitute for our lives. At the end of postmodernism, David Foster Wallace's "A Radically Condensed History of Post-Industrial Life" opens his short story collection *Brief Interviews with Hideous Men* (1999), framing the book's central dilemma—the near impossibility of sincerity—in the context of late-capitalist, post-mechanical society. "Post-industrial" signifies a changed mode of production in the Marxist sense, beyond a mere change in modes of technological reproduction; it also signifies the changed social relations that come with such a wholesale restructuring of society's economic base in which commodities constitute the economy, their material origins so few and powerless as to have all but disappeared. As a "History," Wallace's story implies that we have been post-industrial for a long time, long enough for the transformation from material relationships between products and people to virtual ones between commodities and information to have wholly reshaped the position of humans in relation to society and to each other. These three texts chart a clear movement: from the loss of the aura of the work of art and art's subsequent liberation from its enslavement to ritual; to the questioning of art's (especially narrative's) ability to communicate anything but itself and its forms; to the crises of subjectivity and relations with the other that result from our unreflective entrapment in the forms of art.

When Square compares art to surgery at the end of *VAS*, he suggests a very different relationship between art and science, and thus a different set of potentials for art, than does Benjamin when he uses a similar analogy at the end of his essay about art in an age of technological reproduction. Benjamin compares the surgeon to the filmmaker, opposing them to the magician and painter, in that the painter "maintains in his work a natural distance from reality, whereas the cinematographer penetrates deeply into its tissue." This penetration of reality by film, which he also describes as "the most intensive interpenetration of reality with equipment,"[20] Benjamin credits with an ability to represent the world more extensively, in greater depth and detail, and more truly than has any other mode of art: "Clearly, it is another nature which speaks to the [motion-picture] camera as compared to the eye," exposing through close-up and slow motion a degree of reality never before observed. This "reality" he accepts as unproblematic, a cognate of "nature," leading him to predict that "*Demonstrating that the artistic uses of photography are identical to its scientific uses—these two dimensions having usually been separated until now—will be one of the revolutionary functions of film.*"[21] For Benjamin, art in the age of technological reproduction has the capacity not just to transmit true knowledge about the real world, but also to uncover knowledge about the physical world that had hitherto been unavailable. "Emancipate[d]" from "its parasitic subservience to ritual," the technologically produced work of art can express more than its aura (as does an original, pre-technological work of art in its original context), can generate more than a social relationship between artist and viewer (as does a live theater performance). Art devoid of aura and ritual use, like the film, can instead present not the reality specific to the work of art or artist but a reality contained in the world.

But this reality is, like the patient's body after submitting to the surgeon's knife, different than it was before the intervention, cut into pieces that are then reorganized into a different whole: "the illusory nature of film is of the second degree; it is the result of editing... the equipment-free aspect of reality has here become the height of artifice, and the vision of immediate reality the Blue Flower in the land of technology."[22] Thus the "interpenetration of art and science" seems to suggest an elevation of art to the level of science, to the level of objectively capturing and allowing meaningful study of the world, while the technology of film also obscures the mediation involved in the construction of that reality. Benjamin's flower is *VAS*'s carnation, only blue, and read with more admiration than abhorrence.

This contradiction in the abilities of technological art lies at the heart of Benjamin's predictions for the future capacities of art. On one hand, his essay celebrates the revolutionary potential of film to fully accomplish what the Dadaists strived for when they "turned the artwork into a missile." Film for Benjamin produces "shock effects" beyond what static art can do, causing the kind of "shock" or "shudder" of the I for which Adorno praised modern art: "'I can no longer think what I want to think. My thoughts have been replaced by moving images.'"[23] Such simultaneous distraction from the I and attention to both the work of art and the collective experience of the work of art that Benjamin claims is characteristic of film results in *"reception in distraction*,*"* which Benjamin identifies as the primary tool of technological art to communicate meaning beyond the self's reflection on itself and on the limited ritual use of the unique work of art. On the other hand, Benjamin's "Epilogue" about the violent consequences of aestheticized art points to the dangerous potential of such reception in distraction, the potential of art to feed ideology disguised by the techniques of art as aesthetics to the distracted masses. Benjamin's solution to this problem is to politicize art—to make art's ideology visible, to align technique with ideology.

Mechanic makes ideology the visible goal of his technique when he creates functionless art that points to the labor behind the art and the function made absent by transforming cars into works of art. Velázquez does the same when he produces a painting that includes the viewer, implies its framing of the viewer's point of view, asserts its production of its own reflected point of view, and demonstrates its domination (and equation) of subject and viewer by displacing the king and queen into an infinity of reflection. That is to say, Tomasula's art shares with Benjamin the aims of shattering aura, freeing art from ideologically determined cult value, and foregrounding the ideological content that Benjamin discovered for film. But it accomplishes these aims by insistently nonfilmic methods, and according to a different understanding of the relationship between technology and art. For Square, technological penetration of reality, specifically surgery, means not the liberation of art from aura but the excision of humanity from the human body. *The Strange Voyage of Imagining Chatter*, the opera within the opera of *VAS*, traces an evolution of modes of art from primitive (nature sounds and chatter) to Realistic (artistic representation of the real) to anti-Realistic (exposure of the tricks of representation), culminating in a projected future, or an extreme version of the present, in which the manipulations of the body by science create a new human body and thus new paradigms for beauty and art. This final act does not represent such a future but embodies it, through the live surgical swapping of the heads of two monkeys, which Square renders in drawings reminiscent of the centerpiece of the Sistine Chapel—a new creation myth. In this vision, surgical penetration and manipulations of the material real as the ultimate technology of science and accomplishment of technological art is a nightmare, not a revelation. It is a use of technology not dreamt of in Benjamin's philosophy, and an example of how far technology itself, and its effects on reproduction and manipulation of art and the human, have evolved since Benjamin's essay.

As in that essay, however, technology and means of technological reproduction in *VAS* are not static; they are *forms* whose manifestations change over time as our expertise in developing technology and our desires for using technology change—just as art changes in form according to evolutions in technology. So the antique microscopes displayed in Square's doctor's office are now "history or art now, not technology," just as his own body is now "passé except as philosophy." Technology in *VAS* has so thoroughly penetrated the real—the human body—in its ability to manipulate and reproduce it on the genetic level that technology has begun to supersede the body, to make the real, unaltered human body a thing of art apart from the real, so that the technological body begins to become a simulacrum, a representation without real origin. It is this context in which Square realizes that his art must "compete with surgery" in the way of the antique microscope, whose unscientific biases—Leeuwenhoek seeing his own face in spermatozoa (365)—we can see only now that we view the mechanism as art, outside the framework of technology. Art's ability to affect the body, our ideas of humanness, and the material world we produce with those ideas depend on our ability to hold art apart from science and its ideological manipulation of our ideas and its physical manipulation of the human body. Thus art must preserve the materiality of the human body and our concepts of it as apart from the surgical interventions of science and the uses to which science would put it. It must continually call attention to the difference between body and ideology, body and narrative, and assert the importance of the material in a world becoming increasingly virtual.

Tomasula draws attention to the material in an increasingly digital world even in the bodies of his books. He does so perhaps most obviously in *VAS* and *The Book of Portraiture*, whose innovative textual designs so clearly depend on their print medium.[24] But he also asserts the importance of physical form when he describes his DVD novel *TOC* as comprising the viewer's readerly encounter with its collage of materials: "it is still a book: unlike a film, it is read as well as watched; like a book (and unlike a film), it is interactive."[25] Perhaps most noteworthy, because most unexpected, are Tomasula's methods of privileging the material medium in his most narratively straightforward book, *IN&OZ*: six pages repeating "$1.00" do more than convert Mechanic's toll-booth tedium into a foregrounding of mimetic devices; by boring the reader across the time and space of serially pointless page-flips, they materialize Mechanic's boredom. Their radical break from novelistic conventions of signification—like the spelled-out gene sequence in *VAS*, or the pointlessly described page flips of *The Pale King*—also pulls the reader out of the narrative to see the book she holds in her hands, its pages filled with confounding rather than naturalizable symbols.

Photographer's impressive linguistic display in Chapter 23, in which he repeats the Marxist motto "Live where you work . . . work where you live" in many of the earth's languages, accomplishes a similar defamiliarization of signification, which points to both our need for a material experience of language and ways in which the novel simultaneously provides and denies it. A cursory glance at the pages filled with examples of alphabetic, pictographic, ideogrammatic and body-dependent translations of the sentences reveals how variously linguistic systems relate signifiers to signifieds, and how far the novel can remove us from the material world, when its signifiers constitute not only signs (letters, pictographs) but also signs for signs (drawings of hand symbols, Morse code, Braille). Meanwhile, the languages represented try to assert their physical presence in the world, by occupying the space of the pages in obviously differing ways. Photographer even seems to assert his own impossible ability to speak them all equally well with his body: quotation marks enclose every iteration of the sentences, even those rendered in hand symbols and hieroglyphs, signifiers that are not usually accompanied by sounds. But the silence of those signifiers and the flatness of the Braille dots remind us of the enormous gap between what the character and novel pretend to represent and the novel's linguistic system of representing it.

Then perhaps it is not surprising that the novel's most eloquent expression of the futility of signs for their own sake comes in the chapter that contains the least written language. Arriving on the heels of the discussion between Mechanic and Designer about their different visions of cars and art—as separate from versus instruments of ideology and commodification—Chapter 12 quietly sides with Mechanic by offering a series of drawings of billboards, whose only redeeming function might be said to be their utter functionlessness as agents of consumerism. These drawings of signs encourage us to read their inherent pun from the first image that demands that we (or the billboards) "Stop Making Cents." The chapter then proceeds to deconstruct the signifier-signified relationship by presenting signs incapable of pointing to anything outside their own impotence: "THIS IS NOT A BILLBOARD," "BILLBOARD!" and "BILL bored" is most of what they have to say. The signs are also quite clearly caught up in the obsessive, solipsistic, self-referential system of signification; in the last two drawings of tightly packed billboards that face each other, the signs can say these things only to each other. In one grouping, support poles of one billboard impede the display of another, resulting in a billboard turned into an "illboard" by the sign that suggests its treatment: "Rx DOSIM REPETATUR," or "treatment dose to be repeated."

At face value, this sign suggests that the only treatment for the illness of consumerist marketing is ingesting more of the same in an endless cycle. But as a sign pointing to yet another sign, the phrase insinuates still more. Its Latin recalls a treatment for a woman's anxiety as suggested by gynecologist Rudolf Chrobak (and noted by Freud in *The History of the Psychoanalytic Movement*): "Penis normalis, dosim Repetatur," or "normal penis, dose to be repeated." The connection between sex, consumerism, and repetitive back-and-forth action is developed by another set of signs in the grouping, whose pole for the "BALLS" sign converts "BILLBOARD!" to "BILL IARD!," complete with a phallic tip. When billboards bore themselves with their own solipsistic, even masturbatory self-referentiality, they critique not just the self-perpetuating cycle of consumerism in which they participate, but also any system of signification that understands them as meaningful, that see them as signs rather than as simply things—which is to say, signs. It's a clever joke, complicated further by the fact that Tomasula makes it using drawings of signs, not words, so that this invasion of narrative by a sign (drawing) depicts a thing (billboard) that fails to function as—or functions only as?—a sign ("This is not a billboard"). What is a sign that refuses to signify? What is the use of signification disconnected from the material world? *IN&OZ* answers that question with all its material ways of meaning, most holistically by using its own physical form to shape the way it signifies. Tall and thin between narrow covers, the book recalls an art book much more than novel: is it a novel about art? Or a piece of art about the novel?

Such assertive embodiedness amplifies the many formal and thematic ways that Tomasula's fiction accomplishes its insistent materiality—emphasizing the physical body and its labor, drawing attention to gaps between the physical world and representations of it, and alerting readers to the tension between narrative's capacity to absorb the reader into the ideology through which its techniques become meaningful, and its ability to reflect upon that tendency inherent in narrative. It is the need for this tension as a mechanism for avoiding the distraction used by narrative to absorb the reader that further differentiates Tomasula's revolutionary methods of print art from Benjamin's vision for revolutionary film. Rather than "reception in distraction," Tomasula employs methods espoused by Theodor Adorno, who argued that "to catch even the slightest glimpse beyond the prison that it itself is, the I requires not distraction but rather the utmost tension."[26] Unlike Benjamin's "spontaneous collective experience" of film,[27] Tomasula's novels require the individual reader to do the difficult work of making meaning through methods of representation that seek not to reproduce a world for the reader to inhabit but to reflect on the concepts and delivery systems of those concepts that shape her world. And they preserve the importance of the individual by requiring an individual experience of the art, as Tomasula emphasizes in his description of reading *TOC*: "Whether a user is reading or watching *TOC* . . . it retains the one-on-one intimacy that a reader has with a book."[28]

Thus, Tomasula's fiction asks to be read as Fredric Jameson proposes reading in "The Political Unconscious"—invoking "metacommentary," or an examination of the "master codes" it perceives in society and uses in its own making rather than interpretation that remains blind to the codes that make it meaningful. Tomasula's works present themselves as cultural artifacts, drawing attention to acts of reading and social structures that shape the text and shape our naturalizing of the text, rather than as aspects of literariness that reproduce a total meaning lying either in- or outside the text. Their methods of doing that work also allow his fiction to resist the "strategies of containment" that Jameson sees texts as using to "project the illusion that their readings are complete."[29] Similarly, his texts refuse to act as element or instrument of today's dominant mode of production, late capitalism, and, further, present neither contained symbolic acts in response to a particular historical moment, nor simply evidence of the workings of a particular ideology in a particular historical society. Rather, Tomasula's texts, by collectively exposing the ideologies of science, consumerism, history, religion, time, and art itself, take as their topic Jameson's concept of history as "the inexorable *form* of events,"[30] making visible not just a collection of discrete ideologies that shape our lives but the condition of form, of framing, of forces that constitute the human experience and that we create, inescapably, much as the characters of *TOC* continually reinscribe their own mortality by creating the universe as Time.

The Future of Form

In his 2010 essay on "innovative literature," Tomasula articulates in theory what I have aimed to show through these readings of his work, that literature can reflect upon the cultural forces that shape it by reflecting on its own form. Innovative literature, according to Tomasula, "takes its own medium as part of its subject matter, . . . or works out of assumptions, including those about literature, other than those of the status quo or mainstream." In contrast to the "traditional novel with its emphasis on authenticity, craft, transparency of language, sentiment, and the text as *trompe l'oeil*, the innovative novel would be the novel more interested in exploring the possibilities of form, the limits of language: a type of literature suggested by Sterne's *Tristram Shandy* that emphasizes text as medium, the material nature of language, and the role of these materials themselves in shaping what we think we know." Its primary goal in exploring possibilities of its own form is to show how "literary form . . . both reflects and emerges from its historical moment" and "embodies epistemological, or ontological positions, or otherwise articulates convictions about how the world works." Innovative or "conceptual" writing, in emphasizing this connection between literary form and the social forms that produce it, "is as often as not an exploration of how these elements come together to help bring the present into being."[31]

Such an approach to writing and reading literature is, as I have argued above, an extension of evolving Marxist-materialist methods of reading texts as expressing and shaped by assumptions of the dominant ideologies of the society in which the texts were produced, and of reading texts as cultural artifacts of those societies (*The Book of Portraiture* as archeological dig). But it is an extension of culturally based ways of reading that are crucially grounded in formalist ones. In this way, Tomasula's fiction, and innovative literature in general, relies on a meeting of the tenets of formalism—reading form as content and the techniques of form as the primary subject of literary criticism—with the fundamental objection to formalism's naïve intrinsicness and self-possession that pushed theory in a variety of ways toward concerns "exterior" to the text. This literature, as Tomasula describes it, seems "to have absorbed the fallout over story form, originality, authorship, and the other hot buttons of an earlier generation the way an earlier generation of writers might have absorbed assumptions about the unconscious with or without ever having read Freud, or the way female pilots flying combat missions embody current assumptions about women without having read Hélène Cixous."[32] One suspects that many writers of innovative fiction have in fact read not just Freud but also Marx, Jameson, Lacan, and perhaps Claude Lévi-Strauss, Hayden White, and Gilles Deleuze, but in any case his point is that certainly culture and especially academic literary culture have absorbed the throughline of theory that has divorced language from direct meaning and discovered ideology in narrative, and narrative everywhere. One of the great tricks of innovative literature, then, is its insistent reminder of the importance of form as the way texts operate in the nexus of cultural assumptions they absorb and/or comment on; it illustrates that no reading of a text is complete without paying due attention to both. As Tomasula points out, "though authors of innovative literature today may draw heavily from popular forms, they tenaciously hold onto the belief that aesthetics matter, and therein lies the difference between literature and other kinds of vernacular loveliness.... They exhibit a (retrograde?) belief that the difference between literature and entertainment or other kinds of writing is the writing, [or,] an intense attention to language."[33]

Perhaps more promising still for the future of literary studies is Tomasula's assertion that innovative literature's ability to reveal form's relationship to ideology will keep the book—and specifically the *print* book—viable in an increasingly digital world. "At a time when the book is being transformed more than it ever has been since Johannes Gutenberg," Tomasula writes, the newly technological and collaborative model of writing "won't mean the end of printed books...rather, it allows some books to be more themselves in the way that photography freed painting to be more itself, i.e., to do things that only painting can do better than any other medium."[34] New and old forms of the book will "remediate each other," as painting and photography do, the latter freeing the former to be "less about documentation" (depicting kings and queens, for example) and more about painting itself; Tomasula demonstrates just this remediation via Velázquez in *Book*. He imagines next evolutions of book forms allowing print books to "become more about their materials, the experience of reading"—perhaps freeing print books from their own historical dictate to "document" reality like the "mirror traveling down the road of life" of Stendhal.[35] Instead of a collection of mimetic tricks, pointing away from narrative's sleight of hand and to a *trompe l'oeil* of the world, books can point to the genre of the print novel itself, and ask how it does the work that it does in relation to other genres and other literary and nonliterary acts of narrative. This is exactly the evolution of mimesis, realism, and materiality I will take up in the next chapter, on material realism.

Such a transformation in the form of books can produce a great boon, for printed books and for the study of literature. The printed book, as a "justification for printed paper,"[36] will differentiate itself from the kind of book that can be "poured into a paper or electronic container like the Kindle"[37] by asserting its materiality and primacy of form, and thus generate a new set of experiences for its readers, and change the relationship of author, reader, and text. Such changes are exactly what catalyze creation and revision in literary theory, in our evolving history of reading and textuality. While we may today scoff at the idea of an "ideal form" into which all existing texts—as if we can pinpoint each and all—nicely fit, we will never unlearn Eliot's revelation that every new text forces us to reread every other text, backward and forward.[38] The emergence of a new genre of insistently physical books at a time when literature, along with everything, begins to move into the digital, will change how we conceive of genre, form, and literature backward and forward in our history of literary form.

And so such literature will also be a great boon to theory and to the study of literature, by illuminating its relevance to our ways of conceptualizing the enormous transformation we are undergoing at the beginning of the twenty-first century, in modes of production—from mechanical to digital, from industrial to information—and in their attending ideological strategies. Books will maintain their status, or assert their newly influential status, as productive tools for registering and understanding human reactions and contributions to what is unfolding as a change in art, society, and their relationships to each other, a change that is at least as transformative as our entrance into the age of mechanical reproduction. Along with other contemporary writers informed by his techniques (as I will discuss in the next chapter), Tomasula is composing, dispersed fittingly across a network of acts of reading and writing, a new manifesto for the work of art after the mechanical age.

Notes

1 Tomasula, *The Book of Portraiture*, 284. *VAS: An Opera in Flatland* (Chicago: University of Chicago Press, 2002) uses similar wording on 167. I will note subsequent references to both books parenthetically.
2 Steve Tomasula, *IN&OZ* (Stirling, NJ: Ministry of Whimsy, 2003), 25. I will note subsequent references parenthetically.
3 Tomasula uses the same hammer analogy in *VAS* (365), attributing it to Heidegger.
4 Tomasula describes *TOC* as a book in "Electricians, Wig Makers, and Staging the New Novel," *American Book Review* 32, no. 6 (2011), 5.

5 Louis Althusser, "Ideology and Ideological State Apparatuses," in *The Norton Anthology of Theory and Criticism*, 2nd edn, ed. Vincent B. Leitch (New York: Norton, 2010), 1354.
6 The other chapters of *Book of Portraiture*, which range from the dawn of alphabetic writing to a future of genetic writing, make related assertions about the problems of Realist art. See my *Succeeding Postmodernism*, 156–9.
7 Tomasula's name for this wholly commodified city cleverly enlists the critique of commodification made by Frank Baum's original *Oz* series, as argued by Stuart Culver in "What Manikins Want: *The Wonderful World of Oz* and *The Art of Decorating Dry Goods Windows*," *Representations* 21 (1988): 97–116. His use of "Technicolor" to describe its fabricated vistas alludes to *The Wizard of Oz* film as one further step in the signifying chain of commodified fantasy.
8 Antonio Gramsci, "The Formation of Intellectuals," in *The Norton Anthology of Theory and Criticism*, 2nd ed., ed. Vincent B. Leitch (New York: Norton, 2010), 1002–8.
9 *VAS* connects this insight forward to the same one in *IN* by quoting Glenda, the good witch of Baum's Oz: "What is looked for is what is found" (248).
10 See, for example, "'Dead Souls Babbling': Language, Loss, and Community in *The Names* and *White Noise*," in *Succeeding Postmodernism: Language and Humanism in Contemporary American Literature* (New York: Bloomsbury, 2013).
11 Recent use (February 2019) by a Chinese researcher of CRISPR technology to edit the genes of human babies, however criticized by the wider scientific and medical community, makes Tomasula's warnings about the use of science to write bodies in terms of ideology all the more urgent.
12 Appropriately, the medical community in the novel refers to the surgery as a "vas," thus converting a conveyor ("vessel" or "duct") of reproductive potential into the surgical procedure that prevents reproduction.
13 The book's production, using a variety of page colors, fonts and fonts colors, and inserted reproductions of documents, implies that it comprises sheets from multiple sources, and from outside the narrative, from the "real world." This technique produces an immediacy, invokes the Real, by dividing the clearly unreal narrative Square is writing from the more real-seeming world outside that obvious fiction, a super anti-Realist method of producing realism that is becoming increasingly common in twenty-first-century literature.
14 Jonathan Culler, "Convention and Naturalization," in *Structuralist Poetics: Structuralism, Linguistics, and the Study of Literature* (Ithaca: Cornell University Press, 1975), 131–60.
15 See Victor Shklovsky's "Art as Device," in *Theory of Prose*, trans. Benjamin Sher (Champaign: Dalkey Archive Press, 1991).
16 Jacques Lacan, "The Signification of the Phallus," in *Écrits: A Selection*, trans. Alan Sheridan (New York: Norton, 1977), 181–91.

17 Similarly, in *TOC,* the Vogue model telling the story of Chronos feels a "chasm of incompletion" between the clock's tick and tock, and longs for "a Möbius-strip twist uniting time and desire."
18 Walter Benjamin, "The Work of Art in the Age of Its Technological Reproducibility," *The Norton Anthology of Theory and Criticism,* 2nd edn, ed. Vincent B. Leitch (New York: Norton, 2010), 1054.
19 Also translated as "technological reproducibility" by Harry Zohn and Edmund Jephcott, but for my purposes I like that Zohn's earlier translation preserves the physical machine in the term "mechanical."
20 Benjamin, "The Work of Art," 1054.
21 Ibid., 1066 (original italics).
22 Ibid., 1064.
23 Ibid., 1068.
24 Tomasula remarked in a 2011 interview that "I've always incorporated the materials of the book into the story. In *VAS*—a novel about the bio-tech revolution we are living through—I made a conscious effort to use the body of the book as a metaphor for the human body and vice versa; if you look at the edge of *The Book of Portraiture,* the pages appear as strata in an archeological dig, which evokes, I hope, the central idea of that novel: the archeology of human representation through layers of history that make up its chapters" (Yury Tarnawsky, "Not Just Text: An Interview with Steve Tomasula," *Raintaxi* 2011, https://www.raintaxi.com/not-just-text-an-interview-with-steve-tomasula/, April 2, 2013).
25 Tomasula, "Electricians," 5. When asked whether he thought of himself as writing a movie script when writing *TOC,* Tomasula again compared the digital book to the print medium: "No—maybe more like a graphic novel, or poetry that uses space as part of its poetics," and later, "I wrote it like any other text-only story for print publication" (Tarnawsky, "Not Just Text").
26 Tomasula's methods of insisting on particularity in art are also in line with Adorno's theory of the "the ugly, the beautiful, and technique." See *Aesthetic Theory,* trans. Robert Hullot-Kentor, ed. Gretel Adorno and Rolf Tiedemann (Minneapolis: University of Minnesota Press, 1997), 45–61 and 244–50.
27 Benjamin, "The Work of Art," 1069.
28 Tomasula, "Electricians," 5.
29 Fredric Jameson, from *The Political Unconscious: Narrative as a Socially Symbolic Act,* in *The Norton Anthology of Theory and Criticism*, 2nd edn., ed. by Vincent B. Leitch (New York: Norton, 2010), 1823.
30 Ibid., 1845.
31 Steve Tomasula, "Where We Are Now," *Études Anglaises,* 63, no.2 (2010): 217, 218, 220–1.
32 Ibid., 222.
33 Ibid., 223. Tomasula's defense of literariness, aesthetically defined, directly opposes Jeffrey Nealon's flat equation of literature, culture, and information, and preserves critical and theoretical space for a kind of literary studies that

I suspect such equation would obliterate. See *Post-postmodernism, or, The Cultural Logic of Just-in-Time Capitalism* (Palo Alto: Stanford University Press, 2012).

34 Tomasula, "Electricians," 5, 6.
35 Tomasula, "Where We Are Now," 217.
36 Tarnawsky, "Not Just Text," np.
37 Tomasula, "Electricians," 6.
38 T. S. Eliot, "Tradition and the Individual Talent," in *Selected Prose of T. S. Eliot*, ed. Frank Kermode (New York: Farrar, Straus, and Giroux, 1975).

3

Material Realism and New Materialism

Literature from the 1990s to the Present

Long before *The Blair Witch Project* (1999) sparked the *cinéma vérité* trend that has occupied film for over twenty years, writer William Gibson collaborated with artist Dennis Ashbaugh and publisher Kevin Begos, Jr. to produce art as found testimonial object. Published in 1992, the "deluxe" edition of *Agrippa (a book of the dead)* appears to be an unearthed, fire-scarred black box, containing a shrouded, partially burned manuscript bearing photographic and linguistic representations of DNA sequences— and a floppy disk. When run, the program on the disk generated a 300-line semi-autobiographical poem based on photographs held in Gibson's father's old album; upon completion, the poem disappeared through self-encryption. Likewise, the ink on the manuscript pages was designed to fade over time. Thus *Agrippa* simultaneously enacts our enduring faith in art as stand-in for the elusive past and material witness to reality, and our late twentieth-century anxiety that technology will make art, its testimony, and perhaps the material world disappear.

Once inalienable and thus invisible, textual materiality becomes, in a digital age against which it must redefine if not defend itself, a literary aspect demanding consideration by authors and readers alike. But self-conscious materiality did not arise in this "post-postmodern" age. While it might not date back to literature's own beginnings, like metafiction arising alongside fiction itself (see Chapter 2), writers have exploited the physical properties of books and language for centuries. Laurence Sterne used blank and black pages to draw attention to their ability to hold or exclude text (*Tristram Shandy*, 1759); William Blake made text three dimensional by blending image and text in engraved plates (*The Marriage of Heaven and Hell*, 1790); and Emily Dickinson in the late nineteenth century ate up whole manuscript pages with boldly wrought words and dashes that belied her poems' seeming meekness. But self-conscious materiality remained an unusual element of literature until it erupted with metafiction in the late 1960s, as modernist formal experimentation—especially an interest in things and the thingness of language, as in work by Gertrude Stein, Ezra Pound, James Joyce, and Samuel Beckett—collided with postmodern suspicion of textual authority and authorial control. As pioneering metafictive writers including John Barth, Donald Barthelme, and Robert Coover experimented primarily through narrative self-consciousness designed to make plain literary devices including plot, narrator, and perspective, other writers were reimagining generic and textual form by making visibly meaningful the *language* of which all texts are made, and the *visual and tactile* features of printed texts.

Indeed, the writer who coined the term "metafiction" in 1970, William H. Gass, often crafted his texts' self-consciousness through their attention to their own physicality. *Willie Masters' Lonesome Wife* (1968), for example, combines different page colors and fonts, images, and creative textual layout in conjunction with the text's awareness of itself as a physical object to create a novella that insists readers pay attention to its body while its narrative voice begs us to pay loving attention to hers. Meanwhile, Raymond Federman, who coined "surfiction" as a rival term for the contemporary trend of self-conscious fiction, constructed a novel whose concretizing typesetting does more storytelling than can its repetitive language (*Double or Nothing*, 1971). Diverse authors such as Kurt Vonnegut (*Breakfast of Champions*, 1973) and Ishmael Reed (*Mumbo Jumbo*, 1971) also expanded the period's anti-Realist innovations by incorporating images and documents, evidence of the material world smuggled into fiction. The British experimental writer B. S. Johnson took his material innovation off the page and into three dimensions, innovating on his books' physical forms: first he created a book whose cut-out pages create wormholes from one textual location and narrative moment to another (*Albert Angelo*, 1964); then he rejected physical containment altogether, with a novel made of twenty-seven loose packets which the reader is directed to shuffle, producing any number[1] of textual readings (*The Unfortunates*, 1969).

But the prevalence of materiality in literature in the "post-postmodern" period differs from these earlier appearances in quantity and quality. What amounted to an interesting but exceptional smattering of materially experimental texts in the late 1960s and early 1970s became an increasingly common feature of 1990s American writing, in increasingly diverse texts: men and women, prose and poetry, short story, novel, art book, and memoir, even children's books began to experiment with the physical qualities of language and of printed text. These many and varied experiments produced equally varied ways of paying attention to textual materiality in the "post-postmodern" period, which can be organized into two main types: texts that recognize the physicality of the medium that contains language, pointing to and often distorting the material aspects of the traditional print book; and those that emphasize the visual and physical properties of language on the page, and its ways of acting materially in the world or materializing the world in language.

The first type draws attention to the physical properties of printed texts as works of art, as things in the world, rather than allowing literature to become synonymous with transparent textuality. In the wake of Barthes's death of the work and the birth of the all-encompassing text, such books instantiate acts of language and of reading, reminding us of our own embodiment as we interact with books in time and space. Such physically assertive literature thus accomplishes what Susan Sontag called for in reaction to the dawning age of interpretation, replacing a "hermeneutics of art" with an "erotics of art."[2]

The second type of materiality is conscious of layout, space, and the shapes of letters, viewing language as marks in and on the world. Consider the murderous view of language in Don DeLillo's *The Names*, when anthropologist Owen reminds us that "character" comes from the Greek for "pointed stake" and cultists kill people according to their initials,[3] or Walter Benn Michaels's book-length rejection of the "identity politics" he sees as inherent in reading "the shape of the signifier" as meaningful:[4] literature that asserts meaning in the physical properties of language implies its ability to impact the embodied world in visceral and contentious ways. In the antihumanist context in which subjectivity is socially inscribed on the body, such literature reminds us of the threat to the individual posed by systems of language and ideology.

Materiality in literature, then, especially at the height of theory, the tail end of high postmodern literature, and the beginning of critical and creative debates about where literature should go next, is more than another kind of formal play or rejection of the literary status quo. It participates in the period's debates about the abilities and dangers of language not just to mean but to impact the real world, and posits new textual responses to those debates. It also demonstrates literary reactions to the rapid transformation, from mechanical to digital, of the means of production, communication, and dissemination of information, art, and entertainment in America.

Material and Digital

The rapid development of electronic literature in the 1990s provides one clear motivation for this new investment in the physicality of language and text. With the World Wide Web becoming publicly available in 1991, electronic literature, initially conceived as stand-alone documents primarily characterized by the hyperlink, began to take advantage of the abundance of possibilities in form, structure, media, reader interaction, and connectivity to other texts and readers afforded by the internet.[5] This shift from merely digital to networked, along with rising computational capacity, resulted in an ever-growing variety of electronic literature and a substantially growing body of electronic work—from a handful of electronic texts pre-1990 to dozens, and now hundreds, published every year (see Eliterature.org). Such digitally composed and delivered texts reimagine the most basic elements of literature. Nonlinear; interactive; enacted by the reader; often eschewing closure, fixed structure, and/or boundaries between text and reader, text and world, text and other texts, electronic literature presents the text as event or performance, dependent on the reader's construction of it and different in every encounter. Whether trying to keep pace, or simply adapting the possibilities for literature afforded by this new medium, print literature of this decade increasingly incorporates the openness, multiplicity, and interactivity in genre and structure developed by electronic lit. Meanwhile, evolving printing technology also enabled print literature to emulate electronic literature's innovations by manipulating the physical aspects of texts—incorporating images, carving out space and depth through typesetting, linking and layering texts and characters through mixed fonts and colors. Yet at the same time, texts began reacting to and even resisting the influence of electronic literature, separating themselves from it rather than embracing it, by emphasizing the materiality of their print medium—drawing attention to the colors, textures, even shapes that pages and bindings can take, and the shapes of language itself. Often texts did both, as N. Katherine Hayles points out,[6] making this simultaneous absorption of and resistance to innovations brought about by literature's movement into the electronic realm a defining characteristic of materiality in literature of the 1990s.

The generic and structural innovations of some texts clearly and consciously mimic those of new media. Carole Maso, for example, first considered publishing *AVA* (1993) as an electronic hypertext, and even in print it creates a kind of hypertextual movement between repeated and related fragments, as Stephen J. Burn has noted.[7] Mark Danielewski actually did originally publish most of *House of Leaves* online in 1999, about a year before publishing the entire text in print in 2000. His is the print novel perhaps most often and adamantly compared to hypertext, its four levels of authorship (Zampanò, Johnny Truant, Pelafina, and The Editors) creating a Möbius-strip structure that can only emerge when the narrators are read as integrally interdependent, the reader jumping from one to the other and back again; its refusal to authorize one author or reading, while linking its narrative to real-world people and encounters, results in the kind of boundary-free text of multiple realities that we associate today with electronic literature.

But even these texts remain firmly grounded in print structure and physical form. *AVA* counterbalances its fragmentation and hypertextual linking with an otherwise Aristotelian structure that gathers its nonlinear mental wanderings into three sections completing a single day, "morning," "afternoon," and "night." Danielewski similarly stresses that he conceived of the book only as print, rejecting offers to buy its rights for film, and composed it using solely mechanical means.⁸ That the book focuses on a series of multiply mediated films, and that Danielewski was himself a filmmaker, further emphasizes how thoroughly he rejected the electronic media he understood, worked in, and considered using for this book, in favor of print. Even the book itself privileges its ultimate print form, noting how much of its anchoring material—primarily Johnny's journal in Chapter XXI—was not contained in the first, online edition.

Other texts of the 1990s feature characteristic structural and formal innovations of electronic literature, suggesting shared influence without expressing interest in or awareness of new media. Perhaps the most prominent example of an innovating author who remained for the most part uninvolved with electronic media is David Foster Wallace, who neither wrote for electronic media nor heavily used the internet before his death in 2008.⁹ Yet his innovations in print narrative resemble electronic ones: his *Infinite Jest* (1996) uses endnotes to create nonlinear reading and a sense of networked information, and relies on a structure defined not just by significant narrative gaps (the meeting between Don Gately and Hal; the climactic events between the tournament and the chronologically final scene of the novel), but by its failure to contain the entirety of the narrative, while signaling an entirety which the reader can build with its parts, requiring the kind of interaction and multiple encounters that characterize electronic literature.¹⁰ Likewise, Wallace's intrusion into copyright notices (as in *Jest* and *Consider the Lobster*) enacts elit's multiplication and blurring of authorial layers in the manner of *House of Leaves*, while "Host"'s flowcharted typesetting reorganizes the page into hypertext. Even the single footnote in "Good Old Neon" explodes the text from the confines of the page. Its final "THE END," delivered two pages before the story's textual ending, inserts a pre-emptive, paratextual culmination that creates a kind of Möbius-strip structure, mimicking the character Neal's verbal descriptions of the workings of time. The footnote also creates a story that either ends twice or goes on forever. The two pages separating the endings are crucial in disrupting a linear timeline, as are the many hundreds of pages separating *Jest*'s main text from its endnotes.

Similarly Lee Siegel, whose *Love in a Dead Language* (1996) is in many ways a precursor to the hypertextual *House of Leaves*, has expressed faith in the fate of the book in an electronic age but not interest in making his books in any way electronic.[11] Indeed, *Love* mocks the possibilities offered by digital media, with a *Kamasutra* website that exploits the least enlightening capabilities of screen and internet,[12] while also mocking, through its inventive innovations in print form, the kneejerk assumption (here made by "Seedy-ROM-Antics Multimedia Development") that "Books . . . are an outmoded and profoundly limited means of conveying information" (146). But not all writers, or readers, share Siegel's confidence in the print book. One consequence of the rise of electronic media and the print book's increasing adoption of its characteristics is the development of what has become an ongoing anxiety about "the death of the book" that is often associated with Robert Coover's 1992 essay "The End of Books." Interestingly, Coover neither mourned the death of the print book—citing George Landow's declaration that "the movement from the tactile to the digital is the primary fact about the contemporary world"[13]—nor recognized print's plucky adaptability to the generic changes happening all around it. Instead, he praised the opportunities for literature introduced by electronic media, and put nail to paper coffin by declaring that "hypertext does not translate into print."[14] But while Coover went on to become a pioneering elit publisher and critic, founding *electronic literature organization* with Scott Rettberg and Jeff Ballowe in 1999, books simply went on, as more recent commentators on the "death of the book" anxiety acknowledge.

Many books that persist as print in an increasingly digital world do so quite self-consciously, invoking the presence and possibilities of the digital while foregrounding their own refusal to play along. Such books cultivate what Jessica Pressman calls an "aesthetic of bookishness," which she defines as a practice of "exploit[ing] the power of the print page in ways that draw attention to the book as a multimedia format, one informed by and connected to digital technologies." In addition to revealing its inherent multimedia possibilities, such a text "take[s] itself seriously as a material object."[15] Certainly *House of Leaves*, coupling its structural hypertextuality and thematic celebration of mediation with a formal insistence on print, is the decade's best example of such a text. But many other books, like *Jest*, do not place their materiality against the context of books' digitization. These insistently material texts of the period exhibit not an "aesthetic of bookishness"—the term itself privileging abstraction over substance, book*like*ness over book itself—but rather keen awareness and clever enlistment of the powers already given to the book by its ability to organize language and its status as a physical object. This constantly renewed vitality of the ancient powers of print thus contributes, along with a new "aesthetic of bookishness," to the book's survival alongside the development of digital textuality, while also connecting literary materiality of the 1990s to earlier anti-Realist experiments that had not yet imagined electronic vistas.

Books and/as Bodies

Raymond Federman's *Double or Nothing* provides insight into the complex roots and intentions of emphatically material literature in the 1990s. Published originally as a typescript in 1971, during that early postmodern flourishing of materialist texts, Federman's novel was revived in 1992 as elit took off and the book was declared terminal. Presumably, it benefited from the growing interest in visual and structural narrative experiments being conducted in electronic literature and from publishing advances that made reissuing the novel more feasible. Federman had originally typed the novel, from handwritten notes, as a single five-hundred-page sentence. Out of this linguistic material he painstakingly sculpted the final novel, which depicts through concrete and pictographic language a writer's obsessive, digressive, and displaced—through multiple layers of invented narrators—attempts to write a story. A "novel of performance," the text is less finished narrative than artifact of the character-narrator's experience of trying and failing to write.[16] The book's affinity with and influence on other experimental fiction of the decade and beyond are evident. Similar techniques for foregrounding material aspects of language and production appear in Richard Grossman's *The Alphabet Man* (1993) and William Gass's *The Tunnel* (1995), which I will discuss below; Chapter 2 demonstrates how Steve Tomasula created book as artifact of experience in *VAS* (2004) and as artifact of the history of language—its body like an archeological dig—in *The Book of Portraiture* (2006). But ironically, the very changes in publishing that brought *Double or Nothing* back to print and spread its influence also destroyed design aspects that best communicated the novel's material meaning. Word-processed and digitally rendered in 1992, the book quietly became a product of the digital, its fonts regularized and spaces standardized, no longer a record of the individually inscribed mark on the page or artifact of the embodied experience—not just the narrator's but those of Federman himself—that hammered the marks over time. This translation of the text from mechanically to digitally produced points out what is lost in the transformation from mechanical to digital art, to ways in which books in the digital age, for all the new realms of representation available to them, are inherently distanced from the material realm that used to produce and hold them, and at least for now holds the bodies that read them.

But Federman's novel also points out how much is gained, not just from digital production and electronic media but from how these changes in media and production enlarge our sense of what any text can be. Quite contrary to the open-ended nonlinearity of books such as *House* that exhibit an "aesthetic of bookishness," or a kind of digital envy, *Double or Nothing* emphatically confines itself to the closure that it sees as inherent in print. Deep into this unorthodox literary experiment, which eschews all recognizable elements of Realism, the text argues that because every novel is "always a question of expressing, of translating something which is already there," and because "all fictitious work forms a block [in which] nothing can be taken away from it nor can a single word be changed," every novel, no matter how anti-Realistic, reproduces the tight economy of Realism. The printed text, in its unalterable inscription, constitutes for Federman "a discourse fixed once and for all," which naturalizes each of its elements according to its rules, however scattered and strange.[17] In the context of digital literature, in which text is never fixed, finished, or "already there," such assumptions about the inherent closure and limitations of what fiction can be or how it can be read become laughable. Here is the revelation of materially experimental print reproduced in a digital age: it exposes the ways in which not only texts written in a mechanical age but even our *ideas* about materiality, language, and the possibilities for literature can never be the same after the advent of the digital. Realism's logic of closure and formalism's logic of unity cannot survive unscathed the invasion of digital tools, production, and culture. But neither can the signifying capacities of print.

Perhaps in compensation for this loss by print, even texts of the 1990s that show affinity for the workings of elit also exhibit, and force readers to experience, intense awareness of the material existence of both reader and text. *Jest*, while hypertextually sending us back and forth between main narrative and nearly a hundred pages of endnotes, also locates us firmly in the physical world: flipping through 1,079 pages is nothing like clicking on a line of blue text. *Love in a Dead Language* exacerbates the aggravation by forcing us to turn the book backward and upside down in order to read the "Wives and Mistresses/Mistresses and Wives" chapters, the latter of which runs on the backs of the pages of the former; elsewhere the novel quotes an entire stanza of poetry printed backward (54). In so doing Siegel materializes two of the novel's key thematic notions: that the arrangement of printed text is inherently hierarchical, should be unfixed and multiple, but really can't be ("Wives" always wind(s) up coming first), and that all written language contains the potential, if not the largely unrecognized realization, of puzzles, secrets, and unseen meaning, if only we could look differently at it, which printed text makes rather cumbersome to do (few readers are going to leave their comfortable chairs to find a mirror). Like Wallace, Siegel makes us aware of the effort and reward of looking awry, as well as of the body that is part of every act of reading, every act of reading an embodied translation.

Several steps down a road put on the map by the entirely linguistic *Pale Fire* (1962), Siegel's novel adds to the combination of text and commentary (in this case, the translated *Kamasutra* and Roth's interpretation of it) another set of annotations informed by a different set of commentaries, some of whose parts are rendered by copies of other texts—newspaper clippings, board game, essays, letters, ads, photos—slipped in to the main manuscript (the translation of and commentary on the *Kamasutra*). This novel is thus not simply one narrative distorting another to exponentially increase the ways of reading the whole. Rather, it also materializes the poststructural insight that all texts are remixes of other texts, revised, in the late age of print, into the proposition that all books are constructed of other books. The novel's scrapbook-like composition both relies on and belies texts' ability as artifacts of the real world to fulfill our desire for something true. In a terminal act of materialization, Roth is killed near the end of the novel by the word whose manifesting had been his life's pursuit—he is hit on the head by a Sanskrit-English dictionary, opened to *kama*, or "love" (325). At that point, his narrative is taken over—invaded, usurped, and colonized—by documents that stand in for his death and for the culmination of his work, chosen and placed by others whose commentaries fix their implications. The reassembled pieces of a torn-up love letter (334), and the six reinserted pages of Roth's journal (237–8), all of which had been crumpled and discarded by Roth, act both as "real-world" artifacts, communicating piercing truths about suffering—we can imagine the tearing and crumpling, whose effects are visible in the documents—and, inserted by others into the text, as betrayals not only of Roth but of the book he had meant to complete.

Love also materializes, through form, this potential for any text to colonize another when Anang's commentary on Roth's book, which had been confined below the page to footnotes until Roth's death, invades the main text on page 331 and occupies that space until book's end. One year later, Richard Grossman, for whom text is often a dangerous weapon, made the same point; his *The Book of Lazarus* is essentially a scrapbook of photos and documents that witness and explain the deaths of the drugged-out members of the "People's Liberation Brigade." But the original scrapbook is co-opted by one of its descendants, who alters it by adding her own explanatory narrative. The book she has produced is then altered by the addition of her death date on the "tomb stone" that opens the final book: her life is the price for seeing the book to print, a conversion of body to language. For both Grossman and Siegel, manifesting language, rather than solving the problems of language, runs the risk of altering or dematerializing body—the body of the text or of the human—a metaphor for the power struggles inherent in every act of writing.

House of Leaves repeats *Love*'s material breakdown of the structural hierarchy of academic writing—reorganizing space on the page—by allowing

Johnny Truant's commentary, like Anang's, to break out of the footnotes and occupy the main text in all of Chapter XXI. Further, Danielewski's interdependent narrative strands in which no one narrator controls the book prevent the hierarchies of power that organize Roth's authors (not just Anang's textual coup but also "Lee Siegel"'s ultimate admission to killing Roth). But *House*'s materialization of textual power, and of the power of text to become material, goes further than this and further than *Love*'s: for Johnny, our most present narrator in *House*, the process of piecing together the book left in a shamble of incomplete pieces by Zampanò *is* a translation of text into body, first when the papers he's working on become a "body" or "a child," then when he becomes the beastly body/belly that houses the book and its first author, and finally when he is reborn in his final story as the baby who can let go, the baby whose brain is as undifferentiated and incomplete as the substance of this book (326, 338, 518). Meanwhile, as Johnny thematically materializes the book, the book materializes on the page the impact of its narrators and even of its own story: just as we can read the check mark on page 97 as a materialization of Pelafina's power to inscribe on Zampanò's narrative,[18] we can read the visual concretizing of the house in the "Labyrinth" chapter and of Navidson's actions in Chapter XX as the *book's* embodiment of its own thematic content through words on the page.

Also like *Love*, *House* is a book made of many documents—including letters, poems, newspaper clippings, photos, and drawings—and is aware of the importance of things and of documents' and texts' abilities to act, like things, on the world. The frontispiece that greets us is a collage of things that motivate, measure, or document the action of the book (compass, measuring tape, drugs, bullet, blood), alerting us from the start that language and texts— acts of representation—yield consequences for the real world, the one in which we are reading. Before we open the book, it warns us of this connection, the front cover half an inch shorter than the rest of the book, so that even when closed the things of the book and the horrors they represent spill out at us, as if crossing the threshold from text to world. The shortened cover also implies that the book can't contain itself, so that, with its blueprint of the house and its endless stairs, it makes the book seem to embody in physical form the central physical and philosophical dilemma of the house: it's bigger on the inside. Thus *House of Leaves* may be about the incommensurability of language and the real world, and the necessity of electronic remediation to recuperate identity and meaning in that world (114). But it also asserts, through insistent thematic and visual materiality and use of physical form to embody the linguistic and existential dilemmas of the text, that the material world remains the site where we can best investigate those dilemmas. Like the theories of social construction of subjectivity that define the academic

1990s, *House* demonstrates that however abstract these dilemmas of identity, language, and knowledge are, they are always written on the body.

Materializing (with) Language

Almost a decade and a half before twenty-first-century print literature became redefined as fundamentally reacting to electronic, Carole Maso read the impact of elit differently, as an opportunity to discover in print literature "a new respect for the mark on the page" and reawaken our "love for the physical, for the sensual world."[19] Her novel *AVA*, even in its structural hypertextuality, expresses this desire to materialize language. Repeatedly citing Hélène Cixous, the narrator associates the liberating power of language with women's bodies, while preserving the memory of her own ebbing life in sensory experience wrought through language. The resulting "semiotic materiality" in a text whose fragmented form embodies the narrator's physical deterioration creates a novel in which, as Victoria Frenkel Harris puts it, "matter matters."[20] Maso's later novel *The Art Lover* (1990) seeks to preserve a connection between the truths of the material world and language by explicitly asking how to "love not things that are certain, but simply things in themselves"[21]—unstripped of their ambiguity by fixed representation— and how to capture that love in art. Peppering her attempts to capture truth in art are examples of how we fail, because of elaborate theories, like her father's modernist use of art to distance us from pain, or worse, our ancient desire to use not just art but our own visions of the world to distance ourselves from reality and its suffering. One recurring example of the dangers of (modernist) art is the repetition of "I saw the figure five in gold" by various characters in conversation. Their ironic deployment of the line traces a vast distance from the embodied experience the words originally denoted, appropriating Demuth's 1949 painting, *I Saw the Figure Five in Gold*, itself an ekphrasis of William Carlos Williams's poem "The Great Figure" (1922)—which Williams claims in his autobiography was inspired by his own vivid experience in New York City.

The novel also critiques the ways we convert the material world itself into art. Pictorial and linguistic images of constellations recur, in "Sky Watch" clippings cut from the main narrator's life and in momentous imagery she supplies for her characters. This imagery alerts us to our human habit of arranging the world to suit our needs for meaning and order: we make pictures out of suns, co-opting entire galaxies to soothe ourselves. This is the annihilation of the real that the narrator wants to avoid in her art: "I've got to feel flesh, bone, hair, earth, somehow in words. The urgency of flesh, bone, hair. The thousand demands of blood" (73). As she searches for a mode of art that will preserve the real, she notes methods of translating and preserving visual, aural, and tactile experience—sign language, grave rubbings, recordings of lovemaking—and of fusing the material into art: Van Gogh's thick pigment transferring height onto canvas (34, 71, 97, 234). Ultimately, Maso solves the problem of art's intimacy with the real by breaking into her novel to tell the truth behind the novel's embedded stories, the story of the death of her dear friend Gary Falk, from AIDS (as Charles Harris argues in "The Dead Fathers"). Though a metafictive solution—a product of abstract textual elements such as generic form and point of view—Maso's self-referentiality ultimately forces the reader to reread the novel as doing exactly what Maso aspired to do in her essay—as recording her own "marks on the page," the result of her "desire to put the body on the pages of a book" (71).

Love in a Dead Language materializes in this way as well, manifesting the linguistic impulse that creates it. For Roth, Professor of Indian studies, translating the *Kamasutra* stands in for his desire to have sex with the unattainable Lalita Gupta, while his eventual sex with Lalita—"India incarnate" (134)—itself stands in for an unattainable intimacy with his life's work, in a Möbius-strip transubstantiation of desire, language, and body. His book frequently relies on outside documents to stand in for what he presumably could not translate into words, for example using a graphic panel to represent "erotic biting and sexual scratching" (123-4), and Lalita's own position on "Positions for Sex," in the form of her class paper on the topic, to represent "Poses and Postures" (126-31). Thus the book is a record of Roth's pursuit of meaning and self through the inseparable tangle of tangible and intangible texts and bodies. His desire manifests equally and cyclically in text and sex, the book materializing his desire for intimacy with both through documents that require our own bodies' participation.

Perhaps even thornier than the problem of how to use art to connect to the real world, or to materialize through abstraction, is the question of what "the real" is and how it can relate to language at all. This linguistic dilemma has long been taken up by the Language poets, whose attention to language as material—as the stuff that poems are made of—and only problematically related to reality grew out of modernist convictions and practices such as Gertrude Stein's, persisting into the twenty-first century and experiencing renewed vigor in the late 1980s and early 1990s. Poems of the 1990s by Charles Bernstein, former editor of the journal L=A=N=G=U=A=G=E and prominent Language poet, poke tenaciously at this disjunction between language and reality, as if with enough persistence the distance between word and thing could finally be fathomed. Whereas one poem in *Rough Trades* (1991) declares that "Only / the imaginary is real," another claims "Only the real is real."²² Then in *My Way: Speeches and Poems* (1999), "This line refuses reality," while two years later, in *Let's Just Say*, a self-reflexive poem declares "It's/ real."²³ What is real for Bernstein? Primarily language, whose materiality—how it occupies space on the page, how it sounds in our heads or ears—is what makes it mean, *is* its reality, not its capacity to express: words are "Fundament be-/ yond relation."²⁴ Similarly, "This Line" (1999) uses irony to illustrate that the poem exists apart from every reading we impose on it: "This line/ is only about itself./ This line has no meaning," but the versified denial of meaning is a poem, and its denial is its meaning. Likewise, "Of Time and the Line" (1991) insubstantiates the literal poetic line—if there is such a thing—by cataloging all the useful "lines" it is not (hem-, picket-, blood-, comic, geometric), then pointing out the "line"'s irrelevance even to poetry, which has become linelessly prosaic. Yet this sequence of lines, too, forms a poem, as does the page that declares only "*THIS POEM INTENTIONALLY LEFT BLANK.*"²⁵ These poems use form to materialize meaning, building the thing itself—the poem on the page—out of the articulation of its denial.

Bernstein intensifies this technique in "The Lives of the Toll Takers" (1994), whose erratic textual layout looks at times like that of *Double or Nothing*, at times like *House of Leaves*, and yet is really the opposite of concrete. Rather than arranging words on the page to mimic visually the idea or action being represented, Bernstein uses placement, word division, and punctuation to force us to see and hear the language on the pages. Punning jokes like "ther / e's / no crime like presentiment" suggest that revelation lies waiting in well-worn phrases just a few letters down the line (of the poem, of signification)—like a poetic invocation of *Pale Fire*'s word golf. Increasingly irksome linebreaks become their own joke when they make a pretentious assertion about irony and idealism even more difficult to follow, rendering the specious as spacious, and full of hot air.²⁶ Interestingly, while many of the poems of Joan Retallack's 1998 *How To Do Things with Words* suggest the combinatory possibilities of the digital—for example, the seemingly random reappearance of words and phrases through the columns of "Shakespeare Was a Woman"—more often the poems, like Bernstein's, delineate subjection to the confines of the page. In "Here's Looking at You Francis Bacon," words lie trapped in boxes, while in "ditto Marchel Duchamp? ditto ditto Gertrude Stein?" words form a box that stands in for the "*memento mori*," a stubbornly fixed *Agrippa*. In rendering content via format in these ways, what such poems do best of all is force us to see each word involved, at times even every letter and punctuation mark, not only revealing the materializing power of poetry but transforming it into letters fixed in time and space, marks on the page.

The multiple fonts of Bernstein's "Mao Tse Tung Wore Khakis" (2000), which seems to collect a series of written statements from various media and voices, make the poem another kind of artifact—not of documents but of words that preserve their original inscriptions. Each differently formatted statement is another kind of hyperlink, a connection to a past articulation *in print*. This is one of many materializing techniques that William H. Gass enlists in his mammoth book *The Tunnel* (1995), whose concretized and versified language demonstrates its devotion to poetry long before the narrator-author declares himself, in the end, a frustrated poet. The novel uses textual effects to materialize the memories out of which its narrator, Kohler, attempts to build a present self (while materializing his own attempt by digging a tunnel in his basement). A childhood memory reveals that Kohler conceived of being in spatial terms from a young age: he is drawn to his relatives' steamer trunk, its very name offering to materialize for him "a torso, a pair of lungs, the vital fluid of the soul," and experiences its internal emptiness as the mystery, inarticulateness, and absence of "pure Being."[27] He climbs into the trunk, hoping it would "make of me a space as well" (590). As an adult, he recognizes his obsessive excavation of a tunnel in the basement of his home as an attempt to recreate that space of pure being, hidden from the real world, at play in his hole in the "realm of the Real" (503). Because Kohler perceives that "the real is harder, indeed, than a dry roll" (416) and views being as an escape from that real, his quest—the tunnel, the journal he writes that becomes this book—becomes an attempt to define himself in relief against everything he is not. It requires materializing a world from past memory and present idea out of which he can carve himself. Digging the tunnel is for Kohler a materialization of the "Nothing" that is being (468) and a substitute for the "hole" of his wife (462), which is itself a substitute for writing history, his life's work. It is also, as Roth's conquest of Lalita and scrapbooked translation were for him, a method for manifesting the being at the root of all his bodily and linguistic desires, even of language itself: Kohler deposits his dirt in his wife's (chest of) drawers (644).[28]

As in *Love*, some material effects function artifactually, as traces of its narrator's embodied experience, such as the smudged and crumpled page, partially obscured by a garbage-bag label, on which he recounts the painful end of an affair (174). At other times, the marks seem to manifest or feed his ideas. One page on which he repeatedly "take[s] note" seems to have been written on a self-identifying notepad that declares "note note note," and another two, on which the narrator remembers his mother doing crossword puzzles, are partially obscured by images of the same (627–8). More often Gass, like Federman, Siegel, and Danielewski, employs textual layout to concretize past experience in language, as when he represents "Mad Meg" as an empty center delineated by words that signify the people—"parents, friends, ... students, critics, colleagues strangers"—his Baudrillardian view of history could not touch (8). In direct opposition to Meg's theory, Kohler also employs language, much like Federman's narrator, to eliminate the distance between word and thing, scattering "pow!" and "pop pop pop" across pages to make present the violence of a Second World War battle and of Kristalnacht (308, 331–2); elsewhere, page numbers become stenciled numerals that recall Holocaust markings on trains (31, 33). Equally materially present for him are poignant memories from his childhood, like "Olio di Oliva" on a grocer's window, which marks his unspoiled sense of freedom and pleasure as a child (61). These words and numbers, recorded in the fonts in which Kohler experienced them in the world, operate, as in Bernstein's poem, not as arbitrary signs pointing somewhere else but as materializations of the actual things—signs as things—that populated his formative experience.

Not surprisingly for Gass, who argued that "the sentence confers reality upon certain relations,"[29] these hundreds of pages of materializations of and through language culminate in the narrator's realization that the problem of fiction is the problem of form. All forms, whether history, narrative, limerick, or even language itself, distort and demean—just as form is language's vehicle for instantiating being. Form allows us to carve meaning out of the deluge of language, like Kohler shoveling a tunnel to make a space in the Real. It is the window that allows us to look at all, even while limiting and shaping what we see ("Why Windows Are Important To Me"). Kohler's "fugue" (239), his random fallings into verse (492–3 etc), his rampant alliteration (like the clicking "c's" that shape the "photo of [his] last face," 356), all sculpt language into forms of delineation and limits, sources of containment, and so create the visual and metaphorical spaces in which we can discover meaning and being. Ultimately Kohler recognizes poetry, with its rules and structures, as the most materializing medium, since it "created a permanent and universal present like a frieze of stone, and was therefore what any one of us might see and feel who followed its lines and felt its forms" (642).

It's hard to find Kohler's discovery redemptive; after all, he's not in the end a poet. Or if he is, he's an entirely secret one, as his gargantuan record of carving self out of language remains hidden in the pages of the history book whose introduction he never writes. Such a solipsistic view of language as unable to communicate beyond the self is so typical of the late postmodern period that we can read literary materiality as employed by Maso, Bernstein, and Gass as registering or resisting this earlier postmodern/poststructural disconnection between language and world. Grossman's *The Alphabet Man* (1993) offers another example of such dissociation, using language, like *The Tunnel*, to materialize its narrator's memories and mental states through concretizing font and textual layout, but leading to murderous self-division rather than self-discovery. Its central narrator, Clyde, identifies with letters before he can walk and early on has the entire alphabet tattooed on his body, literalizing the embodiment of language and language as defining self. But the novel is a catalog of all the ways in which his identification with language obscures more than it reveals. Letters are so "unknowable" to Clyde that his murderous alter egos are able to hide in chapters designated by letters rather than numbers.[30] Unaware of their presence in his journal (or in himself), Clyde is unable to understand his killing compulsion, and is able to conjure via letters only a false and incomplete version of himself, another persona rather than his personhood—a "character," or "pointed stake." Thus he and Kohler suggest the limits, as well as the possibilities, of our attempts to materialize meaning and self in language.

"New Materialism" in the Twenty-First Century

As the continued evolution of digital technology in the twenty-first century increasingly intensified material practices in print literature, a somewhat contradictory philosophical shift away from dematerialization at the end of the twentieth century also began to inform material literary practices. Coined by Manuel DeLanda and Rosi Braidotti in the late 1990s,[31] "new materialism" gathers diverse philosophical, social, and physics-based theories that propose ways of reorienting our thinking about matter, language, politics, natural sciences, social sciences, and ethics by once again focusing on material reality rather than, or as the basis of, language and discourse. While the theorists contributing to this movement differ dramatically in terms of methodology, aim, and focus, uniting them is the core belief that we have lost sight of fundamental aspects of reality because we have been so long fixated on language, and on theorizing language as separate from, standing in for, or constituting the material. As Karan Barad brazenly declares, "language has been granted too much power" and "the only thing that doesn't seem to matter anymore is matter."[32]

Taking quantum physics' observations of matter as her starting point, Barad redefines reality as incommensurate with representationalism, or, "the belief that representations serve a mediating function between knower and known." This "common-sense view"—which undergirds "traditional realist belief"—assumes a fundamental separation between words and things and "displays a deep mistrust of matter, holding it off at a distance, figuring it as passive, immutable, and mute, in need of the mark of an eternal force like culture or history to complete it."[33] Instead, quantum physics recognizes the interrelatedness of all matter, observers, and acts of observation. Certainly art that explores an anti-representationalist concept of reality as posited by Barad's new materialism will engender an entirely new, anti-representationalist, anti-Realist aesthetic as well. For their part, Diana Coole and Samantha Frost recognize that this shift from language to matter necessitates new ways of thinking about the social world, as "the more textual approaches associated with the so-called cultural turn are increasingly being deemed inadequate for understanding contemporary society."[34] They go so far as to recognize one of the three major contexts or causes for new materialism as "a sense that the radicalism of the dominant discourses which have flourished under the cultural turn is now more or less exhausted."[35] As Barth proposed metafiction as a tool for renewing literature after the exhaustion of Realist practices,[36] and Lyotard and Jameson defined the postmodern period in part as resulting from the demise of the radicalism of both modernism and the avant-garde,[37] new materialism's philosophical recognition of the errors and dangers of representationalism and the need for new ways of thinking about matter's relationship with discourse portends profound shifts in aesthetics and techniques that will carry us out of postmodernism and into something new.

Barad arrives at her consequential new understanding of discourse and its relationship with the world by way of contemporary scientific concepts of matter that differ substantially not just from Newtonian ideas but also from our own lived experience of reality. Contrary to the atomism of Democritus, the dualism of Descartes, and the cause-effect of Newton, matter according to quantum physics is inherently relational and fundamentally indivisible—from other matter, from those who observe the matter, and from the apparatuses used to observe it. Barad reminds us that Neils Bohr asserted this anti-atomistic view of reality not as philosophical theory but as a result of *empirical* research (138). Matter is not a separate passive thing we observe or act upon, but is what results from phenomena "intra-acting" with each other (141), rather than "interacting," which Barad claims "presumes the prior existence of independent entities" (139). Matter becomes, rather than merely being, and we are involved in its becoming, just as it is involved in ours: most fundamentally new about Barad's new materialist concept of matter is that it is "agentive," acting in the world with as much agency as any other element of the world, including human beings (137). This idea of relational, inseparable, agentive matter forms the heart of Barad's physics-based definition of posthumanism (136).

The understanding of discourse produced by a quantum-physics concept of matter is likewise relational and matter-based. Barad states that "discursive practices produce, rather than merely describe, the subjects and objects of knowledge practices" (147). The interdependence and relationality of all aspects of the physical world and of our observations and descriptions of it result in an intimacy between discursive and physical, language and the body, that is no longer abstract, as in cultural theory, but is absolute: "Bohr's insight that concepts are not ideational but rather actual physical arrangements is clearly an insistence on the materiality of meaning making that goes far beyond what is usually meant by the frequently heard contemporary refrain that writing and talking are material practices" (147). That is, Bohr's insight asks us to push our concepts of materiality beyond those posited by even our most materially minded cultural theorists, such as Foucault and Butler. Rather than simply viewing meaning as made possible by material practices, Barad by way of Bohr asks us to redefine discursive practices as themselves material, as *"specific material (re)configurings of the world through which the determination of boundaries, properties, and meanings is differentially enacted,"* as *"ongoing agential intra-actions of the world"* (148–9, original italics). Likewise, unlike Butler's theory, which "ultimately reinscribes matter as a passive product of discursive practices rather than as an active agent participating in the very process of materialization" (151), Barad asks us to start with the premise that "neither discursive practices nor material phenomena are ontologically or epistemologically prior"; "matter and meaning are mutually articulated" (152).

Material realist fiction of the twenty-first century materializes these core premises of new materialism in a variety of ways, and with increasing frequency, diversity, and intensity of techniques over material realism of the 1990s. Most obviously, it illustrates the articulation of meaning through matter—meaning's dependence on and interrelation with not just a "real world" but with physical reality itself—by foregrounding its own physicality in ways that are instrumental to the fiction's meaning-making. In so doing, it also wrests our attention away from the purely linguistic or physical—from language games and the threat of the hyperreal—and asks us to pay attention to the physical objects in our hands, which ask to be seen, touched, and manipulated in order to make them meaningful. Unlike Realist fiction, whose formal elements are confined to the words on the page and so familiar to us as to have become invisible, material realist fiction, in drawing attention to its embodiedness, makes form visible and assertive: material realist texts act upon us, demonstrating the agency of matter. This fiction also materializes the fundamental intra-activeness of matter and observer, of book and reader. Barad explains this interdependence by way of the "which-slit detector" experiment, which proves empirically that "the ontology of the electron is changing depending upon how I measure it":[38] as we observe the material world, we can study only interactions, not separate objects. Similarly, material realist books in the twenty-first century have become more interactions than objects, requiring the reader's interaction with them and observation of them to create the narrative, the meaning, even, in some cases, the physical book itself.

Finally, and perhaps most importantly in terms of its influence on contemporary literature, new materialist concepts of ontology are inherently ethical, because they are inherently relational. Coole and Frost, for example, point out that the ethical and political questions raised by new concepts in the natural sciences are one of the three major directions in which material realism is developing;[39] Tomasula's work, as discussed in Chapter 2, takes up many of these bioethical and biopolitical issues that concern new materialism. But Barad argues for the centrality of ethics to new materialism in an even more fundamental way, by recognizing that conceiving of ontology as intra-active and anti-atomistic implies that being itself is a matter of relationship, and every encounter with being is ethical. According to new materialism, "objectivity is a matter of responsibility and not a matter of distancing at all"[40] and quantum physics necessarily leads to considerations of social justice.[41] Not surprisingly, then, material realist fiction in the twenty-first century brings a significant return to questions of feeling, relating, ethics, and justice, as we see the return of the parody, critique, and affect that were so often missing from the language-oriented postmodern pastiche of the twentieth century, and even from earlier material realist fiction, such as *Double or Nothing* or Bernstein's Language poetry.

Material Realism in the Twenty-First Century

The first two decades of the twenty-first century have produced even more materially attentive texts than did the same period at the end of the twentieth, suggesting that writers' interest in using the book's physical form to manifest the real world it witnesses and critiques—often in the context of technology that threatens to eclipse it—continues and intensifies. Many writers in the twenty-first century continue the materializing techniques created in the twentieth, and often to similar ends, so that both types of material realism examined in texts of the 1990s thrive after the turning of the millennium. As I demonstrated in Chapter 2, Steve Tomasula's fiction, so thematically focused on the material aspects of art, making art, and art's relationship with the world, provides an excellent example of both types of material realism in early twenty-first-century fiction. He uses the physical bodies of his books to signify, as with the art-book shape of *IN&OZ*, the implication of archeological depth from the deepening page colors of *Book of Portraiture*, and the complexly signifying colors, fonts, and typesetting in *VAS* and *Book*. He provokes the reader's embodied experience of the text as well, by subjecting her to various temporal experiences in *TOC* and forcing her to share Mechanic's boredom in *IN&OZ*. And like the work of Jonathan

Safran Foer (discussed below), David Foster Wallace (discussed in Chapter 1), and David Mitchell (whose *Cloud Atlas* peaks in its center by placing the sacred orison in the hands of the reader[42]), *VAS* invokes the real by handing over a portion of the book to the reader in the real world: "Cut my [vasectomy consent] form from this book, Square wrote. Fill in your _____ and hold it in your hands. Make it as real a presence in your hands as are the countless other bricks that make up your invisible city," the book reads, in non-typographical handwriting, across the page from a facsimile of the consent form (318–19). The book asks readers not just to inhabit Square's dilemma as our own, allowing the fictional world to touch our real ones, but also to do the opposite, in realizing that the "bricks" that seem so solidly to make up our realities are as fictional as is the dilemma we are being asked to realize. Meanwhile, Tomasula also asserts language's own physical impact on the world, when pages of translations force us to consider how differently languages take up space in the world, and drawings of failed billboards ask us to contemplate the function of a sign that won't signify, in *IN&OZ*.

Merging techniques of Tomasula's *VAS* and Siegel's *Love in a Dead Language*, Debra di Blasi's *The Jirí Chronicles and Other Fictions* (2007) blends artifacts from reality with fake documents that extend the ludicrous real into her only slightly more ludicrous fictitious world, as she provides a much-needed female and feminist perspective on topics that also motivate Tomasula's and Siegel's books: sex, procreation, and power in heterosexual relationships. Indeed, many of di Blasi's documents would be right at home in either of those books, such as the (real) internet ad for "Enlargo" penis enhancer or the (fake) public service announcement explaining female masturbation for the benefit of the (real) Kansas Blue Valley School District, "who are incapable of intelligently discussing with their teens the topic of masturbation."[43] One imagines Lalita Gupta reading the latter while Roth surreptitiously makes note of the Enlargo number, to be found later in the novel on an artifactual crumple of paper.

Elsewhere I have written extensively about Jonathan Safran Foer's crucial, perhaps redemptive reorienting of poststructural fiction away from the failures of language—the gap, the absence, the silence—and toward communication, empathy, and human connection. One of the ways he accomplishes this reorientation, particularly in *Extremely Loud & Incredibly Close*, is by materializing language: the tattooed "yes" and "no," the message translated into a Morse code bracelet, all those unread letters taking the place of the missing body (see *Succeeding Postmodernism*, 153–4). These linguistic images of materialized language, along with actual images of materialized language as traces of characters' bodies (the grandfather's journals, his name written in red pen for his grandson to find),[44] remind us that language is only possible as an act of the body, for another body, in the real world. In *Everything Is Illuminated*, "*We are writing*," repeated to occupy two pages, takes the place of the meaningful history that the shtetl fails to produce as it awaits its nonsensically horrific fate at the hands of Nazis.[45] And before writing these two masterful novels that imagined new ways for language to manifest in and shape the world in productive ways, Foer produced two short stories, "About the Typefaces Not Used in This Edition," and "A Primer for the Punctuation of Heart Disease," whose shared core premise was that the shapes of letters themselves—and symbols, signifiers in general—shape meaning.

This second type of materiality, deployed in the 1990s both subtly, as in Bernstein's Language poetry, and with wild inventiveness, as by Danielewski's house- and character-manifesting fonts, colors, and layout, occurs in a surprising variety of twenty-first-century texts of varying genres. John D'Agata and Jim Fingal's nonfiction book *The Lifespan of a Fact* (2012) appears to be directly inspired by Danielewski's fictional *House*, as its textual layout at its most complex resembles that of *House*'s labyrinth chapter IX, creating windows of text framed by differently colored, multiply sourced paratext, and ending with an empty window. The book documents the running conversation/debate/power struggle between a writer and his fact-checker as they work together to produce an "accurate" story for a literary magazine about a young man's suicide in Las Vegas. The unconventional textual layout, in which the debate about facts blossoms around central fragments of the story draft, at times all but choking out the central, "primary," document—not unlike Johnny bursting out of the endnotes in *House*'s Chapter XXI—itself raises questions about how we privilege certain kinds of writing as "true" or "primary," and about our assumptions about authorship and power. But for readers who have navigated Danielewski's *House*, the textual layout might take on more dimension, the gradual disappearance of the internal "primary" text echoing the disappearance of the dangerous house, the remaining border of commentary echoing the peripheral and paratextual voices that tell most of the story of *House of Leaves*. In yet another genre-blurring act of intertextuality—and a kind of reversal of Tomasula's *VAS: An Opera in Flatland*, which is a novel that imagines an opera inspired by another novel—*The Lifespan of a Fact* spawned a Broadway play that ran from October 2018–January 2019, buoyed by major Broadway talent (Daniel Radcliffe, Bobby Cannavale, and Cherry Jones starred).

Guided by an impulse for constraint that is perhaps more akin to Danielewski's *Only Revolutions* than to his constantly expanding *House*, Lily Hoang has created a collection of texts so severely limited by their shapes on the page that they would be best described as concrete poems. *Changing*

(2008) materializes in language the sixty-four possible hexagrams that result from combining the bagwa, or eight trigrams, of the *I Ching*, a three-thousand-year-old book of Chinese philosophy that worked its way into Confucianism, Daoism, and Buddhism. Each of the eight trigrams—signifying heaven, swamp, fire, thunder, wind, water, mountain, and earth—is a combination of three continuous (yin) or broken (yang) lines; each hexagram combines two trigrams, one on top of the other, to make six lines. These hexagrams represent the construction of the universe and its interactions. The *I Ching* has been used both to learn about the nature of the universe and as oracle: traditionally, one would ask a question, roll a die, and find one's answer by reading the corresponding section. Each of Hoang's sixty-four "poems" takes its title from one of these sixty-four sections of the *I Ching*, and each visually reproduces the shape of that section's trigram. On one level, then, her poems use narrative to materialize the building blocks of the universe, of truth and knowledge, and of fate (a topic she touches on often): stories *are* truth, fate, and fortune. On another, they demonstrate how starting with the building block of narrative—and of translation—enables her book to escape the seeming confines of the original, patriarchal and filial-minded *I Ching*.

Changing presents multiple narrative threads, repeated in no particular order and with unexplained changes, incorporates multiple genres (memoir, fairy tale, creation myth, and the *I Ching*), and defamiliarizes language using pronounced repetition of words and phrases, ungrammatical syntax, and a total absence of punctuation. Thus it illustrates the freedom of invention and change inherent in language and narrative themselves, however constrained they might be by the forces—whether of textual layout or of ancient systems of belief and power—that constrain them. The ambivalence of the "final" image—the book's absolute refusal to provide a single reading or narrative resolution—demonstrates the freedom available in language and form: while the Western reader, proceeding from left to right and top to bottom, will encounter the final, oppressive "lasting image" of "a / man over woman coming near/ completion," if we read from bottom to top as we have been (belatedly) instructed to (we are allowed to read all wrong for a while), we end on a note of lovely resolution: "Jack saying I love even your nihilism & I love you/ still & them at last home."[46] Which is the correct ending? What fate (for Jack and Jill, for the narrator, for the reader) do we take away from the book and head into? Hoang provides one more variety of materializing that might answer such questions, or might make things worse: the appendix offers a diagram of a cup to cut out and assemble and 64 numbered squares to draw out of the cup in place of the ancient die. Thus the "handouts" not only reorganize the book as nonlinear, partial, occasional, and oracular, but they also materialize the act of reading as one that requires our own searching questions to catalyze it, physical accoutrements to accomplish it, and an embodied lifetime of change over which we must revisit the text in order to come to anything resembling completion.

In quite different fashion, when Ramón Saldívar uses Salvador Plascencia's *The People of Paper* (2005) to suggest that writers must invent new techniques capable of representing our inherently fantastic "post-postmodern" world,[47] he is in part acknowledging the need for textual materiality. Saldívar explores the many ways in which the novel breaks down boundaries between genres, characters, and text and world by weaving metafiction and fantasy into the book's Realist representation, but the book's materialist aspects are their own battering ram for the walls that usually exist between fiction and world. As in Tomasula's work, *People* incorporates nonverbal, nonlinguistic elements to represent material acts of narrative communication and structure: drawings of hand signals augment the Table of Contents and new section pages (like the sign language near the end of *IN&OZ*), and binary code stands in for the mechanical tortoise's thoughts on page 97 (like the pages of DNA code in *VAS*; Hayles would call this example, by way of Matthew Kirschenbaum, an example of "formal materialism").[48] And like so many of the texts discussed so far (for example, *Extremely Loud* and *The Tunnel*), *People* also uses images to represent material things or acts encountered in the world of the story, as if to give them a physical presence in the narrative.[49] Like *House of Leaves* and *Everything Is Illuminated*, whose narrators often include stricken or otherwise occluded words, *People* includes typed words that have been scratched out messily by a pen (117, 119, 244), the obliteration providing a trace of a character's embodied act on the text we are reading. Who made these marks and what is that character's relationship to the book we hold in our hands? On what diegetic level does the character exist, and does that narrative plane contain this book? Does it contain me?

This subtle implication of novelistic depths and our own confused location in them becomes more pronounced when we consider the materializing ways in which the novel's most commonly used nonlinguistic element operates. For most of the novel, the black boxes that stand in for the narratives of Baby Nostradamus and Little Merced function as a straightforward visual symbol: the image represents the characters' ability to shield their thoughts from others (23, 160, 164, etc.). But the black box becomes a materializing technique when it no longer perfectly covers the words or thoughts it is blocking. Compare, for example, the monolithic black box of page 23, or the erratic but fully obscuring black box of page 160, with the box on page 187, which obscures only a central portion of Little Merced's thoughts, or the offset box on page 189, which only partially obscures Little Merced's thoughts but also covers a portion of EMF. By page 209, the boxes produced by Little

Merced seem to float somewhat freely over the columns of her thoughts, obscuring and revealing willy-nilly, in some places shielding nothing at all. No longer a simple symbol for a character's thought or act, the black box becomes a material thing generated by a character but physically altering the book itself. That is, the box leaves the internal space of the narrative (its linguistic workings, the level of language) to occupy the physical space of the book.

Such an implication of multiple narrative levels containing various elements of the narrative, as well as the book itself, as well as the reader—and of course the author, who enters the book on page 103—constructs the novel not as flat, linear narrative but as an object of multiple dimensions. This is not a new observation about recent literature—*House* comes to us as Möbius strip or Escher painting; *Everything Is Illuminated* contains wormholes linking its several worlds[50]—but here we see the role materiality plays in constructing not just the narrative, or the physical book, but the surfaces of the book's pages themselves in three dimensions (or more—for an attempt at representing the fourth dimension, see Cixin Liu's *Death's End*). Hayles makes a similar observation about narrative depth using Steven Hall's novel *The Raw Shark Texts* (2007), but with dire consequences. Hayles points out that the shark, itself composed of "ideas, thoughts, fragments, story shards, dreams, memories," and moving through the grass as "a curved and rising signifier, a perfectly evolved fin idea,"[51] is "consistently associated with a form that emerges from the depths," and that "depth is also associated with immersion," as when, during a shark attack, the living room of a character converts to a "conceptual ocean." For Hayles, this association between the shark—as the identification of form and content—and dangerous immersion operates as the novel's warning against the perils of immersive fiction. While using innovative materiality in "defend[ing] the aesthetic of bookishness, [the novel] also presents fiction as a dangerous activity to be approached with extreme care."[52]

Contrary to the redemptive power of materialized language in Foer's novels, or the increased capacity to articulate complex truths that we see in the work of Tomasula, Hoang, and Plascensia, the "immense powers to bring a world into being" that Hayles identifies in *RST*[53] are more akin to the murderous stake of the cultists in *The Names* or the murderous lie of Briony in McEwan's *Atonement*. Not coincidentally, young Briony and the cultists share with the shark a murderous view of language: that to write is to make real, that the sign is the thing. In this way it is not the constructed depth of the narrative but the lack of depth in acts of signifying—the identification of sign and thing, of word and reality—that signals danger. All material realist techniques that remind us of the physical world, and of our physical bodies acting in it amid the book's acts of language, might be seen as an antidote to that old postmodern linguistic threat.[54] Hayles identifies another antidote in her reading of *RST*: the "prophylaxis of decoding,"[55] which counters the dangers of immersion and allows the reader (and characters) to stay safely distant from the maw of the word-beast. Certainly decoding has become an increasingly important aspect of reading practices as metafictional and materializing techniques have become increasingly common writing practices over the past half century (as Hayles predicted in her 1999 *How We Became Posthuman*). But material realist texts of the twenty-first century demand decoding to an unprecedented degree, and less often as a counter measure to protect us from the dangers of immersive fiction, than as a writer's most powerful technique for immersing us into the problems, experiences, feelings, and even subject positions of characters in a textual world or of writers themselves—decoding to produce empathy.

Books as Artifacts and Assemblage: Materializing Reading and Memory

As books of the past decade have begun to use increasingly extreme techniques for materializing language and narrative elements, they have also become more physically strange. Published in boxes, camouflaged as journal or library book, strewn with die-cut holes, or fattened by loose papers and devices tucked into their pages, novels have never more boisterously earned their name. Interestingly, as their physical forms grow wilder, they pretend to increasing sobriety, posturing as found artifacts, historical records, evidence of the "real" past experience of people whose lives we are invited to voyeuristically examine. Not all of these artifactual fictions are particularly literary, whether in the formalist sense of using language to make meaning in ways uncharacteristic of practical writing, or in the more contemporary sense (demonstrated by this book) of signifying in ways that make us rethink what narrative is or how it works. Reif Larson's *The Selected Works of T. S. Spivet* (2010), for example, provides a delightful account of a young boy's cross-country journey, enriched by the many maps, nature sketches, diagrams, and notes running along his journal's margins, but ultimately leaves our notions of storytelling largely undisturbed. Likewise, Jess Stoner's *I Have Blinded Myself Writing This* (2012) masquerades as a marble composition book and marshals many of the innovative techniques used by Foer, Danielewski, Plascencia, Siegel, di Blasi, and other literary materialists (stricken or disappearing text, lines of music, odd textual layout, images, blocked text, real-life documents), but while preserving linear narrative, told by a single narrator, on one narrative plane. Still, her work is unique in imagining an absolute materializing of memory through the body—her narrator loses a memory each time her body must heal a physical wound—so that *I Have Blinded Myself* expresses through story the connection between memory and embodiment, and our continued anxiety about the loss of that connection, that preoccupies other materialist fiction in formal and structural ways that require us to rethink how we read, know, and memorialize.

Anne Carson's *Nox* (2010), for example, flaunts its physical presence while demonstrating that absence constitutes memory. A reproduction of the scrapbook Carson made in response to the death of her own brother, *Nox* tells the story of the narrator's lost brother through photographs, letters, and fragments of both, interspersed among the narrator's (personalized) English definitions of the Latin words that make up the poem *Catallus 101*, and her ruminations on the twin difficulties of translation and memorializing. The book argues that both activities are, like history, equally impossible, equally inexact—metaphorical and akin when you want them to be direct and perfect; articulated more through muteness and hiding than through speech or light. We never get a clear sense of what happened to the brother, and we do not get a full translation of the poem until near the end of the book, but we are invited all along the way to work on them, like the narrator, using the fragments of words and pictures that we have. *Nox* employs both types of material realism. First it draws our attention to the book's physical form with its awkward accordion binding—drop the connected pages at your peril—and the massive gray box that entombs them. Once inside, we encounter rubbings and traces that record the force of the hand that wrote the pages, and language materialized in a wide variety of fonts, on documents that extend beyond the pages' margins, and even in paint (or egg yolk). Kiene Brillenburg Wurth recognizes this first type of materiality as proclaiming the text's "bookishness" in a digital age.[56] But rather than illustrating an "aesthetic of bookishness" that counters the digital with the book's powers of print, the foregrounding of its materiality, according to Wurth, "strangely boils down to [the book's] dematerialization" by presenting its seeming materiality as multiply mediated, as performance. Such loss of authenticity, though, is in line with the other losses that motivate the book—the lost and never retrieved brother, the loss inherent in every act of translation (or memory). But while Wurth's reading dwells on these losses that constitute memory, love, history, writing, and translation—a reading I agree with—we might also say the opposite of the book and of the experience of reading the book: that it invites us to translate the poem using the definitions we are given; it invites us to build a history and image for the brother by joining the fragments of letters and photos we are given; it invites us to construct an understanding of the grieving narrator, who reveals herself only in pieces and traces. If decoding is protection from the danger of immersive fiction in *RST*, it is an invitation to empathy and understanding in *Nox*, placing us in relation to *Nox* in the same position Carson occupies in relation to the fragments that constitute the history of her brother.[57]

While *Nox* uses the book to materialize, rather than narrate, an act of memorializing, *S.* (2013), by J. J. Abrams and Doug Dorst, uses the print book to materialize various acts of reading and writing. In this way, both books present as permanent artifacts, or the opposite of *Agrippa*. *S.* also requires a box, to contain not its accordion spread but the host of separate things that constitute the novel. Like *House of Leaves*, the book comprises multiple stories and narrators piecing together those stories, and requires the reader to crack codes at least as much as she reads narrative. But *S.* takes the assemblage of *House* one step further, not representing one reader's journey through a maze of texts using story and tricksy textual layout, but materializing two readers' acts of reading, which themselves constitute the primary story. Essentially, *S.* materializes the state in which Johnny finds the manuscript of *The Navidson Record* that forms the core of *House of Leaves*. Whereas Danielewski painstakingly describes the mess of papers, fragments, and objects left behind by Zampanò and assembled by Johnny into *The Navidson Record* (xvii), then provides in appendices the journal, poems, letters, sketches, and photographs that the reader must assemble into the narrative of *House of Leaves*, *S.* offers the reader a conglomeration of physical objects, including primary text (the library book, *Ship of Theseus*, by V.M. Straka), ancillary texts (postcards, newspaper articles, letters, a map drawn on a napkin), and devices (primarily, a compass-like code-breaking device I never got deep enough into the book to need), used by the novel's two narrators/readers as they navigate and solve the mystery of Straka, and fall in love.

S. is then both the materialization of the materials used to make fiction, and the artifact of this act of fiction making. In this way, *S.* is also a further step down an evolutionary path linking Borges to Nabokov to Danielewski: Borges told stories driven by encounters with texts that reshape the physical world (especially "Tlön, Uqbar, Orbis Tertius," 1941); Nabokov created a novel that is structurally organized around the remediation of a text, and depicts a character's reshaping of reality and revision of a text through rereading that text (*Pale Fire*, 1962); Danielewski dramatized this process of creating a text by encountering, revising, and assembling someone else's text in *House of Leaves*. *S.* now presents the disassembled pieces that enabled others to create a text and asks the reader to do the assembling, more literally than ever before. With each step beyond Borges's narrated vision of literature's power to shape the world, the text demonstrates that power more aggressively in its structural and physical form; with each step we see the primary point of the narrative move further away from the traditional center of the novel, and the act of creation land more squarely (and literally) in the hands of the reader.

In referring to texts such as *Nox* and *S.* as "assemblage" texts, I am using "assemblage" quite differently than does Hayles in *How We Think*. Hayles is primarily interested in textual assemblage as evidence of the multiplicity of sources and systems required to produce a posthumanist, networked text that produces subjects rather than being produced by them. Such texts are assemblages because they are products of "information multiplicity and media assemblage."[58] I use "assemblage" to describe texts as comprising increasingly physically separate parts that must be assembled to be read. Certainly such texts might also be considered metaphorical "assemblages" in Hayles's information-systems sense as well. But my point here is that materializing such assemblage changes the reader's relationship to the text entirely. We enter into the text and empathize with the characters' own physical (and often painstaking) acts of assembly in ways that, rather than obscuring or displacing the roles of author and reader, make our relationship to author, text, and characters feel more real rather than less. Such texts also materialize reading, writing, and interpretive practices themselves in ways that alter our understanding of how texts come to be, how they mean, and how they matter in the world. We are reminded of our continuity with the physical world, that every act of reading, writing, and interpreting is embodied, relational, and so ethical. This intensified materializing of literature's impact on reality—of the effects on the reader and the world on acts of reading and writing—accounts for many of the technical, structural, formal, and generic changes that the novel has undergone in recent decades.

S. goes to great lengths to hide its identity as contemporary work of material realist fiction, while foregrounding the "unauthored" pieces that will provoke the reader's process of meaning-making. This novel defers to its characters even more than Danielewski did when he ceded the novel's title page to Zampanò and Johnny Truant: Abrams's and Dorst's names appear nowhere on or in the book itself, but only on the box that contains the book/artifact to be read. Similarly, the copyright date is nearly impossible to find. If we look where we expect it, we'll find only the copyright of the artifact, and if we think to look on the book's back cover, where copyright dates typically do not appear, we'll find it only through a diligent search in a stream of fine print. The box contains this information only on its bottom, next to the bar code. Such placement of authors and copyright date creates a distance between the people and time that created this piece of fiction and the piece itself, as if to allow "Straka's" book to slip free from the trappings of reality and out into the world to act upon it as an artifact from a reality that does not exist. If a copy of *Ship of Theseus* were to find its way to the shelf of a used bookstore, readers would have no idea it is part of a larger narrative scheme. Such a boxless *S.* would function like Borges's fictional encyclopedia *Orbis Tertius,* which produced on earth the changes made by *hrönir* on the planet Tlön—it would stand in for a world that does not exist, but that would begin to exist in this world as soon as the book was read. And this book intends to be widely read: rather than opening with Johnny's "This is not for you," *S.* greets readers with "BOOK FOR LOAN." Read in this way, *S.* materializes fiction's ability to reshape the world.

But *S.* operates as historical artifact, bending the space around it with the power of its authentic aura, only when thus shorn of its identifying shell. Read in complete form, as a work of contemporary realism, *S.* materializes the *illusion* required for every satisfying act of reading: the illusion that every act of reading is original, private, and uniquely meaningful. Whereas *Nox* uses hypermediation and the flat page to seem to offer the reader an intimate encounter with the author's material memoir, while really giving only the illusion of that immediacy, *S.* puts the material evidence, fragments, and tools in the hands of the reader and provokes her to construct the story and solve the mystery—if not the mystery of Straka, then the mystery of how these two strangers fell in love while solving the Straka mystery—as if for the first time. Both *Ship of Theseus* and *S.* in its entirety—comprising the network of text, marginal notes, and documents that combined tell the story—come to the reader not just pre-read, but pre-analyzed. It is the reader's job not to read the book *Ship*, or to read it in light of the accompanying documents, or to identify the questions raised and answers provided by this network of texts as discovered by Jen and Eric, but to read the documenting trail of the characters' experience of having figured it all out—the texts pre-digested, the mysteries pre-solved (to the extent that they are solvable). Our task is to analyze the characters' traces of analysis in order to reconstruct their construction: most fundamentally, *S.* asks us to read acts of reading. Doing so absorbs us into the novel's metafictional chain of readers reading readings—first Jen and Eric commenting on the book, then commenting on their earlier comments in multiple layers (signified by varying pen and pencil colors), to which we add our own comments on their readings of their earlier readings as we struggle to keep track of things, taking our part in the chain of readings that operates as the novel's chain of signifiers. The novel even seems to orchestrate our absorption into its fictional world through our act of reading: Jen and Eric's marginal notes quickly swallowed mine, just as the pages bulging with their many devices ate my pencil, which lived invisibly among them (as if transformed into another *hrönir*) until I reopened the book years later. In this way, *S*. demonstrates the postmodern, poststructural assertion that there is no original or unread text, and no original act of reading, while also materializing the absorptive experience of immersive fiction.

But rather than enacting immersion as dangerous, as in *RST*, *S*. illustrates how fiction can reshape the world and the reader in ways that bring understanding, connection, and even love. The book as we encounter it is a history of communication and coming to knowledge through reading—Jen's and Eric's independently of the book, then their reading of each other's notes, and ultimately, in the book's final pages, their reading of each other's faces and bodies, described in marginal notes. The book thus models active reading in positive ways, and anticipates our own active reading of it, as if leading us to read toward the same constructive experiences of illumination and connection that Jen and Eric found through their active reading. Rather than traveling along Freytag's linear triangle, we navigate the constellation of connections that break the boundaries of time, space, and even the book itself, as acts of reading and writing by Jen, Eric, and us external readers jump around in time and space (narratively, as characters travel to find clues, and literally, as we move backward and forward through the book to make connections), and as we remove from the physical book the artifactual tools we need to complete Jen's and Eric's readings, and our own. Gradually these connected readings seem to break the boundary between us and the characters' world as well, as we watch the traces of our reading join the traces of others that make up a large portion of *S*. Thus, the novel also materializes, through traces (and lost pencils) the meeting of reader and writer/narrator that has become a staple of "post-postmodern" fiction at least since Wallace.

If this boxless book were a Tlön-like artifact sent out in the world to reshape it in its own image, how would it change the world? A world in which this book functioned as artifact would be one in which people are still reading books to understand things, answer questions, and right wrongs, as Jen and Eric read *Ship of Theseus*; it would be a world in which knowledge, answers, and justice exist. It would be a world in which people read to connect with others, to empathize with others, to form bonds and communities of shared feeling and experience. And—perhaps most far-fetched of all—it would be a world in which people still linger in libraries, reading and feeling embodied reactions to physical books, books that are passed from hand to hand.[59] This novel does not just imagine, but attempts to create, a world in which fiction retains the power to do good work in it.

The Limits of Literary Materiality

The work that *S.* does as a participant in contemporary realism, however, may be less transformative than we would like. One of my primary motivations for examining technical innovations throughout this book has been to note the ways in which such innovations do or do not contribute to the evolution of literary form and function, rather than simply repeating old habits or, worse, detracting from literariness at the expense of innovation—or what Wallace referred to as the "look-ma-no-hands" approach to fiction, one he went to great pains to avoid being accused of. Material realist fiction illustrates how the risks of formal innovation have changed. Whereas Wallace, like the metafictionists before him, risked drawing attention to his clever language and tricky formal structures and away from the meaning-making being literarily done by both, *S.*, and recent fiction like it, risks holding our attention in acts of decoding for information rather than allowing it to linger in the language and forms that generate literary meaning. On one level, this shift occurs because of the meta-reading position in which *S.* places us: because we read the traces of earlier acts of reading, we do not experience the thrill of discovery that Jen and Eric feel so much as observe it from one step removed. We need only solve, rather than read, the documents we are given. *S.* places the reader in a position akin to that of the formalist critic according to Derrida, reading a map of what has already been read, as the New Critic's formalist analysis constructs a map of what the text is already doing. Rather than providing a space in which to explore the tangle of generative contradictions and aporia that always result from literary language, the pre-digested format of *S.* acts as the "guardrail" guiding but restricting our reading experience.[60]

The novel does provide a "new" narrative for us to read, though—the love story that unfolds between Jen and Eric through their acts of reading. But with a couple of insufficient exceptions (each character at one point writes a long note to the other), that story is primarily confined to short, marginal exchanges—much of them focused on the puzzle the characters are solving. These notes do not provide the sheer volume of *language*, much less the development of narrative structure or form, required for literariness as first defined by Russian formalists such as Shklovsy and Eichenbaum: language that is non-pragmatic, figural, motivated by sound and meter as much as sense, and, most of all, defamiliarizing. Kinbote's notes, after all, far exceeded in length the text he was commenting on, enough to create an entire world. And *House of Leaves* devotes pages, below and above the line, to the literary unfolding of Johnny's working-through *bildungsroman*, pages full of literary language, puns, repetitions, dreams, fantasies, foreshadowing, and extended symbolism (consider the intense suggestiveness of the repeating image of animality/engulfment of the brass bull, deer-shaped locket, and Haitian trapped in the belly of the ship). The experience of reading *S.* suggests that one important difference between novels that use material effects and decoding for entertainment—whether the pleasure of puzzle-solving,[61] or of passively witnessing someone else's literary experience—and those that use it as a twenty-first-century technique for literariness, lies in the ability of the novel as a whole to offer a text that invites the kind of linguistic and literary analysis that opens into complex, unsettled, and evolving meaning rather than producing the neat satisfaction of a completed task.

Another aspect, likely unintended, of literary materiality that can limit its impact on the evolution of literary form and function is a tendency toward a kind of extreme anti-immersion. While decoding can hold us sufficiently apart from the world of fiction to prevent its swallowing us whole (as Hayles has argued of *RST*), sometimes it holds us so far away from the fictional world that its world can no longer touch us. *S.* exemplifies this risk as well: the required decoding is constant and enormously demanding, forcing us out of the book in our hands and into other documents on nearly every page, and back and forth between pages, to locate ourselves in the various timelines of the narrative and gather the pieces we need to construct it. The consequence of this extreme amplification of Wallace's page-flipping endnote effect in *Jest* is that we are never able to immerse in any portion of the fictional world, or of its language, long enough to feel at home there. I do not think it is a coincidence that both Hayles (in *How We Think*) and Ali Smith (in *Artful*) compare narrative form to home.[62] Feeling at home is a large part of why we enter narrative at all, and if a novel can't hold us in its spaces long enough to allow us that orientation and comfort, it is unlikely to hold our attention long enough to make us want to fully traverse it. I still haven't figured out what I'm supposed to do with the compass-like decoder tucked into the back of *S.*

And yet we can make all kinds of fancy arguments about such books. Many compelling arguments have been made about Foer's *Tree of Codes* (2010), which uses extensive die-cutting of words and phrases from every page to excavate a new novel out of Bruno Schulz's *The Street of Crocodiles*. Criticism on this novel already points out many ways in which it uses both types of material realism I have been exploring in this chapter. Wurth places the novel, as she did *Nox*, in the tradition of sculpture made from books by artists such as Doug Beube and Brian Dettmer,[63] but reads it rather against her reading of *Nox*. For Wurth, *Tree of Codes* asserts the power of the print book's physical medium, or, as Foer says, the novel is a "book that can't forget it has a body."[64] Hayles also notes this first type of materiality in the novel, its body asserting an aesthetic of bookishness, while also recognizing some of the novel's ways of materializing language itself, by using the depth created by the holes to materialize the "zoom effect" that is normally accomplished by narrative, and to focus our attention on the morphemes and phonemes of language, or "the molecular dimension of language." These material effects change the way we read, forcing us to read proprioceptively, with our embodied selves, as Hayles points out,[65] and, as Berit Michel argues, asking us to navigate a "map of the urban condition" in a kind of "experiential realism."[66]

Wurth aptly labels Foer's sculptural work in making this novel—his "'writing,' his cutting"—an act of "deep reading."[67] But to what extent does the novel offer an act of deep reading for us? Or does the author's depth of reading and writing interfere with the reader's depth of reading? Certainly the existing criticism on the book indicates that such "deep" reading is possible, and intellectually rewarding, but I would suggest that it is both of those things in limited and qualified ways. The relative dearth of criticism on *Tree of Codes*, now in print for nearly a decade, compared to the mountain of criticism on Foer's two earlier novels, and despite the fascinating arguments some critics have made about it, suggests that the book's challenging structure rather than its intellectual content may account for this lack of critical attention. The barrier to deep reading might be, however, less the challenge of decoding the physical structure than the impossibility of it. My copy can't be the only one whose binding misaligns the pages enough to prevent me from reading the beginnings and endings of a large percentage of words. Even a well put-together copy would be enormously time-consuming to read, a difficulty that is implied by one of Hayles's endnotes, which acknowledges three people who aided her in encoding and analyzing the novel, meaning that it took four scholars to produce a six-page article on this novel. For me, and for my colleagues who have admitted a similar frustration with the book, *Tree of Codes* seems more akin to the "impossible book" that Paul Ardoin, in his response to Hayles's article in the *PMLA*, notes that Foer has been constructing all along[68]—a reading that aligns this book nicely with the anxiety about the capacities and limits of the print book expressed by so many other texts examined here, all the way back to *Agrippa*.

According to this reading, the totally illegible literary sculpture seems more like end point than inspiration for *Tree of Codes*; the recent popularity of such art books, and their comingling with legible books—Barnes and Noble sold several versions (the pages of *Sense and Sensibility* folded to form "love," as one example) during the 2014 holiday season—suggests just such a continuum.[69] But the print book that is probably the most materially daring is one that will never be sold by Barnes and Noble, or anyone else. In 2003, Shelley Jackson began choosing volunteers to become "words" in her short story "Skin," which will only ever be read in its entirety by those who have tattooed its words, as assigned by Jackson, on their bodies. The ultimate equation of body and word, Jackson's *Ineradicable Stain* project materializes language, unifies reader and text, and disperses the text to mutate continuously in space, while shackling it to time. It is a culmination of the meeting of materialized language with the fluidity of elit, which is no surprise from the author whose *Patchwork Girl* (1995) defines electronic literature's first phase.[70] Jackson's work—published by tattoo parlors everywhere—demonstrates dramatically what print literature since the 1990s had already discovered: how radically changes in production alter textual form and meaning, and how the body—textual and human—remains the site for registering and reading those changes.

Works like those by Abrams and Dorst, Foer, Jackson, Beube, and Barnes and Noble also demonstrate how the persistence of hypermaterial texts in the increasingly digital twenty-first century does not simply question the "lateness" of print in the 1990s.[71] In their emphasis on physical form at the expense of traditional readability, these texts also question the signifying capacity of print that self-conscious materiality has aimed to demonstrate since the 1990s. Thus they can seem to exhibit not a defiant "aesthetic of bookishness" but rather an aesthetic of the dead book. Meanwhile, theories of "electracy,"[72] or methods for reading electronic texts, emphasize the role played by materiality—of code, of language, of the embodied and temporal experience of reading electronic literature—in making digital texts meaningful, continuing the argument begun by Hayles in her 1999 *How We Became Posthuman*. In this context, today's insistently and often awkwardly physical texts can repeat rather than resolve the anxiety about the status of the print book as historical artifact that *Agrippa* expressed so well in the 1990s.

How Print Matters

And yet—however much some material realist texts might challenge readers beyond fascination and into frustration, the significance and power of their impact on how we read and write and think about art and the world are undeniable. To recognize books again as artifacts of or witnesses to history, however fragmented, tenuous, or partial, is to recognize in today's material realism the opposite of postmodernism's anxiety about representing the past. It is to read contemporary literature moving from *Agrippa* to *S.*, from history disappearing to history concretized, no longer stuck in Jameson's "nostalgia mode" or even postmodern pastiche: consider the prevalence of productive parody in *House of Leaves* (academia), *Love in a Dead Language* (again, academia), *The Jiří Chronicles* (heterosexual norms), *The Book of Portraiture* (Freudian analysis), all of Foer (Jewish culture, historicizing)—

but parody accomplished by placing in our hands documents that attest to past or present lived experience in ways we are meant to understand through our own physical acts of reading, as we connect the embodied past with the embodied present. To view fiction as asserting the power of language, of letters, of the mark, to shape and even create reality for good and for ill is to posit a direct causal connection between art and reality that has been beleaguered or utterly denied since at least modernism.

Material realism also asks us to rethink and recontextualize our practices of writing, to allow them to take their proper place among a long history of evolving technology, in which we can once again see them as material practices. Jameson implies this point when he describes the six different sections of *Cloud Atlas* as distinguished by their "different material apparatus[es] of transmission," reading the novel as not so much about the massively technological future and present versus the primitive past as it is about the gradual evolution of many phases of material media.[73] Hayles makes a similar point when she reads *RST* as a model for "stories in which writing is not just the medium of communication but the material basis for a future in which humans, as ancient as their biology and as contemporary as their technology, can find a home."[74] Combining contemporary technologies of textual formatting and production with the ancient technology of the print book, these material realist texts harness the capacities of the new to produce complexly physical texts that ground us both in the old material practice of writing and in today's physical world out of which all writing grows. This meeting of old and new produces new techniques, forms, and modes for literature in another opposition to or movement beyond the postmodern proclamation that nothing new would ever be possible again.

In changing the nature of the text, material realism also profoundly changes the role of the reader and the reader-writer relationship. Texts presented as disassembled and/or partial artifacts requiring assembly by the reader provoke reader participation in constructing the text that is akin to but far surpassing the demands placed on the reader by mid-century metafiction (e.g., Calvino's *If on a winter's night a traveller*, Barth's *Lost in the Funhouse*) or even by Wallace's late twentieth-century fiction (e.g., *Infinite Jest*). Recent material artifactual texts do not just demand readers' empathy with the writer's linguistic project (as in Wallace's "Octet"); they physically place readers in the position of their writers or characters, asking readers to construct the narratives, even the conditions of the narrative, using found fragments. We might consider such a technique, as used in *S.*, as the literalization of the reader-writer shoe-swapping imagined by Wallace's narrator in Quiz 9 of "Octet," or a process of creating empathy in the reader by physically putting her in the writer's place. Meanwhile, material realism also provokes a return to important older ways of reading whose import is too often forgotten: material texts make obvious and undeniable the century-old Russian formalist claim that form is content. They force us to once again take seriously the formalist method for literary analysis that has been partially eclipsed by decades of cultural theory and criticism, especially new historicism and cultural studies, that treat literature more as container for evidence of cultural practices than as an art form whose language is the very fabric of its art. Or looked at from that more recent, constructivist, cultural-theoretical perspective, we might say that material texts, in which form is undeniably coincident with content, force us to treat the book as a body, and its constitutive structures as real and consequent, not just as an immaterial emanation of the bodies that made, read, and produced it. In this way, material realist practices elucidate one clear method for distinguishing literature since the 1990s from postmodern literature, while demonstrating how crucial formalism is to making such distinctions.

Finally, and perhaps most significantly, material realist fiction enacts and reflects our changing notions of reality, the real world, and matter itself. After decades during which the material world had been eclipsed (or, temporarily, replaced) by signs and theories about signification, and at a time when the rapid evolution of technology predicts a future in which the virtual will eclipse the material and the artificial will replace the real, material realist texts reorient us toward the presence and power of the physical. They remind us of books' bodies and of our own bodies, and that matter is, at this point in our human history, always required for making meaning. They continue and intensify, to the point of materializing, the conceptual work done through narrative in *The Road* and *Extremely Loud & Incredibly Close*, as I argued in *Succeeding Postmodernism*, and in all of Tomasula's work, as I have argued in Chapter 2 of this book: they assert the presence and primariness of the physical world.

Nineteenth-century realist literature—before poststructuralism and virtual-reality technology—had no need to make such an argument. Instead, it asserted the importance of empirical reality against the dream of fantasy, Romance, and idealism. To acknowledge this change from nineteenth-century realism to today's material realism is to acknowledge a fundamental shift in literature, from focusing on epistemology to privileging ontology. Whereas nineteenth-century realism argues for one method of *knowing* the world over another, material realism instantiates a particular concept of *being* shared by literature and the world: being as material, made of matter, potentially making the world continuous with the matter of language. Karan Barad notes that the movement away from representationalism made by new materialism in general, and her idea of "agential realism" in particular, expresses a similar shift: from a "traditional realist" approach "where, much like the infinite play of images between two facing mirrors, the epistemological gets bounced back and forth, but nothing more is seen," to "questions of ontology, materiality, and agency."[75] Her use of the *mise en abyme* (itself a self-reflexive perversion of Stendhal's Realist mirror walking down the road) to represent the kind of representationalism she aims to move away from echoes my own description of Wallace's and Tomasula's representational shifts from *trompe l'oeil* to *trompe l'esprit*, as their primary methods of escaping the *mise en abyme* of metafictional self-reflection (see Chapter 1, pp. 59–60 and Chapter 2, pp. 84–5). All of this metafictive and material realist fiction implies such a shift from knowledge-based inquiries to being-based ones, which I have investigated so far primarily in terms of technical and formal innovations in representational methods.[76]

Barad's quantum-physics-based framing of this shift allows us to take the inquiry even further: when we redefine material reality, how do we necessitate new definitions and forms of fiction that aim to represent—or participate in, or intra-act with—that new reality? How do quantum concepts force us to rethink literary elements such as point of view, perspective, setting, character, and time? If our scientific notions of reality no longer reflect our embodied experience of it, and if fiction's main aims have been to reflect and reflect upon both reality and human experience, how might fiction reconcile this new gap between the two? Chapters 4 and 5 will address these questions about the technical and formal innovations prompted by literary attempts to render the quantum world, and use them to ask and answer the larger questions they imply—about literature's role in exposing the inherent ethics of being, and literature's significance as an agent of change in a wholly relational, agential universe.

Notes

1 Or, precisely $1.088886945 \times 10^{28}$ different textual orderings.
2 Susan Sontag, *Against Interpretation* (New York: Picador, 1961), 14.
3 Don DeLillo, *The Names* (New York: Vintage Books, 1989), 10.
4 Walter Benn Michaels, *The Shape of the Signifier* (New Jersey: University of Princeton Press, 2004), 18.
5 N. Katherine Hayles, *Electronic Literature: New Horizons for the Literary* (Notre Dame: University of Notre Dame Press, 2008), 6.
6 Ibid., 162.
7 Stephen J. Burn, "The End of Postmodernism," in *American Fiction in the 1990s: Reflections on History and Culture*, ed. Jay Prosser (Abingdon: Routledge, 2008), 228.

8 N. Katherine Hayles, *Writing Machines* (Boston: MIT Press, 2002), 126.
9 Little, Brown did publish "Up, Simba" electronically in 2000.
10 For Wallace's descriptions of *Jest*'s structure, see Burn's *Conversations with David Foster Wallace*, 57 and 72.
11 Stephen J. Burn, "Anatomizing the Language of Love: An Interview with Lee Siegel," *Electronic Book Review*, September 28, 2006: np.
12 Lee Siegel, *Love in a Dead Language* (Chicago: University of Chicago Press, 2000), 155–64. I will note subsequent references parenthetically.
13 Robert Coover, "The End of Books," *The New York Times Book Review*, June 21, 1992: 23–5.
14 Ibid., 7.
15 Jessica Pressman, "The Aesthetic of Bookishness in Twenty-First Century Literature," *Michigan Quarterly Review* 48, no. 4 (2009): 465, 467.
16 Jerzy Kutnik, *The Novel as Performance: The Fiction of Ronald Sukenick and Raymond Federman* (Carbondale: Southern Illinois University Press, 1986).
17 Raymond Federman, *Double or Nothing* (Tuscaloosa: FC2, 1998), np.
18 Hayles, *Writing Machines*, 129.
19 Carole Maso, "Rupture, Verge, and Precipice," *Review of Contemporary Fiction* 16, no. 1 (1996): 63.
20 Victoria Frenkel Harris, "Emacipating the Proclamation," *Review of Contemporary Fiction* 17, no. 3 (1997): 2.
21 Carol Maso, *The Art Lover* (Cambridge: New Directions, 1990), 150. I will note subsequent references parenthetically.
22 Charles Bernstein, *All the Whiskey in Heaven* (New York: Farrar, Straus, and Giroux, 2010), 144, 145.
23 Ibid., 233, 258.
24 *Let's Just Say*, Ibid., 144.
25 Ibid., 8–10, 245.
26 Ibid., 155–7.
27 William H. Gass, *The Tunnel* (Champaign: Dalkey Archive Press, 1995), 590–1. I will note subsequent references parenthetically.
28 Of course, the use of the wife and of Lalita as substitution for Being by Kohler and Roth is not far off from the male narrator of Wallace's "Brief Interview #20" using for his own growth narrative a woman's experience of brutal rape (see Chapter 1, p. 77, FN 33). The objectifying male use of women's bodies to materialize aspects of their selves and desires is, in a misogynistic culture, a theme that often occupies materializing contemporary literature (critiqued or normalized to varying degrees).
29 Gass, "Philosophy and the Form of Fiction," 14.
30 Richard Grossman, *The Alphabet Man* (Normal: FC2, 1993), 91, 275.
31 Rick Dolphijn and Iris van Der Tuin, *New Materialism: Interviews & Cartographies* (Ann Arbor: Open Humanities Press, 2012), 48.
32 Barad, *Meeting*, 132. I will note subsequent references parenthetically. Christopher Breu's *The Insistence of the Material* (Minneapolis: University

of Minnesota Press, 2014) participates in this interdisciplinary effort to shift our focus away from language and back to materiality, specifically as a limit to contemporary biopolitics, while recognizing the limits of language's ability to represent the material. His argument rests on extended readings of Burroughs's *Naked Lunch*, Pynchon's *V.*, Ballard's *Crash*, Bellamy's *The Letters of Mina Harker*, and Silko's *Almanac of the Dead*.
33 Ibid., 133.
34 Diana Coole and Samantha Frost, eds., *New Materialisms: Ontology, Agency, and Politics* (Durham: Duke University Press, 2010), 2–3.
35 Ibid., 6.
36 John Barth, "The Literature of Exhaustion," in *The Friday Book: Essays and Other Non-Fiction* (Baltimore: Johns Hopkins University Press, 1984), 62–76.
37 Lyotard, "Defining the Postmodern" and Jameson, "Postmodernism and Consumer Society," both in *The Norton Anthology of Theory and Criticism* (2010).
38 Dolphijn and van der Tuin, *New Materialism*, 61.
39 Coole and Frost, *New Materialisms*, 7.
40 Barad quoted in Dolphijn and van der Tuin, *New Materialism*, 57.
41 Dolphijn and van der Tuin, *New Materialism*, 59.
42 David Mitchell, *Cloud Atlas* (New York: Random House, 2004), 309.
43 Debra Di Blasi, *The Jirí Chronicles and Other Fiction* (Normal: FC2, 2007), 164, 191.
44 Jonathan Safran Foer, *Extremely Loud & Incredibly Close* (New York: Houghton Mifflin, 2005), 49.
45 Jonathan Safran Foer, *Everything Is Illuminated* (New York: Houghton Mifflin, 2002), 212–13.
46 Lily Hoang, *Changing* (Tuscaloosa: Fairy Tale Review Press, 2008), 130, 129.
47 Saldivar, "Historical Fantasy, Speculative Realism, and Postrace Aesthetics in Contemporary Fiction," 574–99.
48 N. Katherine Hayles, *How We Think* (Chicago: University of Chicago Press, 2012), 91.
49 Salvador Plascencia, *The People of Paper* (New York: Harcourt, 2005), 21, 33, 43, etc. I will note subsequent references parenthetically.
50 As I argued in *Succeeding Postmodernism*, 184.
51 Steven Hall, *The Raw Shark Texts* (New York: Canongate, 2007), 158.
52 Hayles, *How We Think*, 206, 207.
53 Ibid., 207.
54 See *Succeeding Postmodernism* Chapter 1.
55 Hayles, *How We Think*, 209.
56 Kiene Brillenburg Wurth, "Re-vision as Remediation: Hypermediacy and Translation in Anne Carson's *Nox*," *Image (&) Narrative* 14, no. 4 (2013): 22.
57 Zuzanna Jakubowski offers an insightful reading of a similarly photography-based text, *Important Artifacts and Personal Property from the Collection*

of *Lenore Doolan and Harold Morris, Including Books, Street Fashion and Jewelry* by Shapton. See her "Exhibiting Lost Love: The Relational Realism of Things," 124–45.

58 Hayles, *How We Think*, 223.

59 Perhaps we might consider Richard Brautigan's *The Abortion: An Historical Romance 1966* (New York: Simon & Schuster, 1971) to be a predecessor for *S.* in this respect. The novel imagines a library that is open 24/7, run by one dedicated man, whose purpose is to catalog works turned away by publishers and make them available for reading at any time of the day or night. In the comings and goings of readers, the library becomes backdrop and catalyst for all kinds of human connection and its consequences (including an abortion). In 1990, Todd Lockwood materialized that library of unpublished works, founding The Brautigan Library in Burlington, Vermont. After a few closures and physical relocations resulting from the difficulty of being that single 24/7 staffer and funder, Lockwood handed over the collection of more than 300 manuscripts to be curated by John Barber of The Creative Media & Digital Culture program at Washington State University, Vancouver. Today, the internet provides a more practical space for housing the library: see brautiganlibary.org.

60 See Derrida, *Of Grammatology*, 158.

61 See, for example, Zachary Dodson's *The Bats of the Republic* (2015), Roy Leban's *The Librarian's Almanaq* (2015), and Dimitris Chassa (et al.)'s *Journal 29* (2017). The most fully disassembled materializing text I have found so far is Chris Ware's *Building Stories* (2012), a "graphic novel" that the reader builds using sundry materials, including a sort of game board and comic strips in varying formats, provided in its large, heavy, rectangular box. While much more open-ended than the puzzle books listed here, *Building Stories* ultimately feels more like a game or other activity than a book; one does not "read" it so much as play with it. Perhaps it is our best example yet of materializing the *jouissance* that Barthes attributed to language.

62 Hayles, *How We Think*, 219; Ali Smith, *Artful* (New York: Penguin, 2012), 145.

63 Less well known are the many female artists using books to sculpt pieces of art with various degrees of bookishness at the Women's Studio Workshop in Rosendale, NY. In September 2019, the Omega Institute in Rhinebeck, NY offered an exhibit called "A Bindery of Reason," curated by Kathleen Laucius and featuring art books and art made of books by artists including Tona Wilson, Wei Jane Chir, Barbara Leoff Burge, Bisa Washington, Clarissa Sligh, and Kate Horvat.

64 Kiene Brillenburg Wurth, "Old and New Modalities in Foer's *Tree of Codes*," *CLCWeb: Comparative Literature and Culture* 13, no. 3 (2011): 3, 7.

65 N. Katherine Hayles, "Combining Close and Distant Reading," *PMLA* 128, no. 1 (2013): 229–30, 231.

66 Berit Michel, "'PlastiCity': Foer's *Tree of Codes* as (Visual) Multilayered Urban Topography," *Critique: Studies in Contemporary Fiction* 55, no. 2 (2014): 174.
67 Wurth, "Old and New," 4.
68 Paul Ardoin, "Jonathan Safran Foer and the Impossible Book," *PMLA* 128, no. 4 (2013): 1007.
69 Garrett Stewart's *Bookwork: Medium to Object to Concept to Art* (Chicago: University of Chicago Press, 2011), on the other hand, explores the productivity of such art books, demonstrating that they do not make books unreadable so much as they make books differently readable—as conceptual rather than mimetic art, provoking us to rethink our assumptions about reading, making, and representing.
70 Hayles, *Electronic Literature*, 7.
71 As argued by Ted Striphas in *The Late Age of Print* (New York: University of Columbia Press, 2009).
72 George Ulmer introduced this term in *Teletheory: Grammatology in the Age of Video* (Abingdon: Routledge, 1989).
73 Jameson, *Antinomies*, 309, 311.
74 Hayles, *How We Think*, 219.
75 Barad, *Meeting*, 135.
76 The shift from epistemology to ontology that I am describing as a feature of contemporary realism, and so of literature after postmodernism, differs significantly from the movement from modernist epistemology to postmodern ontology, which Brian McHale defined back in 1987 as a primary feature of postmodernism. See Chapter 4, p. 183 for more on this difference.

4

Quantum Realism

On Ted Chiang's "Story of Your Life" and Ruth Ozeki's *A Tale for the Time Being*

How thrilling for a certain kind of reader, one who knows far more about theories of language than about theories of the universe, to stumble across this gem at the end of a dense explanation of why linear time does not exist:

> The feeling that time flows is deeply ingrained in our experience and thoroughly pervades our thinking and language. So much so, that we have lapsed, and will continue to lapse, into habitual, colloquial descriptions that refer to a flowing time. But **don't confuse language with reality. Human language is far better at capturing human experience than at expressing deep physical laws.**[1]

From the perspectives of postmodern literature and poststructural theory, Brian Greene's thinking about language comes as a surprise and a relief. After decades of agonizing over language's inability to connect to the real world, deliver truth, or communicate reliably between people, the idea that language is not simply the only paltry method we have for interacting with the world and with each other but is instead an effective tool for "capturing human experience" seems to restore to language the powers it lost, somewhat ironically, during the linguistic turn in which "*il n'y a[vait] pas de hors-texte.*"

How this might be so is not immediately apparent. On its surface, physicists' struggles to describe the physical universe using a quantum mechanics whose fundamental principles do not align with our daily experience do more to underscore, even explain, postmodern views of the world and of language than to oppose them, as early explorers of quantum fiction have noted.[2] But in his chapter on the "flow" of time, Brian Greene is able to propose his more optimistic view of language because he reconceptualizes not its relationship to our attempts to explain reality (quantum mechanics) but its relationship to reality itself. Of all quantum concepts, including complementarity (matter acts as both waves and particles) and entanglement (particles separated by great distances can affect each other), quantum views of time are most distressingly counterintuitive—because we don't have embodied experience of waves and particles to argue with, but we do have constant embodied experience of time. And the experience of every human being, in every moment, runs directly counter to a quantum understanding of time, which is that it is not linear or directional, but is in some fundamental way static:

> Just as we envision all of space as *really* being out there, as *really* existing, we should also envision all of time as *really* being out there, as *really* existing. Past, present, and future certainly appear to be distinct entities. But as Einstein once said, "For we convinced physicists, the distinction between past, present, and future is only an illusion, however persistent." The only thing that's real is the whole of spacetime. (139, original italics)

Every moment that has ever happened or will happen, from a human perspective, is equally as real as this moment that you are experiencing now; every one of those moments equally exists. It is human consciousness that views those moments as moving from past to future: "Within each individual [spacetime] slice, your thoughts and memories are sufficiently rich to yield a sense that time has continuously flowed to that moment" (140). We impose the feeling of flow, of linearity, of cause and effect—of narrative. That is to say, before we write or speak, before language enters at all, human perception transforms existence—what is, the universe, spacetime—into story, adding change, direction, and causality in the process. From the perspective of quantum mechanics, then, Lacan's Real *is* real, is reality itself, is that which we can never experience directly, let alone represent. Greene literalizes Lacan's theory by pointing out that we in fact never do experience the present moment, simply because of the physics of light: "Anything you see right *now* has already happened. You are not seeing the words on this page as they are now; instead, if you are holding the book a foot from your face, you are seeing them as they were a billionth of a second ago" (133, original italics). Quantum mechanics—or, in this case, physics in general—maps onto the whole of reality the crisis of signification that we literary theorists had been content to despair about merely in the arena of language. Reading quantum mechanics as a poststructuralist means finding out that the terror you thought was safely confined to metaphysics is really the terror of the world—that language and world are one (hooray!), but in the worst possible way: both remain forever outside human reach.

It is in *this* context, a crisis of reality far bleaker than the crisis of meaning for which theorists such as Baudrillard have been blamed since the 1980s, that language is allowed to once again become a beacon of hope and illumination.

Language cannot capture reality (poststructuralism), and human experience cannot embody reality (quantum physics) or the present (Newtonian and quantum physics), but the mistakes language makes in representing the real—adding linearity, causality, and meaningful change where none exists—are the same mistakes we all make in processing experience, in experiencing being itself. In this way, language actually *is* continuous with human experience, not alien to or cut off from it, and is our best way of understanding and interacting with a reality whose "deep physical laws" we cannot comprehend. In this cosmic context, all aspects of language—*la parole* and *la langue*—become entirely, uniquely, distinctively human, an organic emanation straining to connect human being and universe, which may preexist any particular human but does not preexist humanity itself.[3] Such a context does not merely reverse the anti-humanist argument of Heidegger, Lacan, and Derrida that language precedes the human,[4] but rather places that assertion in a context so total and timeless that the causality at its heart makes no sense whatsoever.

If the argument mapped through the Introduction holds—that changes in how we view the world necessitate changes in how we represent the world—then certainly quantum ideas about reality must engender new forms of realism. The conventions of nineteenth-century realism, which predated quantum mechanics, reflect their Newtonian universe: events proceed linearly, through cause and effect, in a knowable universe, often presided over by an omniscient objective perspective. The teleology of Freytag's triangle—all conflicts headed toward climactic revelation and resolution back to stasis—mirrors the determinism that described the universe even through Einstein, who, despite having written the theories of relativity and special relativity that opened the door to quantum mechanics, never accepted the uncertainty that lies at the core of the quantum universe.[5] Quantum realism, however, strives to represent the world not empirically, according to human experience, but as it exists apart from human translation, according to the physical laws of quantum mechanics. Those laws describe a reality that is in many ways disturbingly unfamiliar to us, one that is entirely relative, subjective, complementary (both this and that), a nexus of probability rather than a series of causes, and ultimately unmeasurable, uncertain, unknowable, and—perhaps most mind-bogglingly—only one among infinite possibilities in simultaneous existence.[6] In this universe, just as all moments are equally real, all perspectives of those moments are equally valid, and no truth can be expressed using anything but all possible perspectives. Simply to describe the quantum universe is to begin to appreciate the massive challenge of representing it on the page, and to imagine the kinds of literary methods that might do so: multiple perspective and point of view, fragmentation, unreliable narrators, aporias of unresolved contradiction, nonlinear narrative, confused causality, multiple endings and resistance to closure. So then, is "quantum fiction" just another name for "postmodernism" or "experimental fiction"?

Well, yes and no. The two sustained literary-critical works that examine quantum fiction to date both define quantum fiction (without using this exact term) as essentially a subset of postmodernism, in that it shares all of postmodernism's main tenets (having, in fact, bequeathed those tenets to postmodernism), while aiming itself in a slightly different direction. The more recent of the two, Samuel Coale's *Quirks of the Quantum: Postmodern and Contemporary American Fiction* (2012), goes so far as to give a compelling argument that we can understand the break between modernism and postmodernism as a transition from Newtonian and Einsteinian to quantum physics, in terms of the types of worlds being imagined by literature and its ways of structuring those worlds: "If modernism questions our epistemological apprehensions and perceptions, postmodernism questions the very ontological existence of the world we half-observe and half-create" (36). Coale moves through the main features of postmodern textuality and demonstrates their affinity with cousin ideas in quantum theory: "Derrida's vision" of textuality is quantum "flux"; Baudrillard's hyperreal describes the relationship between "our use of language and the quantum realm"; the poststructuralist theory of language—that signs represent multiple, contradictory things—echoes Bohr's theory of complementarity, in which one observation (reading) detects waves and another detects particles; the fragmented, fluid postmodern self reflects the probability and statisticality of the quantum world (36-8). Rather than attempting to separate fiction influenced by quantum theory from postmodernism, Coale baldly states that "quantum theory is one significant approach to and foundation of [postmodernism]" (12). His book then explores quantum elements of postmodern literature in terms of structure, style, and theme. My work here intends to build on the excellent work begun by Coale and provide a slightly more specific lens for examining the effects of quantum theory on fiction, by examining the ways in which quantum ideas about reality shape realism as a mode of writing, and then by reflecting on what this new mode of realism reveals about how we conceive of language's relationship with the world—in representational and ontological terms—in the early twenty-first century.

Susan Strehle, the first to produce a major study on the effects of quantum theory on fiction, takes a very different tack, and one that in my mind limits the effectiveness of an otherwise insightful argument. In *Fiction in the Quantum Universe* (1992), Strehle proclaims from the start her intention to define quantum-inspired fiction—what she calls "actualism"—as belonging to postmodernism, but in opposition to one of postmodernism's most powerful modes, metafiction. Strehle's largest goal is close to my own, in this book and in my previous one, of discovering new intersections between language and world and recognizing ways in which literature never left the world behind. But we differ dramatically in our understandings of metafiction's role in this dilemma and in its solutions. For Strehle, in 1992, metafiction was the culprit:

> Postmodern narratives appear to many critics to be metafiction: a fiction designed to comment on its own textual and linguistic processes. More generally, critics regard all contemporary writers who have abandoned realism as having abandoned reality at the same stroke. In the prevailing metafictive climate, the world outside of fiction is assumed by some critics of postmodern fiction to be linguistic and textual, by others to be fictive or imaginary, and by virtually all to be beside the point. (ix)

While I would not disagree with this assessment of criticism in the 1980s–90s, I would say (and have argued in Chapters 1 and 2 of *Succeeding Postmodernism*) that such reductive and erroneous readings of metafiction are a problem of criticism, not of the fiction itself. Rather than reread metafiction's role in representing the real world, though, as I have aimed to do in Chapter 1 of this book, Strehle's book constructs it as a strawperson throughout, differentiating the ideas, intentions, themes, and techniques of quantum fiction/"actualism" from those of metafiction at every turn. The problem with this fierce defense of actualism against the (for-her) overly linguistic or fantastic metafiction is that no such stark separation between them exists.

Many of the techniques she defines as "actualist" are essentially metafictive. Robert Coover's "multiple repetitions or complementary variations of episodes," which she reads as suggesting probability rather than causality (69), might be read equally well as a metafictive exposure of drafting, revision, and the author's omniscient control—especially in conjunction with his fiction's contemplation of media forms, as in "The Babysitter." Coover's fictionalizing of history, which Linda Hutcheon has convincingly read as "historiographic metafiction,"[7] Strehle reads as an opportunity to demonstrate "popular fears of relativity and indeterminacy" (70). John Barth's technique of creating multiple overlapping frames of authorship and perspective in *LETTERS* she reads as modeling postmodern/quantum insights about the inability to find a privileged frame from which to observe the world (129), which is true, but how is Barth's highly textually self-conscious technique for doing so not metafictive? Or his creation of himself as a character (221)? Or Barthelme's ironizing of the forms of his fiction (212)? Why, and on what consistent basis, label some examples of self-reflexive work as "metafictive," and thus disconnected from reality and not worthy of our attention, and others as "actualist," hence realist in a quantum way and thus meaningful? How might we more productively differentiate *quantum* fiction from merely *postmodern* fiction, or from *metafiction*?

Strehle relies heavily on statements of authorial intent in drawing this distinction, quoting authors known as metafictionists—Coover, Gaddis, Barth, and Barthelme—on their goals for keeping their fiction engaged in reality, in order to redefine them as productive "actualists." I don't dispute that all of these writers were at least as interested in contemplating the world as they were in reflecting on language; rather, I reject the notion that any writer, however "anti-realist" or experimental in form, must defend her or his interest in the world in order to be taken seriously as a "realist" writer. What is language without the world? What is a writer without it? Rather than defending Barth by reading him as emerging from an ill-advised detour through metafiction to "return to realism" with *LETTERS* (124–5), I would remind us that Barth has talked about himself as a realist writer all long, before and after, not just while, writing *LETTERS*,[8] just as Wallace spoke of himself as a realist writer while writing metafiction throughout his career (see Chapter 1). Similarly, many of the authors Strehle defines as metafictionists, rather than actualists, and thus as unconcerned with the real world or with matters of traditional realism (4), I would read as quite the opposite (for example, William Gass, B. S. Johnson, and Ishmael Reed).

I agree with Strehle's central, crucial point, that "contemporary fiction departs from realism without losing interest in reality," in part because "reality is no longer realistic" (ix–x). But rather than denigrate metafictional techniques, which have proven to be so powerful in contemporary attempts to conjure the world on the page, and rather than invent a confusing taxonomy in which quantum fiction is somehow thoroughly postmodern but not metafictive,[9] despite employing metafictive devices, I propose a less convoluted approach: that we consider metafiction as a set of *techniques* that make the text visible, quantum fiction as a *subset* of literature that addresses quantum concepts thematically, and quantum realism as a *mode* of writing—like traditional realism, magical realism, fantasy, romance, etc—that requires metafictive and other anti-Realist techniques to represent the unintuitive, non-Newtonian aspects of its quantum world. Such a differentiation between the looser category of quantum fiction, which might invoke quantum concepts only thematically, superficially, or briefly, and quantum realism, whose very representational strategies are determined—contorted away from Newtonian realism—by the quantum reality it aims to represent, will also aid this book's larger purpose of considering how changes in our ideas about reality lead to changes in form and produce new realisms.

Quantum Fiction versus Quantum Realism

Adding to the challenge of defining quantum realism versus quantum fiction, and of differentiating both from postmodern fiction and metafiction, is the confusion that can be perpetuated by fiction itself. As a primary example, Vanna Bonta's *Flight* (1995), the first novel to bill itself (on the cover no less) as "a quantum fiction novel," is not quantum fiction at all, if we require fiction to correctly represent quantum mechanics in order to be considered a quantum novel. It does explicitly invoke quantum ideas and theorists, including Heisenberg's uncertainty principle and the work of "Bohm"[10]—though it's not clear that Bonta does not mean Neils Bohr, who was Heisenberg's contemporary, while Bohm was not—and the novel makes frequent use of the observer's effect on the reality observed. But *Flight* consistently uses these principles toward its idealist, dualist, and positivist ends: the world it depicts is completely knowable by the mind and shaped by the spirit. The novel is also deeply political and conservatively moralizing. In its warnings about the power of the media to destroy individual selves while creating whiney special interest groups, it is the kind of monstrous baby that might result from the meeting of David Foster Wallace's media and pop-culture critique with Ayn Rand's objectivism and Nietzche's will-to-power.[11] Bonta distorts quantum concepts to assert the power of the individual to mold the world, to deny the presence of Foucaultian social forces, to blame individuals (especially women and minorities) for any suffering they dare to complain about, and to renew the Victorian call for artists to instruct us with Arnoldian morality. Essentially *Flight* uses misunderstood bits of quantum physics to mount an extreme, naïve, conservative reaction to the antihumanism of postmodernism (which was raging at the time of the novel's publication). Rather than imagining a return to meaning redefined and rendered according to poststructuralist means, Bonta re-energizes liberal humanism with all its class, race, and gender prejudices, tricked out in shiny but erroneous contemporary science. Perhaps it is unnecessary to point out that any formal aspect that initially suggests innovation also collapses into naïve conservatism—not just Realism, but the novel's ultimate assertion that all we have read is a record of lived experience manifested as narrative, with no awareness of translation from mind or body into language. This collapse results in a shockingly monist denial of the separation between language and reality, language and human experience, that forms the basis of Realism as much as of quantum mechanics. Quantum realism must be the opposite of all of these assumptions and practices, and quantum fiction must at least engage accurate quantum principles.

Perhaps not surprisingly, given the more challenging requirements of the latter, far more quantum fiction has emerged than quantum realism. Jonathan Lethem produced an early example of quantum fiction with *As She Climbed Across the Table* (1994), whose story revolves around a void created in a university lab, generating (as one might imagine) a host of competing interpretations by various academics and academic branches and alienating the first-person narrator from his physicist lover Alice, who falls in love with the void. Even this brief synopsis reveals that the story is more concerned with the crisis of signification, a plethora of meanings spawned from a gap, than it is with physics. In his extended examination of the novel James Peacock agrees, calling *As She Climbed* "another novel about writing" in which "language [is] the ultimate compensation for lack and desire." The characters' interpretations of the human-made void—really readings of our agential relation to reality—span the gamut of well-worn postmodern stances: the deconstructionist English professor sees the void as a text to be read, a "pure signifier" without depth; the gender scholar reads Alice's love for the void as a "paradigmatic feminist statement" and the void as a "third gender"; the (perhaps structural) anthropologist enters the void to explore and finds the two men who had wandered into it "perfected" in a "completely closed system"; the materialist physicist sees the void as merely matter.[12]

What is striking about these interpretations is their familiarity: no new ways of knowing are created along with the new reality to be known. Likewise, Lethem glaringly fails to create any new representational techniques to depict the entirely new reality that his narrative enters when several characters enter into it. Most striking is the moment near the end of the novel when the narrative demands a new technical strategy that the novel does not provide. Once Philip, the first-person narrator, "falls" into the void, the novel is clear that he no longer exists as a thinking self, and nothing exists to contemplate: "I was not only in the void, I apparently *was* the void. . . . There wasn't any Philip. . . . The nothing was tangible and timely. Real. Relevant. Thing, on the other hand, was impossible, fraudulent."[13] And yet for the pages between Philip's entrance into the void and his exit (caused by explicitly thinking about himself), the first-person narration of a consciousness contemplating all kinds of things continues. How does this representational strategy make sense? In the context of the novel's quantum setting, it does not, making this novel quantum fiction but not quantum realism, and providing an excellent example of how quantum fiction can call for technical innovations its authors are not ready to hazard.

Judie Newman's reading of John Updike's *Toward the End of Time* (1997) uses many-worlds theory to imagine parallel universes that allow American imperialism to expand into the universe. In so doing, it establishes the novel as quantum fiction rather than quantum realism as well, in that it uses many-worlds theory as plot device—to consider the evils of globalism from a new perspective—rather than to drive technical innovation.[14] Likewise, we see quantum ideas applied in this metaphorical rather than technical way in literary criticism, as when Marshall Boswell suggests that in Wallace's 1996 *Infinite Jest* "it is almost as if U.S. history . . . branched off into one of those countless 'many worlds' hypothesized by quantum physics."[15] The "almost" here is key, because nothing in the mammoth novel explicitly asks us to invoke a quantum framework in reading it; in fact, Wallace's own statements about his technique and form in that novel clearly align them with his desire to represent reality as we experience it, not the counterintuitive reality theorized by quantum physics.[16]

Similarly, Jennifer Egan's *A Visit from the Goon Squad* (2010) invokes quantum mechanics repeatedly but primarily metaphorically, in this case to explain cultural phenomena rather than epistemological or ontological ones. In one extended footnote, former journalist Jules Jones uses entanglement to explain the seemingly simultaneous responses of people to the movements of a celebrity in their midst.[17] But his explanation only deepens the mystery of such cultural behavior since, at the time of Egan's writing, entanglement remained an unproven theory—and one soundly rejected by Einstein, no less (physicists demonstrated entanglement empirically in 2015). Egan's application here is essentially hyperbole through quantum mechanics. Further on in the novel and over twenty years later in its timeline, Lulu uses quantum mechanics to explain the new simultaneity of information travel, claiming that young students must study "particle physics" to grasp the basics of marketing, as the old "mechanical" and "viral" models are outdated.[18] This shift from causal, biological, macro metaphors to simultaneous, disembodied, micro metaphors—from Newtonian to quantum physics—raises provocative questions about the role information and market forces play in the universe. Does the quantum analogy suggest that information dispersal in a digital age and capitalistic use of it to influence people is somehow more natural, more in line with the mechanics of the universe, than ever before? Are we to read Lulu as understanding capitalist and consumerist forces as seamlessly integrated into the fabric of the universe, unimpeachable facts of nature? Pursuing such an argument would make *Goon Squad*, if not an example of quantum realism, certainly a clear demonstration of Fisher's "capitalist realism"—but the novel does not develop the argument it briefly raises using quantum mechanics.

Just as the novel poses but does not take up such questions, so it also suggests but does not establish a fully quantum setting that goes beyond metaphors. We might loosely read as quantum Egan's portrayal of the same characters at different points of their lives in different chapters and from differing points of view as representing the infinite multiplicity of points and perspectives in spacetime.[19] This reading has the benefit of accounting for what can otherwise appear to be tricks or inconsistencies in the novel's uses of point of view, such as the shift from second-person to first-person point of view at the end of "Out of Body," when Rob, from whose perspective the entire chapter has proceeded, drowns (resulting in a problem similar to Philip's impossible first-person point of view in the void); and the completely unexplained, unowned, and singular use of first-person plural point of view in the otherwise fully third-person "Safari" chapter.[20] Combined, such instances could suggest multiple, indeterminate, and/or floating point of view—but without more such instances to ask for such a reading, and considering that some reviewers refer to it as a "story cycle," the book does not offer sufficient evidence of quantum-inspired technical innovation to make it quantum realism rather than (slightly) quantum fiction.

Other recent novels come closer to creating a fully quantum rendering of reality in language. Helen Dewitt's *The Last Samurai* (2000) tells one of our oldest stories—that of a young boy searching for his father—in an assortment of new ways, one of which is quantum. Stephen J. Burn details the novel's quantum aspects and the anti-Realist strategies Dewitt uses to represent them, including the branching possibilities of many worlds, a character's empathy with the in-between state of Schrödinger's cat, and a narration that "layers as many as four different simultaneous 'realities' in a single scene, jostling for the reader's attention, or seems to narrate from different positions in consecutive scenes."[21] But despite characters' contemplation of quantum possibilities and narrative parallels with them, the novel as a whole remains anchored in its two main characters' perspectives, and its narrative progresses through time, however much in pieces and with Woolfian moments of simultaneous experience, to tell the single story of the boy's quest.

Paul Auster's *4321* (2017), on the other hand, does just the opposite, in following a clearly quantum-inspired overall structure while essentially refusing to depart from Realist humanist principles. It follows one character through four lives, each rendered in seven chronologically progressing parts. Most of the character's core qualities remain consistent across all sections, but slight variations in behavior and experiences result in wildly different outcomes in later sections, in one case causing the character's early death: all subsequent pages of that strand go blank. Like the 1998 film *Sliding Doors* and the more recent *Mr. Nobody* (2009), Auster's novel asks us to consider a few of the infinite possible worlds, experiences, and narrative outcomes available to each of us at every moment, and every moment as a turning point, or chance to generate another branch of possibilities. But even while it splinters the Realist narrative into four fragmented branches with multiple possible outcomes, *4321* maintains Realism's humanist commitment to the integrity of the individual self. Whereas Coale convincingly argues for the variety of ways in which the quantum context cannot support such a bounded and/or sustained sense of self (see *Quirks* Chapter 4), Auster's novel smuggles humanist individualism, as well as Realist notions of character, into a quantum setting that cannot rationally support either.

Perhaps most quantum in its perspective on its world, while remaining utterly conventional in terms of form and technique, is Cixin Liu's mind-expanding *Remembrance of Earth's Past* trilogy: *The Three Body Problem* (2007 Chinese, 2014 English), *The Dark Forest* (2008, 2015), and *Death's End* (2010, 2016). Rather than framing its story from the perspective of one or a few human beings, as does all the other quantum fiction discussed here, these three novels tell their epic story from the perspective of the universe, or at least from the perspective of a larger portion of the universe than I have seen accounted for by any book or series before. The central conflict in *The Three Body Problem* is not between people or countries but between planets, Earth and Trisolaris; in *The Dark Forest* human civilization is threatened by all of the universe; by *Death's End*, the battle involves not only multiple universes but also multiple dimensions. Humans' attempts to survive threats of such scale—so enormous relative to our tiny experience—become absurd and beside the point; in fact, the point of the trilogy might be summed up as demonstrating how, with a large enough perspective, there is no meaningful "point," only an infinity of neutral points in spacetime.

Liu asks us to contemplate the importance of scale from the other end by opening the second book of the trilogy from the perspective of an ant. As two people discuss strategies for ensuring the survival of the human species, the ant explores a maze of giant troughs carved in stone. By describing the movements of the ant's completely neutral experience of the cold stone's contours, Liu reveals that the people are standing at the grave of Yang Dong, who played a key role in events from the previous novel. Meanwhile, a spider whose web has been casually destroyed by the conferring humans begins to rebuild: "Ten thousand times the web could be destroyed, and ten thousand times the spider would rebuild it. There was neither annoyance nor despair, nor any delight, just as it had been for a billion years." Absorbed in their unceasing inhuman business, "neither ant nor spider was aware that they, out of all life on Earth, were the sole witnesses to the birth of the axioms of cosmic civilization."[22] By observing the detached actions of the ant and the spider as backdrop for the human mind's leap into cosmic strategizing, Liu demonstrates that every act of human meaning-making depends on and is limited by perspectives and scales of space and time, and remains wholly separate from a vast and apathetic universe.

In these ways, Liu's trilogy is an excellent example of a particular type of posthumanism that Mark McGurl calls "the posthuman comedy." McGurl draws on Wai Chee Dimock's transnational argument that literary works and literary history could best be understood in terms of "deep time," which "dramatically expand[s] the tracts of space-time across which literary scholars might draw valid links between author and author, text and text, and among author, text, and the wide world beyond."[23] Proposing that we reconceive of literary period from such a large scale that "the failure of institutions it predicts . . . comes into view," McGurl envisions the posthuman comedy as "a critical fiction meant to draw together a number of modern literary works in which scientific knowledge of the spatiotemporal vastness and numerousness of the nonhuman world becomes visible as a formal, representational, and finally existential problem."[24] That is to say, McGurl acknowledges that enlarging the scale and perspective in which we contextualize and historicize literature enables us to see the futility and terminality of all ways of understanding, organizing, and attempting to preserve works of art, and the inability of contemporary art properly to represent our experience of this vast scale, given its usual methods. McGurl's posthuman comedy is one way of articulating one of the major arguments that motivates this book's investigation: when we change how we view the world, literature's representational strategies must also change.

Not surprisingly then, McGurl later points specifically to the inadequacy of realism: "from the eighteenth-century forward artistic seriousness in fictional narrative has been strongly associated with realism and realism, in turn, with a reasonable-seeming correspondence between representation and ordinary adult experience."[25] Here, McGurl is more concerned with genre (or more properly, genre fiction) than with technique or form, pointing out that only the "outsize realism of science fiction and horror" is capable of representing what he calls the "third stage" of the sublime, or the death of everything, including reason itself.[26] Certainly Liu's sci-fi trilogy, with a timeline of 18 million years and counting; a physical location that includes at least 647 universes, one of which might or might not harbor the last members of the human species; and a plotline driven for hundreds of pages by various strategical applications of reason, all of which are eventually swallowed up by an uncaring multiverse, neatly demonstrates McGurl's point about the capacity of genre fiction. And the subgenre of sci fi contains numerous fictional accounts that similarly attempt to escape anthropomorphism, in point of view and assumptions about the world, from Italo Calvino's *Cosmicomics* (1965), whose first-person narrators include a single point of spacetime, to Michel Faber's *Under the Skin* (2000), whose focalizing third-person narrator is an alien who picks up men to harvest them for meat, with plenty of Ursula Le Guin in between. But we might also ask more specifically how Realism—depiction of "ordinary adult experience"—is forced to change its genre conventions and techniques when it attempts to convey a human experience of that incomprehensibly vast swath of time and space, or the quantum world. How might authors depict, in language on the page, a human experience of the reality of the universe as we now conceptualize it, when that reality for the most part remains outside of human experience?

The remainder of this chapter will examine several examples of quantum realism, with particular attention to how innovative uses of and changes in language, form, and conventions result from the texts' attempts to represent the quantum world through language and genre. Essentially it is my reshaping of and reflection on the provocative questions Coale poses in *Quirks*: "What happens with quantum theories when ontological realities seem to be at stake? Does literature become more radical still? And can it redesign itself in opposition to or in celebration of the deconstruction of cause and effect?"[27] Given my distinction between quantum fiction and quantum realism, in order to define the latter as the mode used by these texts, with particular techniques, effects, styles, and structures, in their attempt to represent the quantum world, I would rephrase Coale's urgent questions like this: What happens to genre, form, and language when writers try to represent in literature a world that is as alien to human experience as it is to language? How do such attempts intensify the poststructural dilemma? How might they solve it?

Language Is the World We Live in: Ted Chiang's "Story of Your Life"

The promising proposal made by McGurl's "posthuman comic" perspective—that dramatically enlarging our perspective on literature will allow us to see new truths about human being and the universe—does for literature and literary studies what Brian Greene's quantum description of the universe does for language. By taking a cosmic perspective, McGurl suggests newly productive contexts in which to consider human experience and creative production, just as Greene uses a quantum context to reveal the usefulness of language in understanding human experience. Both vectors of this cosmic perspective come together in Ted Chiang's 1996 "Story of Your Life," which reconceives not just the nature of physical reality, but also the relationship between language and physical reality, and uses innovations in form and technique to represent that reconceived relationship. Dr. Louise Banks, the story's linguist narrator, is asked to learn the language of a visiting alien species in order to ascertain its intentions and assess any risk it might pose. Assisted by a physicist, Gary, who is simultaneously working to understand the beings' concepts of physical reality, Louise is able to comprehend the heptapods' language only in tandem with Gary's unfolding comprehension of their basic mathematical and physics systems, which differ fundamentally from human systems because of their different understanding and experience of time. As Louise's ability to communicate and think in the heptapods' language grows, she finds that her experience of lived reality changes profoundly as well, allowing her to experience time in two different ways—human and heptapod, linear and simultaneous—because of her fluency in these two different languages. "Story of Your Life" illustrates, thematically and formally, the intimacy and even interdependence between language and human experience of reality that is implied by Greene's explanation of quantum mechanics: in "Story," language arises from concepts of reality and then shapes our lived experiences of that reality.

At the same time, it suggests that a physical reality exists quite apart from any particular concept, experience, or linguistic representation of it. But this confirmed separation between language and reality functions in striking opposition to the word/thing, image/reality split posited by pessimistic postmodern novels of the 1980s and 1990s, such as DeLillo's *The Names* and *White Noise*. Rather than pointing to the loss of the real, the physics foundation of Chiang's "Story" asserts that a real, measurable world that matters and is made of matter exists, quite apart from our or any other species' ideas and equations. And, just as "post-postmodern" fiction uses its poststructuralist framework to renew language's potential for expression and human connection, so does "Story" enlist its post-Newtonian framework not to emphasize all we cannot know or say about the universe or each other, but to acknowledge the inevitable existence of different ways of knowing and saying. On the largest scale, "Story" also uses this quantum framework to demonstrate that empathy—sharing another's feeling and point of view—is only possible when we are willing to see the world as others see it, and to speak their language, which is almost the same thing.

Chiang was not the first author to dramatize this connection between language and experience, which stretches at least as far back as Samuel Delany's 1966 science-fiction novel, *Babel-17*. There, Delany had already imagined the basic setup from which the action of Chiang's story springs: a female language expert, Rydra, is asked by the government to translate a language never before encountered and used by an alien species that poses a threat. Like Louise, Rydra insists that a snippet of the language will not suffice for translation, that she needs full context of the uses of the language and the beings who are using it; like Louise, Rydra insists that she travel to the place where the language is being spoken and attempt to meet with the beings face to "face." Both women also go into the experiments fully aware that language shapes our physical experiences in the world. Rydra describes that causal relationship with an example that would be at home in Tomasula's *IN&OZ* (see Chapter 2): "If you turn somebody with no memory loose in a foreign country with only the words for tools and machine parts, don't be surprised if he ends up a mechanic."[28] Both women also find their own experiences of physical reality shockingly altered by their acquisition of the new language, specifically in terms of their experiences of time. For Rydra, time slows down (171), past scenes rematerialize (175), and multiple streams of thought exist simultaneously (140–4). But with the single exception of inset text boxes to represent those simultaneous thoughts in the 2001 Vintage edition, all of these insights into the intimate relationship between language and physical reality remain confined to narrative explanation—and the original 1966 text eschews even the text boxes.

In 1989, Jeanette Winterson's *Sexing the Cherry* asserted a similar connection between language and experience of reality, noting that the language of the Hopi tribe has "no tenses for past, present, and future. They do not sense time in that way. For them, time is one," and thus "it was impossible to learn their language without learning their world."[29] Likewise, Winterson also frames her novel with quantum observations about space and time, which account for the narrative's numerous uncontextualized leaps through both, as its first-person point of view floats from one body to another. The unsignaled and unexplained jumps between points of space and time, and between perspectives, keep the reader situated outside any particular timeline, physical setting, or character, observing a multitude of each from afar. That is, as long as we inhabit its world, the book keeps us aware of aspects of our reality that we remain unaware of in real life: what we experience as reality at any one moment is only one point of an infinite number of them; what we experience as self is really only the action of briefly inhabiting one of those massively limited points of spacetime; what we experience as past, present, and future is a trick of the human mind—or more accurately, considering the Hopi, a trick of our most familiar human languages. *Sexing the Cherry* demonstrates the surprising irony that innovations in language, narrative, and literary form might begin to free us from the screens and limits imposed on reality by the human mind—and by the types of language, narrative, and literary form we have become accustomed to, the ones that best reproduce our comfortable, untrue, Newtonian reality. Language and form can screen us from reality, or they can show it to us by making us look at the world anew.

Thirty years after *Babel-17*, Ted Chiang explored this connection between language and experience of reality further still, by taking it as the central theme of his story and then developing formal and technical innovations capable of making its implications for human experience clear for the reader. Rather than using the alien language primarily as the impetus for a classic sci-fi romp, as Delany did, Chiang's story focuses on demonstrating how the language-reality nexus shapes experience and, most importantly, human relationships with each other and with the world. Chiang imagines for the heptapods a "semasiographic" written language ("Heptapod B") whose "visual syntax" does not overlap with its spoken language ("Heptapod A").[30] Consisting of circular "semagrams," each of which expresses a complete idea, or what we might consider a sentence, Heptapod B, as an entirely visual language that cannot be spoken, escapes the inherent linearity of signification as lamented by Lacan in "The Agency of the Letter."[31] Instead, the semagrams demand an extreme simultaneity of understanding, of their writers even more so than of their readers: "the stroke participated in several different clauses of the message ... yet this stroke was a single continuous line, and it was the first one that Flapper [one of the heptapods] wrote. That meant the heptapod had to know how the entire sentence would be laid out before it could write the very first stroke" (122-3).

Tellingly, it is Gary's analogous break-through understanding of the heptapods' physics that enables Louise to identify the fundamental difference between "Heptapod B" and human language: whereas human language is linear, the heptapods' is teleological, a difference that also distinguishes the heptapods' experience of reality from that of humans. Chiang cleverly uses Fermat's principle to draw this distinction (116–19): Gary explains to Louise that one way of understanding why light bends when it hits water is linear—the light hits the water, whose density slows its travel. But another, equally valid explanation is teleological: "*the ray of light has to know where it will ultimately end up before it can choose the direction to begin moving in*" (125, original italics). The first explanation relies on causal (or Newtonian) physical laws, while the second relies on "variational principles"—or what Chiang clarifies in "Story Notes" at the end of the collection is quantum mechanics (277). Once the story reveals that the heptapods' "simple math" is "variational," or quantum, in direct opposition to ours, which is linear and causal (since few people understand non-Newtonian physics and perhaps no one grasps it intuitively), Chiang has completed the story's argument: our perception of physical reality, especially in relationship to how we experience time, gives rise to our linguistic system, which will share the basic structure of our physics. Writing and physics are twin languages for describing the world, birthed by that world. But the discrepancy between the heptapods' physics and writing compared to ours also argues that all systems of physics as well as language are only translations of the real. A real world remains, separate from and untouched by our or any other attempt to represent it, and Chiang's story reassures us that no matter how we describe it, we all live in the same physical reality: "The physicists were ultimately able to prove the equivalence of heptapod mathematics and human mathematics; even though their approaches were almost the reverse of one another, both were systems of describing the same physical universe" (120–1).

According to this argument, despite our shared universe we can only truly understand another's experience of reality by speaking their language. As Louise begins to understand Heptapod B, she begins to experience time as theorized by our quantum mechanics and as experienced by the heptapods, with "no physical difference between past and future" (131). Thus, because her daughter's life from conception to death occurs in this post-Heptapod B epoch that she experiences in moments "as a simultaneity" (141), Louise is able to do what Lauren longs to do throughout DeLillo's *The Body Artist* but cannot (as I will discuss in Chapter 5): she can be present with the loved one who has been lost to death in a causal, linear experience of reality. Chiang has provided a theoretical framework, using quantum mechanics, that allows his fiction to escape the trap of linear, Realist narrative and depict exactly the time travel that DeLillo imagined in his notes but ultimately does not manifest in his novel.

Chiang also demonstrates Louise's nonlinear experience and unbroken connection with her dead daughter through technique and form. Like DeLillo, Chiang uses second-person address to expand the story's diegetic space beyond the distant speech of third person or the mono-directional confession of first. But whereas DeLillo's periodic second-person provocations of the reader might always be explained as echoes of Lauren's own self-reflection, and in any case collapse neatly into third person at novel's end, "Story of Your Life" sustains its second-person address throughout, beginning in the title, as the first-person narrator, Louise, tells her already dead daughter her life story. Chiang divides the story into two stories, each with its own formal characteristics. As Louise tells the pre-Heptapod B tale that led up to her daughter's conception—the aliens' arrival, and Louise's work to understand their language with the physicist who would become her daughter's father—the narrative unfolds linearly in flat past tense, a traditional tale. But surrounding and interrupting this tale is Louise's account of her daughter's life, and this narration shows the impact of Louise's Heptapod B understanding.

Anchored in the story's opening moment, when Louise and Gary decide to conceive a baby, this story of the daughter's life primarily uses the future tense—beginning with the moment that marks the daughter's end: "He and I will drive out together to perform the identification [of their daughter's dead body]"(95). And yet some moments also use past or present tenses to indicate Louise's fluid experience of all of the events she describes: "Boys will stare into those eyes the way I did, and do, into your dad's, surprised and enchanted, as I was and am, to find them in combination with black hair" (121). This mixture of times and tenses positions Louise both in and outside of the events she describes, as if she is living them and narrating them simultaneously, without regard to chronology, as if stepping in and out of the timestream of her life: "Your father is about to ask me the question. This is the most important moment in our lives, and I want to pay attention, note every detail....Right now your dad and I have been married for about two years...I remember the scenario of your origin you'll suggest when you're twelve" (91). The events of the past-tense tale of alien interpretation are done and gone, reduced to information, or memories. But the events Louise describes while telling her daughter's life story, because they are not only remembered but were, are, and always will be experienced through the simultaneity of Heptapod B, exist in every moment of time and remain available to Louise to be present in, as her daughter, dead at age 25, remains alive to be present with. The constancy of this presence, of the present, is further communicated structurally. By opening and closing in the moment of the daughter's conception, that moment becomes the organizing logic of Louise's overwhelming experience of simultaneity, the point in time and space according to which she orients herself and the vast block of memories—the last 50 years of her life—that are constantly available to her after learning Heptapod B.

Chiang also uses the contrast between humans' sense of causality and heptapods' sense of simultaneity to contemplate the attending philosophical implications for free will. Does loss of causality render will meaningless? If we can see our entire histories as simultaneous, do we ever really decide anything? In raising this question, the story raises a similar formal/generic question: if one key characteristic of traditional realism is its "truth effects," or a hermeneutic code that raises questions, delays their answers, then ultimately satisfies our piqued curiosity in order to, as Morris claims, "strengthen the belief that 'truth' does exist and will prevail however difficult the passage towards it proves to be,"[32] how can a story that illustrates simultaneity rather than linear progress toward revelation be "realistic"? How can it provoke and then fulfill our desire for rational, well-won truth? One facile answer might be that Chiang's story portrays a different kind of unfolding, not the revelation of events (we know by the second paragraph that the daughter is already dead) but the revelation of a new way of understanding events.

But a more satisfying answer, and one that does justice to the story's own philosophical musing, is that "Story of Your Life" depicts a different kind of truth—one that does not need to unfold, or be pursued, or chased, or won, to be meaningful.

Louise comes to understand that the heptapods' experience of simultaneity does not preclude freedom but changes it; this total knowledge makes heptapods free, even empowered, to enact the "future" they know has happened, or will happen, or is happening: "they act to create the future, to enact chronology" (137). Theirs is a different view of the world that creates different views of time, language, and power: like small children, heptapods "live in the present tense" (137), and for them "language is performative. Instead of using language to inform, they used language to actualize" (138). Language, and acting, make reality. Chiang remarks, in his story notes on another story called "Dividing by Zero," that finally seeing the derivation of an equation as inevitable—already there, rather than brought into being—brings "a feeling of awe, as if you've come into contact with absolute truth" (277). This is the truth effect his stories often strive to depict: the awe of seeing the truth of what is, was, and will be, as if being able for one moment to glimpse a slice of the spacetime loaf. It is seeing the "inevitability" of narrative not as chasing down and revealing truth but as choosing (and choosing to see) what *is* in the eternal moment. In a causal, linear view of language and reality, in which knowledge is limited to the present and outcomes are unknown, the gap between language and reality provides a space for power: language as a tool for imposing one's own view of truth over time becomes a method to manipulate or dominate others, as a narrator might lead a reader to a story's linear resolution, to accept another's causally created truths. But in a simultaneous, fully known reality that does not need to be revealed, the gap between language and reality provides the impetus for enacting what is and is known by all—language as the making real of what has already been observed as true. In order for narrative to express this different kind of reality and truth, one that diminishes the roles of causality and power, it must also be loosed from linearity, chronology, and causality, as Chiang has done with his looping structure, multiple story strands, and mixed verb tenses.

None of these formal innovations or quantum concepts would be of any interest, however, if the story did not use them to reveal—or better, to observe—an inevitable truth that matters to its readers. Chiang connects his ruminations on language, reality, and truth to core lessons of being human (a characterization that seems wrongly anthropocentric, given the heptapods' quietly wise role in all that Louise learns) by placing at the heart of the story, as at its beginning and ending, the narrator's love for her daughter. The most painful and important inevitability of the story, and of the narrator's fifty-year chunk of post-Heptapod B life, is the death of that daughter. And so every time Louise allows her daughter to do something that will lead (has led, is leading) to her death—the toddler gleefully conquering the stairs, the young woman heading off to the rock climb where she will die—it is an act of acceptance more impressive than any that could be accomplished in a linear, unfolding life that hides our outcomes. It is also a stunning act of parental generosity, a granting of freedom to a child to become who she already is, however much the parent would like to change what that is and will be.

The story connects Louise's selfless love and respect for her daughter to the understanding of the world she has gained by learning Heptapod B. This connection makes the alien worldview a moral compass for human behavior, and it makes empathy gained through language learning and communication the mechanism for transmitting that reality and moral sense from species to species, and from one spacetime experience to another: empathy through language on an interplanetary scale. Louise describes her experience of living with her daughter as "like aiming for a moving target; you'll always be further along than I expect" (115). At first the line seems banal: anyone who's raised a child knows that all children are moving targets; just when you figure them out, you look up and they're in a new phase in which you're newly lost. We don't need quantum mechanics to explain that part of human experience. And yet "Story" uses quantum mechanics to enable us to see the platitude in a new way. The analogy slyly invokes "time's arrow," which physicists tell us doesn't exist in quantum reality, and which certainly doesn't exist in heptapods' reality. The shared nonsensicality of parents' belief that they can ever fully know their children in any given moment, much less predict where they are headed, and of human belief in one singular, shared unfolding of orderly moments of time, reveals the mistaken self-centeredness of both beliefs: that we fail accurately to imagine the realities of our children and of the universe because we cannot hold in our heads how totally particular and wholly insufficient is our perspective on both.

For Louise, who is able to step outside that causal, linear experience once she understands Heptapod B, her child is a point that is always moving in relation to her. Rather than viewing her child on a single linear trajectory whose points she can aim for and fix in relation to her concept of herself and her desires for her daughter, Louise sees herself as observing the many points in time and space through which her daughter will move, all of which are removed from herself. In this way, being conversant in Heptapod B allows her to relate to her daughter as she relates to all facets of reality:

> The semagrams seemed to be something more than language; they were almost like mandalas. I found myself in a meditative state, contemplating

the way in which premises and conclusions were interchangeable. There was no direction inherent in the way propositions were connected, no "train of thought" moving along a particular route; all the components in an act of reasoning were equally powerful, all having identical precedence. (127)

Likewise, we might see Louise's way of relating to her daughter as an echo of the heptapods' manner of relating to humans—quietly observing, interfering only when necessary, gradually teaching their language and revealing their world in accordance with the other's capacity for understanding. Both relationships leave Louise transformed. But it is a transformation accomplished through mutual observation and communication, in which "all the components . . . were equally powerful," without intention to direct or change, a model of influence through empathy that works equally well for the human-alien encounters and the parent-child ones—which, as "Story" demonstrates by recounting conversations between Louise and her daughter at various alienating ages, can feel like the same thing. "Story of Your Life" asks how communication, teaching, learning, love, and coexistence might look in a world freed from the tyranny and power dynamics of linear, causal time. It also asks, what might narrative, and what might Realism look like, if freed from the constraints of linear unfolding? What new truths and new methods for attaining truth might it discover?

Quantum Mechanics and Buddhism in Ruth Ozeki's *A Tale for the Time Being*

Ruth Ozeki's *A Tale for the Time Being* (2013) is an extended asking and answering of such questions. As with Chiang's "Story," quantum mechanics is a crucial element of the novel's world and its manner of considering and representing truth. And like "Story," *Tale* invokes quantum principles not simply to represent a larger quantum physical world, but as a tool that empowers it to better tell its human, metaphysical story. Herself an ordained Soto Zen priest, Ozeki employs quantum mechanics to set her novel in a physical reality that can make Buddhist concepts of reality visible. Nonbinary, interconnected, uncertain, and averse to striving and completion, such a Buddhist reality also requires Ozeki to stretch the genre of the novel in odd and interesting ways in order to escape the tight causal logic and closure of Realism. Her unique combination of quantum concepts and technical innovations results in a novel that does not simply imagine such Buddhist paradoxes for the first time in fiction, or provide an excellent example of quantum realism, but also suggests a profound connection between the two accomplishments.

Ozeki establishes these twin underpinnings of the novel's setting, quantum and Buddhist—two ways of describing the same reality, one physical and the other spiritual—early in the novel: Nao, the Japanese teenager whose diary forms one half of the novel, refers us to "Appendix A: Zen Moments," in the novel's first section, so that by page 7 we are asked to read her diary and the entire novel with the "granularity of the Zen view of time" in mind. Fittingly— as her reader, Ruth, will experience the weird time loops of quantum computing "later" in the novel—it is not Nao but Ruth who connects this Zen view of a moment as "a very small particle of time"[33] to quantum mechanics; by page 62 we are guided to "Appendix B: Quantum Mechanics," which reads "superposition," "entanglement," and "the measurement problem" (in which observations alter reality) as another way of understanding Master Dōgen's teachings on moments, interconnection, attention, and not knowing (409). In a subsequent reading of the novel, we can also identify this section as bringing in the quantum-Buddhist connection because it opens and closes with the appearance of the Jungle Crow, a Japanese bird whose presence in Canada at this point in the narrative makes the bird seem merely misplaced, rather than, as it will come to seem later in the novel, superpositioned (as I will argue below).

These quantum elements are so integral to the novel that to overlook them is to significantly misread it.[34] One such misreading, by Marlo Starr, demonstrates the novel's crucial connection between Buddhism and quantum mechanics, when misunderstandings of the former result in blindness to the latter (or vice versa). As one key example, Starr reads Nao's eventual passivity in the course of a brutal attempted rape as evidence of the anti-feminism of Buddhism (14). In fact, Nao's description of her response to the attack (277) is strikingly similar in words, phrases, and ideas to her great uncle's depiction in his journal of his own beatings and sexual assault while being trained as a kamikaze pilot (318–21). By connecting his response to the wisdom of Dōgen's *Shōbōgenzō* (319), he places them both in a long line of teachers and students of Buddhism, in which context Nao's and Haruki #1's passivity is not capitulation to rape, but recognition of their "inner power" to endure what they are powerless to stop and accept whatever is in any moment. In fact, it is Nao's total letting go into a meditative state—what she and her great grandmother Jiko, a Buddhist nun, call her "supapawa"—that ends her abuse, scaring her schoolmates into thinking they've severely harmed her and so causing them to flee. Nao's acceptance in this moment is instrumental as well as wise.

It also might be a bit quantum. We can't see the similarity between Haruki #1's experience and her own until nearly fifty pages later, when we read Haruki #1's secret diary. At that point Ruth points out that Nao herself can't have read the secret diary, because she does not yet know some of its content (328). At the same time, Ruth wonders how the secret diary came to be in the bundle with Haruki #1's "official" diary, and Nao's diary, which washed up on a British Columbian shore in a Hello Kitty lunchbox. We are never told in the novel how the secret diary came to be in that bundle, but later in the book we do see Ruth convey the secret diary to Nao across time and space—in a dream that seems to manifest quantum reality, guided by a crow (354). If the presence of the secret diary in the bundle that came from Nao and was found by Ruth confirms the wormhole workings of quantum mechanics in the book, then so should Nao's prescient echo of a secret diary she had not yet read, but would, and so also had. As I will argue below, such paradoxes, unexplained parallels between characters, and disorderly causality express the physical consequences of both Buddhist and quantum principles of interconnectedness and entanglement, attention and observer effects, and nonduality and superposition. They also demonstrate, on the largest level, the novel's commitment to depicting a world conceived and experienced as bothness: self/no-self, material/immaterial, individual/community, body/disembodiedness. What Nao and Ruth need, to escape the alienation and identity confusion that plague them, is not (as Starr argues) to abandon "ineffective" immaterial solutions (cyberspace, Buddhism, no-self) for an effective material one (the embodied connection of transnational feminism).[35] What they need is to abandon the dualistic thinking that keeps them physically and spiritually separate. The element that Ozeki adds to the novel to allow her to enact this nondualistic way of being is quantum physics.

While *Tale* creates a quantum setting in which its characters experience quantum effects in the novel's larger structures, these effects are most easily visible on the level of narrative and plotting. Central to the novel as a whole, and crucial for the salvation of the suffering teenager Nao, is the empathetic relationship between Nao and Ruth, which is constructed fundamentally as a reader-writer relationship: Ruth has found Nao's diary and demonstrates her empathetic aim immediately by deciding to read the diary at the pace at which Nao wrote it. Meanwhile, Ruth, a professional writer past middle age, struggles to write her own memoir about her caretaking of and the death of her mother. Soon her interest in Nao and research into Nao's identity overtake her writing, though, so that Ruth primarily becomes the reader and witness of Nao's suffering. Meanwhile, footnotes translating and commenting on Nao's diary, which we eventually realize were written by Ruth, and Ruth's first-person epilogue, addressed to Nao, combine to make an exterior editorial shell, created by Ruth, that houses Nao's primary document—ultimately both Ruth and Nao are writers and producers of the book, and readers of it and of each other. On its own, such a setup is not unique, and might mark *Tale* as part of a recent pattern of novels that imagine entwined acts of reading and writing, including *Everything Is Illuminated*, *House of Leaves*, *Cloud Atlas*, *S.*, and *The Brief Wondrous Life of Oscar Wao*, to name a few. But *Tale* adds a new dimension to this structure by converting passive, sequential readerly influence to active, nonchronological, material influence by creating a reader-writer relationship as a model of quantum *entanglement*.

Initially, Nao's influence on Ruth's writing seems traditionally passive, as Ruth absorbs words and ideas expressed by Nao. Ruth opens her section with words or phrases that ended the section of Nao's diary she has just read ("freeter," 82-3; "leaking away," 195-6), or with the results of research into a topic Nao has just mentioned. Interestingly, this influence seems to intensify during and after the chapter in which the quantum Jungle Crow appears, when Ruth begins to see all creatures, including whales and trees, as time beings (58, 59). Eventually, Ruth's and Nao's experiences in relation to each other's reading and writing begin to break our Newtonian laws for time and space: early in the novel, Ruth dreams Jiko's answer to a question Nao has asked Jiko in the diary, but which will not have come to Nao—or, Ruth will not have read in Nao's diary—for quite a while in the narrative, and which does not come until over a hundred pages later in the novel (38-40, 194). A similarly impossible triangulation involves Nao, Ruth, and Haruki #1. Near the end of the novel, Nao expresses the same thought that Haruki #1 has recorded in his secret diary on the eve of his kamikaze flight: "Time is so interesting to me now that I have so little of it. I sit zazen . . . counting with beads and breath the moments until my death. . . . . At the moment of my death, I look forward at last to being fully aware and alive" (324). A few pages later, Ruth reads the similar sentiment written by Nao, who has decided to end her life: "There's nothing like realizing that you don't have much time left to stimulate your appreciation for the moments of your life. . . . Time disappeared and it was like being born into the world all over again" (332). The similarity and proximity of the ideas and images first suggests that Nao has been influenced by reading Haruki #1—until we remember that she has not read the secret diary (yet?), but Ruth has, making Ruth, or spacetime, the conduit through which these ideas flow from Haruki #1's writing into Nao's.

Eventually Ruth and Nao become so entangled as reader and writer that the existence of each seems to depend on that of the other—both physically and spiritually.[36] As Ruth reads Nao's diary by the light of a kerosene lamp during a prolonged and fierce storm that induces a blackout and a nearly hallucinogenic state in their little ocean-side cottage, Ruth discovers that the diary has gone blank at the moment when Nao caught up with herself in narrative time. On one level, the sudden blankness reinforces Ruth's sense all along that she had been living the present moment of the story she was reading, materializing the intensity of immersive fiction and syncing the reality of the diary's diegesis—it had run out of story—inside the diegetic space of Ruth's narrative. But the last entry of the diary before the blankness does not just record Nao catching up to herself in time; it also records her desperate sense of loneliness, as she loses the faith in her reader that had been sustaining her up to that point, as she sits alone at a bus stop waiting to be transported to the temple to say goodbye to dying Jiko: "I know you don't exist and no one is ever going to read this" (340). The suddenly blank pages, which had not been blank before, also materialize Nao's loss of belief in her reader, without whom she cannot exist. Ruth and her husband Oliver feel the same connection in reverse. As Oliver puts it, "if she stops writing to us, then maybe we stop being, too" (344). This dependence on the observer for existence morphs reader-writer entanglement into reader-writer observer effect. Unlike earlier examples of reader-writer empathy and influence, *A Tale for the Time Being* creates a quantum world in which characters affect each other not sequentially or linearly but over vast distances and time, as if to write, to read, and to be read enact material effects between participants that can only be explained by quantum entanglement or observer effects, or Buddhist oneness—which the novel suggests are two different explanations, physical and metaphysical, of the same reality.

The novel's complicated ending, specifically its epilogue and appendices, extends this quantum framework by adding *superposition* and *many worlds* to the book's setting—a combination that makes sense given that, as both Brian Greene and the novel itself explain (in "Appendix E: Schrödinger's Cat"), the many-worlds theory was originally proposed to solve the "problem" of superposition: rather than theorizing that wave functions inexplicably collapse into particles, Hugh Everett proposed "that the superposed quantum system persists and branches." Once again, Ruth's (and Ozeki's) explanation of quantum physics presupposes its intimacy with Buddhism: "At every juncture—in every Zen moment when possibilities arise—a schism occurs, worlds branch, and multiplicity ensues. Every instance of *either/or* is replaced by an *and*. And an *and* . . . adding up to an infinitely all-inclusive, and yet mutually unknowable, web of many worlds" (415, original italics). Ruth's epilogue—already a nonending, considering the provocation of worlds and theories of worlds that follow it in the book's several appendices—provides a suitably complex "ending" for the story and the entangled relationship it has constructed, by turning that relationship inside out. In the end, Ruth addresses Nao and imagines she has conjured her, adding a layer of possibilities for authorship (and readership) akin to that added by Pelafina in Danielewski's *House of Leaves*. At the same time, the epilogue offers elements of both closure and openness, resolution and irresolution, for the novel as a whole. Ruth's postscript verifies what Nao guessed on her first page ("I do have a cat, and he's sitting on my lap, and his forehead smells like cedar trees and fresh sweet air," 403), and mirrors Nao's second-person address of Ruth throughout the novel, as if closing the loop. But Ruth also ends by imagining Nao like Schrödinger's cat (perhaps also like her own cat, who is named Schrödinger, and was, for a few chapters, missing, and from her perspective neither dead nor alive)—Ruth imagines Nao is of indeterminate position unless she decides to allow herself to be found and observed by Ruth. Ruth also ends by both accepting that "I'd much rather *know*," and acknowledging that "not-knowing keeps all the possibilities open. It keeps all the worlds alive" (402, original italics). Ultimately, this "ending" implies that Nao's story, like all stories, and Ruth's story, and the reader's story, can end in an infinite number of ways, or, more radically still, *does* end in an infinite number of ways simultaneously. The true ending of the book—the book's truth—is infinite and unknowable; it is "*and*," not "*either/or*."

Along with these narrative-based elements, Ozeki uses several larger structural elements to create the novel's nonbinary, multidimensional world. Like many recent novels, *Tale* complicates the reality it represents by multiplying perspective, narrators, and diegetic registers, while also using more than one kind of point of view. Ozeki blurs the reader's position in relation to the characters and texts she encounters by providing Nao's first-person diary, but telling the story of Ruth's reading of the diary—and her editing of it, and presumably her authoring of the appendices and possibly her arrangement of the entire novel—using third-person point of view. She then adds another layer of confusion between not just fictional worlds but also fictional and nonfictional worlds by creating a third-person reader and writer who shares many details of her own life, so that the author Ruth Ozeki hovers about the novel as another possible narrator. Multiplying narrators, perspectives, and even planes of existence (themselves multiplied by the novel's many-worlds ending and quantum-computing changes to the reality that is multiply narrated in the book) creates the sense that the novel contains multiple realities, greatly multiplying the similar effect created by Foer in *Everything Is Illuminated* (as I argued in *Succeeding Postmodernism*, 181–4). It also creates the sense of multiple observers and perspectives that create these multiple realities, demonstrating through narrative devices what empirical evidence suggests is true about the universe: that the observer determines the reality observed, and all truth is relational and a matter of perspective. In such a reality, binarism and dualism are simply impossible.

From the perspective of the novel's later logic, the novel's opening also becomes a conundrum to be solved by a quantum/Buddhist framework: how do we make sense of the fact that we encounter Nao's journal first, before Ruth, the observer who brings the journal into existence, has found it and started to read it? One rather facile answer might be that the novel's ultimate quantum context suggests that, due to the nonlinearity of quantum time and superposition, all elements of Nao's narrative and of the novel's other texts exist and don't exist in various worlds and times. But it is more interesting, and perhaps more true to the novel's focus on quantum entanglement, to solve this puzzle using the observer effect: as Ruth is the reader/observer who brings Nao and her journal into being, so *we* are the more external reader/observer who opens the book to bring Ruth and her acts of observation into existence, rather like Schrödinger opening his box to find his cat dead or alive.[37] In so doing, we fix all these particular narrative elements in place, while participating in their loops of entanglement, extending the reader-writer intimacy to us, and bringing us into the novel's quantum world.

Ozeki combines the complexities of point of view and of multiple layers of readers and writers in the epilogue, which uses the former to gesture toward the latter. Here, Ruth takes first-person point of view for the first time, signaling her ownership of the role of writer. Her use of second-person address indicates her faith in her external reader. Having been trained by Nao's similar use of second-person to address her reader, we as faithful readers of Ruth can't help but feel ourselves addressed, that we are being seen as the openers of this box containing all the other acts of reading and writing. In other words, for a while—for the time it takes us to read three lines, to be exact—that reading is true. Then Ruth imagines her addressee in ways that identify her as Nao, and that big, metafictional framework in which we exist within the realities of the novel collapses into the smaller system of Ruth and Nao reading and writing each other. For that moment, though, we had been open to all possibilities: Who is the reader? Who is the writer? "Who had conjured whom?" (392), and when, and where, and how? Certainly readers have felt drawn into fiction for decades, even centuries, through the various metafictional devices that blur the lines between fictional and nonfictional worlds; Chapter 1 in this book has examined some of those devices. But crucially different in *Tale* is the expansion of the book beyond its physical pages, and of the narrative beyond even its multiple implied diegetic spaces, to include the time and space in which the reader is situated, not through simple (or even complex) metafictional address, but through the book's creation of a reality in which characters can move through space and time in and out of many worlds—at least one of which must hold the reader.

Language, Reality, and Materiality in *Tale*

As in "Story," the medium in the novel that allows such spacetime travel is language. But *Tale* imagines language as conduit between worlds differently, by imagining language as part of the matter of the universe in which characters live and move. In this way, Ozeki imagines a materiality of language unlike any of the examples examined in Chapter 3. Certainly *Tale* deploys many instances of metaphorically material language, such as Nao and Ruth's shared anxiety that the words they are reading will fall off their pages (63, 343); the substitution of the government's painfully inadequate words for the missing body of Haruki #1 in the box meant to return his remains (248);[38] Ruth's perception of Nao's journal as warm, like a living body, until she finishes reading, at which point the book/body turns cold (392–3); and the suddenly blank journal pages that reveal to Ruth her entangled dependence on Nao. *Tale* even uses changes in text size, font, and spacing to materialize Ruth's lived experience, much like *House of Leaves* (228–9, 238). But to these textual and tropological examples of material language, Ozeki adds another type, which alters not how she uses language to represent reality, but rather what language *is* in relation to reality, or the ontological status of language. This shift—the depiction of language as not a separate reflection of reality but continuous with the matter of reality, so that one can move through and shape it, and reality along with it—is possible in the novel, like making Buddhist non-dualism visible, only because of the novel's quantum setting.

Prior to Ruth's climactic dream, in which she travels through language to alter the futures (and pasts) of Nao and her father, the novel offers a pair of contrasting concepts of language, both figured as animals that communicate the "kotodama" or "speech souls" of their words. Nao's idea of the "now" fish, formulated when she was a child, communicates the old postmodern pessimism about language's inability to represent the real. Always slipping away or threatening to swallow all the littler fish in its path, the "now" fish represents our inability to write or say the now, because "no matter how fast you write, you're always stuck in the *then* and you can never catch up to what's happening *now* . . . saying *now* obliterates its meaning" (97–8, 99, original italics). But Ruth intuits a very different kotodama for the Jungle Crow, whose cry she hears as "*Ke…Ke, ke*" (96, original italics). One of the four *kana*, or written characters representing the fundamental sounds of Japanese, *ke* manifests the crow's cry as materialized human language, the transformation of idea and character into sound waves moving through the world. At this early point in the novel, Ruth's friend Muriel has already floated the idea that the misplaced Japanese crow is the fabled shape-shifting ancestor who saved an abused girl's life, and Ruth has already dreamed once of the nun on the verge of transfiguring into a crow (40), connecting Jungle Crow to the abused Nao's salvation. When Ruth later encounters the now fish and the Jungle Crow in her final, transformative dream, both as materialized language, we must consider what these kotodama say about language's power or impotence to help Ruth come to the aid of Nao, who at this point of the novel is in crisis.

Ruth's final dream is the meeting of Buddhism, quantum mechanics, and language. It begins with her Buddhist and quantum contemplation, "what does separation look like?"—separation being the lived experience of everyone but the truth of neither Buddhist nor quantum concepts of reality. Then in trying to separate herself, she "push[es] through" paper, making our primary linguistic medium as integral to the fabric of the undifferentiated universe as waves and particles, or Buddhist oneness. After swimming through words and the materialized sounds of words, she lets go of one past she might recover—Jiko's—by letting go of its words, then finds and follows the now fish, in her quest to find and join the timestream of Nao. Tellingly, the now fish leads her astray, to false and threatening images, but out of nothing—"a gap, more like an absence" (349)—comes "the word," a crow, or a crow in the shape of "CROW." It is the word-crow that leads her to Haruki #2, Nao's father, whose suicide Ruth prevents by reporting what she has read in Nao's diary, that his daughter will do the same if he does; so Ruth saves Nao's life as well. The word-crow-guided dream also saves Nao by changing her past, in that it is in this dream that Ruth inspires Haruki #2 to create the quantum software ("Mu-Mu the Obliterator," 382) that will "obliterate" all evidence of Nao's humiliation at the hands of her schoolmates from the internet, as Ruth has found her own internet search results obliterated (352). The dream also saves them by changing their future, making it one in which they have read Haruki #1's secret diary, inspiring Nao's father to tell her the truth about his firing in California, leading to Nao's understanding and admiration of her father, and her father's decision to develop programming that will do good in the world.

Thus Ruth's intervention into one point in Nao's and her father's lives through this dream changes many other points in their lives before and after that intervention. It also creates three wormholes in time, in which Ruth inspires Haruki #2 to create the software programming whose effects she has already encountered, gives Nao the diary that Ruth seems to have already received from her, and provides Nao with the faith and life to write the end of the diary, which had already existed when Ruth first opened it. All of these positive changes are possible because Ruth abandons the misleading now-fish and follows the word-crow, whose multiple associations thus far in the novel connect Ruth's ability to bring about such change to her pursuit of and belief in the transformative powers of Buddhist belief and of language to act upon the real world. But once again, these powers only make sense because they take place in an identifiably quantum world, every element of which is equally an aspect of matter and of spacetime.

In the reality of the novel, the dream is more than a dream; it is a moment in spacetime when Ruth actually moves through time and space to effect change in the matter of the universe, all made possible by the physical medium of language. This blending of being, time, and language is explicitly Buddhist: it is the last in a sequence of dreams in which Ruth puts on the Buddhist nun's glasses; the words Ruth encounters are Buddhist sayings; her mocking, unrecognizable reflection forces her to turn away from her fixation on self; and she becomes the nun/crow that is also oneness, with black sleeves "big enough to hold everything" (354). The dream is also explicitly quantum, as Ruth moves through "subatomic particles," waves, and "fractal patterns" (346, 348) as much as she moves through materialized words. By depicting Buddhist belief and quantum theory as two different languages for describing the same reality, and imagining language as the medium through which we move in time and space—in dreams, reading and writing, and conversation; on paper, in speech, and on the internet—Ozeki creates a world in which to acknowledge the truth of the physical universe is to acknowledge the interconnectedness of all beings, and in which acts of language are our primary method for placing ourselves in the positions of others, for empathizing.

"Appendix E: Schrödinger's Cat," which is nearly the end of the book, ends with a similar contemplation of truth in quantum, Buddhist, linguistic, and ethical terms. Like Ruth's epilogue—and like a Zen koan, a paradoxical expression that has no rational solution—this contemplation also gestures simultaneously toward closure and infinite openness:

> The astrophysicist Adam Frank told me that what's important to remember about quantum mechanics is that while there are many interpretations, including the Copenhagen and many-worlds hypotheses, quantum mechanics itself is a calculus. It's a machine for predicting experimental results. It's a finger, pointing at the moon.
> Professor Frank was referring to an old Zen koan about the Sixth Patriarch of Zen, who was illiterate. When asked how he could understand the truth of the Buddhist texts if he couldn't read the words, the Sixth Patriarch raised his arm and pointed to the moon. Truth is like the moon in the sky. Words are like a finger. A finger can point to the moon's location, but it is not the moon. To see the moon, you must look past the finger. To look for the truth in books, the Sixth Patriarch

was saying, is like mistaking the finger for the moon. The moon and the finger are not the same thing. (415-16)

In this twin formulation, quantum mechanics is a language for describing reality, just like words. They are a "finger pointing at the moon," not the moon itself; neither calculus nor language should be mistaken for the world itself, or for truth itself, as "the moon and the finger are not the same thing." Up to this point, "Appendix E"—like the now fish—has repeated the pessimistic postmodern formulation of the gap between words and things, language and world. But then Ruth imagines old Jiko healing the wound of that gap by completing the koan: "'Not same,' old Jiko would have said. 'Not different, either'" (416).

This koan reaches back to include the rest of the novel when we connect this story to earlier, unexplained references to it: once again out of order, in the way of quantum experience, Ruth seems to have intuited the koan's complex truth early in the novel. Or we might say that the disorderly distribution of bits of the koan, like Louise's disorderly memories/experiences of her alive/dead daughter (who is herself a kind of Schrödinger's cat) defies the tradition of unfolding Realist "truth effects," instead mimicking the truth of a quantum universe in which everything exists in the spacetime loaf, to be observed as one might from one's various points in space and time. First, at the end of her first dream of the nun, Ruth describes Jiko in a way that only becomes meaningful once we have read "Appendix E": "The smooth skin on her shorn head caught the light. From a distance, where Ruth stood, it looked like two moons, talking" (40). With Adam Frank's explanation of quantum physics in mind, along with Jiko's koan-making extension of it, we can see that Ruth views Jiko as the embodiment of this quantum/Buddhist truth. Undistracted by calculus, words, or fingers, Jiko *is* the moon, is one with being and the universe. "Appendix E," in combination with Ruth's early and late dreams that nearly bookend the novel, suggests that Jiko's transformative powers—she nearly transfigures into a crow in the first dream, and by the last she seems to have done so—lie in this simple ability, to be one with what is.

Later in the novel, another use of Frank's image suggests that by sharing the beliefs that give his mother her power to be present with what is, Haruki #1 is never without his mother's presence: "I don't want to die, Maman! I don't want to die! . . . I'm sorry. I was just talking to the moon" (322). Haruki #1 and Jiko—and Ruth, who has compiled (or written) the words of them both—demonstrate that, while no explanatory system can substitute for reality, wise ones can help us understand how to conceive of our relationships to reality, and how to change our ways of interacting with it and with each other, not unlike Louise's reorientation toward empathetic acceptance after learning Heptapod B. Language, or quantum physics, or Buddhism, or our experience of reality, is not reality, but they are not *not* reality, either. As separate as they are from the reality of the universe, they are our best tools for recognizing and enacting the truths of the universe—especially the truth that we are continuous with it. *Tale* uses quantum realism to communicate the complex truth that because we are part of the fabric of spacetime, we are unable ever fully to see or know it, but least inaccurate in our seeing and knowing when we frame our attempts from the cosmic perspective in which what we know is always relative, uncertain, complementary, and one limited possibility among an infinity.

Quantum Realism, Ethics, and Ontology

All of these examples of quantum realism easily confirm one of the hypotheses with which this book began, that to frame a narrative and imagine a world in terms of quantum mechanics is to imagine a new reality of time and space that is altogether different from the one we experience every day, and so to necessitate new methods for rendering this world that Realism had never dreamt of. But these quantum realist texts also illustrate another shift, not simply in literary technique and form, but also in their depictions of what it is to be (human or otherwise). As we saw from the many recent examples of material realism examined in Chapter 3, changes in technique and form accompany changes in our ideas about reality, and thus signal a corresponding shift from questions of epistemology to questions of ontology. Likewise, at the hearts of all of these examples of quantum realism are ontological inquiries—whether by invoking an entire metaphysical belief system, as in *A Tale for the Time Being*'s quantum manifesting of Buddhism, or challenging particular notions of self and relating selves, as with "Story"'s redefinition of power and truth through language, and *Sexing the Cherry*'s redefinition of self and gender as multiple and changing.

Even more interesting, because less conspicuous, is the suggestion that changes in our understanding of reality—of physical, universal being—entail corresponding changes in our human notions of ontology—of human being— and so also of our metaphysical or spiritual understandings of reality. For to read the "truth effects" of "Story of Your Life" as demonstrating our ability to choose to become aware of the eternal moment, as I argued above, is to locate a strikingly Buddhist concept of reality implied by Chiang's quantum reality but never explicitly expressed by the story.[39] Thus in discovering this shift from epistemological questions to ontological ones through my quantum realist readings of these novels, I have reached a conclusion that shares terms with

Coale's, but differs dramatically in those terms' inflections. Coale identified a shift from modernist questions of our "epistemological apprehensions and perceptions" to postmodernism's (and thus, for him, quantum fiction's) questioning of "the very ontological existence of the world we half-observe and half-create."[40] But quantum realism as I have characterized it is much less concerned with questioning the *existence* of the world, and more interested in considering what the quantum nature of the real world—which, according to quantum physics, definitely exists—can teach us about our own *being* (which also exists), and about our relationships to all being.

This ontological shift can also teach us something about "post-postmodern" fiction. For the concepts of being that recent quantum realism posits and queries differ significantly from those described by Brian McHale when he characterized postmodernism, early on, as newly ontological. Though his *Postmodernist Fiction* (1987) notably defined ontology as the new "dominant" of postmodernism, in reaction to modernism's epistemologic focus, the ontology he describes in *Constructing Postmodernism* (1992) remains distinctly linguistic, which is to say, abstract, theoretical, and, to my mind, still epistemological in important ways—being that is an issue of representation or a matter of belief, rather than empirical or material experience. Of the "literary models of the self" produced by postmodernism's ontological shift, McHale wrote that "if we posit a plurality of worlds, then conceivably 'my' self exists in more than one of them; if the world is ontologically unstable ... then perhaps so am I."[41] Once this "plurality of worlds" becomes physically real, as it does in quantum theory and specifically in many-worlds theory,[42] rather than linguistic or figural, as in poststructuralism (language and knowledge are inexact), postmodernism (all experience is partial and contingent), and the culture of the spectacle (images proliferate and substitute for the real), the self becomes more productively multiple than suspiciously unstable— more like time-traveling, savior Ruth than like the ultimately scattered and impotent Oedipa Maas (or Pierce Inverarity, for that matter).

In fact, as we have seen in "Story" and *Tale*, it is exactly the materializing of multiple worlds, multiple selves, and the continuity between selves and language that allows quantum realism to posit being as fundamentally relational, ethical, and productive, as opposed to the dire consequences of the multiplicity of self that McHale describes as postmodern ontology:

> Fragmentation and dispersal of self occurs in postmodernist fiction at the levels of language, narrative structure, and the material medium (the printed book), or between these levels, rather than at the level of the fictional world. In other words, postmodernist fiction prefers to represent the disintegration of the self figuratively, through linguistic,

structural, or visual metaphors, rather than literally, in the persons of characters who undergo some kind of literal disintegrative experience.[43]

Quantum realism, on the other hand, prefers to represent characters' disintegration of self as literal and material—as accomplished (in *Tale*) or attempted (in *The Body Artist*; see Chapter 5)—in their attempts to connect to others.

The complex interiority required for characters to both articulate their unorthodox visions of such an inherently multiple world and navigate it in ways that allow them to connect and empathize with others points to another significant change from the postmodern fiction McHale describes. Focused on "exploring and problematizing the ontologies of worlds and texts," postmodern fiction, and especially science fiction, has according to McHale "appeared to evade the consequences of its ontological pluralism and experimentalism for its model of the self." He goes so far as to claim that "'the disappearance of character (in the traditional sense) from contemporary ('postmodern') fiction . . . is one of the ways in which SF and the more 'serious,' experimental fiction have come close together.'"[44] The increasingly frequent adoption of thematic and generic science-fiction elements by respected literary writers over the past two decades should be proof enough that literature is no longer postmodern in the way that McHale defined it in 1992.[45] That materialist, and especially quantum, literature requires complexity of form and character precisely in order to fulfill its realist aims further indicates that its ontological inquiries are at least as much about the nature of the self and being as they are about the nature of "worlds and texts."

Quantum realism is ontological in that it starts with the assumption that we exist specifically in relation to everything, much less everyone, else that exists. It is therefore also inherently ethical, as Karan Barad has argued through "new materialism" (see Chapter 3). Quantum realism illustrates and develops the ethical dimension that Barad identifies as central to material realism by creating its entire fictional world as the relational, agential, intra-actional quantum reality that Barad identifies as inescapably a matter of ethics. According to this thinking, Ozeki's use of materiality to link language, quantum reality, and Buddhist belief as an argument for the ethics of empathy might make *A Tale for the Time Being* the best literary example of "new materialism" so far. By using its quantum setting to manifest its Buddhism, the novel demonstrates Coole and Frost's new materialist assertion that "there is no definitive break between sentient and nonsentient entities or between material and spiritual phenomena."[46] In making language a material conduit for spiritual phenomena between points in physical spacetime—and for the moving relationship between Nao and Ruth—*Tale* also illustrates one of

Karan Barad's core assertions about the inherent ethics of reality, that "matter entails entanglement."[47] In this way, *A Tale for the Time Being* does not just imagine aspects of reality and being as defined by quantum mechanics; it instantiates an immediate access to that reality, and intimacy between self and reality, language and reality, and self and self, that postmodern fiction could not fathom. Thus *Tale* and other quantum realism uses language in the twenty-first century to posit the existence of things and ethical ways of being and relating that had been rendered impossible by theories and fiction of previous decades.

Reading this fiction enables us to—even demands that we—inhabit these new worlds and their new ways of relating to others and to that world, and occupy the many different and simultaneous subject positions required to construct them. The intensely defamiliarizing metafictional and materialist methods used to construct these worlds, which require readers' persistent attention to and participation in that construction, reposition us as continuous with those fictional worlds, intra-actional in them, part of the agential and relational fabric of the universe in which any act of reading or writing is only one of infinite connected and materializing acts. In being so repositioned, in being required to view the world, ourselves, and all other beings from such a different perspective, how are we changed? As examples of quantum realism proliferate and reading more commonly becomes an act of such radical reorientation, how might we begin to see or make the world differently?

Like Borges's encyclopedia of Tlön and the teleological language of the heptapods, quantum realism has the capacity to reshape the real world. To say so is, on one level, simply to recognize in it the power wielded by every language used to represent reality, as Saussure recognized that the world is shaped by our mechanisms for dividing the "uncharted nebula" of thought into units of language.[48] But by reconfiguring the reader as active and agential, and language as continuous with the matter of the universe, quantum realism is poised to intensify that impact far beyond what can be done by a passive "mirror to nature." Science fiction has long expressed our anxiety about the murderous power and speed of change brought about by self-aware technology; Wallace acknowledged it himself and located it specifically in the technology of writing, when he compared metafiction to the cataclysmic self-awareness of *Terminator*'s Skynet and declared its end to be "Armageddon."[49] But by asking us to inhabit the eternal now and to read and act with awareness of our continuity with and responsibility toward all other beings and matter, metafictive quantum realism creates fiction as a space for observing and experiencing empathy, and so also for reshaping the world in its ethical image.

Notes

1. Brian Greene, *The Fabric of the Cosmos: Space, Time, and the Texture of Reality* (New York: Palgrave Macmillan, 2005), 142 (emphasis added). I will note subsequent references parenthetically.
2. See, for example, pages 16–24 in Samuel Coale's *Quirks of the Quantum: Postmodern and Contemporary American Fiction* (Charlottesville: University of Virginia Press, 2012), which I will discuss below.
3. Mark McGurl's concept of the "posthuman comedy," and the geological scale on which it is based, provides one recent new context for conceiving of human language as characteristic of human being, in the context of a vast and ancient universe that humans and their language have occupied only microscopically and briefly. See his "The New Cultural Geology," *Twentieth-Century Literature* 57, nos. 3–4 (2011): 380–90, which I will discuss below.
4. See for example Heidegger's "Language," in *Poetry, Language, Thought*, trans. Albert Hofstadter (New York: Harper & Row, 1971), 210: "Man [sic] speaks only as he [sic] responds to language."
5. Greene, *Fabric*, 112.
6. For excellent overviews of quantum mechanics, particularly as it relates to literature, see pages 7–14 of Susan Strehle's *Fiction in the Quantum Universe* (Chapel Hill: University of North Carolina Press, 1992) and 14–30 of Coale's *Quirks*. Rather than reproducing their fine work I will simply enlist and describe the main ideas here. I will note subsequent references to both books parenthetically.
7. Linda Hutcheon, *A Poetics of Postmodernism* (New York: Routledge, 1988), 12, 16.
8. See, for example, interviews with Enck, "An Interview" and Reilly, "An Interview with John Barth."
9. Or maximalist. Indeed, Strehle's reading of the "actualism" of *Public Burning* as "uneconomical" (73) also raises the question of "actualism"'s relationship to maximalism in the postmodern period.
10. Vanna Bonta, *Flight: A Quantum Novel* (San Diego: Meridian House, 1995), 118, 333.
11. Ibid., 244–5.
12. James Peacock, *Jonathan Lethem* (London: Manchester University Press, 2012) 61, 62, 125, 182, 202.
13. Jonathan Lethem, *As She Climbed Across the Table* (New York: Vintage, 1997), 206, 207 (original italics).
14. Judie Newman, "Updike's Many Worlds: Local and Global in *Toward the End of Time*," *The John Updike Review* 1, no. 1 (2011): 53–67.
15. Marshall Boswell, *Understanding David Foster Wallace* (Columbia: University of South Carolina Press, 2003), 125.
16. See Stephen J. Burn's *Conversations*, 60, 129, 151. My thanks to Stephen for pointing me to Newman's article, reminding me of Boswell's quantum com-

ment about *Jest*, and introducing me to Dewitt's *The Last Samurai*, which I will discuss below.
17 Jennifer Egan, *A Visit from the Goon Squad* (New York: Anchor, 2011), 168–9.
18 Ibid., 317.
19 My thanks to Ralph Clare, whose discussion of the novel with me sparked this reading.
20 Egan, *Goon Squad*, 81.
21 Stephen J. Burn, "Encyclopedic Fictions," in *American Literature in Transition, 1990-2000*, ed. Stephen J. Burn (Cambridge: Cambridge University Press, 2018), 119.
22 Cixin Liu, *The Dark Forest*, trans. Joel Martinsen (New York: Tor, 2015), 15, 16.
23 McGurl, "The New Cultural Geology," 533.
24 Ibid., 537.
25 Ibid., 543.
26 Ibid., 539.
27 Coale, *Quirks*, 43.
28 Samuel Delany, *Babel-17* (New York: Vintage, 2001), 215. I will note subsequent references parenthetically.
29 Jeanette Winterson, *Sexing the Cherry* (London: Grove Press, 1989), 189.
30 Ted Chiang, "Story of Your Life," in *Stories of Your Life and Others* (New York: Vintage, 2016), 108, 109. I will note subsequent references parenthetically.
31 Jacques Lacan, "The Agency of the Letter," in *Norton Anthology of Theory and Criticism*, 2nd edn, ed. Vincent B Leitch (New York: Norton, 2010), 1175.
32 Morris, *Realism*, 110.
33 Ruth Ozeki, *A Tale for the Time Being* (New York: Penguin, 2013), 407. I will note subsequent references parenthetically.
34 Yet, surprisingly, criticism on the novel tends to do just that. One study of subjectivity in the novel attributes its "fluidity" to the "governing mechanics of the postmodern epoch," specifically Baudrillard's concept of hyperreality (Mojca Krevel, "A Tale of Being Everything: Literary Subject in Ruth Ozeki's *A Tale for the Time Being*," *Brno Studies in English* 43, no. 2 (2017): 111). In my reading below, the novel's pronounced materiality, rendered through its quantumness, precisely prevents us from reading its world as governed by the postmodern simulacrum, and instead insists that we read it in the "post-postmodern" context of the ethical-material. Another reading likewise converts all evidence that I read as the novel representing physical aspects of the quantum world into an abstract literary trope, magical realism (Petra Fachinger, "Writing the Canadian Pacific Northwest Ecocritically: The Dynamics of Local and Global in Ruth Ozeki's *A Tale for the Time Being*," *Canadian Literature* 232 (2017): 54).

Only one critic to date, Hsiu-chuan Lee, considers the quantum aspects of the novel in a sustained way; while his reading reaches conclusions similar to mine, he also ultimately sees *Tale's* quantumness as more trope than aspect of the reality the novel strives to realistically represent. His "Sharing Worlds through Words," *ARIEL: A Review of International English Literature* 49, no. 1 (2018): 27–52, published after this chapter was completed, recognizes that the novel conceives of "words as quantum particles" (27), a point on which I will elaborate in terms of the novel's overall materiality; he also examines how the novel "attends to the philosophical implications of quantum theory," implications I will explore in terms of quantum philosophies of new materialism. Rather than considering these insights in relation to the formal consequences of the novel's attempt to represent a fully quantum reality, however, Lee argues that the novel uses quantum mechanics as a "trope" to demonstrate its "cosmopolitics" (30).

Sue Lovell's "Toward a Poetics of Posthumanist Narrative Using Ruth Ozeki's *A Tale for the Time Being*," *Critique: Studies in Contemporary Fiction* 59, no. 1 (2018): 57–74, considers the novel's quantumness in a more limited way, as one facet of its ability to create for the reader more expansive subject positions—posthumanist positions—than liberal humanism could imagine. My reading of the novel's ethical materiality (again, completed before Lovell's article was published) is thus an expansion of this concept of ethical posthumanism.

Critics' omissions of quantumness from their readings of DeLillo's *The Body Artist* will wreak even more havoc; see Chapter 5.

35 Which does not even occur in the novel: the two women never meet.
36 Ruth and Nao's entanglement points to another misreading caused by neglecting the novel's quantum elements. Starr asserts that the Buddhist letting go of self that Nao practices through meditation is anti-feminist in that it prevents the communal connections required for women to make change by acting in solidarity. Yet, it is only through Nao's meditative practices—and her learning of them from Jiko—that she is able to relate to her father and write the diary in which she extends herself to Ruth, enabling Ruth to save her father's life, and to the reader.
37 Ursula Le Guin constructed a whole short story out of this scenario: see her 1974 "Schrödinger's Cat," in *Postmodern American Fiction*, ed. Paula Geyh, Fred Leebron, and Andrew Levy (New York: Norton, 1998), 520–5.
38 This substitution of words for body strongly echoes that in *Extremely Loud & Incredibly Close*, when Oscar and his grandfather fill their father's/son's empty coffin with the grandfather's unread letters.
39 DeLillo's *The Body Artist* suggests a similarly implicit Buddhism through its more overt quantum framework; see Chapter 5.
40 Coale, *Quirks*, 36.
41 Brian McHale, *Constructing Postmodernism* (New York: Routledge, 1992), 253–4.

42 Which is itself more of a theory to describe reality than a fanciful thought experiment: more than half of physicists believe Everett's many-worlds theory explains the seeming collapse of waves into particles, that is, that it describes the real world we live in.
43 McHale, *Constructing*, 254.
44 Ibid., 254; 255 citing Christine Brooke-Rose, *A Rhetoric of the Unreal* (London: Cambridge University Press, 1981), 102.
45 I do not mean to support the sci-fi/literature divide by invoking it here, only to illustrate how absurd the traditional ghettoization of "genre-fiction" is by pointing out how increasingly blurred these lines are, by writers including David Mitchell (*Cloud Atlas, The Bone Clocks*), Jennifer Egan ("Black Box"), Don DeLillo (*Zero K*), Margaret Atwood (*Oryx and Crake* trilogy), Ali Smith (*How To Be Both*), Ian McEwan (*Machines Like Me*), Jeanette Winterson (*Frankissstein*), and of course all the writers mentioned in this chapter.
46 Coole and Frost, *New Materialisms*, 10.
47 Barad, *Meeting*, 160.
48 Ferdinand de Saussure, from *Course in General Linguistics: The Norton Anthology of Theory and Criticism*, 2nd edn, ed.Vincent B. Leitch (New York: Norton, 2010), 856.
49 Burn, *Conversations*, 30.

5

Quantum Realism Case Study

On Don DeLillo's *The Body Artist*

By the time *Zero K* arrived in 2016, Don DeLillo's published oeuvre comprised fifteen novels (not counting the pseudonymous *Amazons*), three plays, and one short story collection, and had generated an abundant critical response that is equally unusual in the intensity of its disagreements and the clarity of its consecration. Whether reading DeLillo as prophet of contemporary secular spirituality or harbinger of postmodern nihilism, critics of contemporary American literature tend to agree that the canon in all its nascence and contention must contain Don DeLillo, because his books contain contemporary (and future) America. So it's no wonder that we feel so compelled to chip through the tonal ice he seems by now to produce like breathing—one reviewer calls his cool stylings a "tic" or "trademark," comparing him, wonderfully, to Werner Herzog[1]—in search of what warm living thing might be bubbling underneath. No DeLillo work has thwarted critics in that endeavor as much as *The Body Artist* (2001). I will argue that criticism on the novel misses its mark because, with one limited exception,[2] it fails to read the novel as quantum realism. As with Ozeki's *A Tale for the Time Being*, the various misreadings that are exposed when one considers the novel's quantum setting, and the provocative ideas about truth, reality, and narrative's capacity for capturing both that such a reading reveals, illustrate the power of quantum realism as a literary mode and a critical lens.

Given the ambivalence and coyness of DeLillo's entire oeuvre, it is perhaps not surprising that, unlike the fiction examined in the previous chapter, *The Body Artist* is not a clear example of quantum realism. We might say it aspires to quantum realism more than realizing it, or that it realizes nothing so clearly as the challenges entailed by the mode. It thus provides an excellent example of what is at stake in reproducing a quantum world in language and the difficulties and limits of doing so through realism. While the novel itself makes only one glancing mention of quantum mechanics,[3] DeLillo's archive housed at the Harry Ransom Center, with its many folders stuffed with DeLillo's notes on quantum mechanics, their implications for human experience, and notes on the novel connecting the two, proves that the novel emerged at every step as a contemplation of quantum reality. Similarly, we find few and scattered obvious disruptions of traditional realist form in the novel—until we reach the end, and then only if we consider the novel as a whole and its enigmatic ending in light of the archive evidence. Indeed, those who have studied the archive will subsequently find the novel virtually unreadable without it, their own earlier guesswork about the novel's mysteries incomplete if not laughable. And yet so far, with the notable exception of Samuel Coale's, every published critical consideration of the novel—and, one imagines, nearly every private reading—proceeds without benefit of the archive as guide. Overwhelmingly, the novel that has been read to date is not the novel DeLillo wrote. Where critics stumbled through a familiar landscape using trusty old tools for illumination—metaphor and grief, supernatural and trauma—DeLillo had created a different world altogether, with different rules and assumptions, requiring new tools and lenses to become visible. Thus *The Body Artist* is to the archive what human experience is to quantum mechanics: we can't possibly see the truth of it without opening our minds to and informing ourselves of its underlying workings and texture, none of which will be immediately apparent or what we expect to find. For these two reasons, along with a third—the enigmatic, economic brilliance of the novel's language and form, which deserve extended explication—I devote this final substantial chapter to a reading of *The Body Artist* in the context of quantum realism.

The novel itself offers little to go on in terms of plot. With only 126 wide-margined pages, it is the physically sparsest of all DeLillo works, and yet its pages contain the largest world of them all because they conjure all of space and time and because, somewhat paradoxically, they encourage the reader's presence in every particular point of both. In that entirety of spacetime, fittingly, not much happens: a woman breakfasts with her husband, who kills himself; she grieves and practices body work; a strange man appears in her house; they talk; he disappears; she performs her body-art piece; she imagines her dead husband present with her for a moment. Without archival guidance, the book's focus on one character's contemplation can seem to result in more empty space than plot points, and so to invite the reader to connect those points into whatever picture comes to mind: novel as Rorschach blot. And so, the novel's nearly twenty post-publication years have produced a body of criticism which, when read in a good long stretch, can seem to spin its own accompanying narrative that hovers above the novel slightly awry.

In the first (and still the most formally astute and lovely) article on the book, Philip Nel notes that early reviewers of the novel primarily analyzed or attempted to hide the confusion it induced more than the book itself.[4]

Years later, critics' own collective confusion is on display. This is in part a result of the remarkable diversity of their frameworks, which range from organic approaches such as Nel's formalism, inquiries into the book's Heideggerian philosophy of being (Bonca), its neurobiological notions of vision (Burn), and its treatment of trauma (Di Prete) and grief (Smith), to more esoteric readings stemming from ideas that seem rather outside the book's demonstrated concerns, including hospitality (Kessel), threatening exteriority (Fujii), and the paranormal (Keskinen). Some readings seem to stretch beyond the concerns of not just this book but DeLillo's entire output: in 2007, Longmuir called the novel DeLillo's "most political to date," using Kristeva to read it as a staunchly feminist novel that restores the individual female speaking subject, an argument Radia augments through the lens of spectacle. DeLillo's oeuvre offers many things to admire by way of language, style, and prescient social critique, but given its habit of drawing female characters as objects of use by men seeking comfort or identity through domination (*Americana, White Noise, Point Omega, Zero K*...), feminism is not among them.[5]

Such confusion is never more visible than in critics' diverse, sometimes outlandish, and often—as I will argue—textually dubious readings of the book's most enigmatic character, the foundling Mr. Tuttle. In early articles, he is primarily understood as mentally incompetent, whether through childlikeness[6] or from some more profound physical damage: Nel compares him to "an Alzheimer's patient,"[7] while Cowart crassly calls him a "nameless retarded man" who has had a "cerebral accident." Cowart offers a third possibility—Mr. Tuttle as "emissary from beyond"[8]—which several other critics also take up, transforming his inscrutability into incorporeality: Di Prete calls him a "phantom" or "phantasmatic figure," comparing him to Morrison's character Beloved;[9] Keskinen reads the entire novel as supernatural inquiry, in which Mr. Tuttle is "specter," "hallucination," or "ghost";[10] and Breitbach seems to understand Mr. Tuttle as the book's primary example of the "spirituality" and "mystery" that she argues "liminal realism" accommodates.[11]

But most often, critics make sense of the book's central enigma using the tools most readily available to them: they convert the real, problematic person/character into allegory, theme, or metaphor. In Di Prete's trauma-based reading, Mr. Tuttle disappears into Lauren, becoming "a psychotic formation within her own unconscious."[12] Similarly, Smith claims that Lauren's despair is "materialized in the character of the young man," making Mr. Tuttle an ontological rather than psychological enactment of her grief.[13] For Radia, he is less man than an "allegory of the mourning process," just as the most challenging ability ascribed to him—to move from one reality to another—is for her a metaphor for "an othering process."[14] Kessel converts the story of this extraordinary man who lives outside normal time into an elaborate metaphor for ordinary hospitality, while Fujii reads him as a metaphor for "exteriority as threatening topos."[15] Longmuir treats Mr. Tuttle as plot device, the catalyst Lauren requires to begin working through her grief at losing Rey, despite the fact that evidence of Mr. Tuttle's *physical* presence in the house—the hair in her mouth and the noise upstairs[16]—appears *before* Rey's death. Meanwhile, the book's back-cover description, which archival drafts suggest was at least largely written by DeLillo, twice refers to Mr. Tuttle as a "man," "together" with whom Lauren undergoes a profound "journey into the wilderness of time—time, love, and human perception." For DeLillo, here and in the archive, as I will detail below, Mr. Tuttle is neither ghost nor metaphor, but a man whose peculiar relationship with Lauren lies at the center of the book.[17]

Still, the larger thematic questions that inspire these reaching readings of Mr. Tuttle seem to me to be the right ones, the main questions that *The Body Artist* is asking: what is the meaning of Lauren's performance of *Body Time*, and is it redemptive, and of what? Does it enable her to overcome her grief, or does it merely distract her from it, or reproduce it? How do we read the novel's ending: is Lauren "successful" in her endeavors, or resigned to their failure? And how exactly would we define those endeavors? Is the novel—as an example of a work of art, as an act of language—successful in what it is trying to accomplish, and in what terms? But then, how does reading a main character as ghost, madman, hallucination, projection, or metaphor for any number of other concerns contribute to the book's ability to pose and answer these questions? And what evidence in the book asks us to read Mr. Tuttle in any of these peculiar ways?

So far, only Coale's reading of Mr. Tuttle as possibly "contemporary fiction's first quantum character"[18] begins to do justice to the novel's strategies for asking and answering these questions, not only because DeLillo's drafts and notes for the novel insist on such a reading, as Coale argues, but also because, as I will argue, this reading is best supported by the textual evidence given to us by the published novel. If we focus on direct descriptions of the man, rather than on the more abundant depictions of his function in relation to Lauren, we find a character who is only scantily built of physical description, but rounded out with attention to his uses of language, modes of perception, and relationship to reality. About his physicality we know only that he is "smallish and fine-bodied . . . and sandy-haired" (43); "his chin was sunken back, severely receded . . . and his hair was wiry and snagged, with jutting clumps" (47). He has armpits, chest, arms, belly, and all the parts of a man, which she names and touches (70), and "his eyes were gray but what did it matter" (87). This simultaneous anatomical specificity and categorical elusiveness (he is young and old, masculine and androgynous) creates the "thinness of address" that plagues the novel (48): he is a real man, but he doesn't act in the world like one, so what does that mean? Rather, Mr. Tuttle solidifies as a character not out of physical description but from the very particular and inexplicable ways he interacts with the world through language. Struggling with tenses, and thus with grammar and syntax (50–1), reporting future conversations (83), and unable to include in his speech the larger contexts available in narrative (67), Mr. Tuttle is unable to understand or communicate in linear time. Requiring "many levels of perception" to be understood (52), and unable "to measure himself to what we call the Now" (68) or to "shape and process and paint" things into a "story we want to believe" (82), he not only perceives and relates to reality strangely but also is barred from telling a story of how and what he perceives. Mr. Tuttle is a man who occupies time and space differently than we do, and thus relates to Lauren in ways she can't quite comprehend, while also occupying the narrative in ways we don't immediately comprehend either.

DeLillo's archive dramatically bolsters such a reading of Mr. Tuttle as a real man experiencing a real time and space, a reality, outside our own experience. It thus suggests clearer ways of answering the larger questions raised by the novel than have been offered so far, in two ways: it reveals the enormous extent to which DeLillo's research on quantum theory influenced his thinking as he developed and wrote the novel, and, as I will illustrate below, it shows DeLillo considering thoroughly and painstakingly how he could construct in a traditional realist novel a character living in and demonstrating reality as described by quantum theory. Read through the lens of the archive, *The Body Artist* becomes DeLillo's effort to depict a *physical reality* that is dictated by contemporary quantum theory, but is very different from our practical understanding of the physical world and time. Thus, we can most productively read Mr. Tuttle not as metaphor or concept but as a regular element of realism, a character given particular physical and psychological traits that define his interaction with his fictional world, though that realism reproduces a very different reality than the one that dominates our daily experience and the fiction that mimics it. That is to say, though DeLillo is interested in thinking about the implications of quantum reality on the elements of life we typically experience in terms of time and narrative—death, loss, grief, identity, intimacy—the novel's strange qualities, especially Mr. Tuttle, are not metaphors for these things, or effects of these things, but are instead the framework in which these very normal parts of human life occur.

We might, then, read *The Body Artist* as a setting-driven novel, shaped by its rendering of a quantum world in the way that *A Tale of Two Cities* is defined by French-Revolution London and Paris or *Point Omega* is shaped by the desert, more than as a trauma- or grief-driven novel, and certainly more than as a ghost story. In this way and others, reading the novel in light of the archive shifts the focus of the novel, and generates significantly different readings of the novel than have so far been offered, with the exception of Coale's—which I aim substantially to expand and develop. Likewise, though the novel is, like all DeLillo novels, interested in language's role in perceiving and interacting with and within this different physical reality, the novel as read through the archive is driven and shaped not primarily by theories of language, but rather by (quantum) theories of the real world, making it an interesting kind of exception in DeLillo's oeuvre.[19]

In enlisting the archive so extensively to read the novel, I do not mean to weigh authorial intention more heavily than the text, but rather to show how the text itself gives ample evidence of that intention, if only we stop reading it as other things and let it be the unexpected thing that it is. I also do not intend to suggest quantum theory was the only defining framework DeLillo employed for the novel. In fact, in a 2012 conversation with Jonathan Franzen at the New York Public Library, DeLillo spoke of *The Body Artist* as "a novel of time and loss" that emerged from his desire to depict "an intimate relationship" through the "language that develops from these characters."[20] Never does he mention quantum theory. And yet what the archive shows is that, in the case of this novel, the reality he sculpts out of sentences is quantum.

Because the novel itself is so enigmatic, critical confusion about it so pronounced, and its peculiar enlistment of quantum realism so complex in relation to the texts discussed in the previous chapter, a significant amount of work on the novel itself must be done before we can fruitfully consider what it accomplishes through and allows us to conclude about quantum realism. Thus, this chapter will first demonstrate how evidence from the archive illustrates DeLillo translating quantum theory into his fiction's characters, settings, and conflicts. Next, it will offer a detailed reading of the novel in light of this quantum mechanical framework, considering how that framework shapes the questions posed by the text and the possible answers it attempts to provide. Finally, it will consider how DeLillo's desire to express quantum principles in language, specifically using the mode of realism, impacts the structure of that realism and points to the need for and challenges in producing a new kind of realism, quantum realism. Because the novel is one of the most formally beautiful and interesting ones I know, yet is often overlooked when we teach or talk about the best contemporary fiction (or even simply the best of DeLillo's fiction), my textual reading will be thorough, at the risk of seeming to do to the novel what Kinbote's fantastical commentary does to Shade's sober and far superior poem. But the magnitude of the commentary required to unfurl the mysteries of DeLillo's tight little novel strikes me as yet more evidence of its inherent quantumness. Like Kinbote's bloated commentary—or more germanely, like the unfolded proton that fills a planet's skies in Liu's *The Three Body Problem*—this maximalist reading is the microscopic examination that *The Body Artist* requires to reveal the many worlds it almost invisibly contains.

The Body Artist's Big Bang and Repercussions

Samuel Coale accurately described the archival materials as focused around "the randomness of existence, the mysterious nature of human perception, and the nature of time."[21] Still, I find the details of the archive worthy of note because of the telling ways they ask us to read facets of the novel, and simply because, in demonstrating the extent to which DeLillo was contemplating these ideas and working to integrate them into the novel, they compel us to reevaluate the novel's characters, setting, and conflicts in light of their evidence—to read the novel as expanding outward from the dense core of the research materials.

The archive materials are remarkable for the sprawling composition timeline they suggest and the breadth and depth of research on quantum theory they document. Articles on quantum theory snipped from *The New York Times* date from 1984 to 2001, and jotted ideas for the novel go back even further: one line in his notes folder, "The world is self-referring," appears in his 1982 *The Names*.[22] These materials alone indicate that DeLillo was researching and thinking about the ideas that generated *The Body Artist* for roughly 20 years—long before he began writing the novel,[23] and even beyond its publication—while consulting a wide variety of sources. His notebook contains notes on and quotations about quantum theory and time from seven popular science books (including three by Paul Davies), and two magazines (*Scientific American* and *Forbes*), as well as notes on three philosophy and anthropology books on similar topics, all also roughly contemporary (1962-99). To Coale's more general list of main topics in the research I would add these more specific ideas, which repeat often in the notes and then show up quite plainly in the novel: from Davies and Morris, DeLillo takes the idea that there is no real difference between past, present, and future; from Davies and others he notes the theorized existence of multiple worlds, or "overlapping realities." From Prigogine, he notes that time is a human construct and illusion, and he clips and cites many sources that consider the possibility of time travel. All of these ideas are implied by a quotation (of Hermann Weyl) to which DeLillo returns again and again, "The world simply is; it does not happen," underscored (as Coale notes) in a clipping of Lehmann-Haupt's review of Nick Herbert's *Quantum Reality*, but also transcribed in notes on two different Davies books.

Tucked into these two folders containing dozens of pages of "Research Material" and "'Time' notes" are seven pages of ideas for the novel DeLillo imagined crafting out of these concepts. These ideas appear to come quite early in his writing process for the novel: along with the "self-referring" line, we also see DeLillo consider at this point the title "The Ivory Acrobat," which he wound up using for a short story published back in 1988. This perhaps original vision for the novel differs from the novel he published in surprising and telling ways. Most dramatically, it seems to have aimed to capture the time-defying sprawl of a total quantum world, rendered in three parts:[24] in part 1, "The future, Boston as Bombay," DeLillo imagined a post-apocalyptic scenario involving "poisoned water," "people . . . constantly detained," "trains carrying bodies," and "the arrow of time / time is a virus"—that last clause enclosed in an emphatic box. Part 2 would take place in "The present. Upstate New York," with an "elderly man living in a shingled house," whom "children say . . . is living backwards" and with an "alien mentality (?)." Naturally then, part 3 would take place in "The past?" Other pages of novel ideas in these folders explore ways of developing quantum concepts in narrative: DeLillo drafts time paradoxes that would result from living backward, and considers the greater importance of "cosmic history" over "human history" in the twenty-first century.[25] This structural sketch suggests that DeLillo considered making his time-traveling man part of a larger world that was experiencing the consequences of time running amok, and whose reversed timeline was echoed in the novel's overall structure. Of course, as Martin Amis's *Time's Arrow* (1991) illustrates, even writing an entire plot backward does not solve the print novel's problem of closure and teleology. But DeLillo's early sketches of plot and structure indicate that he entered his novel aiming to try.

That he wound up writing only the middle section, did not construct Mr. Tuttle as a man visibly living backward, and shifted the novel's emphasis away from the time traveler and onto his observer, Lauren, suggests that rather than attempting to write a novel that would place the oddities of time and a quantum world front and center for our contemplation—a feat whose difficulty, perhaps impossibility, it is easy to imagine—DeLillo chose the opposite approach, the more Realistic approach: he wrote a novel that offers scant evidence for the quantum world it represents, and filtered even that through the uncomprehending eyes of a human observer living in our familiar Newtonian universe. In this way, DeLillo's writing of only part of the original novel he planned is emblematic of his entire writing strategy for this book, which was one of constant whittling away and reduction, from the massive archive of quantum mechanics research and explicit ideas for manifesting them in character, plot, and structure to the wisp of a novel with faint echoes of an alternate reality that he created out of them.

The green spiral notebook in the archive demonstrates how DeLillo directly applied his research on quantum mechanics to elements of the novel he was building. By the time DeLillo was producing the notes that fill that notebook, he seems to have confined his plot to the middle, "present" section of the outlined story and settled on the characters that occupy the final novel: the notebook's pockets contain stacks of small notes paper-clipped into bundles labeled "Rey Robles," "Lauren," and "The Stranger" (previously "Dunlop," ultimately "Mr. Tuttle"). These loose papers along with notebook pages list aspects of the characters as we know them in the published novel, but using unambiguous description rather than the novel's enigmatic evasiveness. They ground those descriptions in the research about time and quantum theory that also occupies the notebook.

In the context of the novel's evasive portrayal of Mr. Tuttle, and the collective critical chaos of reading him, notes about "The Stranger" are the greatest revelation; certainly they support Coale's assessment of the character as "quantum." Several notes attach Mr. Tuttle to "overlapping realities," indicating that he occupies or has access to realities other than Lauren's or our own. And DeLillo places him firmly outside our chronological model of time and of our sense of time as part of reality, in comments scattered through paper notes and pages: "Mr. Tuttle instructs her on time. An illusion"; he "comes from the future" and is "trying to develop a new sense—time. Seventh sense"; "time does not flow for him. Time is a culture." These descriptions of the character do not merely allude to general concepts from DeLillo's research on quantum theory; as in the novel itself, these character notes quote that research directly. "Overlapping realities" (appearing on p. 84 in the novel) is Davies's phrase, and Mr. Tuttle's instruction to Lauren that "time is an illusion" is a quotation of Einstein, by way of Prig's *The End of Certainty*, which DeLillo notes elsewhere in the notebook. Near the end of the notebook, DeLillo answers all questions of Mr. Tuttle's sanity very clearly: "He's not mentally ill" (which he emphatically boxes again in the middle of the page). Rather, Mr. Tuttle is, from our perspective, a time traveler, who "lost identity in the journey thru time."[26] It is exactly this link between time and identity that the novel will explore, by constructing Mr. Tuttle as lacking both and Lauren as desperately wanting to jettison both in her attempts to enter his reality, as I will argue below.

The research notes and drafts also show DeLillo crafting a quantum setting for the novel, a world in which quantum qualities that remain confined in our experience to theory and imagination become visible and consequential. One folder in the archive contains an extensive series of structural outlines and chapter lists and synopses, whose elements repeat with only subtle changes in wording and order, and accurately predict the shape and contents of the final novel. One of these many chapter outlines places all of the novel's main events in the context of "Overlapping realities," which DeLillo has penned as a heading to the page (see Figure 1).

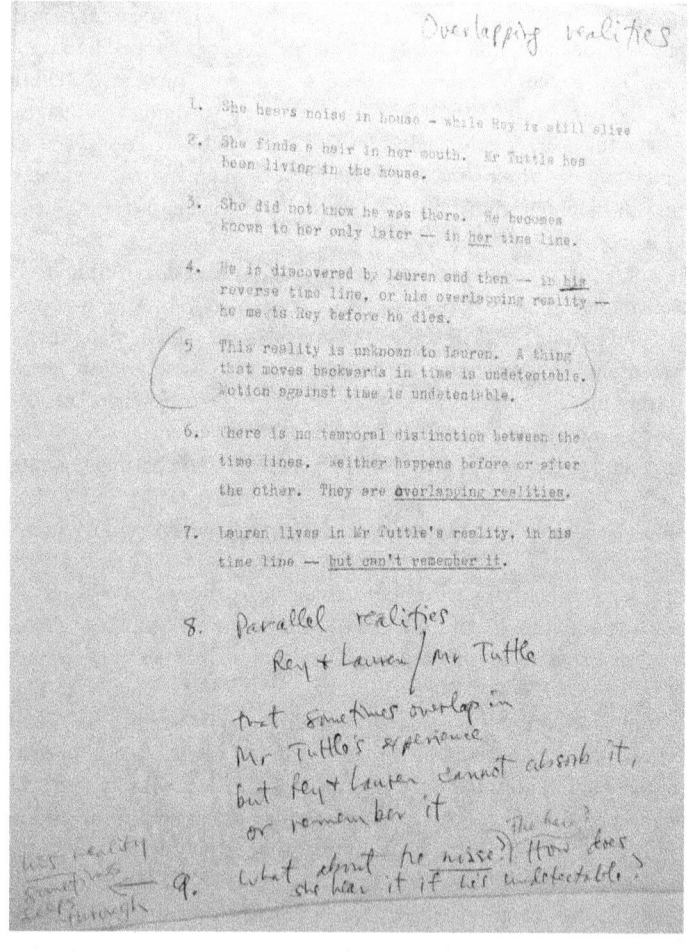

Figure 1 Ideas for depicting "overlapping realities" in *The Body Artist*. Don DeLillo Papers, Container 8.5, Harry Ransom Center, The University of Texas at Austin.

This page seems to make explicit what is implied by the reappearance of "overlapping realities" throughout DeLillo's notes and outlines for the novel (a note with the phrase is even taped to the inside front cover of the notebook): that the plot he devised for the novel—hair in mouth, Mr. Tuttle channeling Rey and predicting the future, Lauren imagining the return of Rey—was meant to signify at least the possibility (if not, as I read the archive, the necessity) that the world of the novel allows for and expresses the experience of multiple simultaneous realities. It suggests that DeLillo created a novel that imagines what our experience would be like in a world in which "these parallel universes are as solid and real as our own," as a physicist theorized the quantum realm in a 2000 *New York Times* contained in DeLillo's research file.[27]

The archive also suggests, as Coale has pointed out, DeLillo's construction of a world in which linear time is an illusion; past, present, and future are linguistic constructs; and, as he often quoted from Weyl/Davies in his notes, "the world does not happen; it simply is." But, as with "overlapping realities," it is not the research notes themselves but the drafts and outlines incorporating those research ideas that demonstrate the ideas' inclusion in the novel. On the question of the novel's concept of time and what that says about the novel's reality, the archive is wonderfully clear. In fact, one set of facing notebook pages seems to present a record of DeLillo transforming quantum concepts into plot and character elements (see Figure 2).

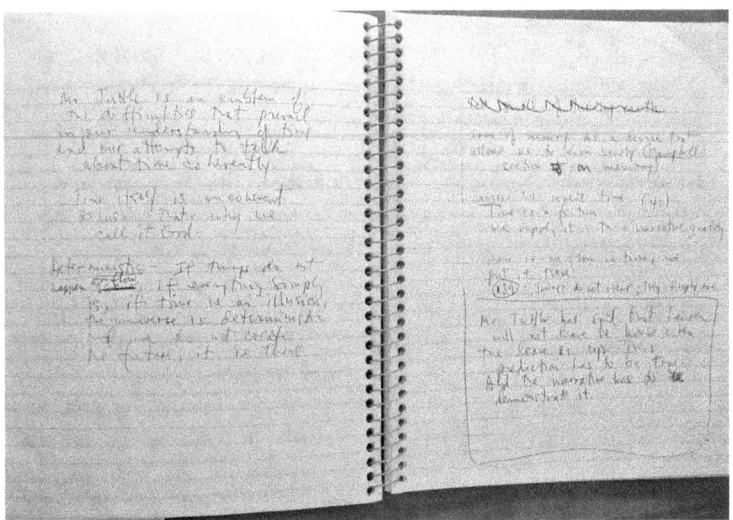

Figure 2 Ideas for constructing Mr. Tuttle outside linear time. Don DeLillo Papers, Container 6.5, Harry Ransom Center, The University of Texas at Austin.

He notes a set of ideas and quotations (some also repeated elsewhere) drawn from his research: "loss of memory as a device that allows us to live sanely (Campbell's section on memory)"; "(Davies) We invent time. Time is a fiction. We supply it with a narrative quality (46). There is no flow in time; we put it there. 189 [circled] things do not occur; they simply are." He seems to conclude on the facing page that these ideas are "<u>deterministic</u> – If things do not happen or flow, if everything simply is, if time is an illusion, the universe is deterministic and we do not create the future; it is there." Then, once again boxed for emphasis, DeLillo records this plot idea:

> Mr Tuttle has said that Lauren
>   will not leave the house when
> the lease is up. This
>   prediction has to be true.
> And the narrative has to
>   demonstrate it.

This is exactly what happens in the novel. The first time Mr. Tuttle talks to Lauren, he mentions the house and tells her she will not (first he says "did not," then "do not," 51) leave it after the lease is out. One of the last things she contemplates in the novel before attempting to instantiate Rey in her present (or join him in their past) is that she has fulfilled Mr. Tuttle's prediction, as if recognizing that Rey's appearance depends on her living in the nonlinear world described by Mr. Tuttle (114). But without DeLillo's blunt description of this sequence in the archive as evidence that Mr. Tuttle exists in a reality outside linear, unfolding time, the episode reads (as it has for most critics) as Lauren's dream, or proof of Mr. Tuttle's madness or supernatural abilities.

However, Lauren's thoughts and responses to this quantum possibility significantly complicate its implications, while further establishing the quantum setting by adding the phenomenon of observer effect:

> She has extended the lease, in whatever words he'd used, and she knows she has taken this action to fulfill the truth of his remark, which probably invalidates whatever truth there had been. It is not circumstances that has kept her here, or startled chance, but only the remark itself, which she barely recalls him making. (114)

Lauren's participation in Mr. Tuttle's prescience suggests her need for his foresight to be real, in order to maintain her hope that in living outside linear time he can know, carry, and return Rey. But it also triggers a conundrum: by consciously acting in a way that causes his prescience, and which creates a deterministic world in which all of time seems to exist simultaneously, a world that "does not happen," but "simply is," and therefore a world in which returning to Rey becomes possible, she must acknowledge this world's, and this possibility's, causal dependence on her (as Ruth discovered Nao's dependence on her). Lauren's awareness of that participation, her sense that it is necessary, and her suspicion that what she is proving is only a linguistic formulation, then belie her tentative belief. Whatever Mr. Tuttle may in the novel's reality be, the novel centers on Lauren's perceptions of him and of everything else; she is the observer who brings Mr. Tuttle into existence and shapes that existence through observation: "could the solidity of reality really be dependent on the presence of observers?" asks one 2000 *New York Times* article, on the quantum tenet of observer influence. If so, and if "the existence of the real world is . . . a tenet of faith," as one of DeLillo's articles on science and religion posits,[28] then the quantum reality of Mr. Tuttle is for Lauren a matter of observation and fickle faith. And then we, confined for the most part to her perspective, would emerge from the novel more certain about the inescapability of observer bias and of the uncertainty principle than we can be of the true nature of Mr. Tuttle or how his quantumness might impact the experience of those of us confined to the Newtonian realm.

But Lauren's role in the novel goes beyond simply playing the observer whose presence makes the quantum Mr. Tuttle visible in our Newtonian experience by fixing his existence in space and time. Her conundrum in feeling barred from living or believing in a reality whose existence depends on her observation and belief points to the central conflict of *The Body Artist*, one that is far more profound than its superficial manifestations (grief, trauma, lack of awareness or of female empowerment) that have occupied criticism on the novel so far. What DeLillo finds in his research on quantum mechanics, and what Lauren realizes in the novel—and what the novel finds in struggling to articulate Lauren's realization—is a gap more universal than the old language/reality gap that motivates DeLillo's earlier novels. Here we also find the unbridgeable division between the reality of the universe and the reality of human experience, as Brian Greene articulated in his overview of quantum mechanics (see Chapter 4). The novel also asks whether we can bridge that gap, and how that gap relates to the language-reality gap with which we and postmodern literature are already so familiar.

In the universe, according to DeLillo's research notes, "all conceivable states are present at once," "the world simply is," grammar and verb tenses are a convenience, time is a "psychological illusion," and reality is multiple, infinite, and made in the image of the observer. And however counterintuitive they are to us, these aspects of the universe are, according to the clippings, "real" in every sense of the word. Likewise, DeLillo's underscoring of remarks by Walter Sullivan on a lecture by Stephen Hawking about the relationship between time and gravity suggests DeLillo's fascination with the *materiality* of time.[29] Human experience, however, comes to us not by way of such universal laws, but through other frameworks for experiencing reality, primarily language and time—both of which are (according to thinking at the time) precisely *not* real. The materials DeLillo collected and his annotations of them suggest that he was fascinated by this problem of the unreality of human experience. The archive also notes in two places how human reality is filtered through and contained in time, which is also an illusion, according to quantum theories of reality. Twice, DeLillo links Mr. Tuttle's loss of identity to his "journey through time,"[30] implying that identity and selfhood—the human experience—can only occur within the illusion of time. That is to say, as surely as language or any form of representation can be considered a mediation of the unrepresentable Lacanian Real, of the Derridean exorbitant that escapes metaphysics, of the poststructural meaning dispersed endlessly down the signifying chain, human experience of the world, organized and contained by time and the body, mediates the reality of the quantum universe. "Physics concerns itself only with what we can say about nature—not what nature is. We're a step removed; we screen nature," DeLillo notes, from Davies's *Other Worlds*.[31]

Human experience is also characterized by suffering, which, as the research notes point out as well, also occurs only in time. One method of escaping the suffering of time is art, as DeLillo notes by underlining a description of a Dutch still life in which "reality is liberated from suffering."[32] His annotation then connects the painting's method for escaping suffering to Lauren's: "her piece, checking watch hailing cab." He will echo this insight in his novel ideas in the green notebook—"art is the cure for time"—and in his early drafts folder, where he has handwritten this challenge for himself: "If art is the only way to stop time and to defeat death, or make it contemplative, then body art must show this etc. Take it out of suffering and into what? I don't know."[33]

I read *The Body Artist* as imagining both this possibility for escaping suffering and mortality through art, and its dubiousness. Its uncertainty results from the novel's quantum attempts to answer the question DeLillo posed here as he developed ideas for the novel: escape "into what?" This passage is one of the places where we can see DeLillo contemplating what happens when we bring the problem of our inability to access universal reality to bear on the problems of human suffering, and of the insufficient solace of art. For these are the two methods for sidestepping suffering attempted by Lauren: escaping human experience into art, and escaping time and its mortalities—our primary framework for human experience—into the quantum realm. DeLillo's bemused query in his notes—"take it out of suffering into what?"—and Lauren's linking of these two possible methods of escape suggest an equivalence between the two escapes (as I will argue below). But is leaving the illusion of time and identity, is stepping outside the human experience of suffering, the same thing as revealing and joining the cosmic reality of the quantum universe? Is removing one "screen for nature" the same as removing the other?

The novel, and the archive, say "not necessarily": the human experience of reality in time is not simply a screen behind which lies the totality of the quantum universe, such that any departure from that screen reveals the universal reality behind it. Instead, the novel indicates that there is more than one way for a human to depart from human reality, that abdication of our human experience of time and suffering does not necessarily equal joining a larger, "truer" universal reality. Thus Lauren's stepping out of time through her body work and art is not necessarily her stepping into the quantum world, but might be merely abdication of her human one. And as imagined by the final novel, these methods of salving the suffering self—by uniting art and the body, or by departing the body and time—interfere with each other and end in failure, not just thematically for Lauren, but seemingly also structurally, for the novel as a whole. That is, the novel's attempt to heal human suffering of the double screen of language and time by rendering a quantum realm containing neither, demonstrates the tenacity of both in any literary attempt to circumvent them. Thus it also demonstrates the problematic need to escape Realism in order to imagine entrance into the Real.

The Limits of Quantum Solace

The novel's stunning first chapter has been read as illustrating various kinds of deep truth: Bonca reads it as Lauren's discovery of Heideggerian Being, while Coale asserts that it uses "quantized style" to demonstrate the reality of the quantum universe. In fact, it illustrates how thoroughly *outside* of both these versions of immediate reality Lauren is. The novel opens with a description of the world that is exactly wrong from the perspective of quantum mechanics. "Time seems to pass"; the design of the spider web seems to imply inherent order; the world seems to bestow certainty to human understanding: "You know more surely who you are on a strong bright day after a storm when the smallest falling leaf is stabbed with self-awareness" (1). The end of the chapter echoes this assertion, its linguistic repetition invoking on the scale of the chapter the same divine order DeLillo has implied at the level of the sentence, where he layers intricate visual and aural echoes: "the spider rides the wind-swayed web."[34] But the airtight circularity of Lauren's logic in this chapter will become ridiculous the moment we turn the page and find out what happened just after this scene of breakfast-table intimacy between wife and husband, what she in her certainty could not fathom—that her husband would leave that table and kill himself. How little she saw, how little she knew, how little she understood of the world she lived in.[35]

Then we might go back through the chapter and recognize all the ways in which she was never present during that scene of supposed quotidian intimacy. She obsesses over words that escape her ("the toaster thing," 10; "the lever sprang or sprung," 12) or piles up too many ("the flesh, the mash, the pulp," 17); she thinks into sensory information (smelling the soya, 15; considering Rey's tobacco smell, 21) yet "forgot to taste" the food in her mouth (21). She "insert[s] herself into certain stories in the newspaper" (16) and into stories of her own making: "she carried a voice in her head that was hers and it was dialogue or monologue" (18). And she lives inside habit and pattern, which are the opposite of awareness: "She took the kettle back to the stove because this is how you live a life even if you don't know it" (14). Meanwhile, the possibility of existing outside these screens of language, thinking, stories, and habit—of being truly present in a moment—exists, and she is intermittently, even concertedly, aware of it.

Others have noted the importance of the birds in this chapter,[36] that they are the only thing that escapes language for Lauren, for whom they "broke off the feeder in a wing-whir that was all *b*'s and *r*'s, the letter *b* followed by a series of vibrato *r*'s. But that wasn't it at all. That wasn't anything like it" (19). Nothing else in the chapter interrupts her internal reverie enough to make her truly see: "she could nearly believe she'd never seen a jay before"; "she thought she'd somehow only now learned how to look" (19). To this general suggestion that the birds invoke a moment of presence for Lauren, I add the more pointed observation that Lauren conceives of the jay who looks into her house as occupying the position of the human looking out or in to the vast, unknowable universe, a being forced to shake off the limitations of its knowledge and being in order to attempt to comprehend the endless, alien world it sees before it:

> When birds look into houses, what impossible worlds they see. Think. What a shedding of every knowable surface and process. She wanted to believe the bird was seeing her, a woman with a teacup in her hand, and never mind the folding back of day and night, the apparition of a space set off from time. (24)

Herself a creature of time and passing, however, she loses the clarity almost as soon as she achieves it ("She was making [the ending] happen herself because she could not look any longer"). Then the stylistic collapse of the chapter from the fat, pregnant paragraph about that vision into the string of single-sentence paragraphs that ends the chapter signals the decoherence of her mind. We see her shift from clarifying focus on the bird and its fully present way of being to the scattershot fragments of her own usual state: newspaper, radio, food, thinking, all—even the thinking—outside her conscious attention.[37] But she has glimpsed an alternative way of being, seeing, and thinking—*before* Rey's suicide tears her apart—so that the novel suggests that the fragmentation she needs to fix is a result not only of that imminent particular grief, but of the universal human condition.

Read this way, the obituary that follows Chapter 1 derails her possible transition into habits of being and presence learned from the birds, as much as it might, as others have suggested, also enact the traumatic unselfing from which she needs to recover. Then Chapter 2, most of which happens before the entrance of Mr. Tuttle, shows Lauren falling back on all those old habits of organizing self and experience as she tries to ground herself in the wake of Rey's death. The second-person address that seemed in the opening of Chapter 1 to include us in her certainty becomes, after the obituary, a signal of her self-alienation, just as her momentary freedom from time in that opening, a freedom that will become her goal later in the novel, here illustrates how untethered she is from reality and her need to bind herself to it again. Thus by Chapter 2 the book has raised a question that will occupy it to its end: to what are we best tethered—the reality of the unknowable universe, of grief, of self-alienation; or the comfortable human experience of certainty, organized time, and defined self?

Tellingly, Lauren's grief-stricken disconnection from reality manifests simultaneously as an exile from narrative and epistemological certainty—from what we usually call reality—and as an openness to a different sort of reality altogether. Profoundly disassociated from her self in the present moment—"seeing herself from the edge of the room or standing where she was and being who she was and seeing a smaller hovering her in the air" (36)—she repeats and exaggerates the techniques she used in Chapter 1 to ignore the dissociation: she fixates on language ("the fucking ice thing," "always thinking into tomorrow") and marvels at the truth of bread crumbs (36, 37). But her inability to make sense of a world in which Rey is absent leads her to a skepticism about that world that goes beyond her disconnection from it at the breakfast table: "Things she saw seemed doubtful—not doubtful but ever changing, plunging into metamorphosis, something that is also something else, but what, and what" (38). This meditation on Lauren's doubt is also an excellent description of the quantum universe—always in flux, always changing, and always simultaneously multiple things at once. It's as if DeLillo signals that Lauren's untethering from the reality of human experience leaves her open to the truth of quantum reality, but that truth has not yet entered her narrative.

Instead, she defends herself against the truth of this radical skepticism and groundlessness by attempting to re-cement herself in knowable (but unreal) things, such as time. "The plan was to organize time until she could live again" (39) indicates her awareness that organizing time is not the same thing as living. Likewise, her addiction to watching the time-stamped live video feed from Kotka, even in the middle of night when nothing was happening, especially when nothing was happening ("the dead times were best"), underscores the fact that she is drawn to exactly the opposite of human intimacy and immediacy, of being fully present in a moment with others and the world—that she is drawn not to human experience but to the *forms* that contain and mediate it: "It was the sense of organization, a place contained in an unyielding frame"; "It was interesting to her because it was happening now…facelessly." The live video feed of Kotka is the opposite of the birds at the feeder, offering immediacy with no possibility of intimacy, only pure mediation of the now. That she "imagined that someone might masturbate to this" (40) suggests her awareness that media can manufacture a sense of intimacy that is entirely unreal yet powerful enough to move our bodies, to blend images so thoroughly with embodied experience that we feel "both realities occurring at once" (41). But here, unlike in other novels such as *White Noise*, what makes the video of Kotka "real" to her is less the dominance of the hyperreal and more her desire to enter organized forms of reality to deny the painful content of reality itself.[38]

She also takes refuge in her body, doing her breathing exercises, orienting herself physically in space (as with her repetitive gesture of touching the newel, 35), and feeling gratitude for her reembodiment through food poisoning. But the novel indicates that the body, too, is a false refuge. Her intense bodywork causes the opposite of awareness and presence, as "the world was lost inside her" (39). The world outside remains unreachable as well: "At night the sky was very near . . . but she didn't see it the way she used to, as soul extension, dumb guttural wonder, a thing that lived outside language in the oldest part of her" (39). No longer a part of her, and no longer apart from language, the universe is for Lauren in her grief as inhuman as language. In the context of the book as a whole, Lauren's reaction to Mr. Tuttle at the end of this chapter will become further evidence of how misguided her attempts to rejoin her life are at this time. For, initially his presence is another source of order and understanding, "her perceptions all sorted and endorsed" (43), rather than the truer disruption of them that he will become.

Thus the two-chapter exposition has drawn a character who, having glimpsed the possibility of real awareness, ducked into the false refuges of mediation and control to deny the total flux of reality. Then the entrance of a character who eludes all frameworks that might be controlled can't help but seem to offer a solution to Lauren's problem. At first, Lauren tries to subdue the mystery Mr. Tuttle represents, using all of her well-worn devices for framing and controlling reality. She corrects his tenses and grammar, imagines an explanatory backstory for him, names things for him, and of course names him as well—fittingly, after her high-school science teacher—in order to "make him easier to see" (50). And she tries to anchor him inside his body, reading to him from human anatomy books and naming his parts while running her hands over them, like a sculptor creating human form out of clay. But the ambivalence of her relationship to reality—her simultaneous defense against it and peripatetic openness to it—continues. As she resists his transience and mutability, she also starts to learn what he is and how to understand it, by learning to listen to him ("It took many levels of perception," 52), contemplating his contentless uses of language ("Say some words to say some words," he says, 57), and trying to "see things through his eyes" by taking him to the mall (66).

At this point Lauren begins to realize not that the man models a different way of being in reality, but that he lives in a different kind of reality altogether. Here, almost exactly halfway through the novel, the quantum world enters the book overtly. "Maybe this man experiences another kind of reality where he is here and there, before and after, and he moves from one to the other shatteringly, in a state of collapse, minus an identity, a language," she thinks; "maybe he lived in a kind of time that had no narrative quality" (66-7). His perceived freedom from linear time prompts her to consider that "maybe it was a physicist she needed to talk to," and when she then describes the "strange . . . discontinuity" between the vocal fragments on Mariella's answering machine as a "quantum hop" (69), we know that Lauren has begun to wonder whether Mr. Tuttle is not a human behaving strangely but a person whose access to a physical realm unreadable to the rest of us makes him unreadable as well.

Complicating her relationship to him significantly, Lauren also experiences Mr. Tuttle's strangeness in another context: as embodying the original, ubiquitous dilemma of the human's disconnection from the real, from the present moment, and therefore from human reality and from other human beings. For, while Lauren is simultaneously trying to fix Mr. Tuttle in a familiar framework and exploring whether she might learn to open up to his, she is also putting up bird feeders. In fact, Chapter 4 opens and nearly closes with the birds and their own alternative reality. First, she reflects on their manner of being, which is unlike both her way of being and her attempts to comprehend Mr. Tuttle ("They weren't looking or listening so much as feeling something, intent and sensing," 55). But most telling is that, as soon as she realizes she might need a physicist to comprehend Mr. Tuttle, her mind moves directly to the birds "going crazy on the feeder" (69). Here we seem to see Lauren connect Mr. Tuttle's potential quantumness with her original, non-quantum dilemma from Chapter 1 of how to be present in a moment, outside the frameworks of time, thought, and language. Similarly, at the end of the chapter, right after making her first request that Mr. Tuttle use his quantum facility with spacetime to conjure Rey, Lauren observes that the birds exist beyond language (73). Later in the novel, when she begins to use Mr. Tuttle's voice on the telephone, it is "a dry piping sound, hollow-bodied, like a bird humming on her tongue" (103).

Lauren's pairing, even equation, of Mr. Tuttle and the birds, which begins when she questions his quantumness, suggests that Lauren views Mr. Tuttle and his existence in a reality that lies outside human habits of time and thinking as a potential answer to her twin problems of presence and absence: the difficulty of being present in any one moment of one's life; the absence of Rey from every moment of hers. The parallel drawn between birds as emblems of pure Being[39] and Mr. Tuttle as quantum being outside the human construct of time suggests that, to Lauren at least, the latter might provide human access to the former: that bridging the gap between human experience and quantum reality might bridge the gap between human representation through thought and language and pure being; that entering the quantum realm might be equivalent to entering the Real.

Once she has connected one dilemma to the other using Mr. Tuttle, Lauren seems to see the strange man as a solution to both—how to be in the moment, and how to transcend time and death. But even in articulating these dilemmas side by side, their mutual exclusivity becomes clear: how can you be both *in* the present and *outside* time? How can you be fully aware of your human life while escaping it and its finitude? Lauren only discovers this contradiction, though, by struggling to embody it herself, through learning more about Mr. Tuttle and trying to become more like him. Most fundamentally, she begins to recognize that he exists outside all the framing devices that had been her refuge: "She didn't think his eye was able to search out and shape things. Not like normal anyway. The eye is supposed to shape and process and paint. It tells us a story we want to believe" (82). Like the birds, Mr. Tuttle sees without imposing himself on what he sees, without making sense of it. He is incapable of managing any representational system, including language, which for him refuses to signify—to allow one thing to substitute for another—by generating tautology: "Say some words to say some words" (57) and "The word for moonlight is moonlight" (84), he says, as if finding it unbearable to convert the real into a sign. The only frameworks she does employ to understand him by this stage in the novel are quantum ones: "She found it interesting to think that he lived in overlapping realities" (84); and she finally amends the book's opening blunder: "Time is supposed to pass, she thought...It is a kind of time that is simply and overwhelmingly there, laid out, unoccurring, and he lacks the inborn ability to reconceive this condition" (79). As she understands more of what he is, she imagines she understands what he offers, how she might learn from him ways of being that she can productively apply to her non-quantum dilemmas of being in the moment and missing Rey.

We witness the former at the beginning of Chapter 5, when Mr. Tuttle gives a verbal performance of mixed verb tenses, aural echoes, repetitions, and linguistic conundrums designed to shatter the confines of language and expose the being inside it:

"Being here has come to me. I am with the moment, I will leave the moment. Chair, table, wall, hall, all for the moment, in the moment. It has come to me. Here and near. From the moment I am gone, am left, am leaving. I will leave the moment from the moment." (76)

Here, Mr. Tuttle's language-busting language and Lauren's enchanted reaction to it are this novel's transporting glossolalia, akin to Wilder's "ancient dirge" and "ululation" for an awed Jack, James's son Tap's ecstatic neologisms at the end of *The Names*, or the boy's cries at sunset that move Jeffrey in *Zero K*.[40] Lauren calls Mr. Tuttle's speech "singing" and "pure chant"; she feels loosed from her body and drawn "out of laborious thought and into something nearly uncontrollable"; she is released from the confines of language and self "to fall in and out of time" through this "wedge into ecstasy, the old deep meaning of the word, your eyes rolling upward in your skull" (76, 77). By harnessing Mr. Tuttle's quantum timelessness to generate a moment of ecstatic, extralinguistic unselfing through language, DeLillo turns quantum mechanics into his newest avenue for achieving his oldest fascination, connecting human beings to the world beyond language.

Ironically, however, the quantum setting of the novel also seems to thwart any such transcendence by insisting on the materiality of everything: the audacity of *The Body Artist* is its insistence that every truth manifest in the body, quantum revelations notwithstanding. For, unlike Jack or James or Jeffrey, it is not enough for Lauren to conceive, through Mr. Tuttle's glossolalia, of a place beyond language and the frameworks of human experience, in a quasi-religious or intellectual experience. Instead she moves quickly from concept to embodiment, viewing Mr. Tuttle as mechanism for both. Once she has experienced his ability to evade language and time, she stops commanding him to "'Do Rey'" using impersonation (73) and begins to expect him to *be* Rey, in his vocal reproductions of Rey's last words: "It did not seem an act of memory. It was Rey's voice all right. . . . It is happening now . . . . Rey is alive now in this man's mind, in his mouth and body and cock . . . and it is nearly real to her" (89–90). The shocking intimacy of "cock" indicates how deeply Lauren believes that Mr. Tuttle can conjure, is conjuring Rey, and how very much that conjuring is about making Rey's body present in her present moment in time. Once again, the archive bolsters this reading with DeLillo's numerous notes that Mr. Tuttle must "carry Rey," to the point of his own suffering of the burden. Thus we see again the contradiction that Mr. Tuttle's quantumness represents for Lauren—an avenue outside time, language, and the body into pure being, and a way of making one mortal body present in another and within a moment of time. Meanwhile, we also see her constant ambivalence about the possibilities Mr. Tuttle represents. She resists them through thinking ("The laws of nature permit things that in fact, in practice, she thought, never happen. But could. But could not. But could," 79), language ("she found herself describing the scene, mentally," 83), and organizing frameworks (she makes up an explanatory backstory for him, 80–2). But she resists all that Mr. Tuttle implies about reality and about possible ways to save her from her suffering in no way more fiercely than through her own body, in her body work.

"Time Is in the Body": *Body Time* and the Limits of Art

Lauren's body work in preparation for her performance art runs throughout the novel and provides its focus, signaling a shift in DeLillo's intentions from early notes and lists of titles that put Mr. Tuttle (then "Dunlop") at the novel's center. A separate folder of research on body art, containing magazine and newspaper articles and screen shots from the first live internet feed, the "JenniCam," indicates DeLillo's fascination with the topic;[41] another folder contains notes he solicited from a friend about waxes, depilatory creams, and other products women use to erase bits of themselves, usually for the pleasure of others.[42] Thus DeLillo anchors the book in the body work as surely as Lauren seems to anchor herself in it, amid the quotidian challenge of distraction and the surreal disorientations of sudden loss and of finding in her house a visitor from a different reality. So it is no surprise that critics have often looked to her body work and her performance piece, *Body Time*, for evidence of how to read the novel's central conflicts and resolution of those conflicts.

As with the novel as a whole, Lauren's body-art and performance piece are most often read by critics in terms of processing grief, and as successful in doing so.[43] But the entrance of a quantum character with time-traveling abilities that are envied and then imitated by Lauren, specifically in the hope of reanimating her dead husband, means that *Body Time* is *not* a "working through" of grief, or even a flawed articulation of it, but is her attempt to circumvent it. And the piece is neither "epiphanic" (as Cowart claims[44]) nor even merely successful, not because of her grief but because woven through it is a logical contradiction that neither she nor the novel can resolve, but can only perform, as I will argue below. Certainly the quantum setting underscored by the archival materials requires that we read both body work and body art quite differently than they have so far been read. But as with all the readings I have offered that are informed by that quantum research, these rely most heavily on the novel itself, in which we see—perhaps made more visible when read in the light of the quantum setting—the ways in which Lauren's body work had put her at odds with her desires for herself all along, and the many reasons why *Body Time* is neither the transformation nor the redemptive articulation that critics so badly want it to be.

The novel suggests that Lauren's bodywork was never the salve she wanted it to be, even before Rey's death and Mr. Tuttle's arrival significantly complicated her disorientation and suffering. From the beginning, her bodywork was not a method of being aware of the truth of her human experience, but was her most concentrated attempt to dominate and control every facet of it, using her body: "I think you are making your own little totalitarian society, Rey told her once, where you are the dictator, absolutely, and also the oppressed people, he said, perhaps admiringly, one artist to another" (59). As she surrounds herself with bird feeders, the better to learn the secrets of avian Being, her bodywork ironically takes her farther from the world and from the present moment: "her bodywork made everything transparent . . . there was little that needed seeing and not a lot to think about" (59). This is the opposite of meditative awareness derived from the body, in that it isolates her being entirely from the present, her "eyes shut tight against the intensity of passing awareness" (60).

As her desire to be aware grows, while becoming significantly complicated by Mr. Tuttle's revelations about the true nature of the reality of which she is trying to be aware, her bodywork notably continues to operate as the primary site of her existence. By the beginning of Chapter 6, Lauren has begun to see the world—at times—through the lens of Mr. Tuttle's quantum world. The paperclip meditation that opens the chapter, again in second person, ascribes to our shared understanding the knowledge that perception is not the same thing as fact, that human experience (hearing and feeling the falling paperclip) does not necessarily describe the actual world (there is no paperclip). Then her account of seeing a bird, truly only an account because the seeing never actually happened, reverses the revelation of the phantom paperclip: we might perceive something then find no evidence for it, but we also might invent an account to explain evidence that evaded perception: "She thought she saw a bird," then realizes "she saw it mostly in retrospect because she didn't know what she was seeing at first and had to recreate the ghostly moment, write it like a line in a piece of fiction." Her revision of "seeing" here as a fiction written to justify a nonexistent reality—seeing as font of the hyperreal, rather than empirical evidence of reality—points to that gap between experience and reality, a gap we can never close: "how would she ever know for sure unless it happened again, and even then, she thought, and even then again" (93). That this insight comes from her (possible) observation of a bird connects it to that very human struggle to immerse oneself in Being. But the dilemma she describes here, of never being able to perceive the real because of a kind of physical gap between perception and the stories we tell ourselves about it, echoes Brian Greene's point about the inability of any creature to perceive the present moment, not because of our seduction by distractions and forms but because of a physical law of the universe, the speed of light. In her frustrated inability to experience the bird directly, Lauren seems once again to overlap the two gaps—between being and perception; between experience and quantum reality—that motivate her contradictory attempts at bridging them throughout the novel.

Then it is striking that, in the wake of her acceptance of Mr. Tuttle's version of the universe, her body work becomes a defense against that awareness as well. After she has discovered his temporal simultaneity (79), "overlapping realities" (84), existence outside forms of experience (82), and lack of self (87), after her reveries on the maybe-bird and the paperclip indicate that she looks for evidence of that reality in our own, her retreat into denial through bodywork says a great deal about how to read that practice and the performance piece that comes out of it. While "working her body," she repeatedly rehearses her disbelief in Mr. Tuttle's quantum reality: "It isn't true because it can't be true. Rey is not alive"; "it can't be true that he drifts from one reality to another, independent of the logic of time"; "Time is the only narrative that matters" (93–4). And she describes that disbelief in terms that reveal the extent to which her bodywork enables or requires her to exist in ways that directly oppose Mr. Tuttle's way of being. She thinks of him as a "walking talking continuum," in that "distinguish[ing] one part from another, this from that, now from then . . . by making arbitrary divisions . . . is exactly what he doesn't know how to do" (93). Of course, making arbitrary divisions is exactly what Lauren does in her bodywork, by enacting quotidian gestures, such as checking her watch, so slowly and repeatedly that they lose all meaning, and simply by fixating in those gestures on time, our most ubiquitous and dictatorial system of arbitrary divisions. While reshaping her body for her bodywork and art, this time by scraping her tongue, her denial continues; she even denies her denial ("This was not a defense against the natural works of the body"), and does so using the illogic of tautology ("It was necessary because she needed to do it. This is what made it necessary" 99, 100). Thus, when she begins to mimic Mr. Tuttle, perhaps even to attempt to embody his way of being—she stops eating, as he does; she begins to speak in his voice—the purpose and potential of her body work once again become a question: is Lauren trying to embody Mr. Tuttle and share his time-traveling powers, or is she asserting her very different humanness? What is the role of her body work, in her quest for presence or Being, and in her quest to rejoin Rey? Can she pursue both simultaneously? Only the final performance, *Body Time*, can answer those questions—which is why it is especially significant that DeLillo writes the performance piece so that it absolutely cannot.

The book's title, repeated attention to Lauren's bodywork, and consistent enlistment of that work as a reaction to or defense against the things that pain her (whether Rey's absence or Mr. Tuttle's presence), prepare us to encounter *Body Time* as evidence of Lauren addressing her suffering, and to look to it for evidence of whether she is successful in her endeavors. Occupying the penultimate section of the novel, the performance sits, according to the conventions of traditional realism, at the pinnacle point of Freytag's triangle, suggesting it serves as climax of the conflict that will bring the story to resolution. And yet, the performance fails to function in this way for several significant reasons, none more damning than the fact that this potentially most meaningful aspect of the story is the only episode we do not get from Lauren's perspective. Instead, the only information about *Body Time* we receive comes from Mariella's review of the performance, thus couched not just in an external perspective but in the trappings of rhetoric and the review's own conventions as well: our view of the art is at least doubly mediated. In a quantum world in which nothing can be true or measurable apart from the observer's determination of it—Schrödinger committing a cat to life or death by lifting the lid of a box—viewing *Body Time* through the lens of Mariella says exactly nothing about what the performance means to Lauren. It's as if Mariella's and Lauren's experiences of the performance constitute not just two perspectives on the same event, but two entirely separate realities: when DeLillo chooses in this quantum setting to mediate *Body Time* through Mariella, he chooses to excerpt it from our understanding of Lauren.

Worse, even outside the quantum context, Mariella is an unreliable narrator for Lauren, her review demonstrably uninterested in the art it supposedly promotes and evaluates. Several rhetorical devices and allusions indicate that Mariella is more interested in hooking a particular kind of reader, cultured and well-off, than she is in considering the art or its artist. Twice she mentions the trendy ethnic food they're eating—Lauren's goat cheese salad and her own baba ghanouj—and she repeatedly addresses her audience, inviting them into the article with a wry wink that includes them: "Can I use the word 'albino' and eat lunch in this town again?" (106); "What *is* baba ghanouj?" (109, original italics). Her supposed attempt to place Lauren's work in a larger artistic context also turns into a kind of winking dismissal, collusion with her middlebrow audience's distaste for challenging art. She compares Lauren's body art to that of a man who gets shot in a gallery (DeLillo lists the real artist's name, Chris Burden, in the archive[45]), a woman who paints with her vagina, a man who wears "women's bloody underwear." After each example Mariella repeats "This is art," the repetition increasing its sarcasm (106–7). Her "personal disclosure" makes fun of another "useless," alienating discipline, philosophy, when she describes her past self dabbling in this subject that Lauren was "twisted enough to major in" in college (108). At one point, Mariella even uses a verb tense that depicts Lauren's contributions to the interview as interruptions to the writer's own clever observations—"'I don't know if the piece went where I wanted it to go,' she is saying . . ." (106)—as if Lauren's contemplation of the work itself is a boring detour that Mariella's review must patronize.

But we needn't wonder why Mariella bothers to watch and review such weird and difficult art; her motivations become clear in her repeated allusions to Rey's suicide. The introductory bio of Lauren leads with this fact ("Hartke, 36, was married to the film director Rey Robles when he committed suicide . . ." 106), and she asks Lauren about the event repeatedly, despite Lauren's obvious pain at the question (110). But we should not be surprised to discover Mariella's use of Lauren in this way, and her lack of empathy for Lauren's grief. After all, Mariella displayed a lack of understanding of Lauren's suffering early in the novel, in a conversation with Lauren during her "first days back" after Rey's death (39), when she offered comfort by pointing out that "'You didn't know him that long. This could be a plus'" (42). The combination of Mariella's unempathetic fixation on the sensational aspect of Lauren's life, the mockery of Lauren's art, and her willingness to put her desire to entertain readers over her desire to connect with Lauren and genuinely represent her work, results in a piece that postures as an art review but is really a kind of tabloid trash in erudite disguise, audience-driven and thinking-averse. In it, *Body Time* becomes not Lauren's achievement or expression but merely the subject of this novel's version of the tabloids that surround Jack in the bleak end of *White Noise*.[46]

Should we attempt to use the evidence of this fake "review" to read the piece, despite the biases and disqualifications of its framing, the results are equally unhelpful. Mariella's accounts of and ruminations on the piece contradict themselves. First, she tells us that "Hartke clearly wanted her audience to feel time go by, viscerally, even painfully. This is what happened . . ." (106), and then allows that watching the piece may leave you "feeling physically and mentally suspended" (108). She claims that in the piece Lauren is "acting, always in the process of becoming another or exploring some root identity" (107), but ultimately concludes that the piece is "about who we are when we are not rehearsing who we are" (112), or the opposite of acting. Mariella's account contradicts not only itself, but also Lauren's descriptions of the piece, which offer only uncertainty in place of Mariella's decided assertions. Explaining what the piece is doing with time (as depicted by Mariella, seemingly in response to her urgent question about baba ghanouj), Lauren offers more questions than answers:

> "Maybe the idea is to think of time differently. . . . Stop time, or stretch it out, or open it up. Make a still life that's living, not painted. When time stops, so do we. We don't stop, we become stripped down, less self-assured. I don't know . . . Doesn't time slow down or seem to stop? What's left? Who's left?" (109)

Everything that isn't a question here is either a contradiction ("When time stops, so do we. We don't stop") or a series of mutually exclusive possibilities (to "stop time" is not the same thing as to "stretch it out" or "open it up"). Which did Lauren mean to accomplish? How did she intend to depict the human's relationship to time?

Lauren is much clearer about her intentions for her viewer's relationship to art. When she claims that "It ought to be sparer, even slower than it is, even longer than it is. It ought to be three fucking hours," or "Why not eight?" (108, 109), Lauren's desire to create an art object that is practically unreadable in its entirety, perhaps even unendurable for any one viewer and viewing, brings to mind the unbearable concerts from Tomasula's *IN&OZ*—or *24 Hour Psycho*, from DeLillo's *Point Omega*. All of these pieces are attempts to break free not just from our expectations about art, but from the conventions of time, space, and perception that structure our human experience of the world. Perhaps in *this* way, then, *Body Time* is analogous to the novel as a whole, and in this way we can see DeLillo making connections between such performance art and his efforts at quantum realism, both of which expose and then break conventions of art in order to do the same for our habitual frameworks of experience. Still, asked to explain what this means in her art, Lauren expresses only uncertainty ("Something about . . . ," "I don't know," 109); prompted to accept Mariella's reductive conclusion that the piece is really about Rey's death, she provides no alternative yet protests that "I can't and I can't and I can't" (111).

That evasive denial is Lauren's last word on the piece (or the last we are given). Mariella, of course, floats plenty of her own interpretations, including one that would play well to her baba ghanouj-eating audience: "At times she makes femaleness so mysterious and strong that it encompasses both sexes and a number of nameless states" (111). Nothing that we know about Lauren's bodywork or this performance suggests that the piece is about "femaleness," and Mariella's own initial description of Lauren as "colorless, bloodless, and ageless," "rawboned and slightly bug-eyed," with "terroristic" hair (105), suggests that her intention has been not to enact femaleness but to escape gender altogether. The appealing feminist reading is exactly wrong, as is, it seems, Mariella's seemingly profound final claim that "it is about who we are when we are not rehearsing who we are": DeLillo's notes in the research on body art stipulate that "LH's body art is not 'real.' She is acting."[47] So we emerge from Lauren's performance without a clear way of reading what it has meant to her or what, if anything, it has allowed her to achieve in terms of any of the goals—to attain presence, to process grief, to bypass grief by conjuring Rey—she has used her bodywork to try to accomplish. Primarily *Body Time* seems to be, for Lauren, a method of enacting both her desire to use her body to escape embodiment and time—to become/become like Mr. Tuttle—and the futility of that desire. Counter to Mariella's proclamation that "The power of the piece is Hartke's body" (111), Lauren seems to demonstrate the problem of the body, that the body traps us in time. All her efforts amount to an impersonation of Mr. Tuttle—not time travel, not a radical unselfing that might release her from her grief or join her with Rey.

The archive once again underscores such a reading of her body work, while complicating it considerably. "Time is in the body" appears only once in the research on time, yet recurs frequently in DeLillo's notes as he later works through ideas, outlines, and drafts for the novel. One page of those draft ideas repeats his own earlier discovery of the idea in Campbell's *A Wide-Awake Inquiry into the Human Nature of Time*—"Green notebook Time is in the body (back of book),"—as well as his earlier note in the notebook that "We carry time; it does not carry us." This latter statement he connects backward to a character from his previous novel, *Underworld*, whose philosophical rumination seems to be a warm-up for the fully quantum Mr. Tuttle ("Bronzini in UW 235"), and forward to a character he was developing at the time: "202 etc.—Rey's suicide carried through time." DeLillo's explicit connection between these quantum ideas and his novel in progress seems to explain some passage he has already written (or planned to write) in the manuscript in terms of this quantum understanding of the body's relationship to time (see Figure 3).

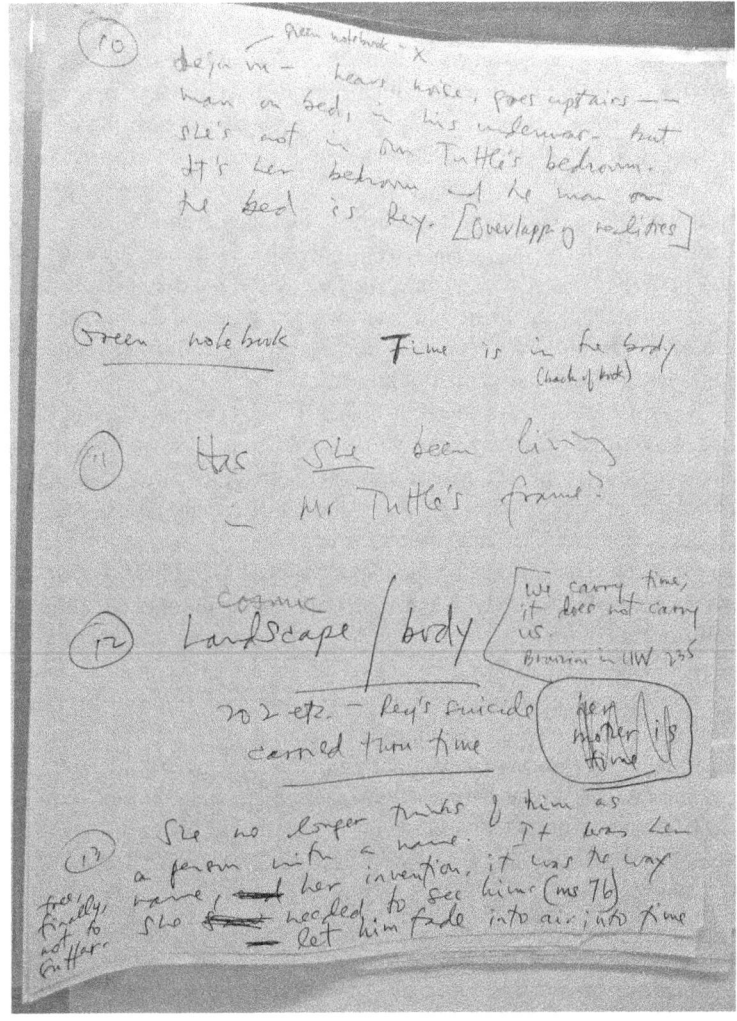

Figure 3 Ideas for demonstrating that "time is in the body." Circa 1998–2000. Don DeLillo Papers, Container 7.1, Harry Ransom Center, The University of Texas at Austin.

In the novel, it is Mr. Tuttle's ventriloquism of Rey's last words to Lauren that convinces her that Rey lives on through such moments, which are, she believes, exactly not echoes or repetitions, but present access to a past event through the body of Mr. Tuttle: "It did not seem an act of memory. It was Rey's voice all right, it was her husband's tonal soul, but she didn't think the man was remembering. It is happening now" (88). For Lauren, Mr. Tuttle is able not to repeat Rey's words but to *embody* them, as if he is somehow also carrying the body that could think them and produce them, as if he is carrying Rey from that moment into this through his access to "overlapping realities." In that context, a seemingly later page from this drafts folder indicates that DeLillo imagined Lauren would attempt to do what Mr. Tuttle had done—to inhabit overlapping realities and so carry Rey into her present reality. In one of several outlines of the book's final events, DeLillo typed "Must involve the body.... She can't just become her stories.... Must find time in the body—body narrative."[48] Here we see DeLillo describing Lauren's belief that embodying the new understanding of time that she has seen Mr. Tuttle demonstrate—making it more than a story—will allow her to embody things lost to the past as well, including Rey.

Two other uses of this sentence in the notes suggest a similar character arc for Lauren—that she learns from Mr. Tuttle the need to move from feeling she is outside of time, and carried by it, at its mercy, to carrying it herself. Under a draft page containing the paragraph that occupies pages 102–3 in the novel, in which Lauren confronts the terrifying unfathomability of all of time and space represented by the night sky, DeLillo has handwritten and boxed "time is in the body." We might read here the distance she needs to travel, or the fantasy of it: from viewing with "fear and shame" all of time out there, and how only the "bedtime language of childhood can save us" from it, to experiencing time in the body, to be articulated as she pleases. The clause reappears in his notes among phrases that connect it to Lauren's fantasy of regaining Rey, phrases that appear in the novel when Lauren is attempting to imagine Rey back into existence: "Rey would be sitting on the bed ... in his real body, smoke in his hair and breath" ("First draft," Container 7.1); "that's where Rey was intact, in his real body, smoke in his hair and clothes" (*TBA* 123). For Lauren, carrying "time in the body" means the promise of carrying her body back in time "where Rey was intact," of materializing the past, or moving to a past material moment.

In light of the archive's optimistic deployment of the idea that "time is in the body," the novel may seem to prepare us for Lauren's ultimate attempt to instantiate Rey through occupying overlapping realities, by illustrating her growing belief that the body is where time materializes and becomes real, and so is the site where she can materialize the alternative reality/time in which Rey is still alive. Her musings on time during her body work, and her attempts to dominate her body and to manifest Mr. Tuttle by dominating his, then can be read as her choice to inhabit her body and time in order to attempt to manipulate them for her own devices, of materializing Mr. Tuttle's time-traveling reality. But even if this is the case, her efforts lead to the body-art performance in which she discovers the futility of her attempt.

So climax becomes letdown, and raises the question of what the novel can accomplish and whether it can complete its Freytag's triangle with the single remaining chapter. This question of the novel's ability to come to resolution in its own terms in fact lurks from the moment it divulges its quantum setting. For, however challenging we might find the implications of quantum theory on the novel's characters and larger themes, those implications put most pressure on the structure of the novel itself. In creating a world in which linear time is an illusion, multiple realities exist, and travel among them and among points in time seems possible, DeLillo has posited a world in which escaping narrative and its closures—of plot and of death—must also be possible. But how can a narrative escape narrative? How can a story escape plot? How can a linguistic construct escape language? Most specifically for *The Body Artist,* which deviates far less from conventional Realist structures than any of the quantum realism analyzed in Chapter 4, how can Realism escape the limits of Realism? In creating his novel's largely Realist world as quantum, he has created the novel as paradox, or at least one that threatens to be. How can a novel whose setting prohibits narrative chronology and closure produce a comprehensible plot? Or a comprehensible total novel? That is, how can it possibly end?

Not with a Bang, but a Whimper: Quantum World's End

The end of *The Body Artist* presents two interpretive challenges: reading Lauren's end and reading the novel's, both of which are significantly shaped by the quantum setting, reinforced by the archive. Lauren enters the final chapter askew, in the uncertainty and skepticism generated by *Body Time,* having disappeared from the review as mysteriously as Mr. Tuttle disappeared from the novel a few pages before it. Again, she grounds herself in the frameworks that solidify and contain her: she reassures herself by matching her watch with the time she holds in her head (114, 121), in a sly revision of Jack's sense of well-being at the ATM in *White Noise.* Again she lives in stories, soothed by the understanding that every newspaper account provides "another framework altogether" (117). When the rental house owner appears, she imagines another story in which he will explain Mr. Tuttle and all that he signifies (122–3). She feels "an easy alertness, a sense of being inside the moment," but is really only present in her expected narrative: when the landlord mentions the furniture he came for, she thinks, "This is not what he was supposed to say" (121). As the novel begins to end, the profound ambivalence about being with which she began the novel continues.

Meanwhile, she also continues to contemplate the possibility of escaping her grief by entering the quantum realm. Once again, critical interpretations based in trauma read Lauren's grief in Chapter 7 against the archive and the novel itself, viewing her grief as the potentially ruinous thing against which she must defend herself through her body work, rather than as her avenue to Mr. Tuttle's timeless reality.[49] But if *Body Time* is Lauren's successful Freudian "working through" of her grief,[50] why does her grief return with force in Chapter 7, after the performance?[51] If her grief is "an abyss of meaninglessness,"[52] then why does DeLillo describe it, from Lauren's perspective, as the most meaningful and true element of her current experience?

> Why shouldn't the death of a person you love bring you into lurid ruin? You don't know how to love the ones you love until they disappear abruptly. Then you know how thinly distanced from their suffering, how sparing of self you often were, only rarely unguarded of heart, working your networks of give-and-take. (118)

No reader who has experienced significant loss, if asked Lauren's first question, would hear that question as purely rhetorical: the truth of death is that it temporarily undoes its survivors. And the truth of the novel—if we remember back to the first chapter, with its give-and-take of soya, newspaper, and counter space, and Lauren's reveries crowding Rey out of her experience—is exactly what Lauren has learned from Rey's death: that we must learn to be present with those we love. Then the novel seems to have set us up to read the next set of questions literally rather than rhetorically as well—as evocations of truth, rather than demands for socially acceptable behavior:

> Why shouldn't his death bring you into some total scandal of garment-rending grief? Why should you accommodate his death? Or surrender to it in thin-lipped bereavement? Why give him up if you can walk along a hall and find a way to place him within reach?
>
>   Sink lower, she thought. Let it bring you down. Go where it takes you. (118)

Because this passage leads to the ominous assertion that "I am Lauren. But less and less" (119), we might be tempted, as Di Prete and Smith are, to read grief in this passage as paralyzing and self-eradicating, in the way of Freud's unproductive melancholia and Caruth's trauma. But that reading cannot account for the mocking judgment of "thin-lipped bereavement," its pressed lips implying that anything less than full-throated mourning is false, repression in the name of manners. Nor does it explain the fact that the passage holds out hope for re-encountering Rey in some real way, of "plac[ing] him within reach," not through self-annihilation so much as by becoming a different sort of Lauren.

DeLillo's notes in the archive on this section underscore this idea which is, as are so many of the novel's strangest ideas, retained in the novel only in the faintest form. His notes state more baldly that "she needs to sink down into some primitive self unrehearsed…to encounter Mr. Tuttle where Rey is intact."[53] In this "sinking," grief is not the thing she must resist or suffer in order to be transformed back into articulability and selfhood that have registered but not given into the loss. Rather, grief is the reality to which she must fully submit herself in order to unself enough, deconstruct narrative time enough, to inhabit a realm in which she can make Rey exist again. It is exactly not mourning productively, not moving beyond trauma and loss. It is unselfing through grief so fully that she might escape the human strictures of time and identity, thus opening the possibility of arriving at a different place and time, where Rey is still alive.

But as before, even when she begins to try to enter Mr. Tuttle's quantum reality, to access another slice of spacetime, she falls back on her comfortable frameworks of story and narrative: "This is the day it would happen"; "This is what would happen"; "She knew how it would happen," she chants (115, 116, 123), and her obsessive repetition is more reminiscent of Jack's delusional plan to rescue his masculinity by killing Mink in Chapter 39 of *White Noise* than it is a revelation of her ability to abandon the forms and frameworks of her human, time-bound life. In such a context, her attempt to abandon human framings is doomed, which we will see played out in the end of the novel. Lauren begins to understand in this final chapter that these two kinds of being she has pursued throughout the novel—inhabiting the present, human moment; and freedom from time to inhabit other moments—both depend on escaping the confines of human frameworks of experience, while also being entirely incompatible with each other. The first roots us in body and time, while the second requires abandonment of human experiences of both. This is one of the central discoveries made by the quantum setting of the novel, that to be out of the body and time is to be in some fundamental way inhuman, to "violate the limits of the human" (102) (making Lauren's shocking physical appearance in *Body Time* yet more evidence of her intentions for that piece). Then we should not be surprised when DeLillo ends Lauren's narrative by dropping her back into time and her body. That the novel ultimately seems forced to drop back into narrative past tense indicates a causal connection between the novel's abandoning of its quantum principles and its overall formal elements.

In the novel's final pages, DeLillo represents Lauren's last attempt to conjure Rey—this time, notably, not by contorting her body but by manipulating her mind—by breaking from the narrative past tense that has dominated the novel to narrate her encounter of a reanimated Rey in present tense. This sustained use of present tense aligns the Rey sequence with the present-tense, second-person sequences that open the first two and last two chapters of the novel: chapters 1, 2, 6, and 7. All of these passages express perceptions of reality that further information or experience will reveal to be misperceptions: "Time seems to pass" (1); "All the cars including yours seem to flow in dissociated motion, giving the impression of or presenting the appearance of" (33); the fallen "paperclip" (91); the burlap "squirrel" (113). Their second-person point of view implies we share this habit of misperception. The bracketing of the novel by present-tense musings and their absence from the middle three chapters suggests a kind of circularity, that Lauren's journey through the novel, her attempt to come to some kind of authentic being (whether Heideggerian or quantum), has led her away from the habit of misperception, only to have her end up there in the end. This association of the Rey episode in Chapter 7 with all these examples of misperceiving the moment—of being most wrong when we think we are most aware—itself hints that the present-tense recuperation of Rey will turn out to be another misperception, that is to say, only another perception.

And yet, in the narrative moment, Lauren is convinced, as are we. DeLillo renders Lauren's mental experience of the experiment in minute detail, while suggesting once again that in trying to conjure Rey, Lauren also struggles to conjure some pure form of awareness, as if they are the same thing. She experiences the mental conjuring as a "chant, a man's chanted voice," recalling the moment of ecstasy triggered by Mr. Tuttle's quantum glossolalia (122). Moving to the room where she expects to find Rey, "she was aware of the world in every step" (123)—her hopeful revelation again echoing Jack Gladney's series of false epiphanies during the shooting-Mink chapter of *White Noise*. But Lauren's belief, in contrast to Jack's, lies not in her cooption by waves and radiation, but in her faith in Mr. Tuttle's world of waves and particles, whose uncertain, immeasurable, unfixed state in spacetime means she can move between them as she moves between times, "fitting herself to a body in the process of becoming hers" (123). She moves toward the bedroom with this faith intact: "His time was here, his measure or dimension or whatever labored phrase you thought to call it" (123).

All along, the novel, and Lauren, has viewed language as a key method for registering Mr. Tuttle's quantum reality, as well as his primary method for materializing that reality: he convinces her of his time travel by predicting her future and re-creating her past, through speech. Thus, somewhat as Ozeki does in *A Tale for the Time Being*, DeLillo has empowered language by the end of the book to be the medium that might materialize Lauren's time travel right in our hands and under our eyes. He has built the novel not out of the ephemeral, approximate, detached language of poststructuralism, which can never touch reality, but out of a language that might—according to the logic Mr. Tuttle lives, Lauren has learned, and we, through those second-person passages, have absorbed—materialize a new kind of reality altogether. This is the faith Lauren carries into her experiment, and us along with her. Thus, when she stands at the threshold of that room, the present-tense narrative voice pushes the possibility of her escape into another time, materialized in language, so far that it seems to bulge off the page like the second-person address in the epilogue of *Tale*. Language here presses against the boundary between the world inside the book and the world outside where we are reading, even as Lauren is pressing the boundary between her human, time-dependent, mortal experience and the timelessness of the quantum world:

> Are you unable to imagine such a thing even when you see it?
> Is the thing that's happening so far outside experience that you're forced to make excuses for it, or give it the petty credentials of some misperception?
> Is reality too powerful for you?
> Take the risk. Believe what you see and hear. It's the pulse of every secret intimation you've ever felt around the edges of your life. (124)

As we've been conditioned to by those other second-person, present-tense passages, we feel this inquisition directed at us, at least as much as it represents Lauren questioning herself. And in this moment, the novel prepares us to accept not just that its character is about to jump into another point in the spacetime loaf—which is not all that unusual, given the number of science-fiction texts in which characters do this and more—but more radically, the novel prepares us to expect that this character will break out of the cage of the human's bodily experience of linear time while staying confined to the more-or-less Realist narrative that has so far contained her.

The archive suggests that at some point DeLillo intended to do just that. We might read his early plan for *The Body Artist* as sprawling science-fiction novel as one idea, ultimately abandoned, for escaping the limits of realism in imagining his quantum world. But multiple drafts of the ending indicate that he also aimed to allow Lauren to escape Realist human/Newtonian experience through the more focused narrative he wound up writing, possibly even envisioning an ending that he didn't finally execute. In the green spiral notebook, whose notes seem to predate those in the "First draft" folder, one page is titled "END," in a circle. The page imagines that Lauren "Goes upstairs. He is there, at the edge of the bed, in his underwear.... It is <u>Rey</u>, getting out of bed.... She has entered Mr. Tuttle's time frame (realities that overlap)" (see Figure 4).

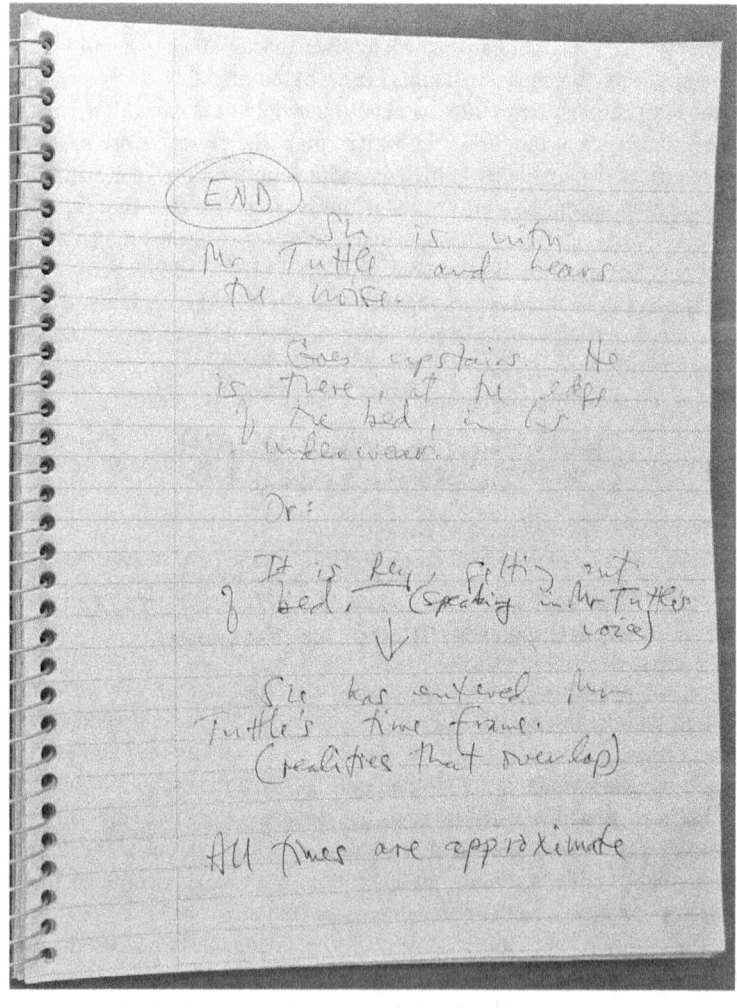

Figure 4 Ideas for final scene of *The Body Artist*. Don DeLillo Papers, Container 6.5, Harry Ransom Center, The University of Texas at Austin.

This draft differs significantly from the final novel, in that it describes Lauren's discovery of Rey in the bedroom and her entry into Mr. Tuttle's quantum state not as a possibility in her imagination, but from an external perspective that describes these things as actually happening. In this ending, Lauren accomplishes what she has set out to do, transcending the strictures of chronological time, undoing Rey's death, and obviating her own grief. But in the later "early drafts" folder, we find nearly a dozen brainstormed, outlined, even fully drafted portions of the novel's end—not the entire last chapter but just the final five problematic pages—that move away from that redemptive ending to its exact opposite: Lauren's inability to find Mr. Tuttle, or rejoin Rey, or leave the time of her own suffering. It is fascinating to watch the reanimated Rey of early drafts disappear from the novel as his return becomes increasingly dubious in DeLillo's thinking.[54] Conditional language enters, first through clauses ("Rey is alive in this room, *if* she can find it," then through verb tense ("Rey would be sitting on the bed. . . . She knew how it would happen.") Another page comes closer to the version DeLillo will put in the book, with its flat declaration of past-tense failure: "when she saw that the room was empty, the bed empty, the sheets mussed and fumbled [?], she went to the window and opened it. . . . It was time to let Rey die."[55]

Ultimately, Lauren fails to enter Mr. Tuttle's time and so also fails to return to Rey for thematic and formal reasons that both pertain to the novel's quantum setting. The novel suggests that Lauren's failure to attain the timeless state in which "They are two real bodies in a room," as she imagines at the end of that present-tense interlude, reflects her inability to be the observer who witnesses and brings into existence her own quantum experience. Tellingly, the page of present-tense narrative is interrupted and briefly halted by a past-tense narration depicting Lauren as no longer *in* her imagined, recuperative moment, but as observing it: "She stopped at the edge of the doorway, aware of the look on her face." She seems briefly to work her way back to the present-tense, past-altering reverie ("It is the simplest thing in the world when she goes out to his car and takes his car keys and hides them"), before once again being catapulted back into narrative past—a past in which Rey is unalterably dead—by her self-awareness: "But before she stepped into the room, she could feel the look on her face. She knew this look, a frieze of false anticipation" (125). In the novel's quantum framework, which Lauren at this point has not just accepted but willfully attempted to enter, to witness the self is to fix the self in time and space, as the scientist fixes the wave as a particle with specific location, or Schrödinger observes the life or death of the cat. Lauren's witnessing of herself in this nearly quantum moment becomes the culmination of her role as witness throughout the novel—of Rey, of Mr. Tuttle, even of us, through repeated second-person point of view. Turning her observation on herself fixes and defines her in a moment of space and time, and as a character, as surely as did the *Body Time* review in which Mariella played *her* observer. This analogy suggests that Lauren's observation of self might be as false as Mariella's, and is certainly as determining: she becomes a character to an authoring other, part of a narrative, and so confined to a told past.

Accordingly, the novel drops back into its flat past tense, as Lauren drops out of her expansive attempt at alternative being—pressing to leap off the narrative page and out of determined time—and back into thinking. Only at this point does she accept that Rey is gone. She does not look into the room, choosing instead her old, familiar refuges, not just "thinking"—a word that repeats several times in the book's final paragraphs—but thinking about language ("the word *motes*") and stories ("Her mother died when she was nine. It wasn't her fault. It had nothing to do with her"). But in the context of this failed attempt to leap into the quantum in order to retrieve Rey, Lauren's collapse from present-tense possibility into past-tense fixity might be read as another kind of victory, one that is attainable only after letting go of her other quest. For the novel ends with Lauren moving from failed quantum leap, to familiar mental retreat, to a new way of being that might be, in the framework of this novel, the only kind of awareness available to her—that of the physical world around her, one in which Rey is finally absent and quantum salvation is no longer possible (the "true colors of the walls and floor," the "empty bed," "sheet and blanket swirled on her side . . . which was the only side in use"). From there, she moves to the window and opens it, to "feel the sea tang on her face and the flow of time in her body, to tell her who she was" (126).

Critics reading the novel outside its quantum setting interpret this ending as Lauren's triumphant return to self.[56] But if the goal of the character and the novel in a world of quantum, time-traveling possibility is to be loosed from time and enter alternate, multiple, immortal existence, this ending that fixes Lauren in time and her body is a failure. In that context, the ending can be a success for Lauren only by default: in failing to bridge the gap from human experience to timeless quantum reality and thus rejoin Rey, she becomes fully aware of her body in time, thus bridging the gap between human perception and the reality of embodied experience. Her position at the window, site of her reflections on being and the birds, and her elimination of the pane that had separated her from them, underscores this reading. But Lauren's entrance into being and presence remains ironically trapped in the past tense of narrative, a philosophical contradiction at the level of form that points to the fundamental conflict between tale and presence theorized by Jameson (see Introduction) and demonstrated by DeLillo's attempt to deliver his character to the latter through the former. The archive materials, which strengthen this reading of Lauren as failing to attain her theorized quantum freedom, also suggest that the novel as a whole demonstrates another fundamental limitation—not just a woman coming up against the limits of human perception of quantum reality, but the novel finding the limits of traditional realism's ability to represent that human perception of or entrance into the quantum universe. Thus, in using Realist narrative to attempt to depict the reality of the quantum universe, *The Body Artist* reveals the incompatibility of Realism with quantum reality, and the incompatibility of narrative with being.

"Otherwise it's only words"

However much the archive materials appear to depict DeLillo dithering about the novel's end, they remain consistent and clear about what is at stake throughout, in terms of both Lauren's body art and her ending. The sentence "Otherwise it's only words" appears at least fifteen times on notes and drafts in the archive, typed and handwritten, in bits of passages and lists of plot points—more than any other phrase or sentence, by my count. One of these iterations appears on a piece of paper stuck to the inside cover of the green spiral notebook (see Figure 5), and at least twice more the sentence occurs on slips of paper tucked into the notebook's pockets. The rest of the repetitions occur in the drafts and notes for drafts, spread throughout them but always in conjunction with only two moments of the novel as DeLillo planned and ultimately wrote it: the review of *Body Time*, and the novel's last few pages in which Lauren imagines finding Rey alive in the bedroom. Taken together, these repetitions of "Otherwise it's only words" become a chant that imbues DeLillo's novel drafts with a clarity of intention that does not materialize in the published novel. Read in conjunction with the two novelistic sections they cluster around, they underscore one of the quantum novel's essential discoveries: that art, whether written or embodied, is another screen for the real, not a way to inhabit it.

This sentence occurs seven times in drafts of the *Body Time* review, implying that the point of Lauren's performance is to embody, not imitate, ways of being (the Japanese woman, the woman hailing a cab), concepts of time and multiple reality, and Mr. Tuttle and his strange relationship to time. The repeating sentence starts to read like DeLillo's reminder to himself throughout the writing process that the novel must provide a bridge between the theoretical quantum possibility of Mr. Tuttle and its lived experience,

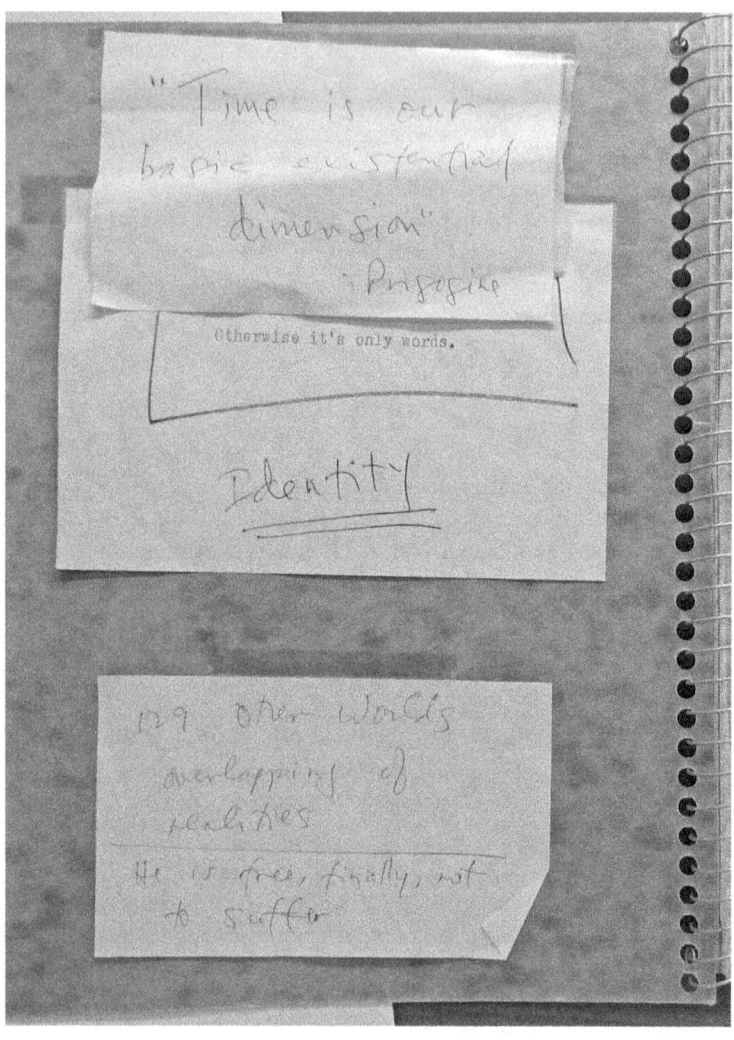

Figure 5 Inside cover of notebook: "Otherwise it's only words." Don DeLillo Papers, Container 6.5, Harry Ransom Center, The University of Texas at Austin.

and that Lauren's performance might—perhaps must?—enact that bridge. When DeLillo's notes twice suggest that the sentence will become the last or penultimate statement of Mariella's review, this mandate seems to sum up the entire intention of the piece.[57] Taken together, these repetitions of "Otherwise it's only words" in relation to the review of *Body Time* suggest that part of what the performance was intended to do was make real and embodied—for Lauren and for her viewers—the alternate reality of Mr. Tuttle and its consequences to our human lives. In that case, Lauren's "seizure that apparently flies the man out of one reality and into another" at the end of her piece is none of the metaphors suggested by critics but is rather Lauren's earnest attempt to enact with her body the freedom from time in which Mr. Tuttle lives. But if "time is in the body," as the archive repeatedly states and the novel demonstrates, any attempt to embody timelessness is doomed. Perhaps this aporia, the gap between her idea/intention and what her body can do, lies at the heart of Lauren's uncertainty in explaining the piece. It might even provide another way of making sense of DeLillo's decision to represent *Body Time* only through the eyes of someone who does not understand it or even want to understand it: the performance art that was meant to have an embodied impact on its viewers becomes, in the novel, entirely abstract, a conundrum.

That the mandate "Otherwise it's only words" appears five times in notes about the novel's final few pages seems to imply that the ending offered another chance—for DeLillo? For Lauren?—to translate the idea of quantum reality, and the possibility that it might shield us from suffering, into embodied human experience. All of these instances connect to Lauren's need to manifest Rey by embodying Mr. Tuttle or his quantum way of being; three changing outlines of the ending attach the sentence to the same plot point, the reappearance of Rey in the bedroom. Each of them repeats that Rey must be conjured as "real body," not just idea ("there must be real bodies"; "Rey would be sitting on the bed . . . in his real body"; "Must involve the body . . . . Must find time in the body…Body," and this requirement makes it into the novel: "that's where Rey was intact, in his real body" (123); "They are two real bodies in a room" (124, see Figure 6).

These draft outlines also indicate an evolution away from stories to bodies, with DeLillo using the sentence to literally underscore several notes about Lauren's and Mr. Tuttle's stories. The paragraph symbol next to it also implies his intention to include not simply the concept but the sentence itself in the novel (see Figure 7).

But as with *Body Time*, Lauren faces the inherent contradiction of attempting to materialize an embodied reality—for herself, for Rey—by occupying the timelessness of a quantum universe. The last two outlines seem to acknowledge this impossibility, adding drafts of the paragraph that will end the novel, in which Lauren discovers the empty bed and moves to open the window.[58]

The archive's fifteen instances of this sentence, and their close association with *Body Time* and the novel's final scene, strongly indicate that for DeLillo,

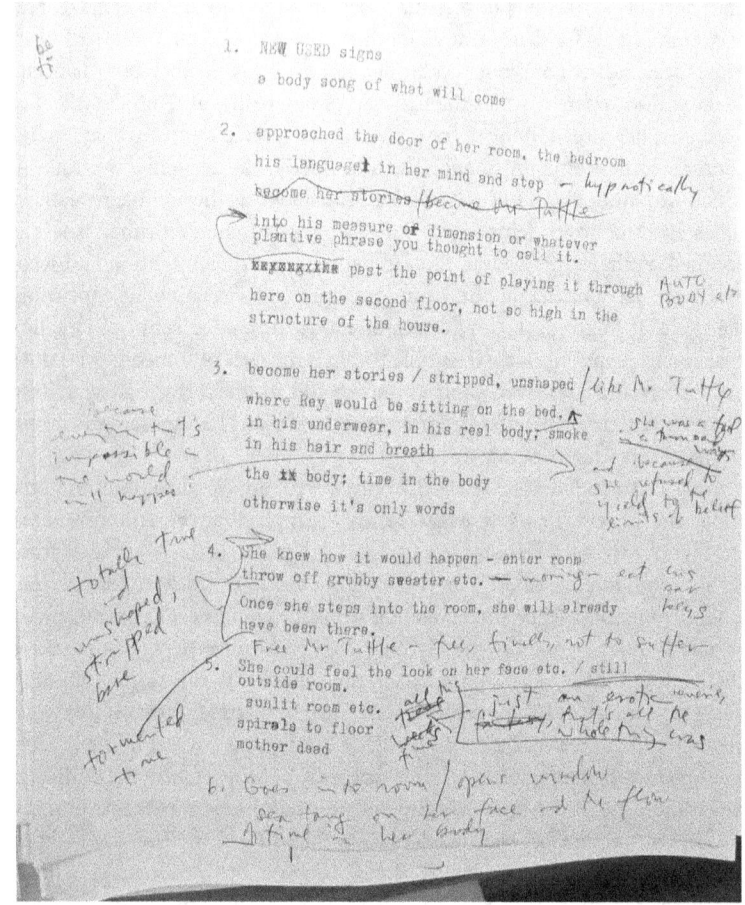

Figure 6 Outline of final pages of *The Body Artist*. Circa 1998–2000. Don DeLillo Papers, Container 7.1, Harry Ransom Center, The University of Texas at Austin.

and/or perhaps for Lauren, none of the novel's ideas about the redemptive power of art or the liberating possibilities of quantum reality makes any difference to our human suffering unless they can become part of our embodied experience. And yet, neither art nor quantum reality ultimately offers relief or impacts human experience: *Body Time* remains elusive in Lauren's experience and mocked in print; Mr. Tuttle's quantumness, along with Mr. Tuttle himself, disappears from the novel. DeLillo seems to have planned, in at least one draft, to end the novel with the insistent statement

Quantum Realism Case Study

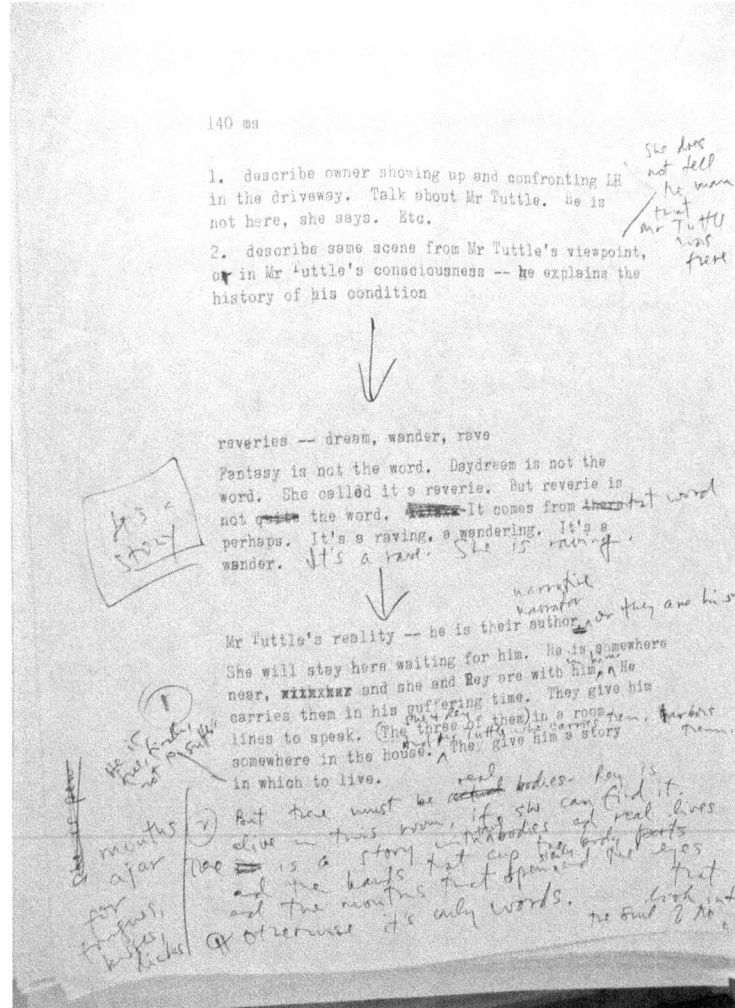

Figure 7 Ideas for final chapter of *The Body Artist*. Circa 1998–2000. Don DeLillo Papers, Container 7.1, Harry Ransom Center, The University of Texas at Austin.

that "Otherwise it's only words" (see Figure 8). But ultimately the novel ends, as all novels do, with mere words, and ones that cannot enact the ways of being Lauren had been pursuing through most of the novel.

Indeed, this sentence that haunts the drafts never appears in the published novel. In light of the archive it peppers, its absence from the novel might be

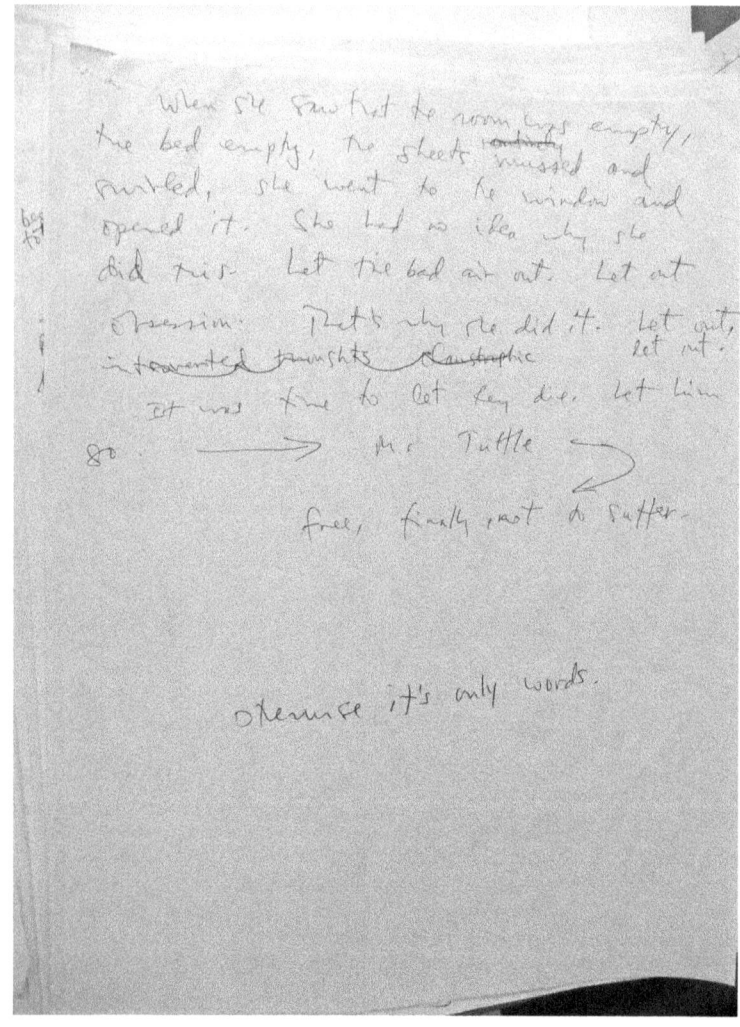

Figure 8 Handwritten draft of the end of *The Body Artist*. Circa 1998–2000. Don DeLillo Papers, Container 7.1, Harry Ransom Center, The University of Texas at Austin.

understood in two contradictory ways: either the clarity of Lauren's urgent need to embody Mr. Tuttle's quantumness in order to return to Rey makes it redundant, or her unavoidable inability to do so makes it irrelevant. In either case, its dropping out between drafts and final novel points to the most urgent thing the novel needed to do—transform language to embodied experience—yet fails to do. Is this failure a result of the limitations of Lauren's abilities, or of her performance piece? Of the unbridgeable gap between quantum reality and human experience? Of the gap between language and human experience? Or of the limitations of the Realist novel?

On the largest level, my argument has been that the quantum setting and the archive that clarifies that setting require that we read the novel's plot as a series of failed attempts in its own terms: first, Lauren is not able to embody Mr. Tuttle's time-traveling quantumness through her body art; next, she is unable to conjure Rey through her belief in the possibilities of that world. If, as DeLillo noted in his research, "the existence of the real world is . . . a tenet of faith,"[59] and "only the language of religion can express" the oddities of the quantum universe,[60] then Lauren's faith in Mr. Tuttle's world is insufficient. Ultimately neither art nor quantum reality is a viable alternative to human experience or human suffering. Even so, and perhaps more importantly, the novel has depicted both as impossible and undesirable, because each in its way takes us out of the realm of the human. Lauren's scrubbed, shorn, seemingly desanguinated state when she performs *Body Time*—especially when she embodies the "naked man, emaciated and aphasic"—makes her a forerunner to Artis and the other wasted, naked, shaved bodies who would be transformed into art, mounted and posed, in *Zero K*. If Lauren's relationship to her art remains unclear to us at the end of *The Body Artist*, it should be easily clarified by DeLillo's latest novel, a scathing indictment on art and science as timeless escapes from the suffering of life. Thus, in the end, *The Body Artist*, rather than a celebration of the power of art to allow us to process grief, transcend suffering, and establish identity, is much more akin to Keats's "Ode to a Nightingale," a fantasy about the transcendent power of art to evade human suffering through nature and art—the nonhuman—that can only lead the dreamer back to the confines and suffering of a self that can be escaped only through death.

But the quantum setting that sets Lauren up to fail at these endeavors, by virtue of its inhuman impossibility, also and paradoxically empowers art and validates human experience as real and true. Both novel and archive construct analogic relationships in which human experience is to quantum reality as language is to human experience: by setting the novel in a world that exhibits a quantum reality beyond human experience to which we have very limited access, DeLillo creates a layered universe in which our human experience becomes more real by comparison to the theoretical quantum, and language's and art's ability to conjure that human experience for us thus becomes more precious than insufficient. Like McHale's "paraworlds"[61] and my "poststructural realism" (see *Succeeding Postmodernism* Chapter 5), the quantum realm as materialized by Mr. Tuttle in *The Body Artist* makes our familiar world—human experience, which hinges on time, causality, and measurability—into only one of multiple worlds existing side by side, a kind of many worlds within one universe, only one of which feels real and immediate to us. But the important difference here is that DeLillo does not create multiple realities in which one emerges as real because the other is obviously a representation or product of language. Rather, he depicts two versions of physical reality—human and universal; Newtonian and quantum—that vie for recognition as "true" and "real" in very different terms: one is true because we experience it as real, while the other is real whether or not we can accept its truth. It is a contradiction of physical laws that the novel turns into a philosophical conundrum for its human character—which reality is authentic? how does quantum mechanics change our efforts to access "authentic" experience?—that can be solved only in human terms, since this novel, like nearly all fiction, proceeds according to human perspective and frameworks of knowledge.

The inability of both quantum reality and art to enact escape from human suffering, and the book's final depiction of Lauren outside of both, finding solace precisely in the bodily experience she sought throughout the book to escape, suggests that being awake to the reality of human experience—however painful, and however untrue in cosmic terms—is the truest thing we can do. This is one aspect of quantum realism demonstrated by *The Body Artist*: the addition of a quantum realm, a cosmic reality we can theorize but never fully inhabit, bestows upon our "unreal" or inaccurate human experience of existence, which can never be a direct or immediate perception of reality, the authenticity and urgency that are missing when we view it as merely a screen for the reality of the universe.

The Body Artist accomplishes a similar resituation of reality in relation to the genre of the novel and its mode of traditional realism as well. Lacking multiple narrators, looping structures, or extreme leaps through time and space, DeLillo's novel distorts Realist conventions more subtly and less pervasively than do the novels examined in Chapter 4, which may be part of its strategic brilliance. It lulls us into the quiet patterns of Newtonian realism, making us comfortable in its largely linear tale, only to disturb us here and there with sudden disruptions of our literary expectations, as if we occasionally stumble into a looking glass through which we can glimpse a reality beyond our imaginations, like Louise gazing at the heptapods. Documents stand in for two of the novel's most significant scenes—the obituary for Rey's death; the review for Lauren's art—but, rather than anchoring the narrative in some implied "real world," like "The Custom House" that prefaces *The Scarlet Letter* or the framing letters of *Frankenstein*, these documents take such distant or distorting perspectives that the real events they mean to represent remain conspicuously unknowable. And like Wallace, DeLillo multiplies uses of point of view and perspective, but less blatantly and to different ends—primarily to imply the uncertainty and observer dependence of the quantum realm. The numerous second-person passages simultaneously dramatize Lauren's alienation from her own experience, or her experience's distance from reality, confuse and multiply the owner of that experience, and insinuate that this confused alienation is a universal human characteristic. His use of third-person free indirect discourse for the rest of the novel variously emphasizes and elides the fact that we are viewing the entire novel from Lauren's perspective, while also multiplying that perspective. Unlike first-person point of view, which would anchor the story in Lauren's singular and biased perspective, third-person free indirect discourse adds another layer of observation to Lauren's: we, or the narrator, or both, observe her observing her life, and so (especially having learned from the obituary and the *Body Time* review) we are constantly aware of the gap that exists not just between her experience and her articulation of it but also between her articulation and its third-person representation of it. So much is being lost, all the time: we see so little of anything. Further, the free indirect discourse is neither constant nor clearly delineated from objective third-person description (it is difficult to tell whether anything in the novel counts as "objective third-person description"), so in many moments, perhaps in any moment, we are left wondering who exactly is narrating or focalizing, and when or whether these functions overlap.

Meanwhile, shifting verb tenses illustrate not just the chaotic timelessness of Mr. Tuttle's quantum existence, but also the multiple levels of reality and simultaneity of experience that characterize even non-quantum human existence. The present-tense, second-person passages that open four of the seven chapters all describe the gap between human perception and reality, aligning the present tense with immediate human experience and implying that such experience is only one version of the experiences and/or realities available to us. Elsewhere the novel uses the present tense to dramatize Lauren's thinking, usually about Mr. Tuttle, and often even labeling this use of the present tense as such ("She liked to think" 85, "This is what she thought" 89, etc). But even this obvious employment of the present tense winds up complicating and multiplying narrative registers, by crafting the present-tense thinking as another reality in which Lauren lives simultaneous with the reality being narrated in the past tense. For example, one of the present-tense reveries in Chapter 1, "Sometimes she doesn't think of what she wants to say to him until he walks out of whatever room they're in . . .," comes immediately on the heels of a simple past-tense description of the same situation: "When he walked out of the room, she realized there was something she wanted to tell him" (26). This present-tense elaboration upon a quickly established past-tense fact reads as Lauren's mental expansion of or deliberation, in "real time," about an event that has just happened in the narrative that contains her. Whether we read this layering of levels of experience as metafictional—the character seeming to deliberate upon the action that has just been ascribed to her, or ontological—the narrator signaling the internal experience occurring inside and alongside the external, observable one, such repetition of events in multiple verb tenses insists that we recognize multiple levels in lived human experience and in narrative on which every simple event might occur, and/or, multiple simultaneous realities in which every event is occurring.

Thus it makes sense that Lauren's ultimate attempt to escape the determined past in which Rey is dead doubles as the novel's attempt to break free from the closure of narrative past tense that characterizes Realist narrative: in order for Lauren to escape the dead past, the narrative must find a way ultimately to contain her in indeterminate time, or multiple time, or an infinity of possible narratives. I have argued in Chapter 4 that Ozeki's *A Tale for the Time Being* does just that using technical and structural devices and Buddhist koans that escape the confines of Realist narrative, as does, to a lesser extent, "Story of Your Life" with its looping ending, nonchronological mixture of events and tenses, and consistent second-person address. But *The Body Artist* does none of these things, ending instead in classic, flat, concluded, dead narrative past tense—and one that comes as a shock after the pages in which its narrated reality shimmered between worlds with Lauren's present tense. What does it mean that a novel whose archive indicates the author's desire to move beyond such narrative, and whose main character baldly imagines doing so, ultimately so conspicuously does not?

Form Is Emptiness; Emptiness Is Form

One way to read the traditional realist ending in the context of the novel's attempts to escape those narrative confines, and the archive's urgent desire to escape the boundaries of human experience, is as evidence of the limits of Realism. The novel's collapse out of temporal possibility and multiple perspective back into linear, causal, chronological narrative focalized solely through Lauren implies that ultimately Realism is incapable of representing the quantum, non-Newtonian reality that Mr. Tuttle lived and Lauren glimpsed, coveted, but abandoned. Because Mr. Tuttle's atemporal quantumness also represents for Lauren the possibility of pure awareness and being outside the stream of time, the collapse into flat past tense also signals the inability of narrative to represent atemporal being—or, as Jameson might put it, the failure of realism. Read in this way, the quantum setting, with its conflict between atemporal reality and temporal human experience, makes the novel an explicit exemplar of Jameson's concept of realism as a dialectic between the temporal impulse of storytelling and the atemporal scenic impulse to represent pure affect (see Introduction and Chapter 1). The triumph of temporal human experience thus becomes the dominance of the teleological tale, at the cost of pure being, affect, and our engagement with the deeper reality of the quantum world. It also reinforces the schism between narrative meaning and embodied experience. When Jameson rereads Sartre's *Nausea* as demonstrating that "it is not existence and meaning which are incompatible here . . . it is allegory and the body which repel one another and fail to mix" (37), he makes the same claim for realism's inability to merge signification and material world: the body can't mean. Affect remains confined to the body while meaning is abstracted into narrative, estranging human experience, feeling, and truth from narrative, specifically Realism. With only a slight shift in perspective we might also read the novel's past-tense, third-person FID ending not so much as the limits of the novel's narrative mode as of Lauren's—and our own—inability to escape her Newtonian, temporal experience of reality, in which we observe ourselves acting and thus fix ourselves in time and space, as Lauren ultimately fixes herself in a time and place in which Rey no longer exists.

And yet, read in the context of all that has come before—of Lauren's protracted denial of Rey's death, her attempts to escape the point in spacetime that contains that death, and her related body-art attempts to escape her self and her own humanity—the flat past-tense declarations also imply that Lauren ultimately inhabits her Newtonian reality in significantly more complex ways than she had before. For these statements communicate new revelations about her world ("She could see the true colors of the walls and floors. She'd never seen the walls before") and new acceptance of the irrevocable loss of Rey ("The bed was empty. She'd known it was empty all along but was only catching up," 126). Prefaced by this new knowledge of truths about the reality she lives in, Lauren's decision in the final paragraph to open the window and feel the wind on her face and the "flow of time in her body" is a choice to inhabit the truth that is newly available to her, the truth of the suffering, mortal body, even though she knows it is an incomplete and even illusory truth. Thus the truth she sees in the empty room and feels in the "sea tang" is not simply the old, partial truth with which she began the novel, and which fuels every Realist novel—the inevitability of suffering, the pain of mortality, the trap of time, the impossibility of escaping the flow to inhabit the affective moment. Rather, it is the complicated, paradoxical truth that the closest a human being can get to inhabiting the full reality of the universe is to know she can never inhabit the full reality of the universe. Likewise, the novel's paradoxical final truth is that the truest narrative depiction of reality must acknowledge the inability of narrative to realistically depict reality, or to be in the end anything but a somewhat tired narrative mode.

Read in this way, the novel ends not in failure but in paradox, and thus, despite its seeming structural collapse from anti-Realism into Realism, it sustains the many paradoxes it has established throughout. Those include Lauren's discoveries that being present in the moment requires being present in the body that lives in the human flow of time; that to become aware of that presence is to observe the self and no longer be present; that any attempt to escape one's human suffering—through art or the quantum—requires a loss of humanity; that the reality we attempt to represent through art is itself a screen for a truer reality to which we have no access. The novel's ending in Realism after its concerted attempts to depart from it also recasts as an affirming paradox what had seemed like a core, problematic contradiction about the potential of the novel or of any art. Art's inability to enable escape from human suffering or to accurately represent reality becomes art's, and realism's, power to allow those doomed attempts, from which we learn new truths about the universe: that its reality expands far beyond human knowledge and perception; that anything we know or say of it is always partial and only transiently true.

Thus *The Body Artist* uses a different formal structure, and departs differently from Realism, while demonstrating the same paradoxical quantum truths constructed by *Tale* and "Story." In contrast to the endlessly looping structures and irreducibly multiple (even infinite) perspectives maintained by Ozeki and Chiang, DeLillo's decision to sustain these paradoxes within a form that imagines new possibilities for Realism before ultimately settling back into that formal Realism becomes conspicuous and significant. The novel's return to chronology, linearity, singular perspective, and the teleology of the tale, after having pressed the boundaries between fiction and reality, tale and affect, temporality and presence, implies that the novel uses realism not as an insufficient, outdated mode that needs to be eclipsed by something altogether new, but as itself the medium in which the struggle to represent the paradox of experience and reality for both human and novel can best be communicated. Its form demonstrates the power and the limits of its form.[62]

This largest paradox is the koan at the heart of *The Body Artist*. We might even say it is *The Body Artist*'s version of the Heart Sutra: form is emptiness and emptiness is form.[63] In *Tale*, Nao first encounters this piece of the sutra when it is chanted at her "funeral" organized by her ostracizing peers. She explains it, through Jiko's teaching, as meaning "that nothing in the world is solid or real, because nothing is permanent, and all things . . . are just kind of flowing through for the time being" (106–7). Nao experiences its truth more directly after Jiko's death: "one moment old Jiko was form and the next moment she wasn't" (364). In response to reading Nao's account of Jiko's death, Ruth likewise comprehends the paradox by remembering her mother's death, recalling the sight of the chimney during her mother's cremation through the lens of the Heart Sutra: "There was no smoke coming from it, but they could see a dense column of shimmering heat, which was all that was left of her mother's body as she became air . . . in this etheric form she could ride the trade winds back to Hilo and be there in no time" (372).

In Buddhist terms, the paradox means that the only truth is change; not even the physical world is "solid or real." Consequently, our perceptions of separate selves are illusory, as we are also transient parts of a constantly changing whole, and must learn to widen our perceptions outside the self to see that truth. In terms of science and quantum physics, it means that we are all temporary arrangements of matter that at any time can be (will be, are being, have been) dissolved and rearranged. Likewise, we are all made of the same matter, the matter of the universe. A person is as much a particular materialization of circumstance in the spacetime loaf—a random orderly arrangement of particles in one moment and place—as any observed particle is only one possible fixation of a wave among infinite possibilities in spacetime. Human beings are as transient and microscopically comprehensive of the universe as is any particle in any one of the infinite worlds of the universe, of the infinite universes. The Heart Sutra unites Buddhist belief and empirically demonstrated quantum theory in asserting that people, particles, knowledge, worlds, reality, truths are always simultaneously form—existing/true/defined/knowable/real, and emptiness—existing, true, and real only in relation to all that is not particular, not human, not knowable, and only for this moment, only from the perspective of this point in the spacetime loaf.[64]

From this massive perspective, the question of the efficacy of a particular novelistic form—the question we are left with at the end of *The Body Artist*—becomes only one of infinite ways to parse this much larger question of the relationship between any one arrangement of things in the universe and all possible arrangements. The relationship of the form of the novel to reality (or, the question of how well any particular form, mode, or theory of representation can reproduce the truth of the real world) becomes one atomic version of this universal question from Buddhism and quantum mechanics, whose answer is, among other things, the paradox: form is emptiness and emptiness is form. Every form is both true and untrue, both a false and accurate reflection of the truth of the universe, depending on when you encounter it and where you are standing. In that context, rather than viewing *Tale* and "Story" as managing to do something that *The Body Artist* does not, by articulating the truth of this paradox both in theme and ultimately anti-Realist form, we might instead view *The Body Artist* as reminding us that the ability of a novel such as *Tale* to teach us this lesson of the form/emptiness paradox depends upon a tradition, norm, system of measurement, and model of form and content against which it can construct its paradox in contrasting and therefore newly illuminating ways. Anti-Realism requires Realism (and Realism requires anti-Realism) in order to be differently meaningful just as quantum mechanics requires the linearity, causality, and order of Newtonian physics as the system against which its atemporal, chaotic, infinite possibilities can become visible. Each of these two novels, by turns Realist and anti-Realist, communicates the paradox in its own way; each novel requires the other to complete the paradox.

This requirement of the assertion of one form or framework (whether generic, ontological, or epistemological) for a new form to emerge, and the need for both to express an always changing and partial truth, is a productive revision of Jameson's dialectic of realism. Read in relation to and in service of anti-Realist techniques, realism does not so much kill off earlier narrative modes and so render itself impotent (as Jameson argues), as it spawns new techniques and modes that simultaneously enlist and defy it, rendering it along with themselves newly productive. On a larger scale, it is also a contextual shift of Derrida's crucial, impossible, endlessly generative attempt to escape the dialectic of metaphysics through deconstruction. This reading of *The Body Artist*'s ultimate realism in relation to the anti-Realism of *Tale* and "Story" discovers at the level of narrative Jameson's and Derrida's aesthetic and philosophical models, which emerged from and define poststructuralism in its fundamental drive to escape the binary, as an engine of quantum realism. To point this out is also to recognize that the same poststructural drive to escape the binary fuels all of the new realisms I have explored in this book, in fiction that has used technical and structural innovations in point of view, perspective, voice, tone, textuality and intertextuality, materiality, generic structure, and metafiction itself to blur the divisions between fiction/reality, language/material, truth/perception, past/present/future, self/other, and being/nonbeing.

But reading *The Body Artist* in comparison with *Tale* and "Story" also points to an important difference between it and these other more technically anti-Realist texts, and so to the perhaps most defining factor in any act of realism: perspective. "Story of Your Life" escapes the confines of illusory linearity, limited point of view, and closure—of Realism—by placing Louise's Newtonian human experience in relation to the quantum experience and perception of the heptapods, such that the insufficiency of her limiting human perspective becomes clear to her as well as to us, in the context of the heptapods' teleological experience. *A Tale for the Time Being* stages a similar escape by providing the Buddhist and quantum perspectives from which Ruth's seemingly linear experience of reading Nao's journal becomes looping and infinite. In contrast, the ultimate closure and past tense of *The Body Artist* expresses the same anxiety that permeates the archive in DeLillo's notes on quantum theory: that it is the isolated *human* perspective that cannot comprehend the truth of the universe. The frustration we feel at the end of this once shockingly quantum but ultimately Realist, Newtonian novel is his frustration, and ours, at this discovery, that what any one of us experiences or communicates of the world is never the world itself.

The other side of this feeling of emptiness, however, is the feeling of urgency it engenders, an urgency for new form—which is also emptiness. In this way, "Story of Your Life," *A Tale for the Time Being*, and *The Body Artist* together illustrate that narrative needs to escape Realism and its traditionally limited perspectives, just as (and because) we, like Lauren, need to escape our own habitually selfish, insufficient, human-centered perspectives. Such an argument has never been more important, as events in the real world—including global warming, mass immigration, the evisceration of truth and the advent of "fake news," and the (not unrelated) empowering of alt-right groups all over the Western world; and their corresponding movements in literary studies—including ecocriticism, animal studies, evolutionary studies, globalization and transatlantic studies, cognitive literary studies, and media studies—make clear. In this context, we might see all these new realisms as what happens when narrative, which has traditionally been singular, linear, and immaterial, and reading and writing, which have been seen as solitary, abstract, and disconnected from each other, are reimagined as necessarily multiple, embodying and embodied, interconnected, paradoxical, and instruments for recognizing and communicating an urgent need for change. This book has attempted to describe the formal and technical ways in which fiction has already changed in response to contemporary notions of language and the world. What remains to be seen are the ways in which the concepts of relational matter and ethical ontology that undergird them might change the world.

Notes

1. Meghan Daum, "Death and Don DeLillo," *The Atlantic*, May 2016. https://www.theatlantic.com/magazine/archive/2016/05/death-and-don-delillo/476367, November 15, 2018.
2. Samuel Coale has published a quantum reading of *The Body Artist* in two places: "Quantum Flux and Narrative Flow: Don DeLillo's Entanglements with Quantum Theory," *Papers in Language and Literature* 47, no. 3 (2011): 261–94 and *Quirks* (2012). It is evidence of how compelling I found some of his arguments that I found his treatment of this novel and its relationship to the archive frustratingly limited. In offering my own much extended reading of the novel as quantum and in relation to the archive, I hope to fill in some of Coale's lines of reasoning with additional and, I think, crucial (and in some cases just really fascinating) evidence, and to add to those arguments my own observations about the novel itself and about what it tells us about quantum realism.
3. See page 69 of the novel and page 191 of this chapter.
4. Philip Nel, "Don DeLillo's Return to Form: The Modernist Poetics of *The Body Artist*," *Contemporary Literature* 43, no. 4 (2002): 737 FN 1.
5. DeLillo struggled to sum up the book himself. In a letter to a translator on December 22, 2000, he resorted to quoting Wallace's parabolic fish joke ("what the fuck is water?") to do so, writing "I guess this is what The Body Artist is all about." Wallace had used that fish joke to describe *The Body Artist* in a letter to DeLillo dated just 10 days earlier, and had incorporated it into his 1996 *Infinite Jest* as well (and would repeat it in his 2005 Kenyon College speech). DeLillo does not attribute the joke to Wallace ("Don DeLillo's Papers," containers 9.1 and 101.1).
6. Nel, "Modernist Poetics," 746; David Cowart, "DeLillo and the Power of Language," in *The Cambridge Companion to Don DeLillo*, ed. John Duvall (London: Cambridge University Press, 2008), 205.
7. Nel, "Modernist Poetics," 746.
8. Cowart, "DeLillo and the Power of Language," 203, 208, 204.
9. Laura Di Prete, "Don DeLillo's *The Body Artist*: Performing the Body, Narrating Trauma," *Contemporary Literature* 46, no. 3 (2005): 488, 483.
10. Mikko Keskinen, "Posthumous Voice and Residual Presence in Don DeLillo's *The Body Artist*," in *Novels of the Contemporary Extreme*, ed. Alain-Philippe Durand and Naomi Mandel (New York: Continuum, 2006), 31, 32.
11. Julia Breitbach, *Analog Fictions for the Digital Age: Literary Realism and Photographic Discourses in Novels after 2000* (New York: Camden House, 2012), 111.
12. Di Prete, "Don DeLillo's *The Body Artist*," 488.
13. Rachel Smith, "Grief Time: The Crisis of Narrative in Don DeLillo's *The Body Artist*," *Polygraph: An International Journal of Culture and Politics* 18 (2006): 101, 100.

14 Pavlina Radia, "Doing the Lady Gaga Dance: Postmodern Transaesthetics and the Art of Spectacle in Don DeLillo's *The Body Artist*," *Canadian Review of American Studies* 44, no. 2 (2014): 204, 206.
15 Hikaru Fujii, *Outside, America: The Temporal Turn in Contemporary American Fiction* (New York: Bloomsbury, 2013), 87.
16 DeLillo, *The Body Artist*, 12, 20. I will note subsequent references parenthetically.
17 Confoundingly, the misreading of the novel is perpetuated by the back cover as well, as it prominently features a quotation from a critic who describes the book up as "a metaphysical ghost story about a woman alone."
18 Coale, "Quantum Flux," 287.
19 Without entering quantum territory, Burn also explains the novel's oddities through physical frameworks that reflect the material world we live in, rather than grasping at abstract ways of reading. His reading adds a biological/neurological dimension to the linguistic slipperiness that has long underpinned postmodern skepticism, or, as Burn remarks, "underwrite[s] a neurophysiological postmodernism" ("The Neuronovel," *American Literature in Transition, 2000-2010*, ed. Rachel Greenwald Smith (London: Cambridge University Press, 2017), 173). My quantum reading of *The Body Artist* adds a quantum dimension to that postmodern skepticism, while also proposing a potential "post-postmodern" quantum framework that moves beyond it.
20 Don DeLillo, "The Angel Esmerelda: Don DeLillo in Conversation with Jonathan Franzen," New York Public Library, October 24, 2102: 15, 14. https://www.nypl.org › files › livedelillofranzen_10.24transcript_0.doc, April 20, 2016.
21 Coale, "Quantum Flux," 269.
22 "'Time' notes and research material," Container 6.4, Don DeLillo Papers, Harry Ransom Center, University of Texas, Austin.
23 The HRC dates his "first draft" as spanning "8 September 1998" to "5 January 2000" ("Papers" 6.6-8, 7.1-2).
24 In a 2012 interview, DeLillo stated that he did not plan his books' structures much, which, if true, would make *The Body Artist* with its folders full of notes on ideas of the book's overall structure an exception in his oeuvre (Nance, "Living in Dangerous Times," *Chicago Tribune*, October 10, 2012).
25 "'Time' notes and research materials," Container 6.4.
26 "Notes in notebook," Container 6.5, Don DeLillo Papers, Harry Ransom Center, University of Texas, Austin. A version of this comment appears on one of the paper notes in the spiral notebook, but also, and most likely previously, scrawled on a playbill for a May 1999 showing of *The Book of Hours*, placing this idea and his reminder of it in the middle of the first drafting period.
27 "In quantum feat, atom seen in 2 places at once," 2000, Container 6.4, Don DeLillo Papers, Harry Ransom Center, University of Texas, Austin.

28 "'Time' notes," Container 6.4.
29 "Is There a Past in the Future?," 1986, Container 6.4.
30 Playbill for *The Book of Hours*," 1999, Container 6.3; "Notes in notebook," Container 6.5.
31 "'Time' notes," Container 6.4.
32 Ibid.
33 Notes from "First draft," Container 7.1.
34 For an extensive and delightful formal analysis of DeLillo's language in this chapter, see Nel, "Modernist Poetics."
35 The novel underscores this reading near its end, when Lauren reflects on "how sparing of self" and "only rarely unguarded of heart" she had been with Rey (118), as I will discuss below.
36 See Cornel Bonca, "Being, Time, and Death in Don DeLillo's *The Body Artist*," *Pacific Coast Philology* 37 (2002): 62, and Nel, "Modernist Poetics," 743.
37 While I do read this chapter as using style and structure—repetition of sounds, letters, words, and phrases, and movement from full paragraphs to fragmented paragraphs—as doing a lot of the work of communicating main ideas of the chapter (namely, Lauren's belief in order, inherent meaning, and certainty, and her movement out of a moment of awareness into the rush of habitual thinking), I do not read DeLillo's style here as "quantized," as does Coale (*Quirks* 44). In my concept of quantum realism, fiction is not quantum, and its representative strategizes are not quantized, until the text has established its quantum setting: it is the struggle to materialize the quantum setting that causes the innovations in style and structure that I would consider quantum realism. Since the setting of this novel does not become explicitly quantum for us until it does so for our observer Lauren, around page 69 (see argument below), I read DeLillo's style and structure in this chapter as enacting the potential for presence and awareness—human access to an immediate present—rather than mimicking the quantum world.
38 Here I read Lauren's view of the Kotka feed differently than does Nel, who views it "as if the broadcast were an unmediated representation, bridging that gap between experience and reality better than words ever could" (755). I would argue that nothing in the novel asks us to read this bit of pure, nearly contentless mediation as anything but mediation, which fascinates Lauren for the same reason that the mechanical voice in the answering machine fascinates her, both of which she incorporates into her performance piece, *Body Time*, which I will read below as failing to connect her to the real.
39 As Bonca argues, "Being, Time, and Death," 62.
40 Don DeLillo, *White Noise* (New York: Penguin Books, 1985), 78; *Zero K* (New York: Scribner, 2016), 274.
41 JenniCamLive screenshot, May 3, 1998, Container 6.3.
42 Letter from unidentified source, undated, Container 8.5.

43 Nel first read *Body Time* as a "metaphor for mourning," and one Lauren creates "to purge herself of grief" (756), and equates Lauren's body work with DeLillo's famous sculpting of reality using language, both projects of self-definition (748); Longmuir argues that Lauren's successful recuperation of Rey through her antiestablishment art is not a personal victory but an artistic and feminist one (533); Radia reads Lauren's parroting of Mr. Tuttle as a recuperation of the "potential of spectacle" (195) to dismantle the gender and social expectations that define us. Di Prete maps Cathy Caruth's theory of trauma onto the novel, thus reading Lauren's piece as speaking the language of trauma and opening a space for witnessing and working through; Smith reads the art in the same vein, concluding it is a "necessary failure" because it illustrates the impossibility of articulating the truth of grief and trauma (also a Caruthian/de Manian formulation) (101). Only Bonca reads the piece as truly failing in its endeavor because of the trap of grief, but that is because he argues that the goal of the piece is not productively to mourn but to "find her way back to [Heideggerian] Being" (63), which her grief prevents. Notably, Bonca offers no reading of the performance piece itself.
44 Cowart, "DeLillo and the Power of Language," 207.
45 Notes in "Research material," Container 6.3.
46 This reading of Mariella's selfish mediation of Lauren's body art obviously precludes Di Prete's argument that the review "bears witness" to the difficulties presented by the performance to readers and viewers, and to the difficulty of gaining knowledge about trauma (509).
47 Notes in "Research materials," Container 6.3.
48 "First draft," Container 7.1.
49 Di Prete views Lauren's grief as the "annihilating" force against which Lauren protects herself by relating to Mr. Tuttle (508); Smith reads her desire to "sink lower" (*TBA* 118) into the obliteration of grief as balanced by the opposite choice of "organizing time," and reads *Body Time* as illustrating how Lauren's experience of potentially nihilistic grief points to the importance of attempting to speak (101).
50 Di Prete, "Don DeLillo's *The Body Artist*," 504.
51 Likewise, if Mr. Tuttle "affirms the need for communication, interconnectedness, and sharing against the annihilating power of grief" (508), then why does he disappear in Chapter 6, when Lauren remains in the grip of her grief? Further, I find it difficult to read Mr. Tuttle, who is repeatedly described as machinelike and disaffected, as emblematic of empathy and human connection. He is, to me, much more like Drinion in Wallace's *The Pale King*—able to "witness" Lauren's suffering precisely because he remains disconnected from it and does not care.
52 Smith, "Grief Time," 100.
53 "First draft," Container 7.1.
54 In this reading, I am assuming, perhaps erroneously, that I can establish a kind of order of the draft materials in this "early drafts" folder, the

evidentiary minutiae of which argument seems too vast and uninteresting to document here. Nevertheless, I admit that different scholars might read these archive materials and their sequencing differently. My general assertion that Rey's return moves from certainty to doubt to erasure in these drafts does not depend on the detailed sequencing of that broad transformation that I suggest here, however.

55 "First draft," Container 7.1 (italics added).
56 Nel reads the novel as ultimately proving the "salvation" of art and Lauren's ability "to purge herself of grief" (757); Bonca reads Lauren as experiencing an "unironic, existential renewal" (66); Cowart sees her failure to imagine herself back in Rey's company as her narrow escape from "some irremediable descent into solipsism" and "madness" (208); Smith reads Lauren as ultimately experiencing "the limit that corporeality interposes," which "resists narrative withdrawal . . . and insists upon an engagement with the world" (107); Longmuir's Butlerian reading of the novel as feminist sees Lauren as using her body art as a "political aesthetic" that "springs in part from the subject's own body" and "restores the individual speaking subject" (542).
57 "First draft," Container 7.1.
58 Interestingly, DeLillo's ideas for the ending evolve from Mr. Tuttle-centered to Lauren-centered, like his ideas for the novel as a whole, as we see especially in two different drafts of the last paragraph. In one, she opens the window to "let Rey die" and make "Mr. Tuttle free, finally, not to suffer" (Container 7.1); this last idea repeats through many drafts and outlines of the novel's end, only to drop out of the novel.
59 "'Time' notes," Container 6.4.
60 "Notes in notebook," Container 6.5.
61 Brian McHale, "1966 Nervous Breakdown; or, When Did Postmodernism Begin?" *Modern Language Quarterly* 69, no. 3 (2008): 410.
62 This reading of *The Body Artist* blending ant-Realist and Realist techniques to expose the limits of Realism, and the necessity of both for the productivity of any act of realism, is a quantum version of my reading of contrapuntal metafictive realism of *The Pale King* (see Chapter 1).
63 Interestingly, the one critic who has examined Buddhism in DeLillo's work, Robert Kohn, describes *The Body Artist* as perhaps the least Buddhist of all the DeLillo novels he analyzes ("Tibetan Buddhism in Don DeLillo's Novels: The Street, the Word and the Soul," *College Literature* 38, no. 4 (2011): 156–80). Instead, he points out ways in which the novel mocks Buddhism and then situates the novel in the spectrum of modernism-postmodernism-hypermodernism. In arguing for what I see as a profound, if subtle, connection between the quantumness of *The Body Artist* and its Buddhist koanic structure, as I do below, I do not mean to assert that DeLillo intended to write a Buddhist novel or that the novel is most productively analyzed as pervasively Buddhist. Rather, I am observing that core Buddhist and

quantum concepts share so many similarities that to write a quantum novel, whether overtly, as did Ozeki, or covertly, as we might say DeLillo did, is to some extent to write a novel that will also be illuminated by Buddhist concepts. For the similarities (and key difference) between quantum mechanics and Buddhism, see Victor Mansfield's "Relativity in Madhyamika Buddhism and Modern Physics," *Philosophy East and West* 40, no. 1 (1990): 59–72.

I also acknowledge that I employ Buddhism here and in Chapter 4 as called for and delineated by the novels in question. I do not pretend to bring a full consideration of Buddhism as belief system or practice to bear on my readings. Certainly several of the novels examined in this book and many other contemporary novels would benefit from such a Buddhist-centered reading, a project for another time.

64 Such a concept of truth and meaning essentially adds a quantum-Buddhist framework to the fundamental shift from presence-absence to pattern-randomness that Hayles first articulated in her 1999 *How We Became Posthuman*.

Conclusion

Realism and Periodizing after Postmodernism

> *"What a vapid idea, the book as the image of the world."*
> –Gilles Deleuze and Félix Guattari[1]

The central argument of *Succeeding Postmodernism*—that poststructural fiction continues the ethical, communicative, and empathizing work of realism—was contentious when I conceived of it, felt urgent as I prepared it for publication in 2013, and yet already begins to feel quaint a few years later, as critics more generally acknowledge fiction's renewed investment since postmodernism in earnestness and ethics. *The Moral Worlds of Contemporary Realism* has aimed to look more closely at the details of the territory that the earlier book mapped out, the technical and formal innovations that emerge from decades of literary attempts to render reality in language within a poststructural framework. These innovations coalesce around two major features, one focused on language and the other on the world: metafiction, as a set of strategies that use attention to language and literary devices as tools for invoking the real; and materiality, or emphasis on language's physical reality and ability to shape reality, and on the matter of the world, the matter that literature is made of, and the continuity between them. One significant influence on this materiality is quantum physics, a scientific concept of physical reality that has been increasingly enlisted by writers in imagining their fictional worlds, thus necessitating new representational forms and techniques. One significant consequence of this quantum-physics influence is a profound multiplication and expansion of literary perspective. Together, these innovations demonstrate not just the poststructural insight of the previous book, that changing notions of language impact our ideas about reality and our literary depictions of them, but also the reverse: that changing concepts of reality and real advances in technology change literary technique and form as they strive to more accurately represent that reality, in turn reshaping the real world.

These aspects of realism after poststructuralism also demonstrate contemporary fiction's continuity with fundamental characteristics of the fiction that it defines itself against. Like nineteenth-century realism, poststructural realism emerges from faith in and fascination with the real, physical world, such that even its characteristic metafictional techniques invoke that world. Like postmodernism, it reproduces the dialectic it struggles to escape, its structural paradoxes and perspectival shifts attempting new solutions to a conundrum at least as old as Western metaphysics. The proliferation of "realisms" proposed since the transition out of postmodernism began in the 1990s further speaks to a widespread desire by critics and writers to connect their acts of creating and theorizing literature to the realism that preceded modernism, while retaining postmodernism's undermining of the connection between literature and reality, and structuralism's and poststructuralism's alienation of signification from the real. That these decades have seen a multiplying of "realisms" rather than, say, proliferating varieties of "anti-realism," "anti-novels," or "irrealism," likewise implies a desire to see these literary modes, so technically distinct from Realism, as new methods of making language reflect the real world and real human experience. It also provides strong evidence that "realism" has finally broken free from nineteenth-century claims to ownership and settled into the broad and somewhat problematic meaning proposed by critics as diverse as Jakobson, Abrams, and Morris, that "realism" has come to stand for any writing that intends to reflect a real world. But despite these terms' attempts to classify poststructural representative modes using (to-date) more than twenty different qualifiers, their cooption of "realism" imports its periodizing and definitional dilemmas, making today's coinages at least as problematic as they are promising.

The contradictions and challenges of defining "realism" that the Introduction discovered by examining over a century of attempts can be distilled into five distinct problems. From Steven Moore's alternate history of the realist novel, which identifies thirteenth-century Icelandic sagas as the ancestors of nineteenth-century European realism, we see that periods are always produced historically, but often applied ahistorically. Reading Howells's and James's theories of realism against their own fiction and that of their contemporaries, we see that periods are not necessarily accurately defined by their practitioners. From Auerbach's valorizing of Woolf's "modernist realism" over the "incompetent" experiments of her successors, we see that we tend to periodize according to the aesthetic values and worldview of our critical moment, and fail to consider that such values and visions are always changing. René Wellek and other mid-century theorists demonstrate how defining realism according to ideas or thematic agendas, in an effort to be more historically specific than formalist analysis allows, often results in a loss of literary and generic specificity. And work by more recent critics, including Eric Sundquist and Pamela Morris, illustrates that reading texts written during one historical-critical moment through lenses from another can cause unintended misreading. These pitfalls in periodizing "realism" elucidate problems of periodizing in general, by revealing that every period is structured according to multiple dimensions that are themselves inflected by multiple perspectives. Periods are variously limited according to historical, social, cultural, and economic contexts; aesthetic values and practices; concepts of language and representation; and concepts of reality. These dimensions of periods are viewed and defined differently by fiction writers, by texts themselves (which do not always say what their writers thought they were saying), and by critics and theorists, all of whom are bound by the above dimensions of their own historical periods. The prevalence of "realisms" in and after postmodernism suggests that today's fiction comprises and is shaped by the same multidimensional conflicts that characterize nineteenth-century realism. That connection also underscores the perhaps most problematic aspect of the term: that "realism" is often and most convincingly defined in terms that apply to all fiction. Thus it loses its power to define itself or to operate as an origin or standard against which other periods might react and distinguish themselves. Yet to a large extent, our framework for periodizing fiction and differentiating its modes is based on it. Meanwhile, as we see from Moore's Icelandic "realism," every act of naming takes place in a pre-established system—a periodizing version of Saussure's *la langue*—in which all terms and periods gain meaning only in relation to others, some of which are as problematic as "realism."

In 2018, an American Comparative Literature Association conference panel convened to discuss our field's current quandary of naming and periodizing contemporary literature. The proposals it generated further delineate problems of periodizing in general. Papers clustered around three main arguments: we should choose a new dominant around which to organize the contemporary period; we should enlist or resist particular dominants already in place (e.g., Jeff Severs's use of traditional literary history to propose Pynchon as the father of "post-postmodernism"; Alissa Karl's rejection of the industrial/post-industrial divide as a meaningful periodizing marker); we should resist dominants altogether and instead identify multiple strains of writing as characteristic of the period. None of the proposals for new dominants offered a satisfying alternative to ones already in place. One offered a solution that was in part an unwitting restatement of the problem: it suggested we conceive of periods as comedies, characterized by a proliferation of characters and marriage, rather than tragedies, characterized by the rise and fall of a single dominating character—as if the marriages that traditionally close off comedies are not one of the most common forms of closing off possibility and domination (of plot lines, of characters, of women) in literature. Another stopped short of specifying what its proposed grand gesture should be. A third, by Danielle Brandeis, proposed a compelling concept—"situated realism," or formally traditional realism that focuses on material and affective experience, which sounded to me like evidence of Jameson's affect-based realism persisting within contemporary writing. But since much of today's literary fiction is not formally Realist, such a concept can at best characterize only one facet of the great diversity encompassed by the period in question.

Those papers aiming to avoid reinventing the domination that literature since postmodernism has been so obviously trying to avoid offered more useful responses, such as Laurin Williams's discussion of the anthropocene as framing device in criticism and fiction, and of the focus on perspective it brings to periodizing. The most radical suggestion, and the one I most wanted to agree with, was David Rudrum's proposal that we simply stop periodizing altogether, and avoid the various pitfalls—many of which had been illuminated, knowingly or not, by other papers on the panel—necessitated by every act of periodizing. But however appealing such a wholesale rejection of the flawed system is, it would ultimately be too thoroughly pacifying. For if periodizing is in fact a system, a kind of *la langue* for talking about an entirety of literature so vast and varied as to be incomprehensible in its totality by any one reader (*contra* Eliot's quaintly egotistical notion of "ideal form"), then it is as indispensable to those of us who wish to interact with literature and with each other in terms of literature as language is to those of us who wish to interact with the world and with each other in that world.

If we can't tear down the system and build one that makes more diachronic sense, how can we best make more synchronic sense out of the one we have? And how can we do so in a way that acknowledges the obvious investment of so much of anti-Realist contemporary literature in the realism that preceded modernism? I can imagine three possibilities, of various scopes, usefulness, and plausibility. We might define and name this new period of literature after postmodernism in a way that marks a decisive split from the realism-modernism-postmodernism framework that has been in place for decades. This would mean ceding "realism" to the nineteenth century and inaugurating a new classifying logic that would escape the morass we are currently in, like grafting a sleek new limb to an old gnarly tree. But what would that logic be, and—more importantly, as Williams asked in her ACLA paper, and as papers advocating for a new dominant notably failed to ask—*whose* logic would it be? Alternatively, we could continue the stutter of postmodernism and capitulate to the term "post-postmodernism" that most critics use now (whether as a placeholder or with commitment). This approach would identify the current period as another step down the signifying chain away from its (false) modernist origin. Though the least helpful or accurate, this option seems most probable: print is a powerful canonizer. But capitulating to "post-postmodernism" feels to me like handing over today's big-hearted, aggressively alive and embodied fiction to the zombiefied afterlife of a period that is already dead.

A third, more ambitious approach would aim to remedy simultaneously the dilemmas of periodizing contemporary literature, clarifying "realism," and elucidating the relationship between the two. In essence, it would reconceptualize nineteenth-century realism as one subset of a larger, multifaceted evolution of forms used to depict reality in language (following both Eichenbaum and Jameson), and would require renaming old "realism" and thus also new "realisms" in related ways. Doing so requires taking a much broader view than has been imagined by the realism-modernism-postmodernism framework from which the proliferation of contemporary "realisms" sprang. Much as Mark McGurl's use of geologic time allowed him to delineate the subgenre of the "posthuman comedy," or art that recognizes the inhuman components of human experience, widening our perspective of literary periods would help us recontextualize the divisions we have been drawing between them in newly meaningful ways. For example, if we focus not on the many obvious differences between these new realisms and their namesake—the plethora of technical and formal innovations examined in this book, along with the fundamentally different notions of reality they represent—but on what they have in common, we see an important continuity running through all of these forms of realism: their belief in and commitment to representing a material world that is primary and defines human experience, and that is if not continuous with, at least fundamental to language, literature, and acts of reading and writing. Even our most forward-thinking concepts of literary representation and their attending notions of subjectivity remain grounded in this primary materiality:[2] N. Katherine Hayles repeatedly emphasizes the constitutive embodiedness of our experiences of technology, reading, and subjectivity, and Donna Haraway's cyborg requires the material realm in order to achieve its liberating transgression. Wai Chee Dimock's transnational studies "across deep time" and the anthropocenic philosophy and politics of Timothy Morton and Jedediah Purdy, like McGurl's geologic posthumanism, all orient around the experiences of bodies in time and space, however much they enlarge their scales.[3]

These frameworks expand our individual body-based perceptions of the world by taking up different positions in relation to technology and history, to bridging self and world, *not* by leaving the body or the material behind. In this way, poststructural literature and all its new realisms remain in fundamental agreement with Realism about the nature of reality and our relationship to it through language, in ways that unify human experience rather than splintering it into a compendium of subject positions. From this macro view, essentially what has changed over the centuries of literary expression so far are our concepts of that material world, our confidence in language's ability accurately to reflect it, and our technical and technological ways of expressing the relationship between the two. How will art change once we no longer consider the material as the basis of reality? How will realism change once we leave our bodies?

This seems to me to be the epochal shift that will shatter and remake our notion of realism, or literary representation of reality. In comparison, our recent movement from the positivism of nineteenth-century realism to the linguistic and philosophical skepticism of poststructuralism and all of its remade realisms becomes a trivial modification. Imagining such a reframing is more pragmatic than fanciful: literature and art have been leaving their bodies behind increasingly, at least since the advent of digital and electronic literature in the 1990s, and human experience is not far behind, as recent developments in virtual-reality and AI technology attest. Literature and film have been pondering the implications of such human-virtual interfacing for quite a while, as in *Blade Runner* (1982), *Her* (2013), *Ex Machina* (2014), *Blade Runner 2049* (2017), *Machines Like Me* (2019), and *Frankissstein* (2019), and of our own departure from our bodies, as in *The Girl Who Was Plugged In* (1973), *Neuromancer* (1984), *Snow Crash* (1992), *eXistenZ* (1999), *The Matrix* (1999), *Transcendence* (2014), and *Zero K* (2016); the *Black Mirror* series (2011–present) frequently ponders both. But these examples remain products of our current poststructural, "post-postmodern" moment, in which we remain grounded in the body and materiality, while considering the emancipatory and oppressive potentials of full movement into virtuality. Only art created in a fully virtual world, or one in which human experience has become thoroughly virtual, can reveal to us the representational techniques and philosophies of ontology and epistemology that will characterize the next new realism, virtual realism.[4]

For now, we might use this broader perspective that anticipates our shift away from the material and into the virtual to reconsider how we might more productively differentiate today's new realisms from their nineteenth-century namesake. United in their commitment to material reality, and to their shared project of representing that reality through language, they can most meaningfully be distinguished by their very different ideas of how that representation works and, to a lesser extent, by their differing concepts of that materiality. Whereas nineteenth-century realism expresses faith in the referential capacity of language to connect to and reflect the truth of the world, contemporary realisms operate according to the skepticism and dialectic of poststructuralism. While Realism expresses the positivist belief that we can empirically know and intellectually comprehend the truths of the Newtonian world we live in, today's realisms offer multiple, contradictory possibilities of partial truths, and confounding evidence of the quantum world we may theorize but cannot experience. Rather than maintaining a panoply of scattered new realisms opposing a titanic, originating "realism," then, we might consider a more fruitful framework that places all of these realisms in relation to each other, and orients them toward the next massive shift to come: empirical, poststructural, and virtual realism. Adopting such a scheme would free us from our subjugation to old, ill-fitting frames, prevent emerging periods from being contorted by old ones, and delineate a space—poststructural realism—large enough to encompass all of the innovations that we generate for invoking this material world and our embodied experience of it as humans and as readers in the ongoing poststructural-material era.

Poststructural Realism and "Post-postmodern" Literature

I suggest "poststructural realism" again in this book as a term for differentiating today's realisms from nineteenth-century realism because, along with their commitment to the materiality of the world, language, and their print forms, and their use of metafiction to articulate that commitment, attempts to think or represent their way outside the dialectic Derrida sought to escape through deconstruction mark another crucial commonality of the contemporary realist fiction examined here. Whether through the endless binary of metafictive realism, or the Möbius-strip authors and readers of material realism, or the looping structures, paradoxes, and koans of quantum realism, all of these examples of contemporary realism seek to escape singularity, linearity, binarism, and closure by encompassing multiple or even infinite perspectives, voices, planes, or narratives, as if to place the reader in an infinity of subject positions from which to observe the phenomena of their worlds. This fiction continues to use the basic tools of realism, including character, setting, plot, tense, and point of view, and to require recognizable naturalizing strategies, including reality effects and self-reflexivity, to gesture toward the infinite perspective and total uncertainty that the tools themselves cannot construct—perhaps somewhat like Hal Foster's postmodern notion of traumatic realism, in which language can only point to the absence of the traumatic real: however strongly the koans and looping structure of Ozeki's *A Tale for the Time Being* suggest many worlds in which everything has happened completely differently, the pages we read offer only one bound and unchanging set of experiences for Ruth and Nao. In this way, contemporary realism remains to some extent stuck acknowledging the same representational challenges performed and bemoaned by postmodern fiction.

We must also acknowledge, though, how "post-postmodern" fiction, like that last flat sentence of *The Body Artist*, places its limits and frustrations—and the ways it is exactly *not* the real world—in a larger context in which every encountered limit triggers another attempt to transcend and so yearns toward future forms, as each deconstructive reading engenders another. As it is fair to see the last half century of literary theory as a sustained attempt to think outside the Hegelian dialectical model of subjectivity in which one's selfhood must always come at the expense of the other's, we might see the past quarter century of literary realism as an ever-evolving attempt to escape the language/world, truth/fiction,[5] reader/writer binaries that underlie the very notion of realism. But as Hardt and Negri argued in their theory of Empire—that postmodern hybridity fuels late capitalism rather than resisting it, and Deleuze and Guattari demonstrated in failing to produce the rhizomatic work that was their expressed intention,[6] it is far easier to theorize the dialectic in which theory and literature have been eddying at least since postmodernism, and to illustrate its systematic oppressions, than it is to effect an escape. If we cannot say today's metafictive and materialist realism escapes it entirely, we might see their attempts as creating a new dialectic no longer confined to the abstract realms of theory, language, or literature, but one that rather strives to expand to encompass the entire material world. For on the largest level, these readings of contemporary realisms have demonstrated their sustained and multivalent efforts to construct an unprecedented intimacy, even continuity, between language and the material world.

Metafictive realism as practiced by David Foster Wallace in *The Pale King* illustrates this continuity by using language to provoke readers into awareness of their own embodied experience and of the "realest, most profound parts" of themselves and of the world. Material realism does so by transforming reading into a physical experience that reorients readers in time and space, requires their diligent physical participation, and positions them as constitutive parts of a world made in part by the matter of language. Quantum realism intensifies the continuity between language and matter, and literature and reader, further still by demonstrating how each literally shapes the other, to the point of entanglement. It also illustrates how theories of the material world (such as quantum mechanics) generate concepts of being (such as new materialism) that carry their own implications not only for what the world *is* but for how we *ought* to be in that world (as suggested by Buddhism). When *Tale* offers Buddhism and quantum mechanics as two languages to describe the same reality—one spiritual and one physical—Ozeki makes this connection between material and moral ontologies overt. "Story" demonstrates their interdependence more covertly by revealing the ethical implications of Louise's experience of simultaneous time, in which she must accept and even choose outcomes and people she would like to change. We might read the end of *The Body Artist* as Lauren's discovery of a similar lesson that she must choose and accept the life available to her, after her painful and even inhuman attempts to contort it into an escape from linear time. Thus, connecting many of these disparate examples of metafictive, material, and quantum realism is not only an attempt to make language continuous with the material world but also a correlating argument for an ethical way of being that is implied by such a wholly relational world. These texts demonstrate, however tacitly, the benefits to the self and the other of a world not made of individuated selves, in which every vision—human and literary—knows its insufficiency, and every act—in language and in the material world—is aware of both its power to affect others and the limits of its wisdom.

More than a catalog of technical innovations and generic change, reading contemporary realisms in the context of a long history of realism reveals how ideas about the nature of reality generate literary techniques for representing it that themselves demonstrate both what the world is and how we ought to live in it. At the same time, ideas about how language relates to the physical world, and the literary techniques developed to represent both the world and its relationship to language, shape the literature that endeavors to represent and connect us to our physical world—the one we can never immediately or entirely experience—and to expand our awareness of what that world is, and of our place in it. If the cycling dialectic of poststructural realism is, as I argued at the end of Chapter 5, an engine fueling all these contemporary realisms, then this dialectical relationship between material world and language is the larger dialectic containing that engine. Perhaps this is a version of what Jameson means to say with his dialectic of realism. But rather than predicting an end, however zombified, for realism after modernism, I see this larger material-linguistic dialectic as one that will continue for as long as there is a material world, and humans living materially in it and striving through story to know, experience, and comprehend the world beyond the terribly limited means offered by our absurdly miniscule and particular embodied perspectives.

So, my central formulation in *Succeeding Postmodernism* was incomplete. After postmodernism, language does become the solution to the problem of language, but not on its own, and not solely because authors began to turn poststructural linguistic techniques toward realist ends. Writers have also been using form and technique to reinvent realism itself, motivated by cultural and technological changes in the real world, and by newly influential ideas about the nature of that material world that insist we see it as inherently ethical, and that allow us to conceive of a continuity between language and the world that had been lost since structuralism. The ultimate result of all these theories of language, literature, and reality is renewed intimacy—between reader and writer, between language and reality, between beings in the world—an intimacy produced not in spite of but because of the productive engine of poststructural realism. Like quantum mechanics and language, which Ozeki reminds us are not the world itself but only "a finger, pointing to the moon" (415), literature and its engine, realism, are not the same thing as reality. But as old Jiko would remind us, they are "not different, either."

Notes

1. Gilles Deleuze and Félix Guattari, *A Thousand Plateaus: Capitalism and Schizophrenia*, trans. Brian Massumi (Minneapolis: University of Minnesota Press, 1987), 6.
2. Morris's theory of realism presumes materiality and embodiment as well: "Realism can and does rationally refer to a material domain beyond representation and can and does communicate knowledge of that extra-textual reality" (*Realism*, 141).
3. See Hayles, *How We Became Posthuman* (1999), *Writing Machines* (2002), and *How We Think* (2012), among other works; Haraway's "A Manifesto for Cyborgs" (1985); Dimock's *Through Other Continents: American Literature across Deep Time* (2008); Morton's *Hyperobjects: Philosophy and Ecology After the End of the World* (2013); and Purdy's *After Nature: A Politics for the Anthropocene* (2015).
4. "Virtual realism" is, of course, itself a placeholder for fiction created in and aiming to reflect a reality that remains today largely beyond our imagination, let alone our capacity for naming.
5. The breakdown of the fiction/nonfiction binary is another major facet of contemporary realism, which this project has neglected in the interest of doing justice to the metafictive, material, and quantum elements on which it focuses. But I want to at least acknowledge that a great deal of work can and should be done on the blurring of fiction and autobiography that also characterizes "post-postmodern" literature, notably in Rachel Cusk's *Outline* trilogy (*Outline*, 2014; *Transit*, 2016; *Kudos*, 2018); Karl Ove Knausgaard's six-volume *My Struggle* (published 2009–2018 in English), and of course Ozeki's own *A Tale for the Time Being*.
6. See *Empire* (2000) and *A Thousand Plateaus* (1980), respectively.

Bibliography

Abrams, Jeffrey Jacob and Doug Dorst. *S.* London: Mulholland Books, 2013.
Abrams, Meyer Howard. *A Glossary of Literary Terms*. 1st edn. New York: Holt, Rinehart and Winston, 1957.
Abrams, Meyer Howard. *A Glossary of Literary Terms*. 3rd edn. New York: Holt, Rinehart and Winston, 1971.
Abrams, Meyer Howard. *A Glossary of Literary Terms*. 6th edn. New York: Harcourt, 1993.
Adorno, Theodor W. *Aesthetic Theory*, translated by Robert Hullot-Kentor, edited by Gretel Adorno and Rolf Tiedemann. Minneapolis: University of Minnesota Press, 1997.
Alter, Robert. *Partial Magic: The Novel as a Self-Conscious Genre*. Berkeley: University of California Press, 1975.
Althusser, Louis. "Ideology and Ideological State Apparatuses." In *The Norton Anthology of Theory and Criticism*. 2nd edn, edited by Vincent B. Leitch, 1335–61. New York: Norton, 2010.
Ardoin, Paul. "Jonathan Safran Foer and the Impossible Book" [letter to the editor]. *PMLA* 128, no. 4 (2013): 1006–8.
Auerbach, Erich. *Mimesis: The Representation of Reality in Western Literature*, translated by Willard Trask. Princeton: Princeton University Press, 1953.
Auster, Paul. *4321*. New York: Henry Holt and Co., 2017.
Barad, Karan. *Meeting the Universe Halfway: Quantum Physics and the Entanglement of Matter and Meaning*. Durham: Duke University Press, 2007.
Barth, John. "The Literature of Exhaustion." In *The Friday Book: Essays and Other Non-Fiction*, 62–76. Baltimore: Johns Hopkins University Press, 1984.
Barth, John. *Lost in the Funhouse*. New York: Anchor, 1988 (1968).
Barthelme, Donald. "At the End of the Mechanical Age." In *Sixty Stories*, 267–74. New York: Penguin, 1993 (1976).
Barthes, Roland. "The Death of the Author." In *Image, Music, Text*, edited and translated by Stephen Heath, 142–8. London: Fontana, 1977.
Barthes, Roland. "The Reality Effect." In *French Literary Theory Today*, edited by Tzvetan Todorov, 11–17. Cambridge: Cambridge University Press, 1982.
Baudrillard, Jean. *Simulations*, translated by Paul Foss, Paul Patton, and Philip Beitchman. Boston: Semiotext(e), 1983.
Baum, Frank. *The Wonderful Wizard of Oz*, illustrated by W. W. Denslow. New York: George M. Hill Company, 1900.
Becker, George J. *Realism in Modern Literature*. New York: Frederick Ungar Publishing, 1980.
Beilin, Katarzyna Olga. "Disquieting Realism: Postmodern and Beyond." In *A Companion to the Twentieth-Century Spanish Novel*, edited by Martha Eulalia Altisent, 186–96. Woodbridge: Tamesis Books, 2008.

Benjamin, Walter. "The Work of Art in the Age of Its Technological Reproducibility." In *The Norton Anthology of Theory and Criticism*. 2nd edn, edited by Vincent B. Leitch, 1051–71. New York: Norton, 2010.

Bernadete, Jane, ed. *American Realism*. New York: G P Putnam's Sons, 1972.

Bernstein, Charles. *All the Whiskey in Heaven*. New York: Farrar, Straus, and Giroux, 2010.

Berthoff, Warner. *The Ferment of Realism: American Literature 1884-1919*. New York: The Free Press, 1965.

Birke, Dorothee and Stella Butter, eds. *Realisms in Contemporary Culture: Theories, Politics, and Medial Configurations*. Berlin: de Gruyter, 2013.

The Blair Witch Project. Directed by Daniel Myrick and Eduardo Sánchez. Haxan Films, 1999.

Bolaño, Roberto. *2666*, translated by Natasha Wimmer. New York: Picador, 2004.

Bolger, Robert K. and Scott Korb, eds. *Gesturing Toward Reality: David Foster Wallace and Philosophy*. New York: Bloomsbury, 2014.

Bonca, Cornel. "Being, Time, and Death in Don DeLillo's *The Body Artist*." *Pacific Coast Philology* 37 (2002): 58–68.

Bonta, Vanna. *Flight: A Quantum Fiction Novel*. San Diego: Meridian House, 1995.

Borges, Jorge Luis. *Collected Fictions*, translated by Andrew Hurley. New York: Penguin, 1988.

Borgmann, Albert. *Crossing the Postmodern Divide*. Chicago: University of Chicago Press, 1992.

Boswell, Marshall. *Understanding David Foster Wallace*. Columbia: University of South Carolina Press, 2003.

Boswell, Marshall, ed. *David Foster Wallace and "The Long Thing": New Essays on the Novels*. New York: Bloomsbury, 2014.

Boswell, Marshall and Stephen Burn, eds. *A Companion to David Foster Wallace Studies*. New York: Palgrave Macmillan, 2013.

Bourriaud, Nicolas. *Altermodern*. London: Tate, 2009.

Bowen, Deborah. "Photography and the Postmodern Realism of Anita Brookner." *Mosaic: A Journal for the Interdisciplinary Study of Literature* 28, no. 2 (1995): 123–48.

Bowen, Deborah. *Stories of the Middle Space: Reading the Ethics of Postmodern Realisms*. Montreal: McGill-Queen's University Press, 2010.

Brandeis, Danielle. "Is There a New Cultural Dominant?" *Always Periodize? Methods and Implications of Literary History*. American Comparative Literature Association Conference, UCLA, May 2018.

Brautigan, Richard. *The Abortion 1966*. New York: Simon & Schuster, 1971.

Breitbach, Julia. *Analog Fictions for the Digital Age: Literary Realism and Photographic Discourses in Novels after 2000*. Rochester: Camden House, 2012.

Breu, Christopher. *The Insistence of the Material: Literature in the Age of Biopolitics*. Minneapolis: University of Minnesota Press, 2014.

Brodhead, Richard. "Hawthorne among the Realists: The Case of Howells." In *American Realism: New Essays*, edited by Eric Sundquist, 25–41. Baltimore: Johns Hopkins University Press, 1982.

Brooke-Rose, Christine. *A Rhetoric of the Unreal: Studies in Narrative and Structure, Especially of the Fantastic*. Cambridge: Cambridge University Press, 1981.

Brooks, Neil and Josh Toth, eds. *The Mourning After: Attending the Wake of Postmodernism*. Amsterdam: Rodopi, 2007.

Brown, Kevin. "Finding Stories to Tell: Metafiction and Narrative in *Cloud Atlas*." *Journal of Language, Literature and Culture* 63, no. 1 (2016): 77–90.

Buford, Bill. "Dirty Realism: New Writing in America." *Granta* 8 (1983): 4–5.

Bukiet, Melvin Jules. "Crackpot Realism: Fiction for the Forthcoming Millennium." *Review of Contemporary Fiction* 16, no. 1 (1996): 13–22.

Burn, Stephen J. "Anatomizing the Language of Love: An Interview with Lee Siegel." *Electronic Book Review*, 28 September 2006.

Burn, Stephen J. *David Foster Wallace's* Infinite Jest: *A Reader's Guide*. 2nd edn. New York: Continuum, 2012.

Burn, Stephen J. "Encyclopedic Fictions." In *American Literature in Transition, 1900-2000*, edited by Stephen J. Burn, 107–23. Cambridge: Cambridge University Press, 2018.

Burn, Stephen J. "The End of Postmodernism." In *American Fiction in the 1990s: Reflections on History and Culture*, edited by Jay Prosser, 220–34. Abingdon: Routledge, 2008.

Burn, Stephen J. *Jonathan Franzen at the End of Postmodernism*. New York: Continuum, 2008.

Burn, Stephen J. "The Neuronovel." In *American Literature in Transition, 2000-2010*, edited by Rachel Greenwald Smith, 165–78. Cambridge: Cambridge University Press, 2017.

Burn, Stephen J., ed. *Conversations with David Foster Wallace*. Jackson: University Press of Mississippi, 2012.

Cady, Edwin H. *The Road to Realism: The Early Years 1837-1885 of William Dean Howells*. Syracuse: Syracuse University Press, 1956.

Calvino, Italo. *Cosmicomics*, translated by William Weaver. New York: Harcourt Brace, 1976.

Calvino, Italo. *If on a winter's night a traveler*, translated by William Weaver. New York: Harcourt, 1981.

Carlisle, Greg. *Elegant Complexity: A Study of David Foster Wallace's* Infinite Jest. Los Angeles: Sideshow Media Group Press, 2007.

Carson, Anne. *Nox*. Cambridge: New Directions, 2010.

Carter, Everett. *Howells and the Age of Realism*. Philadelphia: J B Lippincott Co., 1950.

Carton, Evan. "*Pudd'nhead Wilson* and the Fiction of Law and Custom." In *American Realism: New Essays*, edited by Eric J. Sundquist, 82–95. Baltimore: Johns Hopkins University Press, 1982.

Caruth, Cathy. *Unclaimed Experience: Trauma, Narrative, and History*. Baltimore: Johns Hopkins University Press, 1996.
Caruth, Cathy, ed. *Trauma: Explorations in Memory*. Baltimore: Johns Hopkins University Press, 1995.
Castle, Gregory, ed. *A History of the Modernist Novel*. Cambridge: Cambridge University Press, 2015.
Cazzato, Luigi. "Hard Metafiction and the Return of the Author-Subject: The Decline of Postmodernism?" In *Postmodern Subjects/Postmodern Texts*, edited by Jane Dowson and Steven Earnshaw, 25–41. Amsterdam: Rodopi, 1995.
Cheyfitz, Eric. "A Hazard of New Fortunes." In *American Realism: New Essays*, edited by Eric J. Sundquist, 42–65. Baltimore: Johns Hopkins University Press, 1982.
Chiang, Ted. "Story of Your Life." In *Stories of Your Life and Others*. New York: Vintage, 2016.
Christensen, Inger. *The Meaning of Metafiction: A Critical Study of Selected Novels by Sterne, Nabokov, Barth and Beckett*. Oslo: Universitetsforlaget, 1981.
Clareson, Thomas D., ed. *SF: The Other Side of Realism: Essays on Modern Fantasy and Science Fiction*. Bowling Green: Bowling Green University Popular Press, 1971.
Coale, Samuel. "Quantum Flux and Narrative Flow: Don DeLillo's Entanglements with Quantum Theory." *Papers in Language and Literature* 47, no. 3 (2011): 261–94.
Coale, Samuel. *Quirks of the Quantum: Postmodern and Contemporary American Fiction*. Charlottesville: University of Virginia Press, 2012.
Cohen, Samuel and Lee Konstantinou, eds. *The Legacy of David Foster Wallace*. Iowa City: University of Iowa Press, 2012.
Cohen, Samuel S. *After the End of History: American Fiction in the 1990s*. Iowa City: University of Iowa Press, 2009.
Coole, Diana and Samantha Frost, eds. *New Materialisms: Ontology, Agency, and Politics*. Durham: Duke University Press, 2010.
Coover, Robert. "The End of Books." *The New York Times Book Review*, June 21, 1992: 23–5.
Cowart, David. "DeLillo and the Power of Language." In *The Cambridge Companion to Don DeLillo*, edited by John Duvall, 151–65. Cambridge: Cambridge University Press, 2008.
Crane, Stephen. "The Open Boat." In *Norton Anthology of American Literature*. 7th edn, vol. C, edited by Nina Baym, 1000–16. New York: Norton, 2007.
Crockett, Clayton. "Postmodernism and the Crisis of Belief: Neo-Realism vs. the Real." In *The Mourning after: Attending the Wake of Postmodernism*, edited by Neil Brooks and Josh Toth, 263–83. Amsterdam: Rodopi, 2007.
Culler, Jonathan. "Convention and Naturalization." In *Structuralist Poetics: Structuralism, Linguistics, and the Study of Literature*, 131–60. Ithaca: Cornell University Press, 1975.
Culver, Stuart. "What Manikins Want: The Wonderful World of Oz and The Art of Decorating Dry Goods Windows." *Representations* 21 (1988): 97–116.

Cusk, Rachel. *Kudos*. New York: Picador, 2019.
Cusk, Rachel. *Outline*. New York: Farrar, Straus and Giroux, 2015.
Cusk, Rachel. *Transit*. New York: Picador, 2017.
Danielewski, Mark Z. *House of Leaves*. New York: Pantheon Books, 2000.
Danielewski, Mark Z. *Only Revolutions*. New York: Pantheon Books, 2006.
Daum, Meghan. "Death and Don DeLillo." Review of *Zero K*. *The Atlantic*, May 2016. https://www.theatlantic.com/magazine/archive/2016/05/death-and-don-delillo/476367. November 15, 2018.
de Cervantes, Miguel. *Don Quixote*, translated by Edith Grossman. New York: Harper Collins, 2003.
Delany, Samuel. *Babel-17*. New York: Vintage, 2001 (1966).
Deleuze, Gilles and Félix Guattari. *A Thousand Plateaus: Capitalism and Schizophrenia*, translated by Brian Massumi. Minneapolis: University of Minnesota Press, 1987.
DeLillo, Don. *The Body Artist*. New York: Scribner, 2001.
DeLillo, Don. Letter to translator ("Harry"). December 22, 2000. Container 9.1 Don DeLillo Papers. Harry Ransom Center, University of Texas, Austin.
DeLillo, Don. *The Names*. New York: Vintage Books, 1989 (1982).
DeLillo, Don. *Point Omega*. New York: Scribner, 2010.
DeLillo, Don. *White Noise*. New York: Penguin Books, 1985.
DeLillo, Don. *Zero K*. New York: Scribner, 2016.
DeLillo, Don and Jonathan Franzen. "The Angel Esmerelda: Don DeLillo in conversation with Jonathan Franzen." New York Public Library, October 24, 2102. https://www.nypl.org › files › livedelillofranzen_10.24transcript_0.doc. April 20, 2016.
Den Tandt, Christophe. "Pragmatic Commitments: Postmodern Realism in Don DeLillo, Maxine Hong Kingston and James Ellroy." In *Beyond Postmodernism: Reassessments in Literature, Theory, and Culture*, edited by Klaus Stierstorfer, 121–41. Berlin: Walter de Gruyter, 2003.
Derrida, Jacques. *Of Grammatology*, translated by Gayatri Chakravorty Spivak. Baltimore: Johns Hopkins University Press, 1974.
Derrida, Jacques. "Structure, Sign, and Play in the Discourse of the Human Sciences." In *The Critical Tradition: Classic Texts and Contemporary Trends*, edited by David H. Richter, 959–71. New York: St. Martin's, 1989.
de Saussure, Ferdinand. From *Course in General Linguistics*. In *The Norton Anthology of Theory and Criticism*. 2nd edn, edited by Vincent B. Leitch, 850–66. New York: Norton, 2010.
Dewitt, Helen. *The Last Samurai*. Cambridge: New Directions, 2000.
D'Haen, Theo. "European Postmodernism: The Cosmodern Turn." *Narrative* 21, no. 3 (2013): 271–83.
Diakoulakis, Christoforos. "'Quote Unquote Love…a Type of Scotopia': David Foster Wallace's *Brief Interviews with Hideous Men*." In *Consider David Foster Wallace*, edited by David Hering, 147–55. Los Angeles: Sideshow Media, 2010.
Di Blasi, Debra. *The Jiří Chronicles and Other Fiction*. Normal: FC2, 2007.

Dimock, Wai Chee. *Through Other Continents: American Literature across Deep Time*. Princeton: Princeton University Press, 2008.

Di Prete, Laura. "Don DeLillo's *The Body Artist*: Performing the Body, Narrating Trauma." *Contemporary Literature* 46, no. 3 (2005): 483–510.

Dolphijn, Rick and Iris van Der Tuin. *New Materialism: Interviews & Cartographies*. Ann Arbor: Open Humanities Press, 2012.

Dowson, Jane and Steven Earnshaw, eds. *Postmodern Subjects/Postmodern Texts*. Amsterdam: Rodopi, 1995.

Dubey, Madhu. "Post-Postmodern Realism?" *Twentieth-Century Literature* 57, no. 3–4 (2011): 492–515.

Egan, Jennifer. "Black Box." Twitter, May 2012.

Egan, Jennifer. *A Visit from the Goon Squad*. New York: Anchor, 2011.

Eichenbaum, Boris. From *The Theory of the "Formal Method."* In *Norton Anthology of Theory and Criticism*. 2nd edn, edited by Vincent B Leitch, 925–51. New York: Norton, 2010.

Elias, Amy. "Meta-Mimesis? The Problem of British Postmodern Realism." In *British Postmodern Fiction*, edited by Theo D'haen and Hans Berten, 9–31. Amsterdam: Rodopi, 1993.

Eliot, T. S. "Tradition and the Individual Talent." In *Selected Prose of T. S. Eliot*, edited by Frank Kermode, 37–44. New York: Farrar, Straus, and Giroux, 1975.

Enck, John J. and John Barth. "An Interview." *Wisconsin Studies in Contemporary Literature* 6, no. 1 (1965): 3–14.

Eshelman, Raoul. *Performatism, or, the End of Postmodernism*. Aurora: The Davies Group Publisher, 2008.

Faber, Michel. *Under the Skin*. Eugene: Harvest House, 2001.

Fachinger, Petra. "Writing the Canadian Pacific Northwest Ecocritically: The Dynamics of Local and Global in Ruth Ozeki's *A Tale for the Time Being*." *Canadian Literature* 232 (2017): 47–63.

Federman, Raymond. *Double or Nothing*. Tuscaloosa: FC2, 1998.

Fest, Bradley J. "'Then Out of the Rubble: David Foster Wallace's Early Fiction." In *David Foster Wallace and "The Long Thing": New Essays on the Novels*, edited by Marshall Boswell, 85–105. New York: Bloomsbury, 2014.

Fisher. Mark. *Capitalist Realism: Is There No Alternative?*. Zero Books, 2009.

Fleisher, Kass. *Accidental Species*. Tucson: Chax Press, 2005.

Fluck, Winifried. "Surface Knowledge and 'Deep' Knowledge: The New Realism in American Fiction." In *Neo-Realism in Contemporary Fiction*, edited by Kristiaan Versluys, 65–85. Amsterdam: Rodopi, 1992.

Foer, Jonathan Safran. "About the Typefaces Not Used in This Edition." *The Guardian*, December 2002. https://www.theguardian.com/books/2002/dec/07/guardianfirstbookaward2002.

Foer, Jonathan Safran. *Everything Is Illuminated*. New York: Houghton Mifflin, 2002.

Foer, Jonathan Safran. *Extremely Loud and Incredibly Close*. New York: Houghton Mifflin, 2005.

Foer, Jonathan Safran. "A Primer for the Punctuation of Heart Disease." *The New Yorker*, June 2002. https://www.newyorker.com/magazine/2002/06/10/a-pr imer-for-the-punctuation-of-heart-disease.
Foer, Jonathan Safran. *Tree of Codes*. London: Visual Editions, 2010.
Foster, Hal. *The Return of the Real: The Avant-Garde at the End of the Century*. Boston: MIT Press, 1996.
Franzen, Jonathan. "Why Bother?" In *How To Be Alone*, 55–97. New York: Picador, 2002.
Fujii, Hikaru. *Outside, America: The Temporal Turn in Contemporary American Fiction*. New York: Bloomsbury, 2013.
Gass, William H. "Philosophy and the Form of Fiction." In *Fiction and the Figures of Life*, 3–26. Boston: Nonpareil Books, 1979.
Gass, William H. *The Tunnel*. Champaign: Dalkey Archive Press, 1995.
Gass, William H. *Willie Masters' Lonesome Wife*. Champaign: Dalkey Archive, 1989 (1968).
Gibson, William and Dennis Ashbaugh. *Agrippa (a Book of the Dead)*. Kevin Begos Jr., 1992.
Gladstone, Jason and Daniel Worden. "Introduction: Postmodernism, Then." *Twentieth-Century Literature* 57, nos. 3–4 (2011): 291–308.
Gram, Margaret. "*Freedom*'s Limits: Franzen, the Realist Novel, and the Problem of Growth." *American Literary History* 26, no. 2 (2014): 295–316.
Gramsci, Antonio. "The Formation of the Intellectuals." In *The Norton Anthology of Theory and Criticism*. 2nd edn, edited by Vincent B. Leitch, 1002–8. New York: Norton, 2010.
Green, Jeremy. *Late Postmodernism: American Fiction at the Millennium*. New York: Palgrave Macmillan, 2005.
Greenblatt, Stephen. "Resonance and Wonder." In *The Norton Anthology of Theory and Criticism*. 2nd edn, edited by Vincent B. Leitch, 2150–61. New York: Norton, 2010.
Greene, Brian. *The Fabric of the Cosmos: Space, Time, and the Texture of Reality*. New York: Vintage, 2005.
Grossman, Richard. *The Alphabet Man*. Normal: FC2, 1993.
Grossman, Richard. *The Book of Lazarus*. Normal: FC2, 1997.
Hackman, Paul. "'I Am a Double Agent': Shelley Jackson's *Patchwork Girl* and the Persistence of Print in the Age of Hypertext." *Contemporary Literature* 52, no. 1 (2011): 84–107.
Hall, Steven. *The Raw Shark Texts*. New York: Canongate, 2007.
Haraway, Donna. "A Cyborg Manifesto." In *Simians, Cyborgs, and Women*, 149–82. Abingdon: Routledge, 1990 (1985).
Hardt, Michael and Antonio Negri. *Empire*. Boston: Harvard University Press, 2001.
Harris, Charles. "The Anxiety of Influence: The John Barth/David Foster Wallace Connection." *Critique: Studies in Contemporary Fiction* 55, no. 2 (2014): 103–26.
Harris, Charles. "The Dead Fathers: The Rejection of Modernist Distance in *The Art Lover*." *Review of Contemporary Fiction* 17, no. 3 (1997): 157–74.

Harris, Victoria Frenkel. "Emancipating the Proclamation: Gender and Genre in *Ava*." *Review of Contemporary Fiction* 17, no. 3 (1997): 175–85.

Hayles, N. Katherine. "Combining Close and Distant Reading: Jonathan Safran Foer's *Tree of Codes* and the Aesthetic of Bookishness." *PMLA* 128, no. 1 (2013): 226–31.

Hayles, N. Katherine. *Electronic Literature: New Horizons for the Literary*. Notre Dame: University of Notre Dame Press, 2008

Hayles, N. Katherine. *How We Became Posthuman: Virtual Bodies in Cybernetics, Literature, and Informatics*. Chicago: University of Chicago Press, 1999.

Hayles, N. Katherine. *How We Think: Digital Media and Contemporary Technogenesis*. Chicago: Univeristy of Chicago Press, 2012.

Hayles, N. Katherine. *Writing Machines*. Boston: MIT Press, 2002.

Heidegger, Martin. "Language." In *Poetry, Language, Thought*, translated by Albert Hofstadter, 187–210. New York: Harper & Row, 1971.

Hemmings, F. W. J., ed. *The Age of Realism*. New York: Penguin, 1974.

Hennig, Reinhard. "Ecocritical Realism: Nature, Culture, and Reality in Icelandic Environmental Literature." In *Realisms in Contemporary Culture: Theories, Politics, and Medial Configurations*, edited by Dorothee Birke and Stella Butter, 109–23. Berlin: de Gruyter, 2013.

Hering, David. *David Foster Wallace: Fiction and Form*. New York: Bloomsbury, 2016.

Hering, David, ed. *Consider David Foster Wallace: Essays*. New York: Sideshow Media Group Press, 2010.

Hicks, Heather. "'This Time Round': David Michell's *Cloud Atlas* and the Apocalyptic Problem of Historicisim." *Postmodern Culture: An Electronic Journal of Interdisciplinary Criticism* 20, no. 3 (2010): np. http://www.pomo culture.org/2013/09/03/this-time-round-david-mitchells-cloud-atlas-and -the-apocalyptic-problem-of-historicism/. September 19, 2019.

Himmelheber, Rachel. "'I Believed She Could Save Me': Rape Culture in David Foster Wallace's 'Brief Interviews with Hideous Men #20.'" *Critique: Studies in Contemporary Fiction* 55, no. 5 (2014): 522–35.

Hoang, Lily. *Changing*. Tuscaloosa: Fairy Tale Review Press, 2008.

Hoberek, Andrew. "Introduction: After Postmodernism." *Twentieth-Century Literature* 53, no. 3 (2007): 233–47.

Holland, Mary K. "David Foster Wallace and the Future of (Meta)Fiction." *The First Annual David Foster Wallace Conference*, keynote speech, Illinois State University, May 2014.

Holland, Mary K. "David Foster Wallace's 'Octet' and the 'Atthakavagga.'" *The Explicator* 74, no. 3 (2016): 165–9.

Holland, Mary K. "'By Hirsute Author': Gender and Communication in the Work and Study of David Foster Wallace." *Critique: Studies in Contemporary Fiction* 58, no. 1 (2016): 65–78.

Holland, Mary K. "*Infinite Jest*." In *The Cambridge Companion to David Foster Wallace*, edited by Ralph Clare, 127–41. Cambridge: Cambridge University Press, 2018.

Holland, Mary K. "A Lamb in Wolf's Clothing: Postmodern Realism in A. M. Homes's *Music for Torching* and *This Book Will Save Your Life*." *Critique: Studies in Contemporary Fiction* 53, no. 3 (2012): 214–37.
Holland, Mary K. "Mediated Immediacy in *Brief Interviews with Hideous Men*." In *A Companion to David Foster Wallace Studies*, edited by Marshall Boswell and Stephen J. Burn, 107–30. New York: Palgrave Macmillan, 2013.
Holland, Mary K. *Succeeding Postmodernism: Language and Humanism in Contemporary American Literature*. New York: Bloomsbury, 2013.
Holland, Mary K. "'Your Head Gets in the Way': Reflecting (on) Realism from John Barth to David Foster Wallace." In *John Barth: A Body of Words*, edited by Gabrielle Dean and Charles Harris, 201–31. Champaign: Dalkey Archive Press, 2016.
Homes, Amy M. *Music for Torching*. New York: Harper Collins, 1999.
Howells, William Dean. "Editha." In *Heath Anthology of American Literature*. 7th edn, vol. C, edited by Paul Lauter, 162–73. Boston: Cengage, 2014.
Howells, William Dean. "The Editor's Study." In *Heath Anthology of American Literature*. 7th edn, vol. C, edited by Paul Lauter, 147–8. Boston: Cengage, 2014.
Howells, William Dean. "Novel-Writing and Novel-Reading: An Impersonal Explanation." In *The Norton Anthology of American Literature*. 7th edn, vol. C, edited by Nina Baym, 915–17. New York: Norton, 2007.
Howitt, Peter, dir. *Sliding Doors*. Miramax, 1998.
Hutcheon, Linda. *Narcissistic Narrative: The Metafictional Paradox*. Waterloo: Wilfrid Laurier University Press, 1980.
Hutcheon, Linda. *A Poetics of Postmodernism: History, Theory, Fiction*. Abingdon: Routledge, 1988.
Jakobson, Roman. "On Realism in Art." In *Language in Literature*, edited by Kyrstyna Pomorska and Stephen Rudy, 19–27. Boston: Harvard University Press, 1987.
Jakubowski, Zuzanna. "Exhibiting Lost Love: The Relational Realism of Things in Orhan Pamuk's *The Museum of Innocence* and Leanne Shapton's *Important Artifacts*." In *Realisms in Contemporary Culture: Theories, Politics, and Medial Configurations*, edited by Dorothee Birke and Stella Butter, 124–45. Berlin: de Gruyter, 2013.
James, David. "Integrity After Metafiction." *Twentieth-Century Literature* 57, nos. 3–4 (2011): 492–515.
James, Henry. "The Art of Fiction." In *Heath Anthology of American Literature*. 7th edn, vol. C, edited by Paul Lauter, 238–55. Boston: Cengage, 2014.
James, Henry. "The Real Thing." In *The Norton Anthology of American Literature*. 7th edn, vol. C, edited by Nina Baym, 429–47. New York: Norton, 2007.
Jameson, Fredric. *The Antinomies of Realism*. New York: Verso, 2013.
Jameson, Fredric. From *The Political Unconscious: Narrative as a Socially Symbolic Act*. In *The Norton Anthology of Theory and Criticism*. 2nd edn, edited by Vincent B. Leitch, 1822–46. New York: Norton, 2010.

Jameson, Fredric. "Postmodernism and Consumer Society." In *The Norton Anthology of Theory and Criticism*. 2nd edn, edited by Vincent B. Leitch, 2509–16. New York: Norton, 2010.

Jameson, Fredric. *Postmodernism, or, The Cultural Logic of Late Capitalism*. Durham: Duke University Press, 1999.

Johnson, B. S. *The Unfortunates*. Cambridge: New Directions, 1969.

Karl, Alissa. "A(nother) Case for Economic Periodization." *Always Periodize? Methods and Implications of Literary History*. American Comparative Literature Association Conference, UCLA, May 2018.

Kelly, Adam. "David Foster Wallace and the New Sincerity in American Fiction." In *Consider David Foster Wallace: Critical Essays*, edited by David Hering, 131–46. Los Angeles: Side Show Media Group Press, 2011.

Keskinen, Mikko. "Posthumous Voice and Residual Presence in Don DeLillo's *The Body Artist*." In *Novels of the Contemporary Extreme*, edited by Alain-Philippe Durand and Naomi Mandel, 31–40. New York: Continuum, 2006.

Kessel, Tyler. "A Question of Hospitality in Don DeLillo's *The Body Artist*." *Critique: Studies in Contemporary Fiction* 29, no. 2 (2008): 185–204.

Kirby, Alan. *Digimodernism: How New Technologies Dismantle the Postmodern and Reconfigure Our Culture*. New York: Continuum, 2009.

Knausgaard, Klaus. *My Struggle, Book 1*, translated by Don Bartlett. New York: Farrar, Straus, and Giroux, 2009.

Kohn, Robert E. "Tibetan Buddhism in Don DeLillo's Novels: The Street, the Word and the Soul." *College Literature* 38, no. 4 (2011): 156–80.

Kolb, Jr., Harold. *The Illusion of Life: American Realism as a Literary Form*. Charlottesville: University Press of Virginia, 1969.

Krevel, Mojca. "A Tale of Being Everything: Literary Subject in Ruth Ozeki's *A Tale for the Time Being*." *Brno Studies in English* 43, no. 2 (2017): 111–25.

Kuehl, John. *Alternate Worlds: A Study of Postmodern Antirealism American Fiction*. New York: New York University Press, 1989.

Kutnik, Jerzy. *The Novel as Performance: The Fiction of Ronald Sukenick and Raymond Federman*. Carbondale: Southern Illinois University Press, 1986.

Lacan, Jacques. *The Seminar of Jacques Lacan, Book XI: The Four Fundamental Concepts of Psychoanalysis*, translated by Alan Sheridan, edited by Jacques-Alain Miller. New York: Norton, 1981 (1973).

Lacan, Jacques. "The Signification of the Phallus." In *Écrits: A Selection*, translated by Alan Sheridan, 181–91. New York: Norton, 1977.

Lasch, Christopher. *The Culture of Narcissism: American Life in an Age of Diminishing Expectations*. New York: Norton, 1979.

Latour, Bruno. "Why Has Critique Run out of Steam? From Matters of Fact to Matters of Concern." *Critical Inquiry* 30 (2004): 225–48.

Le Guin, Ursula. "Schrödinger's Cat." In *Postmodern American Fiction*, edited by Paula Geyh, Fred Leebron and Andrew Levy, 520–5. New York: Norton, 1998.

Lee, Hsiu-chuan. "Sharing Worlds through Words: Minor Cosmopolitics in Roth Ozeki's *A Tale for the Time Being*." *Ariel: A Review of International English Literature* 49, no. 1 (2018): 27–52.

Lethem, Jonathan. *As She Climbed Across the Table*. New York: Vintage, 1997.
Lipsky, David. *Although of Course You End up Becoming Yourself: A Road Trip with David Foster Wallace*. New York: Broadway Books, 2010.
Liu, Cixin. *The Dark Forest*, translated by Joel Martinsen. New York: Tor, 2015 (2008).
Liu, Cixin. *Death's End*, translated by Ken Liu. New York: Tor, 2016 (2010).
Liu, Cixin. *The Three Body Problem*, translated by Ken Liu. New York: Tor, 2016 (2007).
Longmuir, Anne. "Performing the Body in Don DeLillo's *The Body Artist*." *Modern Fiction Studies* 53, no. 3 (2007): 528–43.
Lovell, Sue. "Toward a Poetics of Posthumanist Narrative Using Ruth Ozeki's *A Tale for the Time Being*." *Critique: Studies in Contemporary Fiction* 59, no. 1 (2018): 57–74.
Lukács, George. *Essays on Realism*. Boston: MIT Press, 1980.
Lukács, George. *Realism in Our Time: Literature and the Class Struggle*. New York: Harper and Row, 1962.
Lyotard, Jean-Francois. "Defining the Postmodern." In *The Norton Anthology of Theory and Criticism*. 2nd edn, edited by Vincent B. Leitch, 1465–8. New York: Norton, 2010.
Mansfield, Victor. "Relativity in Madhyamika Buddhism and Modern Physics." *Philosophy East and West* 40, no. 1 (1990): 59–72.
Marcus, Ben. "Why Experimental Fiction Threatens to Destroy Publishing, Jonathan Franzen, and Life as We Know It." *Harper's*, October 2005: 39–52.
Markson, David. *Wittgenstein's Mistress*. Champaign: Dalkey Archive Press, 1988.
Marx, Karl and Frederic Engels. From *Economic and Philosophic Manuscripts of 1844*. In *The Norton Anthology of Theory and Criticism*. 2nd edn, edited by Vincent B. Leitch, 651–5. New York: Norton, 2010.
Maso, Carole. *The Art Lover*. Cambridge: New Directions, 1990.
Maso, Carole. *Ava*. Champaign: Dalkey Archive Press, 1993.
Maso, Carole. "Rupture, Verge, and Precipice; Precipice, Verge, and Hurt Not." *Review of Contemporary Fiction* 16, no. 1 (1996): 54–75.
Max, D. T. *Every Love Story Is a Ghost Story: A Life of David Foster Wallace*. New York: Penguin, 2012.
McCaffery, Larry. "The Art of Metafiction: William Gass's *Willie Masters' Lonesome Wife*." *Critique: Studies in Contemporary Fiction* 18, no. 1 (1976): 21–35.
McCaffery, Larry. "An Interview with David Foster Wallace." *Review of Contemporary Fiction* 13, no. 2 (1993): 127–50.
McCarthy, Cormac. *The Road*. New York: Vintage, 2006.
McGurl, Mark. "The New Cultural Geology." *Twentieth-Century Literature* 57, nos. 3–4 (2011): 380–90.
McHale, Brian. "1966 Nervous Breakdown; or, When Did Postmodernism Begin?" *Modern Language Quarterly* 69, no. 3 (2008): 391–413.

McHale, Brian. *Constructing Postmodernism*. Abingdon: Routledge, 1992.
McHale, Brian. *Postmodernist Fiction*. Abingdon: Routledge, 1987.
McLaughlin, Robert L. "Post-postmodern Discontent: Contemporary Fiction and the Social World." *Symploke* 12, nos. 1–2 (2004): 53–68.
McLaughlin, Robert L. "Stalking the Billion-footed Best: A Literary Manifesto for the New Social Novel." *Harper's Magazine*, November 1989: 45–56.
Michaels, Walter Benn. *The Shape of the Signifier*. Princeton: Princeton University Press, 2004.
Michel, Berit. "'PlastiCity': Foer's *Tree of Codes* as (Visual) Multilayered Urban Topography—Performing Space and Time in a Twenty-First-Century Adaptation of Bruno Schulz's Textual Labyrinths." *Critique: Studies in Contemporary Fiction* 55, no. 2 (2014): 166–86.
Miller, J. Hillis. "Narrative." In *Critical Terms for Literary Study*, edited by Frank Lentricchia and Thomas McLaughlin, 66–79. Chicago: University of Chicago Press, 1990.
Mitchell, David. *Cloud Atlas*. New York: Random House, 2004.
Moore, Steven. *The Novel: An Alternative History*. New York: Continuum, 2010.
Moraru, Christian. *Cosmodernism: American Narrative, Late Globalization, and the New Cultural Imaginary*. Ann Arbor: University of Michigan Press, 2010.
Moraru, Christian. "Thirteen Ways of Passing Postmodernism." *American Book Review* 34, no. 4 (2013): 3–4.
Morris, Pam. "Making the Case for Metonymic Realism." In *Realisms in Contemporary Culture: Theories, Politics, and Medial Configurations*, edited by Dorothee Birke and Stella Butter, 13–32. Berlin: de Gruyter, 2013.
Morris, Pam. *Realism*. Abingdon: Routledge, 2003.
Morton, Timothy. *Hyperobjects: Philosophy and Ecology after the End of the World*. Minneapolis: University of Minnesota Press, 2013.
Nance, Kevin. "Living in Dangerous Times" [interview with Don DeLillo]. *Chicago Tribune*, October 10, 2012. https://www.chicagotribune.com/entertainment/books/ct-xpm-2012-10-12-ct-prj-1014-don-delillo-20121012-story.html.
Nealon, Jeffrey. *Post-postmodernism, or, the Cultural Logic of Just-in-Time Capitalism*. Palo Alto: Stanford University Press, 2012.
Nel, Philip. "Don DeLillo's Return to Form: The Modernist Poetics of *The Body Artist*." *Contemporary Literature* 43, no. 4 (2002): 736–59.
Newman, Judie. "Updike's Many Worlds: Local and Global in *Toward the End of Time*." *The John Updike Review* 1, no. 1 (2011): 53–67.
Nichols, Catherine. "Dialogizing Postmodern Carnival: David Foster Wallace's *Infinite Jest*." *Critique: Studies in Contemporary Fiction* 43, no. 1 (2001): 3–16.
Norris, Christopher. "On the Limits of 'Undecidability': Quantum Physics, Deconstruction, and Anti-Realism." *Yale Journal of Criticism* 11, no. 2 (1998): 407–32.
Oppermann, Serpil. "Raymond Federman's *Double or Nothing*: A Prolegomena to a Postmodern Production Aesthetics." *American Studies International* 35, no. 3 (1997): 42–66.

Ozeki, Ruth. *A Tale for the Time Being*. New York: Penguin, 2013.
Peacock, James. *Jonathan Lethem*. Manchester: Manchester University Press, 2012.
Pizer, Donald. *Realism and Naturalism in Nineteenth-Century American Literature*. Carbondale: Southern Illinois University Press, 1984.
Pizer, Donald, ed. *The Cambridge Companion to American Realism and Naturalism: Howells to London*. Cambridge: Cambridge University Press, 1995.
Plascencia, Salvador. *The People of Paper*. New York: Harcourt, 2005.
Powers, Richard. *The Prisoner's Dilemma*. New York: William Morris and Company, 1988.
Pressman, Jessica. "The Aesthetic of Bookishness in Twenty-First Century Literature." *Michigan Quarterly Review* 48, no. 4 (2009): 465–82.
Purdy, Jedidiah. *After Nature: A Politics for the Anthropocene*. Boston: Harvard University Press, 2015.
Radia, Pavlina. "Doing the Lady Gaga Dance: Postmodern Transaesthetics and the Art of Spectacle in Don DeLillo's *The Body Artist*." *Canadian Review of American Studies* 44, no. 2 (2014): 194–213.
Rebein, Robert. *Hicks, Tribes, and Dirty Realists: American Fiction after Postmodernism*. Lexington: University of Kentucky Press, 2001.
Reilly, Charlie. "An Interview with John Barth." *Contemporary Literature* 22, no. 1 (1981): 1–23.
Retallack, Joan. *How To Do Things with Words*. Los Angeles: Sun & Moon Press, 1998.
Robertson, Mary. "Postmodern Realism: Discourse as Antihero in Donald Barthelme's 'Brain Damage'." In *Critical Essays on Donald Barthelme*, edited by Richard Patterson, 124–39. Boston: G. K. Hall & Co., 1992.
Ronen, Ruth. "Philosophical Realism and Postmodern Antirealism." *Style* 29, no. 2 (1995): 184–201.
Rudrum, David. "Towards a New Ahistoricism." *Always Periodize? Methods and Implications of Literary History*. American Comparative Literature Association Conference, UCLA, May 2018.
Saldivar, David. "Postmodern Realism." In *The Columbia History of the American Novel*, edited by Emory Elliott, 521–41. New York: Columbia University Press, 1993.
Saldivar, Ramón. "Historical Fantasy, Speculative Realism, and Postrace Aesthetics in Contemporary Fiction." *American Literary History* 23, no. 3 (2011): 574–99.
Saunders, George. *Lincoln in the Bardo*. New York: Random House, 2017.
Scholes, Robert. *Fabulation and Metafiction*. Champaign: University of Illinois Press, 1979.
See, Fred. "Henry James and the Art of Possession." In *American Realism: New Essays*, edited by Eric Sundquist, 119–37. Baltimore: Johns Hopkins University Press, 1982.
Severs, Jeffrey. *Always Periodize? Methods and Implications of Literary History*. American Comparative Literature Association Conference, UCLA, May 2018.

Shanahan, John. "Digital Transcendentalism in David Mitchell's *Cloud Atlas*." *Criticism: A Quarterly for Literature and the Arts* 58, no. 1 (2016): 115–45.
Shaviro, Stephen. *The Universe of Things: On Speculative Realism*. Minneapolis: University of Minnesota Press, 2014.
Shklovksy, Victor. "Art as Device." In *Theory of Prose*, translated by Benjamin Sher, 1–14. Champaign: Dalkey Archive Press, 1991.
Siegel, Lee. *Love in a Dead Language*. Chicago: University of Chicago Press, 2000.
Slocombe, Will. "Is Metafiction an Other Realism?: The Strange Case of Paul Auster and Mr. Blank." In *Realism's Others*, edited by Geoffrey Baker and Eva Aldea, 227–46. Newcastle upon Tyne: Cambridge Scholars, 2010.
Smith, Ali. *Artful*. New York: Penguin, 2012.
Smith, Rachel. "Grief Time: The Crisis of Narrative in Don DeLillo's *The Body Artist*." *Polygraph: An International Journal of Culture and Politics* 18 (2006): 99–110.
Sontag, Susan. "Against Interpretation." In *Against Interpretation and Other Essays*, 3–14. New York: Picador, 1961.
Starr, Marlo. "Beyond Machine Dreams: Zen, Cyber-, and Transnational Feminisms in Ruth Ozeki's *A Tale for the Time Being*." *Meridians* 13, no. 2 (2016): 99–122.
Steiner, Wendy. "Postmodern Fictions, 1960-1990." In *The Cambridge History of American Literature*, edited by Sacvan Bercovitch, vol. 7, 425–538. Cambridge: Cambridge University Press, 1999.
Stephens, Paul. "What Do We Mean by 'Literary Experimentalism'?: Notes Toward a History of the Term." *Arizona Quarterly* 68, no. 1 (2012): 143–73.
Stern, J. P. *On Realism*. Abingdon: Routledge, 1973.
Stewart, Garrett. *Bookwork: Medium to Object to Concept to Art*. Chicago: University of Chicago Press, 2011.
Strehle, Susan. *Fiction in the Quantum Universe*. Chapel Hill: University of North Carolina Press, 1992.
Striphas, Ted. *The Late Age of Print: Everyday Book Culture from Consumerism to Control*. New York: Columbia University Press, 2009.
Sundquist, Eric J. *American Realism: New Essays*. Baltimore: Johns Hopkins University Press, 1982.
Tarnawsky, Yury. "Not Just Text: Interview with Steve Tomasula." *Raintaxi*, Spring 2011. https://www.raintaxi.com/not-just-text-an-interview-with-steve-tomasula/April 2, 2013.
Terada, Rei. *Feeling in Theory: Emotion after the "Death of the Subject."* Cambridge: Cambridge University Press, 2001.
Tew, Philip. "A New Sense of Reality? A New Sense of Text: Exploring Meta-Realism and the Literary-Critical Field." In *Beyond Postmodernism: Reassessments in Literature, Theory, and Culture*, edited by Klaus Stierstorfer, 29–49. Berlin: de Gruyter, 2003.
Tew, Philip. "Re-acknowledging B S Johnson's Radical Realism, or Re-publishing *The Unfortunates*." *Critical Survey* 13, no. 1 (2001): 37–61.

Thompson, Lucas. *Global Wallace: David Foster Wallace and World Literature*. New York: Bloomsbury, 2017.
Thornton, William and Songkok Han Thornton. "Toward a Cultural Prosaics: Postmodern Realism in the New Literary Historiography." *Mosaic: A Journal for the Interdisciplinary Study of Literature* 26, no. 4 (1993): 119–42.
Tissut, Anne-Laure. "Signs of Time: *VAS*, a Story of Languages." In *Science and American Literature in the 20th and 21st Centuries: from Henry Adams to John Adams*, edited by Claire Maniez, Ronan Ludot-Vlasak, and Frédéric Dumas, 147–56. Newcastle upon Tyne: Cambridge Scholars Publishing, 2012.
Tomasula, Steve. *The Book of Portraiture*. Tuscaloosa: FC2, 2006.
Tomasula, Steve. "Electricians, Wig Makers, and Staging the New Novel." *American Book Review* 32, no. 6 (2011): 5.
Tomasula, Steve. *IN&OZ*. Stirling: Ministry of Whimsy, 2003.
Tomasula, Steve. *TOC: A New Media Novel*. Tuscaloosa: University of Alabama Press, 2009.
Tomasula, Steve. *VAS: An Opera in Flatland*. Chicago: University of Chicago Press, 2002.
Tomasula, Steve. "Where We Are Now: A Dozen or So Observations, Historical Notes and Soundings for a Map of Contemporary American Innovative Literature as Seen from the Interior." *Études Anglaises* 63, no. 2 (2010): 215–27.
Toth, Josh. *The Passing of Postmodernism*. Albany: State University of New York University Press, 2010.
Trachtenberg, Alan. "Experiments in Another Country: Stephen Crane's City Sketches." In *American Realism: New Essays*, edited by Eric J. Sundquist, 138–54. Baltimore: Johns Hopkins University Press, 1982.
Twain, Mark. "Fenimore Cooper's Literary Offenses." In *The Norton Anthology of American Literature*. 7th edn, vol. C, edited by Nina Baym, 294–302. New York: Norton, 2007.
Twain, Mark. "The Man That Corrupted Hadleyburg." In *Heath Anthology of American Literature*. 7th edn, vol. C, edited by Paul Lauter, 92–127. Boston: Cengage, 2014.
Ulmer, Greg. *Teletheory: Grammatology in the Age of Video*. Abingdon: Routledge, 1989.
Vermeulen, Timotheus and Robin van den Akker. "Notes on Metamodernism." *The Journal of Aesthetics and Culture* 2 (2010): 1–14.
Versluys, Kristiaan. *Neo-realism in Contemporary American Fiction*. Amsterdam: Rodopi, 1992.
Wallace, David Foster. "Borges on the Couch." Review of Edwin Williamson's *Borges: A Life* in *The New York Times*, November 7, 2004.
Wallace, David Foster. *Brief Interviews with Hideous Men*. Boston: Little, Brown and Company, 1999.
Wallace, David Foster. "E Unibus Pluram: Television and U. S. Fiction." *Review of Contemporary Fiction* 13, no. 2 (1993): 151–95.

Wallace, David Foster. "The Empty Plenum: David Markson's *Wittgenstein's Mistress*." Afterword for David Markson's *Wittgenstein's Mistress*, 243–75. Champaign: Dalkey Archive Press, 1990.

Wallace, David Foster. *Infinite Jest*. Boston: Little, Brown and Company, 1996.

Wallace, David Foster. "Letter to Don DeLillo." December 12, 2000. Container 101.1. Don DeLillo Papers. Harry Ransom Center, University of Texas at Austin.

Wallace, David Foster. *Oblivion*. Boston: Little, Brown and Company, 2004.

Wallace, David Foster. *The Pale King*. Boston: Little, Brown and Company, 2011.

Wallace, David Foster. *This Is Water*. Boston: Little, Brown and Company, 2009.

Wallace, David Foster. Typescript draft of "Good Old Neon." June 2000. Container 24.3. David Foster Wallace Papers. Harry Ransom Center, University of Texas at Austin, August 6, 2012.

Wallace, David Foster. Typescript draft of "Mister Squishy." June 2000. Container 24.6. David Foster Wallace Papers. Harry Ransom Center, University of Texas at Austin, August 6, 2012.

Watt, Ian. *The Rise of the Novel: Studies in Defoe, Richardson, and Fielding*. Berkeley: University of California Press, 2001 (1957).

Waugh, Patricia. *Metafiction: The Theory and Practice of Self-Conscious Fiction*. Abingdon: Routledge, 1984.

Wellek, René. *Concepts of Criticism*, edited by Stephen B. Nichols, Jr. New Haven: Yale University Press, 1963.

Wharton, Edith. "The Other Two." In *The Norton Anthology of American Literature*. 7th edn, vol. C, edited by Nina Baym, 830–43. New York: Norton, 2007.

White, Hayden. *Figural Realism: Studies in the Mimesis Effect*. Baltimore: Johns Hopkins University Press, 1999.

White, Hayden. "The Structure of Historical Narrative." In *The Norton Anthology of Theory and Criticism*. 2nd edn, edited by Vincent B. Leitch, 1536–53. New York: Norton, 2010.

Williams, Laurin. "Radical Breaks: Periodizing a Non-anthropocentric Anthropocene." *Always Periodize? Methods and Implications of Literary History*. American Comparative Literature Association Conference, UCLA, May 2018.

Winterson, Jeanette. *Sexing the Cherry*. London: Grove Press, 1989.

Wolfe, Thomas. "Stalking the Billion-Footed Beast: A Literary Manifesto for the New Social Novel." *Harper's Magazine*, November 1989: 45–56.

Wood, James. "Human, All Too Inhuman." *The New Republic*, July 24, 2000. https://newrepublic.com/article/61361/human-inhuman. September 19, 2019.

The Wizard of Oz. Directed by Victor Fleming. Metro-Goldwyn-Mayer, 1939.

Wurth, Kiene Brillenburg. "Old and New Modalities in Foer's *Tree of Codes*." *CLCWeb: Comparative Literature and Culture* 13, no. 3 (2011). http://docs.lib.purdue.edu/clcweb/vol13/iss3/14.

Wurth, Kiene Brillenburg. "Re-vision as Remediation: Hypermediacy and Translation in Anne Carson's *Nox*." *Image & Narrative* 14, no. 4 (2013): 20–33.

Yamashita, Karen Tei. *Tropic of Orange*. Minneapolis: Coffee House Press, 1997.

Index

Abrams, J. J. and Doug Dorst, *S.* 135–9, 140, 142, 174
Abrams, M. H., *A Glossary of Literary Terms* 21–3, 252
actualism 154–6
Adorno, Theodore 17, 98, 102
aesthetic of bookishness 114, 115, 132, 134, 140, 142
and Women's Studio Workshop 148 n.63
affect 29, 30, 31, 51, 71–4, 127, 239, 240, 254
Agrippa (a book of the dead) 109, 121, 135, 141, 142
Alter, Robert 50
Amis, Martin, *Time's Arrow* 198
anti-humanism 25, 35, 153, 157
"anti-realism" xv, 3, 15, 26, 30, 33, 36, 38, 40, 50, 70, 72, 156, 252
anti-Realism 47 n.111, 56, 63, 68–70, 76, 82–4, 99, 106 n.13, 114, 116, 156, 160, 240, 242–3, 248 n.62, 254
Ardoin, Paul 141
artifact, literature as 45 n.88, 55, 87, 91, 103, 115, 117, 122, 128, 133–8, 142, 143
Auerbach, Erik, *Mimesis* xv, 9–15, 16, 17, 18, 19, 22, 24–5, 29, 30, 31, 32, 33, 37, 42 n.32. 49, 50, 70, 72, 74, 252
Auster, Paul, *4321* 54, 160–1
awareness 69–70, 75, 185, 203, 206, 208, 213–14, 224, 228, 239, 246 n.37, 258

Barad, Karan 32
Meeting the Universe Halfway 39
and new materialism 60, 124–7, 144–5, 184–5

Barth, John xv, 49, 56, 57, 64, 66, 76 n.16, 110
LETTERS 155–6
"The Literature of Exhaustion" 71, 125
Lost in the Funhouse 58, 67, 143
Barthelme, Donald 49, 57, 110, 156
"At the End of the Mechanical Age" 96
Barthes, Roland 19, 22, 24, 25, 26, 34, 45 n.88, 111
Baudrillard, Jean 14, 57, 122, 152, 154
Beilin, Katarzyna 32, 37
being/Being
in *The Body Artist* 193, 205–15, 223, 224, 228–9, 231, 233, 236, 239, 247 n.43
and Buddhism 180–1
and new materialism 25, 127, 144–5
in *The Pale King* 69
and quantum mechanics 153, 173
and quantum realism 182–5, 242
in Tomasula 85, 91
in *The Tunnel* 122–3
Benjamin, Walter, "The Work of Art in the Age of Mechanical Reproduction" 93, 94, 96–102
Bernstein, Charles 120–1, 123, 127, 129
Berthoff, Warner 15, 16
Beube, Doug 140
bildungsroman 37, 63, 66, 70, 139
The Blair Witch Project 109
Blake, William, *The Marriage of Heaven and Hell* 109

Bohr, Neils   125, 126, 154, 157
Bonca, Cornel   193, 205, 247 n.43, 248 n.56
Bonta, Vanna, *Flight*   157
Borges, Jorge Louis, "Tlön, Uqbar, Orbis Tertius"   65, 135–7, 138, 185
and Wallace   63–5
Borgmann, Albert   32, 33, 37
Boswell, Marshall   159
Bowen, Deborah   32, 46 n.100
Braidotti, Rosi   124
Brandeis, Danielle   254
Brautigan, Richard, *The Abortion: An Historical Romance 1966*, 148 n.59
Breitbach, Julie   193
Brodhead, Richard   21
Brown, Bill   56
Buddhism
and *The Body Artist*   241–3, 248–9 n.63
and *Changing*   130
and *Lincoln in the Bardo*   74
and "Octet"   74
and quantum realism   259
and *A Tale for the Time Being*   171–85, 180 n.36, 238, 243, 258
Buford, Bill   31, 33
Bukiet, Melvin Jules   32, 36
Burn, Stephen J.   112, 160, 193, 245 n.19
Butler, Judith   126, 248 n.56

Calvino, Italo   65, 66, 143, 162
Carson, Anne, *Nox*   134–5, 136
Carter, Everett   15
Carton, Evan   19
Caruth, Cathy   36, 223, 247 n.43
Cheyfitz, Eric   21
Chiang, Ted, "Story of Your Life"   14, 163, 164, 166–71, 182, 238, 240, 242, 243, 259
Cixous, Hélène   104, 119

Clareson, Thomas   xiii
Coale, Samuel   244 n.2
"Quantum Flux"   192, 194, 196, 197, 198, 199, 201, 205
Quirks of the Quantum   154, 161, 163, 183, 246 n.37
complementarity   151, 154
Coole, Diana   125–6, 184
Cooper, James Fenimore   4, 24
Coover, Robert   49, 57, 110, 155, 156
"The End of Books"   114
Cowart, David   193, 213, 248 n.56
crisis of signification,   xiv, 152, 158
Culler, Jonathan   22, 24, 56, 94
Cusk, Rachel   49, 260 n.5

D'Agata, John, *The Lifespan of a Fact*   129
Danielewski, Mark   49, 65, 133
House of Leaves   112–14, 117–19, 121, 122, 129, 131, 135, 136, 139, 142, 174, 176, 178
Only Revolutions   129
decoding   133, 135, 139, 140–2
deconstruction   25, 26, 58, 158, 242, 257
DeLanda, Manuel   124
Delany, Samuel, *Babel-17*, 164–6
Deleuze, Gilles and Félix Guattari   104, 251, 258
DeLillo, Don   34, 35
Americana   196
The Body Artist   69, 167, 191–243, 258–9
archive at HRC   191, 192, 194–205, 212, 216, 218–27, 229–35, 238
birds   206–10, 214, 228
body work/body art/*Body Time*   194, 205, 212–23, 228, 229–32, 235, 237, 247 n.43, 247 n.49
glossolalia   211, 224

grief 192–6, 203, 207–8, 213, 216, 218, 222–3, 227, 235, 247 n.43, 247 n.49, 247 n.51, 248 n.56
"overlapping realities" 197, 199, 200–1, 211, 214, 220, 226
"time is in the body" 218–21, 223–5, 228, 231
trauma 192, 193, 196, 203, 207, 222–3, 247 n.43
and feminism 193, 218, 248 n.56
The Names 111, 132, 164, 197, 211
Point Omega 193, 196, 217
Underworld 218–19
White Noise 91, 164, 193, 208, 217, 221, 223, 224
Zero K 191, 193, 211, 235, 256
Derrida, Jacques 14, 17, 19, 25, 50, 153, 154, 204, 242, 257
Of Grammatology 40, 73, 139, 151
"Structure, Sign, and Play" 18
Dettmer, Brian 140
Dewitt, Helen, *The Last Samurai* 160
dialectic
 Hegelian 258
 of poststructural realism 259–60
 of realism (*see* realism, dialectic of)
Díaz, Junot, *The Brief Wondrous Life of Oscar Wao* 174
di Blasi, Debra, *The Jiří Chronicles and Other Fictions* 128, 133, 142
Dickinson, Emily 109
digital
 age 100, 105, 109, 111, 134, 142, 159
 literature 23, 111–16, 256

printing/technology 14, 79, 81, 105, 124
Dimock, Wai Chee 162, 255
Di Prete, Lauren 193, 222, 247 n.43, 247 n.49
Dōgen, Eihei, *Shōbōgenzō* 172
Don Quixote 1, 49, 52
Dubey, Madhu 32, 35–6, 37, 53

Egan, Jennifer, *A Visit from the Goon Squad* 159
Eichenbaum, Boris xiv, 52, 139, 255
Einstein, Albert 26, 152, 153, 159
electronic literature, *see* digital, literature
Elias, Amy 32, 36
embodiment/embodied 23, 26, 99, 103, 131, 134, 152, 173, 181, 243
 and being or experience 69–70, 87–8, 111, 122, 127, 145
 in *The Body Artist* 208, 211, 218, 220–1, 228–36
 and books/ books as bodies 115–19, 126, 144
 and language 118, 124
 and poststructural realism 239, 243, 255–60
 and reading 40, 136–8, 141–3
empathy
 and material realism 128, 133, 135, 136, 138, 143
 and metafictive realism 49, 56, 58, 59, 61, 63, 64, 74–6
 and "Story of Your Life" 164, 170–1
 and *A Tale for the Time Being* 173–5, 180, 184–5
empiricism 54, 56, 144, 153, 159, 176, 183, 214, 241, 257
emptiness is form, *see* form is emptiness
Enlightenment, the 25, 27, 34, 49

Index

entanglement   28, 151, 159, 172–8, 185, 258
epistemology/epistemological   18, 27, 34, 39, 40, 53, 94, 103, 126, 144–5, 154, 149 n.76, 159, 182–3, 207, 242, 256
ethics/ethical
  and material realism   136
  and metafictive realism   59
  and new materialism   124, 127
  and "post-postmodern" fiction   251
  and poststructural realism   259–60
  and quantum physics   145, 180, 182–5, 243, 259
  and Realism   33, 251
Everett, Hugh   175, 189 n.42
"experimental" fiction   xiv–xvi, 1, 26, 33, 34, 154, 184

Faber, Michel, *Under the Skin*   163
Federman, Raymond, *Double or Nothing*   110, 115–16, 121, 122, 123, 127
Fingal, Jim, *The Lifespan of a Fact*   129
finger, pointing at the moon, a   180–1, 260 (and *passim*)
Fisher, Mark   32, 35, 159
Foer, Jonathan Safran   128, 133, 142
  "About the Typefaces Not Used in This Edition"   129
  Everything Is Illuminated   129, 131, 132, 174, 176
  Extremely Loud & Incredibly Close   128, 131, 144
  "A Primer for the Punctuation of Heart Disease"   129
  Tree of Codes   140–2
form
  and Jameson   22, 28–31, 51–2
  and materiality   40, 110, 111, 113, 116, 118, 120, 121, 123, 126, 127, 132–4, 136, 139–44
  and metafiction   53–4, 66, 74
  and periodizing   xiii, 3, 10, 13, 16–19, 23–4, 26, 27, 36, 37, 40, 53–6, 73, 251–5
  and poststructural realism   251, 260
  and quantum realism   156, 157, 161–9, 182, 184, 192, 224, 227, 228, 240–2
  and Tomasula   81–2, 96–105
formalism, Russian   xii, 4, 12, 18, 52, 53, 103, 116, 133, 139, 144
form is emptiness, *see* emptiness is form
Foster, Hal   32, 36, 79, 257
Foucault, Michel   14, 17, 126, 157
Franzen, Jonathan   32, 36, 54, 196
free indirect discourse (FID)   6, 7–8, 30, 61–2, 72, 237, 239
Freytag's triangle   138, 153, 215, 221
Frost, Samantha   125–7, 184
Fujii, Hikaru   193, 194

Gass, William H., and metafiction   50, 55, 110, 156
  The Tunnel   115, 122–4, 131
  Willie Masters' Lonesome Wife   110
Gibson, William   109
Gram, Margaret   53–4
Greene, Brian, *The Fabric of the Cosmos*   151–2, 163, 164, 175, 203, 214
Grossman, Richard, *The Alphabet Man*   115, 123
  The Book of Lazarus   117

Habermas, Jürgen   17
Hall, Steven, *The Raw Shark Texts*   132–3, 135, 138, 143
Hardt, Michael and Antonio Negri   258

Harris, Charles 76 n.16, 120
Harris, Victoria Frenkel 119
Hayles, N. Katherine 112, 131–3, 255
 How We Became Posthuman 133, 142
 How We Think 136, 140
 and *The Raw Shark Texts* 132–3, 143
 and *Tree of Codes* 140–1
Heart Sutra 241
Heidegger, Martin 17, 82, 153, 193, 205, 224
Heisenberg's uncertainty principle 153, 157, 203
Hennig, Reinhard 32
Hoang, Lily, *Changing* 49, 129–31, 132
Homes, A. M. 33, 37
Howells, William Dean 4–8, 9, 15, 21, 22, 24, 252
 "Editha" 5
 "The Editor's Study" 6
 "Novel-Writing and Novel-Reading" 6–7
hrönir 137–8 (and *passim*)
Hutcheon, Linda xv, 1, 50, 56, 155
hyperreal 126, 154, 208, 214
hypertext 56, 112, 113, 114, 116, 119

I Ching 130
ideology
 of art 80–2, 86–91, 98–102, 111
 and innovative literature 103–4
 and post-modernist realism 35
 and Realism 13, 14, 18, 20, 22, 27
 of science 91–6

Jackson, Shelley, *Ineradicable Stain* and *Patchwork Girl* 141–2
Jakobson, Roman 4, 22
 "On Realism in Art" xii–xiii, 252

Jakubowski, Zuzanna 32, 45 n.88
James, David 53
James, Henry xii, 19, 21, 24, 53
 "The Art of Fiction" 4–5, 7, 11, 15, 17, 24, 252
 "The Real Thing" 6, 19
Jameson, Fredric xiv–xv, 33, 35, 104, 142, 255
 The Antinomies of Realism 9, 27–31, 38, 50–1, 52, 65–6, 70–4, 228, 239, 242, 254, 259
 and *Cloud Atlas* 143
 "The Political Unconscious" 28, 102
 "Postmodern and Consumer Society" 20, 125
 "swollen third person" 51–2, 72–3
Johnson, B. S., *Albert Angelo*, *The Unfortunates* 110, 156

Karl, Alissa 253
Keskinen, Mikko 193
Kessel, Tyler 193
Knausgaard, Karl Ove 260 n.5
koan, Zen 180–1, 238, 241, 248 n.63, 257–60
Kohn, Robert 248 n.63
Kolb, Harold, *The Illusion of Life* xiii, 16–17, 18–19, 21

Lacan, Jacques, "The Agency of the Letter" 14, 17, 19, 104, 153, 166
 and the Real 36, 79, 95–6, 152, 169, 204
 "The Signification of the Phallus" 95–6
Language poets 120–1
Larson, Reif, *The Selected Works of T. S. Spivet* 133
Latour, Bruno 45 n.88, 56–7
Lee, Hsiu-chuan 188 n.34
Le Guin, Ursula 163, 188 n.37

Lethem, Jonathan, *She Climbed Across the Table*   158
linguistic turn   xiv–xv, 4, 16–18, 151
literariness   52–3, 102, 107 n.33, 139–40
literary history   xii, 1, 3, 12, 15, 28, 31, 40–1, 162, 253
Liu, Cixin, *The Dark Forest*   161–2
   Death's End   132, 161
   The Three Body Problem   161, 197
Longmuir, Anne   193, 194, 247 n.43, 248 n.56
Lovell, Sue   188 n.34
Lukács, George   16, 28
Lyotard, Jean-Francois   21, 25, 125

McCaffery, Larry, "Interview with David Foster Wallace"   55, 58, 75
McCarthy, Cormac, *The Road*   144
McEwan, Ian, *Atonement*   132
McGurl, Mark   162–3, 186 n.3, 255
McHale, Brian   149 n.76, 183–4, 235
McLaughlin, Robert   36
Mansfield, Victor   249 n.63
many worlds   158–60, 175, 177, 197, 189 n.42, 201, 236, 258
Marcus, Ben   xvi, 1
Markson, David, *Wittgenstein's Mistress*   39–40, 58–60, 61, 65
Marxism   20, 28
   and Tomasula   87–91, 97, 100–3
Maso, Carole, *The Art Lover*   119–20
   AVA   74, 112–13, 119
materiality
   and artifactuality   133–8, 143
   and assemblage   136, 143
   and *The Body Artist*   204, 211, 242
   books as bodies   115–19, 127–9, 131–2
   and electronic/digital literature   111–14

of language   26, 119–24, 129–31, 178–80, 184, 225, 258
   limits of   139–42
   in literature before "post-postmodernism"   109–10
   and metafictive realism   60
   and new realisms   126, 145
   in post-modernist literature   37–9
   and poststructural realism   251, 255–60
   and *A Tale for the Time Being*   178–82, 184, 187 n.34
   and Tomasula   99–102, 105
material realism, *see* realism, material
memoir   110, 130, 137, 173
metafiction
   and fiction   xv, 1, 13, 17, 27, 49–50, 74–5
   and formalism   52–3
   and Jameson   51–2, 70–3
   and materiality   109–10, 120, 125, 131, 133, 137, 139, 143, 145
   and post-modernist realism   33, 37–41, 47 n.109, 53–5
   and quantum fiction   155–6
   and quantum realism   177, 185, 238, 242
   and Tomasula   85
   Wallace on   55–60
metafictive realism, *see* realism, metafictive
Michaels, Walter Benn   111
Michel, Berit   141
mimesis   xiii, 17, 24, 33, 50, 56, 57, 81, 84–6, 95, 100, 104
mise en abyme   59, 64, 145
Mitchell, David, *Cloud Atlas*   30, 49, 128, 143, 174
Möbius-strip structure   107 n.17, 112, 113, 120, 132, 257
modernist/modernism
   and epistemology   149 n.76, 183

and materiality   109–10, 119, 120
and periodizing   xii–xv, xvii n.8, 3, 20, 31, 96, 125, 252, 254, 255, 259
and quantum fiction   154
realism in   9–14, 17, 24–5, 30, 34, 51–2, 73, 93, 143
Moore, Steven   xvi, 1–3, 9, 252, 253
moral/morality   4–8, 38, 40, 64, 71, 93, 157, 170, 259
Morris, Pam   xvi, 32, 33, 34
Realism   xiv, 1–2, 23–7, 168, 197, 252
Morton, Timothy   255
Mr. Nobody   160

Nabokov, Vladimir, Pale Fire   57, 116, 121, 135, 139, 196–7
Nel, Philip   192, 193, 246 n.38, 247 n.43, 248 n.56
New Critics/New Criticism   xiv, 139
Newman, Judie   158–9
new materialism   60, 124–7, 144, 184, 259
Newton/Newtonian   40, 125, 153, 154, 156, 159, 164, 165, 166, 174, 198, 203, 226, 236, 238, 239, 242–3, 257
nonbinary/nonduality   171, 173, 175–6, 242–3, 257

observer/observation effects   124–6, 154, 157, 172, 173, 175–7, 198, 202, 203, 215, 227–8, 237
ontology/ontological   19, 27, 39–41, 58, 103, 256
and new materialism   39–40, 60, 126–7, 145
postmodern   183–4
and poststructural realism   144–5, 149 n.76, 242–3
and quantum fiction   154, 159

and quantum realism   163, 178, 182–5, 193, 238
Ozeki, Ruth, A Tale for the Time Being   14, 49, 74, 171–85, 191, 225, 238, 240–3, 258–60

paradox   40–1, 172–3, 180, 192, 198, 221, 235, 240–3, 252, 257
parody   71, 127, 142–3
periodizing   xiii, xiv, 1–3, 12, 15–16, 20–2, 27, 28, 41, 52, 162, 251–7
perspective   8, 14, 38, 57, 70
in The Body Artist   199, 203, 205, 215, 222, 227, 236–3
dialogism of (see Wallace, David Foster)
and periodizing   254–6
and poststructural realism   252, 257
and quantum realism   152, 153, 155, 160–3, 165, 170, 176–7, 182, 185, 203, 251
and Tomasula   84, 86–7, 93
and Wallace   14, 38, 57, 60–3, 64–70, 72, 74
Plascencia, Salvador, The People of Paper   49, 131–2
point of view   160, 162, 242, 243, 257
and quantum realism   145, 153, 164, 165, 176–7, 237
and Realism   8, 17, 19
second-person in Chiang   23, 167
in DeLillo   167, 207, 224–5, 227, 237
in Ozeki   176–7
"swollen third person"   51–2, 72–4
and Tomasula   84–6, 98
and Wallace   8, 14, 30, 61–5, 68, 70
and Woolf   10, 12

posthuman/posthumanism
  and Barad 39, 125
  and Hayles 136, 249 n.64
  McGurl's posthuman comedy
    162–3, 186 n.3, 255
postmodern/postmodernism
  culture xv, 96, 191, 258
  fiction 18, 27, 34, 36, 57, 155–7,
    184–5, 258
  and Jameson xiv, 30, 72–3, 125
  and language 178, 181, 203,
    245 n.19, 259
  and materiality 115, 123, 127,
    133, 138, 142–4
  and metafiction xv, 1, 52–3,
    56–7, 60, 71, 110
  and ontology 149 n.76, 183–4
  and periodizing xii, xv–xvi, 3,
    11–14, 19–21, 25–7, 31,
    32–7, 41, 251–7
  and quantum fiction 151,
    154–8
  and quantum realism 164, 181,
    183, 187 n.34
  realism (*see* realism, postmodern)
"post-postmodernism" 3, 12, 14,
  25, 31, 35, 36, 37–41, 49,
  52, 53, 55, 59, 109, 110,
  131, 138, 164, 183, 253–60
poststructural/poststructuralism
  xiv–xv, 18, 19, 21, 23, 24,
  25, 26, 28, 30, 32, 35, 38,
  39, 40, 56, 58, 73, 79,
  117, 123, 128, 138, 144,
  152–3, 157, 163, 183,
  204, 225, 242, 251, 252,
  256, 257
poststructural realism, *see* realism,
  poststructural
Powers, Richard 32, 36, 54
Pressman, Jessica 114
print books 104–5, 110, 114, 135,
  140–1, 143
Purdy, Jedidiah 255

quantum computing 172, 176, 178
quantum fiction 39, 151, 154–63,
  183
quantum mechanics/physics/theory
  74, 151–3, 159, 251, 257
  and *The Body Artist* 191, 192,
    194–6, 203, 205, 211, 221,
    236, 241–3
  and Buddhism 241, 249 n.63,
    259
  and ethics 124–7, 145
  and poststructural realism 260
  and quantum fiction 39, 154,
    156, 159
  and quantum realism 258
  and "Story of Your Life" 163,
    166–71
  and *A Tale for the Time Being*
    171–85
quantum realism, *see* realism, quantum

Radia, Pavlina 193, 247 n.43
realism
  agential 32, 33, 144
  bourgeois 16
  British postmodern 32, 36
  capitalist 32, 35, 159
  crackpot 32, 36
  critical 16
  dialectic of xv, 27–31, 38, 51, 54,
    65–6, 70–1, 72, 73, 74, 84,
    239, 242, 259
  dirty 31, 33
  disquieting 32, 37, 54
  ecocritical 32, 45 n.89
  empirical, 257
  figural 13, 32–4, 35
  hysterical 32, 35, 136
  material 26, 38, 40, 55, 74, 104,
    109–45, 184, 257–9
  meta- 32, 33, 47 n.109, 54
  metafictive 32, 33, 37, 38, 40,
    54, 55, 60, 64, 69, 57, 74–5,
    257–9

metonymic 32, 34
modernist xvii n.8, 9–14, 252
neo- 31, 33
nineteenth-century
 ("Realism") xii–xv, 1–10,
 15–31, 40, 41, 47 n.111,
 50–3, 144, 153, 251, 252,
 253, 255, 256, 257
postmodern 31, 32, 33, 37, 38,
 46 n.100, 54
post-postmodern 32, 33, 35–6
poststructural 32, 33, 38, 54, 56,
 63–4, 235, 252, 256–60
quantum 26, 34, 38–40, 55, 153,
 156, 157, 160, 163–85, 191,
 192, 196, 217, 221, 236,
 242, 246 n.37, 257–9
relational 32, 33, 45 n.88
socialist 16
speculative 32, 33, 37, 39, 54
tragic 32, 46 n.105
traumatic 32, 36, 79, 257
virtual 256–7
Rebein, Robert 33
Reed, Ishmael, *Mumbo Jumbo* 110,
 156
representationalism 39, 40, 124–5,
 144–5, 154
Retallack, Joan, *How To Do Things
 with Words* 121
Rudrum, David 254

Saldivar, Ramón 32, 37, 39, 131
Saunders, George, *Lincoln in the
 Bardo* 74
Saussure, Ferdinand de 17, 19, 22,
 24, 185, 253
Schrödinger's cat 160, 175–7, 180,
 181, 188 n.37, 215, 227
science fiction xiii, 37, 161–3,
 166, 184–5, 189 n.45,
 225
See, Fred 19
separation . . . DNE
Severs, Jeff 253

Shklovsky, Viktor 52, 95, 139
Siegel, Lee, *Love in a Dead Language*
 113–14, 116–18, 120, 122,
 128, 142
Sliding Doors 160
Slocombe, Will 38, 54, 65
Smith, Ali 49, 189 n.45
 Artful 140
Smith, Rachel Greenwald 193,
 222, 247 n.43, 247 n.49,
 248 n.56
Smith, Zadie 34–5
Sontag, Susan 111
spacetime 152, 160, 161, 163, 165,
 169, 170, 174, 178, 180–2,
 184, 192, 210, 223–5, 239,
 241
Starr, Marlo 172, 173, 188 n.36
Stein, Gertrude 110, 120
Steiner, Wendy 36
Stern, J. P. xiii, 18–19
Sterne, Laurence, *Tristram Shandy*
 49, 52, 103, 109
Stoner, Jess, *I Have Blinded Myself
 Writing This* 133–4
Strehle, Susan, *Fiction in the
 Quantum Universe* 154–6
structuralism 17, 22, 23, 83, 84,
 252, 260
Sundquist, Eric, *American Realism*
 19–21, 23, 25, 29, 252
superposition 172, 173, 175, 177

Tew, Philip 32, 47 n.109
thing theory 45 n.88, 56–7
Thompson, Lucas 65
Thornton, Songok Han 33, 37
Thornton, William 33, 37
time
 and art 213–18, 204–5
 and Borges 65
 "deep time" 162, 255
 embodied experience of 111,
 152, 204, 217, 219–21, 224,
 227, 258

and identity 205, 223
and Jameson 49
linear/chronological/"flow
   of" 74, 151-2, 195, 199,
   201-2, 205-6, 208, 209-10,
   214, 221, 225, 227, 228,
   236, 239-40, 259
materiality of 121, 177-82, 204,
   220
narrative 175, 223
quantum 14, 152, 165-70,
   172-4, 177, 192, 195,
   197-8, 202-4, 209, 211,
   214, 223-5, 226-8, 229,
   231, 235-41, 259
"time's arrow" 170-1, 198
and Tomasula 82, 84, 88, 92, 94,
   99-100
and Wallace 73
and Woolf 10-12
Zen or Buddhist view of 172,
   175, 180
Tomasula, Steve xvi, 1, 49, 127, 131,
   132, 144, 145
and anti-Realist practices 79,
   81-5, 145
The Book of Portraiture 60, 80,
   81, 84-7, 92, 100, 103, 115,
   127, 142
IN&OZ 80, 81-3, 87-91, 98,
   100-2, 127-8, 131, 165,
   217
TOC 80, 81, 83-4, 98-100, 102,
   103, 127
VAS 80, 81, 85, 91-6, 97-100,
   115, 127-8, 129, 131
Toth, Josh 33
Trachtenberg, Alan 20
trompe l'esprit 59-60, 66, 85, 145
trompe l'oeil 59-60, 66, 84-5,
   103-4, 145
truth effects 168-9, 181, 182
Twain, Mark 4-5, 9, 15, 24, 72
"The Man that Corrupted
   Hadleyburg" 5-6, 7-8, 19

Updike, John, *Toward the End of
   Time* 158-9

verb tense, shifting 165, 167-9, 195,
   203, 209, 211, 216, 224-9,
   237-9, 243, 257
verisimilitude xii, xiii, 4, 17, 24, 28,
   66, 68
Versluys, Kristiaan 31
virtual reality xv, 23, 100, 144, 256
Vonnegut, Kurt 66
   Breakfast of Champions 110

Wallace, David Foster 34, 40, 83,
   85, 128, 138, 145, 157, 237,
   244 n.5
archive at the HRC 62, 64
and Borges 64-5
"Brief Interview #20" 64,
   77 n.33, 146 n.28
"Brief Interview #48" xii
*Brief Interviews with Hideous
   Men* 65-7, 70, 97
The Broom of the System 57
Consider the Lobster 113
and contrapuntal metafictive
   realism 65-75
"The Devil Is a Busy Man" 64
and dialogism of
   perspective 60-3
"The Empty Plenum" 58-60
and the endless binary 63-5,
   257
and feminism 77 n.33
"Good Old Neon" 61, 63, 64,
   73, 113
Infinite Jest 60, 69, 71, 113, 114,
   116, 140, 143, 159
and metafiction 54-60, 139,
   143, 156, 185
and misogyny 77 n.33, 146 n.28
"Mister Squishy" 61-3
"My Soul Is Not a Smithy"
   62-3
"Octet" 66, 67, 73, 74, 143

The Pale King 65–70, 100, 247 n.51, 248 n.62, 258
"A Radically Condensed History of Post-Industrial Life" 96–7
and realism, and Realism 38, 55, 156
"Westward the Course of Empire Takes Its Way" 57
Ware, Chris, *Building Stories* 148 n.61
Waugh, Patricia 38, 50, 54, 56
Wellek, René xiii, 28, 252
Concepts of Criticism 15–16
Wharton, Edith 7
"The Other Two" 8–9

White, Hayden 17, 32, 33, 35, 37
"The Structure of Historical Narrative" 34
Williams, Laurin 254
Winterson, Jeanette, *Sexing the Cherry* 165–6, 182
Wittgenstein, Ludwig xiii, 17–18, 59
Wood, James 32, 34
Woolf, Virginia 9–12, 14, 25–6, 34, 160, 252
Wurth, Kiene Brillenburg, and *Nox* 134
and *Tree of Codes* 140–1

www.ingramcontent.com/pod-product-compliance
Lightning Source LLC
Chambersburg PA
CBHW050337230426
43663CB00010B/1892